WRITING WAR IN THE
TWENTIETH CENTURY

CULTURAL FRAMES, FRAMING CULTURE
Robert Newman, *Editor*

WRITING WAR IN THE TWENTIETH CENTURY

Margot Norris

UNIVERSITY PRESS OF VIRGINIA

Charlottesville and London

THE UNIVERSITY PRESS OF VIRGINIA
© 2000 by the Rector and Visitors of the University of Virginia
Printed in the United States of America
First published in 2000

⊚ The paper used in this publication meets the minimum requirements
of the American National Standard for Information Sciences—Permanence of Paper
for Printed Library Materials, ANSI Z39.48-1984.

Library of Congress Cataloging-in-Publication Data

Norris, Margot.
    Writing war in the twentieth century / Margot Norris.
        p.   cm. — (Cultural frames, framing culture)
    Includes bibliographical references and index.
    ISBN 0-8139-1991-6 (cloth : alk. paper) — ISBN 0-8139-1992-4 (paper : alk. paper)
    1. War in literature.   2. War and literature.   3. Literature, Modern—20th century—
History and criticism.   I. Title: Writing war in the 20th century.   II. Title.   III. Series.

PN56.W3 N67 2000
809′.93358—dc21   00-31922

To my husband, Rowland Davis,
for sharing these years of peace with me

CONTENTS

ACKNOWLEDGMENTS

For a project with such a global focus, financial and professional support has been surprisingly local. The two small grants I received in support came from the Global Peace and Conflict Studies Program (GPACS) of my own institution, the University of California, Irvine. For these I am extremely grateful, for they speeded the writing of the Hiroshima chapter and gave me the opportunity to visit the Peace Memorial Museum in Hiroshima. But over the years GPACS has given me much more than money. A unique interdisciplinary program focused on alternatives to war as much as on war itself, GPACS has given me the opportunity to learn from engaged social scientists and other humanists, and to meet longtime peace activists, scholars, and writers such as Daniel Ellsberg, Barbara Ehrenreich, Maxine Hong Kingston, and Susan Jeffords on their visits to UCI. I am especially thankful for the encouragement I've received from Keith Nelson, Jules and Doris Margolis, Paula Garb, Herbert Lehnert, Wayne Sandholtz, Pat Morgan, and John Whitely over the years.

In my own department, I have been much nourished by the collegial support of Michael Clark, Gabriele Schwab, and John Rowe. Thomas Keneally, who was our cherished colleague here at Irvine for a number of years, supported our efforts to hold an annual one-day Peace Symposium, and generously returned long-distance phone calls from Australia to answer questions I had about *Schindler's List*. I've learned much from the students in my various classes on war literature, and particularly from a former undergraduate, Eric Matza, whose subsequent work in the Peace Corps and commitment to global understanding and communication have been a source of inspiration to me. I wish also to acknowledge two nonacademic friends no longer alive who were important to this project. Rick Davidson, an architect living in Venice, California, taught me that peace begins at home—in our neighborhoods and on our streets. Rick introduced me to the Los Angeles artist Leonard Cutrow, who shared his Vietnam War paintings with me. Along with much other encouragement, for which I remain warmly grateful, Laurence Goldstein, my former colleague at the University of Michigan, some years ago gave me the opportunity to write about Leonard Cutrow in the *Michigan Quarterly Review.*

Several of the chapters in this book have appeared previously in academic journals and collections of essays, whose editors have at times become encouraging friends. I am especially grateful to two successive editors of *Modern Fiction Studies*—Patrick O'Donnell and William J. Palmer—who gave me the opportunity to edit a special fall 1998 issue, "Modernisms and Modern Wars," and who published my essays on *A Farewell to Arms* and *Apocalypse Now* in that journal. "The Novel as War: Lies and Truth in Hemingway's *A Farewell to Arms*" appeared in *Modern Fiction Studies* 40:4 (winter 1994), 689–710, and "Modernism and Vietnam: Francis Ford Coppola's *Apocalypse Now*" was published in *Modern Fiction Studies* 44:3 (fall 1998), 730–66. A very early version of my chapter on World War I poetry appeared under the title "The Trace of the Trenches: Recovering Modernism's World War I" in *America's Modernisms: Revaluing the Canon,* edited by Kathryne V. Lindberg and Joseph G. Kronick. This collection of essays in honor of my late mentor, Joseph N. Riddel, was published by Louisiana University Press in 1996, and I am grateful to LSU Press for permission to use a revised version of the essay in this book. The journal *Cultural Critique* published two pieces of mine: a rudimentary version of "Military Censorship and the Body Count in the Persian Gulf War" (fall 1991, 223–45) and "Dividing the Indivisible: The Fissured Story of the Manhattan Project," which appeared in winter 1996–97 (5–38). Another early version of my chapter on press censorship during the Persian Gulf War appeared as "Only the Guns Have Eyes: Censorship and the Body Count," in *Seeing through the Media: The Persian Gulf War,* a collection of essays edited by Susan Jeffords and Lauren Rabinovitz and published by Rutgers University Press in 1994. Finally, although I did not reproduce my essay "The (Lethal) Turn of the Twentieth Century: War and Population Control" in this book, I wish nonetheless to thank Robert Newman for inviting its inclusion in his collection *Centuries' Ends, Narrative Means,* published by Stanford University Press in 1996. The experience led to his interest in my project for his series Cultural Frames, Framing Cultures, and to his shepherding my book to publication by the University Press of Virginia. His generous faith in this project has been a significant impetus behind its timely completion. My editor at the University Press of Virginia, Cathie Brettschneider, has been unfailingly patient and responsive to my concern that I be able to bring the book to light in the ways I needed to write it, and Ellen Satrom's wise editorial advice contributed much to its present form. Barbara Salazar's expert copyediting not only greatly improved the book but taught me much about the craft.

My family, of course, merits my most special thanks. My son, Josef Norris, sent me a stream of books and tapes relevant to my work over the years, and my husband, Rowland Davis—a more eloquent writer than I— took time from his own scientific writing to help polish my prose. And Helga, John, and Michael Barisits provide the loving familial support that sustains creativity and productivity. Family, too, has been a more painfully intimate source of inspiration for this project. Growing up in post–World War II Austria and overhearing my gentle grandfather's experiences in prison camps after both world wars, I feared war would be the emotional and historical element of our lives. My family's inability to bury my young father, whose end on the Russian front remains unknown, further haunted me with a need to memorialize. Eventually this personal feeling for specific wartime suffering was submerged in a historical sense of the period's overwhelming violence, and engendered a powerful—if doomed—wish to embrace all the dead and injured of the twentieth century's wars in these pages.

WRITING WAR IN THE TWENTIETH CENTURY

I

WRITING WAR IN THE TWENTIETH CENTURY

An Introduction

The Aesthetic, Critical, and Ethical Problem

LOOKING BACK AT THE TWENTIETH CENTURY, WE MIGHT at first be struck by the incommensurability of two of its hallmarks: modern mass warfare and innovative art. How is the century's burgeoning of rich, new conceptual forms and aesthetic technologies related to the fact that the twentieth has been the bloodiest century in the human history of the world? Was modern war a stimulus to aesthetic revolution, as early twentieth-century artists and critics claimed, or did art become increasingly aghast and defeated by events and spectacles beyond its powers of representation as war became unspeakably immense in scale and unutterably violent in conduct? The multiple answers to this question betray the heterogeneous configurations of art in relation to war during those hundred years, as well as the diverse positions of scholarship and theory in addressing this topic. And art's incommensurability to war—its inability to respond with adequate and appropriate gravity, scale, and meaningfulness—can be seen to vary with the century's different conflicts. There are several outstanding works relating modernism and avant-garde art to the advent of the mechanized warfare of World War I, from Paul Fussell's classic *The Great War and Modern Memory* to intriguing studies by Modris Eksteins, Samuel Hynes, Evelyn Cobley, and—more recently—Allyson Booth. But with World War II,

I

the responses become more complex and tortured, both because its experience is recent enough that the surviving populations have not yet ceased mourning, and because the scale and intensity of the violence threatened to sever art's expressive connection to war altogether. Theodor Adorno's famous, disputed, and misunderstood dictum that poetry became impossible after Auschwitz ("To write poetry after Auschwitz is barbaric")[1] is the most dramatic announcement of this aesthetic threshold—echoed by such critics and artists as Claude Lanzmann, whose documentary film *Shoah* enacts his conviction that the Holocaust must not be represented. Paul Fussell writes, "Conveying an adequate idea of the Second World War is close to impossible because, as war correspondent Robert Goralski has said, 'What we did to each other is almost beyond human conception'" (*Norton Book of Modern War,* 308). The military conflicts of the late twentieth century, particularly Vietnam and the Persian Gulf War, have differently problematized relationships to postmodernism and poststructuralist criticism, as Christopher Norris makes clear in his harsh attack on Jean Baudrillard's problematizing of the "reality" of the Persian Gulf War.[2] Whether art is construed as having become impossible in the face or aftermath of the world wars or whether its constraints, limitations, inadequacies, and impotences have merely been productively exposed, the terrain of critical assessment and scholarship on war writing has itself become an intellectually conflicted and afflicted arena.

As this book explores modern texts that respond to the century's wars, I will remember the critical debates over modern art and war without explicitly adjudicating them, and without attempting to abide by their mandates. My project is itself made problematic by its scope, its aim to function as a *century book* of writing about modern war—a scope impelled by my own intellectual affliction in being haunted by the aggregation of the huge numbers of war dead. When I say that the twentieth century was the bloodiest in human history, I refer to this period's sanctioning of the killing and wounding of well over a hundred million people in a hundred years' time—the equivalent of decimating a nation the size (in people) of Belgium, Chile, or Greece every ten years for a century. I derive the approximate number of 130 million casualties (dead and wounded) from the following tally: World War I is conservatively estimated to have produced 10 million dead and 20 million wounded (Beckett, 9);[3] Paul Fussell writes of World War II:

Killed and wounded were over 78 million people, more of them civilians than soldiers. Close to 6 million Jews were beaten, shot, or

> gassed to death by the Germans. One million people died of star-
> vation and despair in the siege of Leningrad. . . . If the battle of the
> Somme constituted a scandal because 20,000 British soldiers were
> killed in one day, twice that number of civilians were asphyxiated
> and burned to death in the bombing of Hamburg. Seventy thousand
> died at Hiroshima, 35,000 at Nagasaki, and the same at Dresden.
> (*Norton Book of Modern War*, 308)

And Barbara Ehrenreich reports an estimated 22 million dead from the
160 wars that have been fought since the end of World War II (226).

But thinking of modern wars in terms of these numbers is a desperate
and arguably futile gesture, because their status as dead or injured *bodies*
is conceptually irrecoverable or unimaginable in their materiality. They
therefore resist meaningful figuration and representation, as Elaine Scarry
explains: "On the one hand, counting makes an extreme claim about its correspondence with the material realm. . . . On the other hand, numbers and
numerical operations are, presumably with good reason, habitually thought
of as abstract, as occupying a space wholly cut off from the world. Even
forms of counting that claim to have worldly content sometimes seem instead characterized by the complete lack of it: the 'body count' in war is
a notoriously insubstantial form of speech" (*Literature and the Body*, viii).
The census of the war dead resists and exceeds both representation and
attempts at signification—particularly ontological signification. The philosopher Edith Wyschogrod goes further than many modern thinkers by
dilating the numbers when she adds a temporal dimension to the vast numbers of twentieth-century war dead. She thereby formulates what she calls
the "death event"—that is, a warfare phenomenon in which compressed
time plays a new and powerful role in the "systematic rational calculation"
for maximizing human destruction: "scale is reckoned in terms of the compression of time in which destruction is delivered" (x). The death event was
inaugurated by World War I, but it was not abolished after the Great War,
or after Hiroshima and the Holocaust. The very brief but extremely destructive Persian Gulf War of 1991 was a disturbing reminder that the death event
was not only *not* put behind Western culture but had become commonplace
and acceptable. The critic Susan Jeffords notes that

> what distinguished the Persian Gulf War from earlier instances . . .
> is that the strategies of terror that are part of the death-world were

used, not at the end of an already long and brutal war (as in the use of the atom bomb . . .) but as its initial strategy. In this way, the U.S. engagement in the Persian Gulf War moved warfare in the post–Cold War era into a distinctively different and more terrifying phase: the combination of the death-world and the technological world as a philosophy of war. (18)

The twentieth century death event has, in fact, become our conventional warfare.

This threat extending beyond the century's borders into its future—a legacy of the Cold War renewed by the atomic bomb tests of India and Pakistan and the NATO bombing of Yugoslavia in the spring of 1999—invests my study of modern war writing with an anxiety about art's power to address and affect war's unstoppability. *Writing War in the Twentieth Century* derives its ethical edge (and edginess) from this desire to have writing about mass warfare be "ethical" in J. Hillis Miller's sense ("The ethical moment in the act of reading . . . is a response to something, responsible to it, responsive to it, respectful of it" [4]). The challenge to have reading be ethically productive—"the ethical moment in reading leads to an act" (4)—raises the stakes of my critical project to produce critiques with relevance for the possibility of intervening in matters of policy. I am not suggesting that my reading of modern war texts be recognized as an exercise in political activism. I rather endorse having literary criticism, including mine, produce an engaged self-reflection of the sort promoted by Evelyn Fox Keller for the physical and biological sciences when she writes that "we need to understand the enmeshing of representing and intervening, how particular representations are already committed to particular kinds of interventions" (76). This perspective on science reminds us that, however indirectly, literature too is shaped by, and shapes, the ideological constructions that legitimate attitudes that inform public policy. War depends on a tortured logic of relations between ends and means. Literature and culture are not immune to colluding with the doubled and overwritten discourses of military action that themselves inevitably layer nonmaterial issues (security, sovereignty, national identity) over instrumentalities of force and violence (invasions, offensives, strategic bombing, nuclear threats). But while we readily recognize the cruder forms of war rhetoric's deviousness in justifying itself by propaganda, hypocrisy, and patriotic "lying" ("the Old Lie: Dulce et decorum est pro patria mori"),[4] I am more interested in the challenge posed by subtler and less visible textual incriminations and discursive self-incriminations. Even in sincere and compassionate poetic and narrative strategies for representing mass killing, we find that omissions, repressions, disavowals, and displacements may inadvertently produce verbal or discursive violence to suffering populations. "No one can speak for those murdered," Michael André Bernstein argues, "and no one can determine what would count as a further betrayal of their suffering" (44). Even the voices of victims, Jean-François Lyotard argues, may multiply the violence: "There would be no collective witness. From many deportees, there is only silence. From many, there is only the shame felt before the testimony of former deportees" (98).[5]

Then how can one speak at all of twentieth-century wars, and where does one begin? How does one formulate an inquiry, and what does one address in pursuing such a "century" critique? I began by choosing texts: clusters of canonical and popular works and popular mythologies and practices that seemed to me imperfect but illuminating responses to the century's historical catastrophe of manmade mass death. My study follows a chronological trajectory through the periods of the century to include modernist, avant-garde, and trench poetry of World War I, Ernest Hemingway's *A Farewell to Arms,* Erich Maria Remarque's *All Quiet on the Western Front,* the history of the Manhattan Project, John Hersey's *Hiroshima* and Japanese survivor (*hibakusha*) memoirs, the book and film *Schindler's List,* Francis Ford Coppola's film *Apocalypse Now,* and press censorship during the Persian Gulf War. I chose to explore widely read, popular, and "emblematic" war texts (including cultural "stories") as well as some avant-garde art, in order to press beyond exploring merely what art does to consider as well what sort of power it wields in inflecting both cultural attitudes and public policy. "The choice of examples, moreover, and their ordering," Miller points out in *The Ethics of Reading,* "is never innocent" (11). My examples are culpable in advance of a selectivity that does violence to what is left out, what is not honored by inclusion, what appears disrespected by inattention. On a local level, this problem partly results from the impossibility of encompassing so large a field; in nearly every conversation about this project, someone suggests yet another literary text I have not read, another critic or historian I have not yet encountered, another conflict I have not explored. But in the larger, historiographical context this matter of selectivity, prioritizing, and privileging of the century's conflicts is both an ethical and a political problem with the potential to marginalize peoples and silence or ignore voices.

Although a rigorous exploration of the problem of selectivity in the study of modern war is not possible here, even a brief allusion can suggest the scope and significance of its ethical ramifications. At the very least, privileging exempla is a problem of justice—for example, the arbitrary neglect of the suffering of the people of Nagasaki in favor of those of Hiroshima.[6] In other cases selectivity may constitute ideological maneuvers, as when the Western press is criticized for systematically foregrounding the problems and conflicts of industrialized nations over those of the Third World. Sometimes a failure to select may reflect both an inability and a refusal to select. Except for the bombing of German cities, which is widely known and addressed in such fictions as Kurt Vonnegut Jr.'s *Slaughterhouse-Five*, *Newsweek*'s indication that in World War II "3 million German civilians died, perhaps two thirds of them in forced expulsions from Eastern Europe" (May 22, 1995, 30), must seem surprising to many readers. The huge number of civilian casualties of the German expulsions have virtually no narrative or representational form—no facts, images, or stories—for a U.S. readership. The problem is partly historiographic; G. C. Paikert writes of the victims of the German exodus, "Approximately two million of them are still 'unaccounted for'; presumably the majority of these persons either died during their forced exodus, falling victim to starvation, imprisonment, forced labor, or to the hardships of the bitter winter of their migration in 1944/45" (3). Undocumented, these victims of chaos and policy become doubly victimized when the political context of their creation causes them also to become unmourned. The Cold War produced a similar reluctance to mourn Russian victims of World War II. In an effort to highlight the insufficiently global focus of the U.S. perspective on World War II, the *Newsweek* article compared the number of Soviets killed—"10 million soldiers and at least that many civilians"—with U.S. losses, "408,000 troops in both Europe and the Pacific" (30). In yet other cases, selectivity betrays categorical confusions. "Although figures for the First World War usually exclude an estimated 1.5 million Armenians exterminated by the Turks in 1915, those for the Second World War do include an estimated 5.9 million Jewish victims of the Nazi genocide," Ian Beckett notes (9). While this difference admits a range of explanations, the confusion over whether and how to count victims of genocide as war casualties is clearly one of them. Edith Wyschogrod provides a solution for this categorical conundrum by refiguring the phenomenon of modern "man-made mass death" as an "event" that encompasses killing and atrocity beyond the range of combat:

6

I shall define the scope of the event to include three characteristic expressions: recent wars which deploy weapons in the interest of maximum destruction of persons; annihilation of persons, through techniques designed for this purpose (for example famine, scorched earth, deportation), *after* the aims of war have been achieved or without reference to war; and the creation of death-worlds, a new and unique form of social existence in which vast populations are subjected to conditions of life simulating imagined conditions of death, conferring upon their inhabitants the status of the living dead. (15)

This book's problem of selection and exclusion may be simpler, more trivial, and more pragmatic, but it harbors at least a reduced version of the painful condition of maimed and untotalizable mourning that prevents our collective historical healing from the last century's wars. My text is haunted by its gaps and omissions, both large and small, of untold massacres, unaddressed atrocities, unreported holocausts. Even my list of writers omitted is doomed to incompletion and fragmentariness. Virginia Woolf, Robert Graves, E. M. Forster, and Vera Brittain are missing from the discussion of World War I, along with poets and novelists from other European literatures. There is no mention, in my discussion of World War I, of the Armenian massacre, or, in my discussion of World War II, of the infamous 1937 Rape of Nanking, during which the Japanese killed over a third of the civilian population of this Chinese city—an estimated 260,000 to 350,000 people murdered during a seven-week rampage.[7] My discussions of World War II writers omit Norman Mailer's *The Naked and the Dead,* Günter Grass's *The Tin Drum,* Thomas Pynchon's *Gravity's Rainbow,* and the dark comic fictions of Kurt Vonnegut Jr. and Joseph Heller. I treat a popular Hollywood film instead of Elie Wiesel's classic Holocaust memoir *Night,* Claude Lanzmann's remarkable *Shoah,* or the work of Primo Levi. And I selected another popular Hollywood film instead of the serious Vietnam War fiction of Tim O'Brien, or the narratives of Vietnamese writers that Renny Christopher discusses in her 1995 book *The Viet Nam War/The American War.* I leave out the Korean War altogether, do not engage with "nuclear criticism," and fail to contend with contemporary violence in Rwanda, Russia, and Serbia. My list of omissions could go on and on, but even if the list of conflicts and their representations were different, the field would still remain untotalizable.

Although my inclusions are based on a variety of criteria, the most signifi-cant include *recognition* or identification with the conflict (e.g., poetry, Hem-ingway, and Remarque with World War I, Hiroshima and the Holocaust with World War II, etc.) as well as availability and popularity with a U.S. reader-ship. These criteria—partly stimulated by my teaching—lead to other prob-lems, however.

The ethical problem of selectivity affects not only the choice of historical focus and textual material but also the matter of perspective, of critical stance, theoretical framework, and voice. I have felt with some frustration that no matter how cosmopolitan I wish to make my sympathies, it is still difficult—even when writing out of a complex personal and intellectual background—entirely to escape a perspective inflected by Western con-cerns, by a U.S. point of view, by an orientation toward male-centered is-sues, and by a frank pacifist prejudice. I would hope this is less a personal failing than a constituent of the ethical dilemma endemic to the study of the literature of war. Contemporary critics such as Jacques Derrida[8] and Jean-François Lyotard (in *The Differend*) have given us conceptual tools for ad-dressing the aporia that plagues expert knowledge and expertise with the inevitable violence produced when selectivity causes every discourse, every text, to dispute, displace, and silence its alternatives and its opposites. Wrestling with the problem of the justice of one's critical approach led me to adopt very different voices and discursive modes for discussing different kinds of texts and different kinds of war experiences. Because the emotional valences of military and noncombatant casualties tend to differ, I found, for example, that one cannot discuss World War II in precisely the same way one discusses World War I. The style of analyzing war poetry is necessarily different from the critical discourse needed to transmit and summarize a revisionary history of weapons development, like the one I offer in my chap-ter on the Manhattan Project. And I found it absolutely impossible to treat a highly stylized filmic text such as Francis Ford Coppola's *Apocalypse Now,* which is intended to work on a symbolic rather than a realistic level, in the same way one treats Steven Spielberg's *Schindler's List,* which had to fulfill its considerable responsibility for historical fidelity and factual accuracy by having Holocaust survivors as consultants on the set. The result is that al-though my chapters are organized chronologically from the beginning of the twentieth century to its end, their sequence resembles less a continuous nar-rative, coherent thesis, or developing argument than a kind of collage assem-bly of different discursive and representational styles only loosely united by the common topic of war. However, I've tried to impose this diversity of styles of critical writing on an underlying set of recurring and related ethical topics.

One of the challenges in respecting the pressure of tacit counterevidence to any given text—the ramification of Lyotard's concept of the *differend*—is that it obliges one to eschew pressing twentieth-century war writing into service as evidence for an overarching thesis. Although it would be possible to construct a coherent argument about the relationship between representation, numbers, and violence in the literature of modern war, a more nuanced ethical reading is achieved if one avoids the temptation to create a master narrative that gives a single argument victory or justification. An example of such a thesis that crops up repeatedly in a number of my chapters—but that I did not wish to sustain as the overarching explanation for the representational difficulties of modern warfare—argues that instrumental and rationalistic military discourses have colluded with an ideology of hostility to population *as such* that has simultaneously facilitated and disavowed the deliberate destruction of vast numbers of people. Because of its local recrudescence in a number of my discussions of both world wars, this argument is nonetheless worth addressing even if it does not provide a master key to the question of why the killing and wounding of nearly 130 million people was sanctioned in the twentieth century. The hostility to population that appears inscribed in the twentieth-century "death event," as Edith Wyschogrod calls it, seems to have had an overdetermined origin in the eighteenth century in the "actuarial terror" of Thomas Malthus and Romantic fantasies of depopulation, as Frances Ferguson has argued,[9] and in the fear of anarchic masses and mobs produced by the democratizing French and American revolutions of the Enlightenment.[10] These nascent population fears received their formal articulation as a threat to art, culture, and civilized life in Matthew Arnold's nineteenth-century *Culture and Anarchy*, which in turn conditioned both the form and ideology of high modernism in the twentieth. The cultural hostility to population had rhetorical, political, and aesthetic consequences for Western art's response to the massive casualties produced by the twentieth century's world wars. Early in the century, particularly during the early years of World War I, mourning for the vast aggregates of the dead was blunted by a shocking calculus reckoning the massive war casualties as a prophylactic form of population control. In his study of Ezra Pound, John Tytell notes that eugenics theories were widespread in the early twentieth century, and he cites the example of Winston

Churchill as typical: "Winston Churchill was a believer in eugenics and the idea that the earlier stages of the industrial system had created work for an enormous mass of inferior Europeans who were less and less required as the system evolved" (119). The sculptor Henri Gaudier-Brzeska, Pound's friend, published a missive from the front in Wyndham Lewis's avant-garde journal *Blast,* which provocatively extends this argument into a sardonic claim for the Great War's contribution to population control—"THIS PALTRY MECHANISM, WHICH SERVES AS A PURGE TO OVER-NUMEROUS HUMANITY. THIS WAR IS A GREAT REMEDY" (33). But if the proto-modernist and modernist late nineteenth- and early twentieth-century hostilities to excess population were inflected by class hatreds, they transmogrified into race hatreds after World War I. Walter Benn Michaels finds in Lothrop Stoddard's post–World War I tract *The Rising Tide of Color against White World-Supremacy* an obverse eugenic fear: "The Great War, according to Stoddard, was a breeding disaster for the white race since, in killing millions of Nordic soldiers at an age when they were 'best adapted to fecundity,' it had (like immigration) 'prevented millions more from being born or conceived'" (198).

But however tempting, it is untenably reductive to shape this historical trajectory of population ideology into the overarching thesis that the tolerance for immense casualties was underwritten by class hatreds in World War I, by race hatreds in World War II, and by a combination of class, race, and ideological hatreds during the Cold War and post–Cold War conflicts directed against the Third World in the latter part of the century. Nonetheless, it may reasonably be argued that hostility to population compromised experimentation to achieve poetic expressions and representations of the death event. Benedict Anderson's concept of nations as "imagined communities" illuminates the sharp contrast between imaginatively bonding with one's own war dead and imagining oneself in communion with a dead enemy population.[11] The former can have tremendous political potency—for example, the state of Israel's spiritual and emotional communion with Holocaust victims—while the latter tends to be confined to poignant fantasies of individual identification and empathy (for example, Wilfred Owen's "I am the enemy you killed, my friend,"[12] or Erich Maria Remarque's anguished "I have killed the printer, Gérard Duval. I must be a printer, I think confusedly, be a printer, printer" (225). But although population hostility may mediate and deform artistic responses to the massive twentieth-century war casualties, a more nuanced argument locates the difficulties of writing and speaking modern mass warfare in the convergence of several determinants, including three of particular significance: generic limitation or the problem of picturing or imagining dead populations in language; epistemological crises or the inability to know or apprehend the deaths of thousands or millions of persons; and ideological contaminations or the pressures behind cultural and artistic disavowals and legitimations of mass violence.

As an alternative to an overarching narrative, I have opted for allowing my selected texts to produce an aporia that urges they be read against the shadow of some countertext, some other voice of their own kind or of a different kind. This makes it easier to relate the challenges that modern mass warfare creates to the problems and conflicts that haunt its criticism. Throughout this study, I intend to keep the ethical inquiry focused on the literary peculiarities—especially the rhetorical texture and narrative strategies—of my topical texts. Even when one deals with topical or historical issues, questions of justice appear inseparable from the deployment of discourse—as I discovered at the genesis of my project, two weeks after the onset of the 1991 Persian Gulf War. When I learned that we would be given no estimates of enemy casualties, I began to question the relationship between the Pentagon's rigidly imposed press censorship and its refusal to make a body count. It seemed that by coupling an instrumental military discourse to the indeterminability and invisibility of the enemy body, the Pentagon had created a sophisticated strategy for derealizing the war. By transforming mass bombing into a spectacle that would feel to the U.S. public like a simulation, a hypothetical explanation or demonstration rather than a representation of destruction and damage, the military had managed to lighten the ethical valence of its massive bombing campaign. This strategy, mirrored in the writings of Jean Baudrillard, in turn created intellectual controversies over whether this postmodernistic military strategy generated theoretical collusion that required resistance.[13] From the government's point of vantage, the Pentagon strategy struck me as ambiguously successful: it effectively eliminated criticism or protest by making the war "virtual" rather than "real," but at the price of failing to have it register meaningfully as a national experience. This is the reason, in my opinion, why the war's wild popularity failed to neutralize the Bush administration's economic woes in the president's bid for a second term. But from an ethical point of view, the strategy enacted an evasion of responsibility.

This contemporary war exploration sent me back to my own literary period, the early twentieth century, to look into the intriguing relationship of form to numbers in the poetry of World War I. Inscribed in the rigorous economies of poetic form—modernist poetry's extrusion of excess, indulgence, profligacy, and sentiment in poetic language—one finds Matthew Arnold's legacy linking a commitment to high art with ideological repulsion by mass population and mass culture. The discipline and craft of modernist poetry reflect an ideological hostility to excessiveness as a concept—excessiveness readily troped as superfluous and unwanted population that took form, at least in some of the early strains of high modernism, as a frank militarism.[14] This discourse in turn abraded against the lyrical Georgian outpourings of soldier-poets in the trenches. In the dissonance of the ensuing formal debates—particularly the derision and dismissal by the modernists of trench poetry's "realism" as sentimental and effete—one can find the marks of a class hatred that refused to mourn the carnage of an army construed as England's industrial human surplus fighting on a battlefield configured like an industrial slum. One might expect a similar ideological dispute to result from putting two highly popular 1929 war novels into dialogue with each other: Ernest Hemingway's *A Farewell to Arms* and Erich Maria Remarque's *All Quiet on the Western Front*. But the contest between Hemingway's rigorously stripped prose and Remarque's anguished lyrical naturalism fails to replay the combat between the modernists and the trench poets. While the adventures of Hemingway's American in Italy do *not* address the carnage of the trenches, the novel nonetheless stages the ethical crisis of war writing and truth telling in a surprisingly doubled, nuanced, and indirect way—in style, narration, and textual performativity. With a very different agenda, Remarque, emerged from the German trenches, bends the *Bildungsroman* into an innovative *novel of depopulation*—one of the most successful treatments of the war's industrial violence, and one of the most nuanced representations of dying and dead populations that I encountered in my study.

With some exceptions, notably the massacre of one and a half million Armenians by the Turks in 1915, the depopulation of World War I was generational rather than genocidal;[15] Erich Maria Remarque announced that his novel would "try simply to tell of a generation of men who, even though they may have escaped its shells, were destroyed by the war" (1). But the two most conspicuous and emblematic population atrocities of World War II were different: the Holocaust and Hiroshima both resulted from a political willingness to destroy populations of civilians for no instrumental purpose, no strategic gain or military goal. The political ends of these mass killings, however they were publicly or secretly rationalized, can be recognized in distilled form as displays of pure power. I chose Steven Spielberg's academically controversial film of Thomas Keneally's *Schindler's List* as my Holocaust text because I believe it articulates the operational logic of this premise and dilates its subjective effects in a historically illuminating and ethically responsible way. All Holocaust criticism proceeds with anxiety, for the response to the Holocaust—both artistic and scholarly—still exhibits symptoms that might be likened to post-traumatic shock. These symptoms are both expressed and explored in the ongoing critical debates over foundational ethical issues concerning mandates and prohibitions for representation and speech—debates enacted in the paradox between the wide popular approval and sharp academic disapproval of Spielberg's film. But the unique opportunity to interleave Thomas Keneally's historical research, Steven Spielberg's popular-media presentation, and survivor memories and memoirs of the Cracow ghetto and the Płaszów concentration camp make it possible to explore *Schindler's List* as a didactically powerful and emotionally commemorative population narrative.

Hiroshima—a different kind of holocaust—makes its troubling effect on U.S. reaction visible in U.S. censorship, disavowal, and repression. In a 1998 *Los Angeles Times* book review, Greg Mitchell—the coauthor of *Hiroshima in America*—writes that "Hiroshima is America's raw nerve" (4). The cancellation, under military and congressional pressure, of the planned 1995 Smithsonian Museum anniversary commemoration of the end of World War II demonstrated the difficulty of accepting alternative versions of what the historian Barton J. Bernstein has characterized as the "official" Hiroshima story, that the "bombs had been necessary to end the war quickly and avoid the dread invasions with many American casualties; there were no likely alternatives to using the bomb; and the use of the bomb on enemy cities had been necessary, patriotic, and just" (*Judgment at the Smithsonian*, 133). I include a nonliterary chapter on U.S. atomic weapons development in order to draw attention to the contested appropriation of the authority of science to justify atomic warfare as rational policy. Without the story of the Manhattan Project, the story of Hiroshima can be read as a natural disaster narrative rather than as a scientific plot whose sequel transformed postwar Japan into a U.S. research laboratory on the effects of the bomb on human bodies. Even compassionate U.S. accounts of Hiroshima focus on the physics of the event, and John Hersey's deracinated Japanese have history, particularity, subjectivity, and anger restored to them only in *hibakusha* memoirs and poetry.

Vietnamese voices, likewise, rarely break through in U.S. writing about the Vietnam War. But in contrast to the faulty way U.S. Hiroshima accounts grapple with U.S. responsibility, Francis Ford Coppola's *Apocalypse Now* interpolates modernism's great narrative of imperialist self-indictment—Joseph Conrad's *Heart of Darkness*—into a powerful poetic critique of U.S. military adventurism in Southeast Asia.

Theorizing War and the Twentieth-Century Rupture

The texts I have chosen as my exemplary representations and narratives of twentieth-century warfare are, as I tried to emphasize in my survey above, intended to function not as singular voices but as voices in dialogue and dispute with other texts and other voices. Writing about war is itself engaged in a textual condition of war, as it were. One of the predominant pressures against which many of the texts I've selected struggle is the double language of idealism (the appeal of heroism, sacrifice, patriotism, nationalism) and rationalism, the authoritative voice of military logic and political policy since the eighteenth century.[16] My own voice is similarly engaged in dialogue and dispute with other critical and theoretical studies of war and war writing, and although it is possible to make some generalizations about the battle lines, as it were, my intellectual field resists schematization into clear or simple alliances. The dominant discursive universe of twentieth-century thinking about war was shaped by the rationalistic logic of Carl von Clausewitz in the nineteenth century,[17] and much of my implicit and explicit critique of military logic throughout this study is aimed at the vulnerabilities—the virtually inevitable illogicality, hypocrisy, and deviousness—of this instrumental discourse and its fictions of ends and means. By focusing on art's contention (or complicity) with the secondary violence of martial logic, I set my thinking apart from prominent academic discourses both outside and inside the humanities. Although my decade-long involvement with the Global Peace and Conflict Studies Program (GPACS) at the University of California, Irvine, has taught me great respect for the work of historians and political and social scientists, I don't engage in the "professional" academic discourse of war and politics that Jean Bethke Elshtain locates in the field of international relations (IR) and that she subjects to sharp critique:

> But—something happened when realism got pinioned within the academy: it became palpably less realistic, less attuned to the

political and historic landscape than in its classical formulations. Encumbered with lifeless jargon, systems and subsystem dominance, spirals of misperception, decision-making analysis, bipolar, multipolar, intervening variables, dependence, interdependence, cost-effectiveness, IR specialists in the post–Second World War era began to speak exclusively to, or "at," one another or to their counterparts in government service. (88)

Nor, although I admire their contributions, do I ally myself with prominent contemporary studies that offer irrationalistic theories of war's genesis and dynamic, such as Barbara Ehrenreich's primitivist genealogy in *Blood Rites,* Klaus Theweleit's study of fascist violence in *Male Fantasies,* and Gilles Deleuze and Félix Guattari's extra-institutional model of the "war machine." [18] I do not mean to argue that the waging of war is *not* irrational, but I am more interested in why war is pointedly *not irrationalistic* in its self-presentation. I see the rationalizations and justifications for waging war powerfully engaged in disavowal: disavowing disjunctions between ends and means, incommensurabilities between ideals and material effects, and the element of excess that makes the ultraviolence of modern warfare incapable of serving any rational instrumentality. The thinking of Elaine Scarry, with its materialist bias in her analysis of how and what war signifies, has had great impact on my approach to modern warfare and warfare's resistance to representation. The influence of *The Body in Pain* will be in evidence throughout my various arguments—particularly in the sections that interrogate the refusal of military discourse to honor its referential obligation to the wounded or slain human body. Finally, my project—to retrieve from military logic and artistic representation reference both to the material body of entire populations as well as to the subjectivity that modern warfare's death event destroys—obliges me to consider (however obliquely) the paradoxes and conundrums posed by the destruction or maiming of language by trauma. Although the important work of Shoshana Felman, Dori Laub, and Cathy Caruth stands in the foreground of this field, I am most indebted to Edith Wyschogrod's *Spirit in Ashes* for raising the significant ontological question that also echoes through my study:

What is the meaning of death in the twentieth century, when millions of lives have been extinguished and the possibility of annihilating human life altogether remains open? Is there an art of dying which is useful in this time and circumstance? Or does quantitative change, the emergence of the numberless dead, so alter our perspective on death that no interpretation is adequate to the apocalyptic character of the phenomenon except perhaps the gasp of horror, the scream, that in Greek tragedy accompanies the revelation of things unspeakable? (1)

Primitivistic theories of war's genesis have only arguable relevance for modern warfare because they inadequately reckon the changes that technology has brought to the phenomenon of war. For the purposes of this study I need less a theory of war's origins than an explanation of why modern warfare is phenomenologically and ontologically discontinuous with earlier modes of warfare. The answer—that modern weapons technology has fundamentally altered the locus of agency—also addresses the fundamentally altered ethical terrain on which modern wars are waged. To track this change with attention to how agency, instrumentality, ontology, and ethics are simultaneously affected by technology in warfare, I find it useful to begin with a historical moment of warfare that produced a specifically anthropogenetic model of war's genesis: a theory not that war is the result of humankind's unsuppressed animality or bestiality but, on the contrary, that war is coeval with the moment of becoming human. In deriving this moment from the discussion of the master–slave dialectic in Hegel's *Phenomenology of Mind,* Alexandre Kojève sheds light on some of the intractable paradoxes of war's simultaneous idealism and inhumanity. Hegel finished writing the *Phenomenology* while listening to the gunfire of the Battle of Jena in 1806—a moment Kojève turns inside out, as it were: "Therefore, human, historical, self-conscious existence is possible only where there are, or—at least— where there have been, bloody fights, wars for prestige. And thus it was the sounds of one of these fights that Hegel heard while finishing his *Phenomenology,* in which he became conscious of himself by answering his question 'What am I?'" (41). Kojève finds the symbolic status of war as an ultrasignificant phenomenon grounded in the Hegelian notion that the moment of becoming human was situated in an originary fight to the death because the transition from animal to human required the willingness to risk life, to transcend the survival instinct and set immaterial values above material life. This fiction of war's genesis as coeval with idealism has the value of locating the origins of war in a fissure or rupture between the impulses and interests of the body and those of the mind as a subject created by self-consciousness.

This fissure or rupture perdures as the condition of war, with idealism, ideology, reason, and logic providing the self and the nation with transcendentalizing figures and mechanisms that require the material destruction of human bodies and human populations for their symbolic exaltation.

But those bodies were historically male, with significant cultural consequences for the symbolic valorization of gender. Simone de Beauvoir, working within the phenomenological philosophical tradition that transmitted Hegel to Sartre and Merleau-Ponty by way of Alexandre Kojève,[19] recognizes that the gendering of the warrior as male served also to gender the male as human:

> The warrior put his life in jeopardy to elevate the prestige of the horde, the clan to which he belonged. And in this he proved dramatically that life is not the supreme value for man, but on the contrary that it should be made to serve ends more important than itself. The worst curse that was laid upon woman was that she should be excluded from these warlike forays. For it is not in giving life but in risking life that man is raised above the animal; that is why superiority has been accorded in humanity not to the sex that brings forth but to that which kills. (64)

This elaborate explanation produces the simple demotic truth, that war is what makes a man a man. "Here we have the key to the whole mystery" (64), Beauvoir states of this dynamic model of war, gender, and the Symbolic Order.[20] But this gendered model of anthropogenesis as the origin of war may also provide the key to the fundamental difference that makes twentieth-century wars ontologically discontinuous with earlier wars. If before World War II the warrior and his victim were both male and were the same, since World War I they were different. Civilian casualties in World War I accounted for 15 percent of fatalities, according to Barbara Ehrenreich, whereas in World War II the proportion was 65 percent of total fatalities, far more than half (206). This shift had to do in large part with dramatic changes in the technology of weaponry in the twentieth century, changes that effectively deconstruct the concept of the warrior and of combatancy in ways that make the Hegelian gladiatorial and masculinist model of individual one-on-one combat philosophically obsolete and irrelevant for understanding modern war. "One feature of the 'transformed' war of the nuclear age is that it is less likely to be the exclusive province of males or even of adults," Ehrenreich writes, attributing the "de-gendering" of war to the on-going "democratization" of weaponry (229). The gun was the first of these democratizing weapons, making it possible to kill with minimized risk to life. Conversely, the "risk of life" faced by a civilian population vulnerable to atomic weapons attack bears no ontological relation, no related idealizable value, to that faced by a samurai.

Elaine Scarry writes of nuclear arms that it is "only at the 'firing' end of the weapon that human presence is eliminated: their bodies' presence at the receiving end is still very much required" (*Body in Pain,* 152). But the changing configurations of soldiers and victims have had profound impact on the discourses legitimating nuclear war, and on their ethical status. The agency of killing—always already dispersed among politicians, strategists, and soldiers—becomes so extremely dispersed with the deployment of weapons of mass destruction as to become virtually unlocatable. At the same time, the increasingly indiscriminate effects of modern weapons disperse both the nature of their targets and the instrumental rationalization and justification of their use. One could reformulate Elaine Scarry's dictum that in nuclear arms "the *building-in of skill* thus becomes in its most triumphant form, the *building-out of consent*" (152) to say that the building-in of technological agency becomes the building-out of human responsibility. In some significant way, atomic bombs are thought to kill populations without a corresponding human image—a Harry Truman, Leslie Groves, Robert Oppenheimer, or Paul Tibbets—to occupy the place of agency, the place where, in the Hegelian model, transcendence was once earned by risking life.[21] The "risk of life" had to be retroactively replaced with the military argument sharply contested in revisionary histories, that the bomb saved the United States from risking a half-million U.S. soldiers in an invasion of Japan. Since the Germans could invoke or invent no similar justification for annihilating an internal Jewish population that posed no threat and lacked all combatancy, ethical descriptions of the Holocaust can readily assume as one of its characteristics the extreme power differential more proper to the condition of torture than to the condition of war.[22] When modern war refigures combatancy as an atomic weapon aimed at a civilian population, or a military and administrative machine bent on annihilating an internal population, the gladiatorial or ludic model of warfare becomes inoperative; pure slaughter, without risk or instrumental justification, strips war of both rational and idealistic foundations.

But modern discourses of war fail to acknowledge this changed ethical condition. The only moment of rupture occurred in World War I, when the use of chemical weapons scandalized Western civilized pretensions. The widespread recoil from the use of nerve gas recognized that an essentially targetless technology—which kills utterly without discrimination because it usurps the human element, the air—destroys the ludic pretense and the fiction that war functions as a rule-governed contest. But although chemical and biological warfare remain unacceptable, the introduction of aerial bombing in World War I and its increasing use against civilian populations in World War II were accompanied by shifting and shifty rationales that exposed their improvised anteriority to the technology. The initial argument, that the massive conscription of civilians into the war industries made their destruction strategically necessary, failed with the failure of strategic bombing. An instrument that was intended to work as a scalpel worked instead like a bludgeon, according to John Pimlott. "When, in the absence of a weapon capable of hitting anything smaller than a city, the bombers cannot even take out precise targets, this temptation [to go for bludgeon attacks, flattening the city on the assumption that it contains many valuable targets that are not on the planners' lists] becomes operational necessity" (135). As cities were destroyed by weaponry too imprecise to target specific military and industrial installations, the target of instrumental rationalization was widened from factories to workers' homes, to cultural centers whose destruction would demoralize the populace. The destruction of Dresden, called "Florence on the Elbe" for the beauty of its architecture and the wealth of its art treasures, by five massive air attacks in February 1945 remains an emblem of strategic bombing with no defensible military purpose. And had it not been for Secretary of War Henry Stimson's recoil from destroying Japan's ancient cultural capital, Kyoto (the preferred target of the atomic bomb target committee) would have been another.[23] In post–World War II fighting, the discourses justifying or exculpating the bombing of civilian areas tend to invoke indirect rationalizations that make civilian deaths "accidents" or incidental by-products of some other military necessity. The most pernicious—in its manipulation of ethical responsibility—was the U.S. claim that its civilian Iraqi victims had been "human shields" deliberately interposed by Saddam Hussein between U.S. missiles and their military targets during the Persian Gulf War. This same claim was repeated by the NATO alliance spokesman Jamie Shea after NATO bombs killed more than 80 people, most of them ethnic Albanians, in the village of Korisa on May 14, 1999. Paul Watson, a Canadian journalist reporting the attack, likened the

NATO bombings of Yugoslavia to "calling in a plumber to fix a leak and watching him flood the house" ("Witness to War," A32).[24]

Discursive Fractures and the Problem of Genre

How can art assume responsibility for either resisting these instrumental discourses of the military and political establishments or at least calling them to account? Can art turn the tables on political science, and make its own critical capability the voice of "realism" on the subject of war and thereby extricate itself from its unintentional alliance with the ineffectual camp of "idealism" in Elshtain's sense: the pacifists and religious moralists dismissed by academic scholarship of war for their "dangerous if well-intentioned innocence concerning the world's ways" (Elshtain, 88)? Can art overcome its internal constitutive difficulty in addressing the violent, the cruel, and the ugly without transforming it into beauty, without endowing it with aesthetic effects, without arousing pleasure, without bringing to redemption what should be irredeemable? These are formidable challenges for art in the twentieth century, and the extent to which they have been met successfully is as remarkable as the extent to which they cannot be met. While I hope that my study implicitly responds to these questions and delineates art's powers and constraints in the face of this subject, it may be helpful nonetheless to sketch at least a few of the more intractable difficulties that the representation of the extreme violence of modern mass warfare poses to modern art. Among the more egregious difficulties I would privilege a set of related problems: art's epistemological inability to totalize, to encompass all aspects of a phenomenon; the long-standing marriage of art and individualism that makes artistic representation resistant to human aggregations, to populations; and, concomitant with the previous point, art's inability to extend its power to express subjectivity—its power to make the interiority of lived experience available to its expressive media—to the representation of large numbers of people, and particularly to large numbers of the dying and the dead.

Although art shares with other human sciences its inability to perceive war as a whole, in a totalized form, its specific selectivities of focus and perspective tend to carry negative consequences for the authority of its discourses. The complexity of war in the twentieth century has indeed forced the field of military history to broaden and transgress traditional disciplinary boundaries—"Until recent years, the field of 'military history' tended to be narrowly defined as the study of generalship, battles and campaigns—what has been described rather unkindly as 'drum-and-bugle' history," Colin McInnes and G. D. Sheffield write in their introduction to *Warfare in the Twentieth Century*. "However, the realization of the importance of war has led to non-military historians being drawn to the study of warfare and taking paths rather different from the traditional one" (ix–x). Among these paths, magisterial histories that are monuments to facticity remain privileged with indisputable authority as reference works. Its heavy grounding in data and statistics lends Robert Goralski's impressive *World War II Almanac, 1931– 1945* the referentiality of the "real": the dust jacket promises, and the text delivers, "detailed maps, charts and diagrams depicting major battles, invasions and landings as well as production and losses by the individual military powers." The back of the book bristles with lists of all kinds: detailed casualty charts; accounts of monetary costs; "Leading Fighter Aces by Nationalities (With Numbers of Enemy Planes Downed in Combat)" (422); "Weekly Rations for Prisoners in Class II Nazi Concentration Camps" (429); the weights, lengths, tonnages, and speeds of tanks; the cruising ranges of all types of battleships; and much more. Looked at from this perspective, art can be seen to seize *what is left over* for its own terrain, a leftover in the form of the *human remainder*, the affective residue, the suffering that military histories imply but don't voice, the inner experience that can't be mapped, charted, counted, or otherwise quantified. The consequence of this intellectual economy is that the human remainder left over for art belongs to the discredited realm of the private and the subjective—a realm traditionally coded as feminine—while facticity lends history and political science the masculinely coded prestige of the public and the objective.

Modern art's response to this marginalization as a disesteemed war discourse has been diverse, although two particular tendencies to compete with the "harder" human sciences are worth noting. Modernistic prose can be said, roughly, to derive its own tendencies toward concreteness and objectivity from the influence of Gustave Flaubert on the literary front and from journalism on the extraliterary front. Ezra Pound in poetry and Ernest Hemingway in fiction were exemplary modernists intent on bringing the marks of the masculine—coded as hard, dry, concrete, objective, spare, crafted, disciplined language—to their art. Modernism might therefore be seen to have equipped itself with the formal means to meet historiography on its own terms as a fitting discourse of war. I will explore the devious complexities of this proposition later, in my discussion of Hemingway's *A Farewell to*

Arms. But in cruder terms, this tendency explains the privileging of the journalist writers—Hemingway, Martha Gellhorn, John Hersey, Michael Herr, to name only a few—as successful speakers for modern war. At the same time, concern with fiction's inability to match the "truth value" of historical facticity tends to privilege writing that has testimonial power—the memoir, the diary, the letter, the poetry and fiction of the soldier—as we see in the writing of Erich Maria Remarque and the trench poets, for example. Military censorship—such as that exercised rigorously during the Persian Gulf War—is designed to incapacitate both of these forms of "truth-telling" capability, both "objective" journalism and the "subjective" voice of witness. But that very gesture simultaneously bears witness to recognition that significant "truth" resides elsewhere than in facticity, that the transmission of subjective experience has the potency to challenge the rational narrative that military briefings and their disseminations of facts claim as salient knowledge. There is an opening, then, for arguing that art's responsibilities might include the exposure of historical writing's own inability to totalize, whatever tonnage of facts it brings to bear on its telling of war, and to explore the status of history as historiography, inherently as textual, narrative, and metonymic as art itself. The excited response to the "realism" of Steven Spielberg's World War II film, *Saving Private Ryan,* acknowledges that there are "truths" of combat that elude narrative—truths of sounds, noise, motion, touch, imperception, blindness, muteness—that historiography is unable to portray but that are available to genre-bending experiments. This film, in turn, uncovered the silences of trauma where they had been least suspected, among the heroic and much appreciated veterans of the great modern "just war," many of whom now acknowledge that they have not been able to speak of what they experienced.

Art's inability to totalize war experience clashes with history's inability to totalize war experience to produce war discourse as a model of complex fracture, a pattern of uneven and awkward breaks whose points of rupture, like those in a body, are sites of cultural pain. The fractures divide not only by discipline, with history's fictions of policy discontinuous with art's fictions of subjective experience; they divide sharply within disciplines, cleaving official and revisionary histories, amputating memories and memoirs from their historical contexts, making the spheres of war experience and significance incommensurate and incommunicable with each other. How can the hidden U.S. policy—to use an atomic weapon to intimidate the Soviet Union by bombing two Japanese cities—relate to the keloids on the faces of Japanese schoolgirls burned by the blast, except as a narrative fracture? How can art meaningfully relate the politics and policy that continue as war, in a Clausewitzian sense, to the "other means" of the materiality of the fighting on the ground? Erich Maria Remarque's soldiers, resorting to a chivalric model of honor, conclude that wars begin when one country badly offends another country, a concept they cannot decipher analytically. "A country, I don't follow. A mountain in Germany cannot offend a mountain in France." Even seriously they cannot make the connection: "Almost all of us are simple folk. And in France, too, the majority of men are labourers, workmen, or poor clerks. Now just why would a French blacksmith or a French shoemaker want to attack us?" (204–5). How can one cope with a phenomenon like the Holocaust, where the link between the policy and the unstoppable suffering it produced ruptures rationality, any pretense of functional instrumentality, and can therefore be figured only as an ideological pathology? Thomas Keneally's patient and careful labor in reconstructing the historical shape of an era and interleaving it with the quotidian detail of the Cracow Jews' lived experience emerges as one of the more remarkable attempts to "set" the fracture of war narrative and create a fiction that, while it cannot totalize the catastrophe, nonetheless makes a highly integrated version available to the imagination. The Holocaust is a particularly acute site of fracture, in any case, because while the trauma has not yet abated (and will probably never abate) and the event's subjectivity remains largely unexpressed and unmastered, the arena of facticity—assembling the facts of the vast Nazi technology of imprisonment and mass killing—has about it an aura of violation intensified by the pressures put on it by the denials of Holocaust revisionists. Totalization—bringing the layers of war narrative together into a coherent whole—may be not only an impossibility but perhaps also, in some respects, an undesirability.

The discursive fractures that impair our ability to comprehend war as a totality challenge literary writing to produce genres that will be responsive to the mass destruction of warfare. In one sense, the most extreme features of modern mass warfare—its immense scale, its global threat, and the intense suffering it produces—could be said to render modern war writing "postgeneric"—that is, fit only to problematize the very concept of genre, to question the representational and ethical fitness of all genres, as it questions the representational and ethical fitness of art itself. But its postgeneric condition does not obviate the need of war writing to make generic choices nevertheless, even though these choices will be fraught with compromises and complicities, and with the danger of imposing significances preordained by genre upon historical experience. Michael André Bernstein's *Foregone Conclusions* eloquently elaborates the perils and possibilities of generic decisions in relation to the Holocaust, invoking particularly the Bakhtinian caveat against seeing reality through the eyes of genre (10).[25] At the same time, war writing is an inevitably intertexted process, obliged to contend with its own tradition of genres and conventions in the spirit of debt, opposition, or subversion even as it is haunted by the betrayals and inadequacies of its predecessors. The soldiers of Stephen Crane's *Red Badge of Courage* mentally carry Homer's *Iliad* into the Civil War with them, Crane's naturalism thereby playing its minutiae of fear, pain, and bafflement off the clarity of the epic's graphic violence, the grandeur of its national scale and religious significance, and the magniloquence of its poetry. But not only in fiction do war's participants bring genre cognitively to bear on experience, testing their perception against the expectations of film or writing, expressing their sense and feeling through the referent of media. "Mythopathic moment," Michael Herr calls Vietnam flashbacks to, say, John Wayne and Henry Fonda in *Fort Apache* (47). Combatants and survivors of war must themselves contend not only with genre but with their internalization of genre.

> I keep thinking about all the kids who got wiped out by seventeen years of war movies before coming to Vietnam to get wiped out for good. You don't know what a media freak is until you've seen the way a few of those grunts would run around during a fight when they knew that there was a television crew nearby; they were actually making war movies in their heads, doing little guts-and-glory Leatherneck tap dances under fire, getting their pimples shot off for the networks" (Herr, 223)

Because war is a world-unmaking event, a reality-deconstructing and defamiliarizing activity, one of the challenges of war writing is how to make its inherent epistemological disorientation, its sense of experienced "unreality," real. This generic challenge makes artists vulnerable to the temptations of genres of the unreal, the abnormal, and the extreme—the Gothic, the grotesque, the surreal, the expressionistic—that can lend to war writing powerful conventions of horror, fright, and disgust, but that even at their best can carry with them the ideological freight of decadence, pathology, and irrationality. The generic ambiguity of postnuclear television films—such as

24

The Day After and *Threads*—exposes the danger of exteriorizing the horror, representing it as seen but inadequately incorporated into the viewing eye, and thereby straddling the thin line between voyeurism and witness more on the side of the detached viewer of disaster films. Michael Herr's *Dispatches,* conversely, produced prose that veered like a hand-held camera in dizzying implication at what is narratively seen—a technique that strongly influenced Francis Ford Coppola's surrealistic cinematic style in parts of *Apocalypse Now,* and gave Steven Spielberg's opening sequence in *Saving Private Ryan* much of its visceral impact. "It's not just the carnage—the leg off here, the arm off there," Spielberg explained to Hendrik Hertzberg in a *New Yorker* article. "It's the cumulative effect of the shaky handheld camera, the uncoated lenses, the desaturated color. . . . Nothing blurs: when you see an explosion, you see every grain of sand. It's an accumulation of sounds and sights" (31). This technique contrasts with the more traditional shots of war movies, which, according to Paul Virilio, simulate the embrasured perspective of the gunner: "The soldier's obscene gaze, on his surroundings and on the world, his art of hiding from sight in order to see, is not just an ominous voyeurism but from the first imposes a long-term patterning on the chaos of vision" (49).[26] The affective difference between John Hersey's compassionate but cool narration of *Hiroshima* and the narratives in which the *hibakusha* used the Western genres of the Gothic and the surreal to describe what they saw argues the greater visceral power of the latter. In their palpable sense of unreality, their sense that what is happening cannot be happening, survivors of military or genocidal cataclysms witness the deconstruction not only of their material world but also of their conceptual universe—that is, their world has become in some sense a fiction of the genre of the surreal or the fantastic. Fiction depicting this unreal reality is virtually obliged to adopt metafictional gestures to make its point. By putting surrealism and expressionism into the service of allegory, Günter Grass's *Tin Drum* and Volker Schlöndorff's cinematic adaptation of the novel additionally transform effects of irreality into analytical tools and devices of historical explanation.

The generic difficulties of presenting the effects and experiences of mass warfare are aggravated by the inadequacy of fictional traditions to address the fundamental destabilizations of entire populations. Michael André Bernstein disputes this inadequacy, and, by grounding ethical thinking in "deep respect for particular cases," finds the traditional novel an adequate and even appropriate genre for ethically representing the catastrophic life of communities—"literature, consisting, as it does, only of particular cases, is such a powerful repository of the kinds of exempla that the search for an 'ethical condition' requires" (122).[27] But without disputing the powerful integration of the historical and the particular achieved in classic exemplars of the genre—Tolstoy's *War and Peace,* for example—I nonetheless question some of the ethical limitations of the novel's synecdochic procedures in having representative figures stand for the community, with its democratic assumption about the interchangeability of actors in social life. The undergirding premise of the realist novel, its individualistic ideology of the self's agency and power to actualize itself through engagement with plausible agons, for decades pressed the Hollywood war film toward fictions of the heroic warrior, from *Sergeant York* and *Lawrence of Arabia* to *Patton,* the *Rambo* films, and the extremely interesting *Bridge on the River Kwai.* Realist fiction is far less adept at elucidating both the corporate nature of modern soldiering and the corporate nature of the violence it inflicts on bodies whose interchangeability must be painfully reversed by conspicuous acts of specifying memorialization—of which the Vietnam Memorial in Washington, D.C., with its inscription of more than 50,000 names, is the most stunning example. But while naturalism would seem the plausible vehicle for representing the soldier or the civilian population as a collective protagonist whose repressed materiality, dispossessed social condition, and compromised volition are enfolded in a form of structural violence, the best of the modern writers of this genre refuse the condescension that naturalism's scientific and detached perspective turns on its subject. By resorting to first-person participant-witnesses, Erich Maria Remarque and Michael Herr—two of the ablest practitioners of the naturalistic mode—are able to enact the subjectivity, suffering, and introspection of men transformed into organisms of a military species, or cogs in a machine, whose agency is always already programmed elsewhere.

The recourse to "representative" figures for elucidating the war experience in fiction and nonfiction also carries more subtle ideological and ontological implications in its practice. To overstate the problem for heuristic effect, one could argue that the synecdochic use of the "vignette" in war writing inevitably participates, in attenuated form, in the representational stratagems of war propaganda. By producing figures reduced in scope and complexity, the "vignette" creation of a typical ensemble of soldiers or civilians, while gesturing toward their historical and cultural particularities, nonetheless produces deracinated figures in ways that may not be ideologically neutral or innocent. Remarque's fascist critics quickly pointed to his foregrounding of working-class soldiers; Hersey's atomic bombing victims, self-selected by their connection to the Tokyo Jesuit mission, may have been disproportionately Westernized; Herr's grunts coalesce into images of hyper-Americanized adolescence; Spielberg was accused of producing a Manichean vision of good and bad Nazis and reducing his Jewish victims to an undifferentiated mob. The practice of vignetting transcends its limitations only when its scope is sufficiently enlarged to permit the development of conflicts from differences within its representative population—in Norman Mailer's *The Naked and the Dead,* for example. But the emphasis of individualism carries with it both exaltation of the West's liberal and democratic virtues and the obverse threat of depicting the enemy as a "mass." In fascism the opposite of the mass is coded as "culture," according to Klaus Theweleit: "At the 'height' of culture, there is nobility, morality, intellect, heart, feeling, reason, and soul—none of which can exist 'in the depths,' in the mass" (45). But a similar ideological opposition characterized the reciprocal stereotyping that John Dower found operative between the United States and Japan in World War II:

> On the part of the Japanese, this involved singling out the emphasis placed on individualism and profit making in the Western tradition, and presenting this as proof positive that Westerners were fundamentally selfish and greedy, devoted to self-aggrandizement at the expense of the community and the nation as a whole. Westerners, in turn, accepted Japanese emphasis on the primacy of the group or collectivity at face value, and used this as prima facie evidence that the Japanese were closer to cattle or robots than to themselves. One side's idealized virtues easily fed the other side's racial prejudices. (30)

The use of vignettes of characters to function as representative samples of a population also risks embodying potentially dangerous fictions about numbers in relation to mass warfare. The notion of representative samples implies an infinitely large pool filled with interchangeable figures. Edith Wyschogrod argues that Zeno's paradox undergirds the totalitarian logic of the death event: "The premise that the whole—by analogy with a straight line—is infinitely divisible and the supply of parts to be subdivided inexhaustible provides the logical paradigm for the death event" (38). But we might consider that versions of this logic undergird some of the popular, if not the legal, notions of "just war" as well. Aggression in anticipation of greater aggression—the putative prevention of a future "bloodbath" by a present bloodbath—has played a role in "just war" arguments for self-defense and international security as recently as World War II and Vietnam. This prophylactic argument carries with it an existentially problematic arithmetic about the temporal interchangeability of people—a willingness to sacrifice a present number of combatants or civilians on the grounds that some greater, if unknowable, number (a number coded as definitionally of greater innocence or value) can consequently be spared or saved thereby. Leaving aside the ethics of this substitutive algebra, the quantitative assumptions behind urging that the determinate living preempt the place of the proleptic hypothetical dead imply fantasies of population infinitude that, according to Wyschogrod, make genocide seem an impossibility even to totalitarian regimes. "The existential application of Zeno's argument in the death event points up a category mistake that unconsciously dominates totalitarian discourse. A collection is interpreted as a spatial continuum which is conceptually divisible into an infinite number of parts but which in actuality can be exhausted" (38). An understanding accepted for the natural world of flora and fauna, that species of plants and animals can be endangered and exterminated as a totality, appears not yet extended to human communities as a possibility.

Modern Warfare, Death, and Expression

The value of the literary vignette—which reduces the scale and magnitude of modern war violence sufficiently to retrieve an imaginable community of victims available to empathy and identification—risks distorting or falsifying other significant ontological dimensions of the death world. In the aftermath of the Nietzschean "death of god," with its loss of transcendental fictions of death and dying, Martin Heidegger's concept of authentic being-toward-death, in *Being and Time,* opened the possibility of imagining dying as an existential experience that discloses being to itself: *"Death is something that stands before us—something impending.* . . . With death, Dasein stands before itself in its ownmost potentiality-for-Being" (294). Heidegger's depiction of the subject's difficulties in translating the death of others into a singular possibility for the self and investing the conscious acceptance of mortality with the fully apprehended significance of not-being serves as a figure for the reading subject's confrontation with literary or poetic death

as well. But Edith Wyschogrod interrogates the relevance of earlier models
of monadic death and dying to the death event:

> It is tempting in these circumstances to revert to familiar para-
> digms, the *artes moriendi* which have tamed death in the past, and
> to import these strategies into the new context on the hope that
> what serves the dying individual can be stretched to accommodate
> vast numbers, as if numbers did not alter the significance of death
> and the process of dying. But the question "What conception of
> world, experience, and self is required in order for these numbers
> to become possible?" is covered over when a sheerly additive pro-
> cedure is brought to bear upon the problem of scale and the masses
> of the dead are conceived as a sum total of the deaths of monadic
> individuals. (1)

Wyschogrod cites Hobbes as first articulating the notion that "what human
beings fear most is death by violence" (172). Whether or not one believes
that a "natural death" is an oxymoron, that all death is produced by an
agency perceived as violent and aggressive even if that agency is the self's
body, there is a qualitative social difference in the contemplation of death
humanly willed and inflicted on entire populations as enactment of a discursive universe of politics and policy or an expressive universe of hatred and
cruelty.

Neither the paradigmatic "good death" that Wyschogrod describes as
"accepting one's ceasing to be with equanimity and maintaining one's com-
posure until the end" (204) nor the Heideggerian authenticity of being in
dread at the acceptance of the certainty of not being serves as a proper model
for the condition of dying in the death worlds of the twentieth century.
"Each I experiences the possibility not only of its own coming to an end but
also of human extinction in toto as a result of human acts" (Wyschogrod,
211). The ontology Wyschogrod here indicates is given a very specific articulation in Robert Jay Lifton's *Death in Life* when he describes the perception of Hiroshima as entailing another dimension, "a dimension of totality,
a sense of ultimate annihilation—of cities, nations, the world" (14)—that
is, a fear of omnicide. His psychiatric work with atomic bomb survivors convinced Lifton that nuclear war has inaugurated ontological consequences we
have only begun to understand: "What I am suggesting is that our perceptions of Hiroshima are the beginnings of new dimensions of thought about

death and life" (14). In the researches of psychiatrists of war trauma lie the beginnings of a semiotics of the death world experience. The multiplicities of violence in all the registers of the human condition overwhelm the apocalyptic subject in such a way that their translation into the language of the everyday world becomes possible only performatively, clinically, as somatic or psychic symptom. "Massive trauma precludes its registration," the psychiatrist Dori Laub writes, "the observing and recording mechanisms of the human mind are temporarily knocked out, malfunction" (Felman and Laub, 57). Art's ability to register symptoms as disturbances of language may be its best means of expressing the ontological state of the apocalyptic subject. Shoshana Felman finds the symptomatic sign performatively inscribed into the poetry of Paul Celan:

> By introducing silence as a rhythmic *breakdown* and as a displacing *counterpoint* to sound not just *in between* his stanzas and his verses, but even *in the very midst* of the phonetic flow and the poetic diction of his *words* . . . Celan strives to defetishize his language and to dislocate his own aesthetic mastery, by breaking down any self-possessed control of sense and by disrupting any unity, integrity or continuity of conscious meaning. Through their very breakdown, the sounds testify, henceforth, precisely to a knowledge they do not possess, by unleashing, and by drifting into, their own buried depths of silence. (Ibid., 37)

These performative expressions of the confrontation with the death world in turn place extraordinary interpretive responsibility upon the reader and the critic. The listener to the testimony of trauma victims, Dori Laub writes, "must *listen to and hear the silence,* speaking mutely both in silence and in speech, both from behind and from within the speech. He or she must recognize, acknowledge and address that silence, even if this simply means respect" (ibid., 58).

Readers of twentieth-century war writing enter into communion with acts of witnessing that entail both psychological and ethical risks, as well as ontological and ethical responsibilities. The crudest negative risks—of having representations of violence excite pleasure, or having images of cruelty feed what Michael André Bernstein calls an "appetitive fascination with evil" (55)—are most often incurred by war writing that is not testimonial in structure or intention. Louis Menand offered one of the rare excoriations of

Saving Private Ryan in reaction to the audience response he experienced while viewing the film: "There are many heart-wrenching deaths in *Saving Private Ryan,* but they are all American deaths. When Germans are shot, they go down like ten-pins, and they stay down. *Their* deaths are movie deaths. And the more agonizingly the Americans suffer, the happier we are to see the Germans slaughtered. The realism just ratchets up the enthusiasm" (7). But the eyes of witness tend to translate into a more anguished narrative. The Vietnam War correspondent Michael Herr wrote in *Dispatches,* "I went to cover the war and the war covered me." Acting on the serious belief that "you had to be able to look at anything," he discovered "that you were as responsible for everything you saw as you were responsible for everything you did" (20). Herr transformed the temptations of detached journalism into the solitary and painful act of testimony not just to what he saw but to his own experience of seeing. Even when we witness events at some remove, the act of reading can make us vulnerable to penetration by experience, including traumatic experience. "A 'life-testimony' is not simply a testimony to a private life, but a point of conflation between text and life, a textual testimony which can *penetrate us like an actual life,*" Shoshana Felman tells us (Felman and Laub, 2). Reading testimony can therefore alter us, inhabit us, haunt us, augment us more profoundly than other acts of reading. But because of its nature it can also threaten us with the infection of pain, an experience that has its most eloquent implication for the psychiatrist of Holocaust trauma: "The listener to trauma," writes Dori Laub, "comes to be a participant and a co-owner of the traumatic event: through this very listening, he comes to partially experience trauma in himself" (ibid., 57). But although Laub notes that the listener sharing the experience of the victim does not become a victim, Roger Gottlieb, in his introduction to *Thinking the Unthinkable,* addresses the absorption of the self into trauma that afflicts some students of the Holocaust: "The event is remembered but everything else, including the self, is forgotten. We immerse ourselves in images of death. The gas chambers and barbed wire, burnt buildings and burning bodies seem at times to be more real than our own lives. Our daily existence becomes an echo of a Holocaust which never ends" (4).

It could be argued that because the Holocaust is a unique and exceptional atrocity, its power to provoke obsession is also unique. Nevertheless, the Holocaust's transfixations serve as a compelling emblem for the unstoppability of war's effects. Elaine Scarry argues that the perdurance of war's material effects in multiple visible and invisible ways—by familial gaps that

31

mark casualties, by the effects of maiming and scarring upon the bodies and minds of veterans and survivors, by architectural ruins or by the newness of their replacements—all of these signs of a war's pastness, its conclusion, are in fact dynamic and operational requisites for instantiating the outcome of the war, the "making it real" that is necessary for securing nations' consent to abide by its outcome. The effects of this process, however, alter the conditions of peace in such a way that peace itself becomes maimed, as war's activity of injuring continues long after the armistice and the treaty have been signed and the event is designated as "over." As much "home front" literature of the First World War attests—Virginia Woolf's *Mrs. Dalloway* is a premier canonical example—war invades the home front both at the time of its duration and in its aftermath, as veterans carry their wounds and their trauma home and infect their families, communities, and institutions by whatever invisible or dramatic forms their symptoms take. When the home front became the arena of combat in the Second World War, the boundaries that separate war and peace became so thoroughly collapsed and confused that "total war" takes on a temporal as well as an operational dimension, its effects perduring into the future, and into the lives of ensuing generations. In the case of nuclear war, the material and literal perdurance of injury— atomic weapons' effects on the intimate recesses of the body, on blood and genes, sexuality and reproduction, on the bodies and brains of children and grandchildren—symbolizes the ineradicable psychic and spiritual damage that survives all venues of total war. And yet, as Elaine Scarry points out, "while the central activity of war is injuring and the central goal of war is to out-injure the opponent, the fact of injuring tends to be absent from strategic and political descriptions of war" (12). The polity and institutions responsible for inaugurating, promoting, pursuing, analyzing, and recording war explicitly extrude the job of registering the suffering caused by its vast machinery of injuring. This job—and the work of mourning it entails—falls largely to art and to the work of culture. This book is dedicated to elucidating the difficulties, accomplishments, limitations, and failures of this job, and to urge that art and criticism find ways of reinjecting these verbal representations of war and expressions of the injury it produces back into the discourses of politics and policy.

2

THE TRACE OF THE TRENCHES
Revisiting Modernism and World War I

Aesthetics and War

"TODAY THE SOMME IS A PEACEFUL BUT SULLEN PLACE," Paul Fussell writes in *The Great War and Modern Memory*. "When the sun is low in the afternoon, on the gradual slopes of the low hills you see the traces of the zig-zag trenches" (69–70). His book itself is, of course, one of those traces of the trenches that in its study of "trench poetry" both recreates a major discourse of World War I and concedes that its historical referent, "the trench experience," was itself already textualized—"Indeed, if the book had a subtitle, it would be something like 'An Inquiry into the Curious Literariness of Real Life'" (ix). Not only the trench poetry but the competing poetic discourses of modernism and avant-garde writing seemed to preempt and precede the Great War. "You will be astonished to find how like art is to war, I mean 'modernist' art" (4), Wyndham Lewis writes in *Blasting and Bombardiering,* and Gertrude Stein makes a similar point—that the art was the war's historical referent and not the other way around—when she describes it as a cubist painting: "Really the composition of this war, 1914–1918, was not the composition of all previous wars, the composition was not a composition in which there was one man in the center surrounded by a lot of other men but a composition that had neither a beginning nor an end, a composition of which one corner was as important as another corner, in fact the composition of cubism" (11).

Lewis made a similar point. Asked if the fighting was hell, he replied, "It was Goya, it was Delacroix—all scooped out and very El Greco. But hell, no" (180). The war was preceded by its simulacra not only as art but as language. Even the "proper names" that might have overcome its formlessness and become its historical sign—Loos, Verdun, Ypres, Passchendaele, the Somme—fail to cohere as battles. Fussell says later historiography calls them battles to imply that they had a rational causality and "to suggest that these events parallel Blenheim and Waterloo not only in glory but in structure and meaning" (9). Lewis writes of Passchendaele:

> The very name, with its suggestion of *splashiness* and of *passion* at once, was subtly appropriate. This nonsense could not have come to full flower at any other place but at *Passchendaele*. It was preordained. (160)

"It was clear by the end of 1914 that this war would be different—it would be the most literary and the most poetical war in English history," Samuel Hynes writes in *A War Imagined* (28). But this prior textualization contributed to the strange phenomenon of a "Great War" that was present to itself chiefly as a misleading sign—misleading because none of its multiple discourses, themselves in considerable dispute, were able to totalize either its experience or its significance. T. S. Eliot wrote in 1929, "Perhaps the most significant thing about the War is its insignificance" (Chace, 145).

This aesthetic and poetic *en*scription of the war—both before and after the event—raises the question of whether the significant insignificance that Eliot identifies as its outcome is not produced by what Marianne DeKoven calls the suppression of the historical referent in modernist writing. If that referent is identified with the mass dead of World War I—"Nearly 60,000 of these men were to become casualties on the first day of the Somme offensive in 1916" (Stephen, 6)—then the early effects of a kind of Baudrillardian hyperreality[1] may be seen in modernism's construction—or lack of construction—of World War I. The elegant figurations of the modernists—for example, Pound's powerful synecdoche in Canto IV: "Troy but a heap of smouldering boundary stones" (*Cantos*, 13)—tropes the destructiveness of the war as the atomic power of rhetoric itself, capable of reducing the world to a burning stone. This figure so dramatically inverts the ground of the reference (rhetoric as figure of war, or war as figure of rhetoric) that the question of the poem's Nietzschean amnesia can seem itself an ideological violence.[2] Canto IV, written in 1918 and 1919, either "forgets" or pointedly disregards the recent closure of World War I, and the elision of the dead bodies in the self-reflexive figure and poem seems to enact Elaine Scarry's argument about the role of disavowal in the discourses of war. The 10 million war dead of 1918 are the historical referent of the war without having themselves a referent; this gives them the referential instability that allows them to serve what Scarry oxymoronically describes as "their 'fiction-generating' or 'reality-conferring' function" (121). Dead bodies make the issues and outcomes of war real because "the human body, the original site of reality" (121), serves a semiological function as a code of the real. This endows the bodies of the war dead with the power to transfer the signification of reality onto the abstractions that have been the issues of war. The unreality and insignificance of the Great War may thus be implicated in modernism's disavowal of mass warfare's material and affective reference. The dead, whose sign is needed to make war's issues real, must always simultaneously be there yet be disavowed, in order to serve the purely symbolic function (to signify reality) that conceals their lack of instrumental function (to effect control over territory). This lack has never been more glaringly obvious than in this war, in which territorial gains and losses were sometimes nearly zero over the course of a year's unimaginable carnage. Furthermore, the present absence of the killed soldier's body was encoded in postwar England as cenotaphs—memorials in which empty space signified the soldier's body, as Allyson Booth has argued.[3] Modernism's self-reflexive pre-scription of the war as (energetic) formalism may thus have colluded in the phenomenology of the Great War by placing the mass dead's irrational and illogical production under an erasure that itself pre-scripted and, in a sense, pre-dicted World War II. One is tempted to worry that the failure of the dominant World War I discourses to reference the mass dead as anything but unreferential may have contributed to making their reproduction in World War II unstoppable.

Modernism's suppression of the war dead—which was repeated in its suppression of trench poetry—provides a particularly useful example of the collusion of its aesthetic and ideological agendas. Since the mass is the enemy of form, the mass killing of the Great War confronted the modernists with an aesthetic unintelligibility that they nonetheless coded politically as "the crowd" or "anarchy." The modernist resistance to "the mass" and "the masses" has simultaneous formal and historical roots, therefore. Historically, the Victorian coding of the masses as proletarian was transferred to the mass formations of World War I battlefields, which with their physical configurations of crowded, filthy, polluted trenches were easily figured in the public imagination as industrial slums. Paul Fussell argued that much of the disaster of the battle of the Somme—an engagement that the troops renamed "The Great Fuck-Up" (12)—was produced by "the class system and the assumptions it sanctioned" (13). The officers took the largely ill-trained troops of miners and factory workers recruited from the Midlands and "assumed that these troops—burdened for the assault with 66 pounds of equipment—were too simple and animal to cross the space between the opposing trenches in any way except in full daylight and aligned in rows or 'waves.' It was felt that the troops would become confused by more subtle tactics like rushing from cover to cover, or assault-firing, or following close upon a continuous creeping barrage" (13). The upshot was that nearly 60,000 soldiers were killed or wounded in the battle of the Somme on a single day, the first day. Modernism's formal response to the challenge of mass warfare and mass death was to translate the nineteenth-century discourses of population control and quality—Malthusian arithmetic and Darwinian competition, Nietzsche's herd and Arnold's mass culture—into mandates to produce aesthetic formalism and artistic connoisseurship. William Chace explains that Pound's changed sensibility toward the war ("The poet who had once luxuriated in the prospect of violence now rages against war") occurred when the war began to kill artists, in spite of his ideological opposition to Fabian pacifism ("socialists caught up by doctrines of 'mass-men'" [23]). By destroying artists, the war destroyed art and reproduced the operation of mass culture in the voluminous, indiscriminate production of its dead. Modernism responded by replacing representation with performance—both in textual strategy and in institutional practice. Its formal prolepsis or anticipation of the war in violent disjunctions, illogical parataxes, mutilated figurations, and "series . . . of explosive fragments" (Perloff, 187) gave war a rhetorical poetic performance. Modernism's institutional gesture took form as displacement, extrusion, and silencing of the trench poetry that clearly aspired to become poetry *as* historical referent, poetry that defended itself against the lethal intertexts of the very classicism (cf. Owen's attack on Horace's "old lie") that served as modernism's premier episteme.

Yeats's dramatic expulsion of the trench poets from the canon when in 1936 he excluded them from *The Oxford Book of Modern Verse* on the ground that "passive suffering is not a theme for poetry" (xxxiv) staged not only the heteroglossia of the war's poetic discourses, that the field of art itself marked a contested terrain of conflicting aesthetics, but emphasized the doubling of the war's textualization. Old war poetry can shape not only new war poetry but present conduct. As the war's pre-text, poetry can serve an enabling or propagandistic function for war that both Wilfred Owen's and Stephen Crane's intertextual interpolations of the martial classics into their works (Horace in Owen's poetry and *The Iliad* as martial spur in *The Red Badge of Courage*) expose and decry. Poetry, they show, creates ideals, mythologies, expectations, and models of behavior. Virginia Woolf's *To the Lighthouse* ironically invokes the intertext of Tennyson's "Charge of the Light Brigade"—when used, prewar, by Mr. Ramsey chiefly to cast his career into tragic postures: "All his vanity, all his satisfaction in his own splendour, riding fell as a thunderbolt, fierce as a hawk at the head of his men through the valley of death, had been shattered, destroyed. Stormed at by shot and shell, boldly he wrote and well, flashed through the valley of death, volleyed and thundered—straight into Lily Briscoe and William Bankes" (30). But Mr. Ramsey's son Andrew, who may have heard his father blustering "Some one had blundered," has his death ingloriously dismissed by the parenthetical narrative in "Time Passes": "(A shell exploded. Twenty or thirty young men were blown up in France, among them Andrew Ramsey, whose death, mercifully, was instantaneous)" (133). Perhaps it is war itself, Woolf's text implies, that was the blunder. As texts for mass education—Fussell notes that copies of *The Oxford Book of English Verse* were carried into battle like bibles (157–59)—anthologies such as *The Oxford Book of Modern Verse* could have enfolded the disputed poetic discourses of World War I, whose disjointed forms and aims would have dramatized their inability to provide the Great War with even imaginary unities. Yeats's gesture in exiling trench poetry from the canon removed the most eloquent articulation of the Great War's mass violence from the literary spiral that might have (in 1936) rhetorically served as remembering, warning, and prophecy of the mass violence of the imminent Second World War. As it happened, the poetry of the Great War skipped a generation, leaving little trace of itself on the literature of World War II.[4] When it resurfaced rather dramatically in *Apocalypse Now*, the American film that became popular culture's most significant address to

Vietnam, it reappeared in its most oblique, aestheticized, and canonical version as high modernism.

Modernism versus Trench Poetry

W. B. Yeats characterized Wilfred Owen's poetry as "unworthy of the poets' corner of a country newspaper" and "all blood, dirt and sucked sugar-stick" (Yeats to Dorothy Wellesley, Dec. 21, 1936, in Yeats, *Letters*, 874)— a judgment of grimy sentimentality that the schoolbook anthologizing of Owen's "Dulce et Decorum Est" might seem to seal. Yet Owen's powerful poetic gestures to retrieve both the body of the soldier and the immediacy of the trench are, as Fussell contends, "unique" (291), though— unlike Fussell—I would situate their uniqueness not in his homoerotically inflected sensuous identification with the soldiers but in his ideologically charged maneuver of *Deklassierung*. Owen deglamorizes the scene of war precisely by proletarianizing it, by industrializing it, by investing it in codes of beggary, brute labor, filth, and invalidism that impoverish, degrade, numb, and unsex the soldier:

> Bent double, like old beggars under sacks,
> Knock-kneed, coughing like hags, we cursed through sludge,
> Till on the haunting flares we turned our backs
> And towards our distant rest began to trudge.
> Men marched asleep. Many had lost their boots
> But limped on, blood-shod. All went lame; all blind;
> Drunk with fatigue; deaf even to the hoots
> Of gas shells dropping softly behind.
>
> (Silkin, 182–83)[5]

The old-fashioned rhyme scheme, the regular syllable line, the shameless Dickensian appeal for sympathy rendering the sentiment as unsubtle as a Victorian reform tract, all are features likely to set a modernist's teeth on edge.[6] But other critics give Owen credit for innovation with the sustained terminal pararhyme (Crawford, 187–88) and allow him to set his own aesthetic terms when he claims that "the poetry is in the pity" (Crawford 188). Beyond what seems like mechanical sentimentality, like graceless language that may deliberately de-aestheticize the verse, Owen gathers a momentum that dramatically controls narrative time and perspective to produce an extraordinary effect of immediate experience for the reader:

> Gas! GAS! Quick, boys!—An ecstasy of fumbling,
> Fitting the clumsy helmets just in time;
> But someone still was yelling out and stumbling,
> And flound'ring like a man in fire or lime . . .
> Dim, through the misty panes and thick green light,
> As under a green sea, I saw him drowning.
>
> (Silkin, 183)

The gas attack disrupts the limping poem as it disrupts the limping march and makes the detached poetic voice an urgent actor on the scene—as though it were reporting in "real" time, or as though it were—in mid-poem—reliving an experience of trauma. The emergency is cosmic—an instantaneous plunge into a lethal element—the fire, lime, sea of burning air—whose only protection is a crudely half-blinding visor pressed, by the poetic voice, against the reader's face as well as its own. We are thereby made to share the claustrophobic sensation of nightmare, "In all my dreams, before my helpless sight, / He plunges at me, guttering, choking, drowning." There follows a journey into hell that takes form as an imaginative scope inside the soldier's suppurating body—a journey from the outside ("And watch the white eyes writhing in his face"), from the auditory ("If you could hear, at every jolt, the blood / Come gargling from the froth-corrupted lungs"), to the obscene inside of mouth and lungs ("Obscene as cancer, bitter as the cud / Of vile, incurable sores on innocent tongues"). It is as though the poem's prosodic ugliness, its aesthetic maiming, were also a product of incurable sores on the tongue of the soldier-poet.

The hidden ideological impetus behind Yeats's derision of Owen may best be inferred from the dialogical interplay of his own 1919 Great War poem, "An Irish Airman Foresees His Death," with both trench poetry and other modernist poetry. Yeats's poem expels the vortex as much as the trenches—deleting the airplane and other advanced technology ("the war was celebrated by most of the poets and painters who enlisted as the culmination of a thrilling new adventure with technology" [Perloff, xxi]) along with the mass slaughter on the ground. The gesture of Yeats's poem is to abolish the war in the interest of saving poetry from the proletarian masses in the trenches that Owen likens to the Midland collieries ("dark pits / Of war" ["Miners," Silkin, 186]) peopled by blind troglodytes ("Bent double, like old beggars under sacks, / Knock-kneed, coughing like hags" [Silkin, 182]). Yeats replaces the "passive suffering" of the trench soldier with the ephiphanic vision of the seraphic warrior, who is purified into an unbearable lightness of being through a total ideological divestiture of the war:

> I know that I shall meet my fate
> Somewhere among the clouds above;
> Those that I fight I do not hate,
> Those that I guard I do not love;
> My country is Kiltartan Cross,
> My countrymen Kiltartan's poor,
> No likely end could bring them loss
> Or leave them happier than before.
> Nor law, nor duty bade me fight,
> Nor public men, nor cheering crowds,
> A lonely impulse of delight
> Drove to this tumult in the clouds;
> I balanced all, brought all to mind,
> The years to come seemed waste of breath,
> A waste of breath the years behind
> In balance with this life, this death.
>
> (Yeats, *Selected Poems,* 55–56)

The war marks the poem with vapor trails of emptied determinants: political ("No likely end could bring them loss / Or leave them happier than before"), patriotic ("Those that I fight I do not hate, / Those that I guard I do not love"), moral ("Nor law, nor duty bade me fight"), and polemical ("Nor public men, nor cheering crowds"). What remains from the affective erasures that produce perfect equanimity ("I balanced all, brought all to mind") is the autotelos of a pure Nietzschean will-to-power—"A lonely impulse of delight"—that doubles as the poem's empyrean of form: pure symmetry, simplicity, and equipoise. Yeats abstracts the Georgian impulse that made much war poetry a pastoral outpost (see Fussell's chapter "Arcadian Recourses") of a war troped widely as an industrial slum whose fighting was a species of urban violence—"that little shindy of schoolboys with gunpowder" (96), Woolf's Septimus Smith sardonically calls it in *Mrs. Dalloway.* In "An Irish Airman Foresees His Death" Yeats translates the complex political referent, Lady Gregory's Irish son dying in the service of his British colonial master, into the formal stasis of a poem as pure peace. The poem's gestures—enacting Major Gregory's death in the practice of his self-erasure, his lines' chiasmic self-cancellations ("The years to come seemed waste of breath, / A waste of breath the years behind")—reproduce, by discursively killing him into a poetic peace, the perverse illogicality of war as a practice of massive slaughter in the service of peace-production.

This antiphrastic gesture—representing war as peace, the soldier's tenemental troglodyte existence as angelic and solitary suspension in air—owes its ideological coloration, if not its form, to a recrudescent Romantic impulse that in some Georgian poetry took pastoral and elegiac form. The depopulated Romantic landscape—what Frances Ferguson characterizes as a wasteland transformed into "a peopled solitude, anthropomorphizing rocks and stones and trees, without encountering the pressures of competing consciousness" (106)—becomes in patriotic war poetry "the model world" of an England constructed of "rural nostalgia" (Fussell, 232). Paul Fussell identifies this image and mode as a specifically British antithesis to war. "If the opposite of war is peace, the opposite of experiencing moments of war is proposing moments of pastoral. Since war takes place outdoors and always within nature, its symbolic status is that of the ultimate anti-pastoral" (231).The poetic voice of Rupert Brooke's sonnet "The Soldier" (Silkin, 81–82) proleptically invokes the soldier's death ("If I should die, think only this of me") as a hypostatic union with a nationalized landscape— "A body of England's, breathing English air, / Washed by the rivers, blest by suns of home"—unpopulated until disembodied marks of sentiment ("laughter, learnt of friends; and gentleness, / In hearts at peace") people it at the end. This trope of the national construction of the body ("A dust whom England bore, shaped, made aware") anticipates Elaine Scarry's semiotics of the soldier's body as politicized ("the political identity of the body is not easily changed; if another flag is placed in front of British eyes, it will be looked at or away from with eyes looking out from under eyebrows held high" [110]) and thereby able to signify nationally through its injuries or death. What Brooke registers—and what, arguably, may have made his poetry so popular in England both during and after the war[7]—is the hidden logic that makes the human body, in its injury and destruction, the instrument and expression of the nationalization through which the causes, issues, and justifications of war are articulated. In Georgian England, that nationalization was expressed as idealized pastoral imagery.

After savagely exposing the pastoralism of John McCrae's "In Flanders Fields"[8] as "a propaganda argument—words like *vicious* and *stupid* would not seem to go too far—against a negotiated peace," Paul Fussell introduces another poem whose subtle engagement with traditional pastoralism and the lyric tradition of Nashe, Shakespeare, Sidney, Shirley, and Arnold make it, to his mind, "the greatest poem of the war" (250): Isaac Rosenberg's "Break of Day in the Trenches." Leaving aside the poetry of the German avant-garde, I concur with Fussell's assessment, but on somewhat different grounds. Rosenberg, like Brooke, may anthropomorphize the flora and fauna of his landscape in the manner of Romantic pastoralism ("Poppies whose roots are in man's veins" [Silkin, 208–9]), but his aim contrasts markedly with Brooke's idealized nationalization of the landscape. Engaging an anthropo-morphized (but decidedly anti-Romantic) *rat* as his interlocutor, Rosenberg carefully breaks the trenches into a multinational zone peopled by multina-tional literal and figurative bodies. If Brooke's "foreign field" is made English by enfolding the dust of the English body in its earth, Rosenberg's trenches harbor a transnational rat:

> Droll rat, they would shoot you if they knew
> Your cosmopolitan sympathies.
> Now you have touched this English hand
> You will do the same to a German—
>
> (Silkin, 208)

By exchanging perspective with the cosmopolitan rat—exempt from the treasons of narrow nationalisms—Rosenberg allows the poetic soldier-voice to double its perspective in a way that turns both body ("Bonds to the whims of murder, / Sprawled in the bowels of the earth, / The torn fields of France") and mind inside out:

> What do you see in our eyes
> At the shrieking iron and flame
> Hurled through still heavens?
> What quaver—what heart aghast?
> (Silkin, 208)

By seeing through the eyes of the rat, the soldier has transformed himself into witness of himself, witness of his complex, intersected emotions, and witness to the complexities of his own seeing, his own insight. The poem's rhetorical gesture has become one of an utterly denationalized performative

courage. The debonair, lighthearted romantic gestures ("As I pull the para-
pet's poppy / To stick behind my ear"), the delicate evasion of sympathy
("Poppies whose roots are in man's veins / Drop, and are ever dropping; /
But mine in my ear is safe, / Just a little white with the dust") perform the
fragile dance of a civilized heart that has been broken ("What quaver—what
heart aghast"). The "loving" heart that Brooke sentimentally nationalizes ("A
dust whom England bore, shaped, made aware / Gave, once, her flowers to
love") Rosenberg simultaneously eroticizes and de-eroticizes by turning the
rat's eyes sardonically upon the peril of the idealized body of the soldier in
the double guise of his peacetime agon and his wartime agon:

> It seems you inwardly grin as you pass
> Strong eyes, fine limbs, haughty athletes
> Less chanced than you for life,
> Bonds to the whims of murder
> (Silkin, 208)

The reader, invested with the rat's sophisticated eye, is given penetrating, multiple, and transcendent vision—seeing the trenches simultaneously
from below the earth, at the level of roots and soaked blood, from the bowels
of the body of the rat-infested earth, and from above the nationalized conflict
in which the soldier-poet's wise and gentle courage is subdued by the quaver
of a heart aghast at the hurtling iron and flame. The elegiac poignancy of
impending loss was historically literalized: less than two years after writing
the poem, Rosenberg was killed.

Yeats's tacit interplay with trench poetry is one among several dialectical
disputes in the poetic performance of the Great War. While Yeats enacted
Romantic impulses without their form, Wyndham Lewis inflected the war's
challenge to modernistic form through a futuristic mandate (Perloff highlights it as "violence and precision" [87]) he simultaneously denied and enacted. In advance of a gesture Jameson calls poststructuralism's attack on
"the Romantic valorization of organic form" (30), Lewis demystifies the im-
periling of artistic form by violence without precision when he limns what
he calls the romance of war. "It is commonly remarked that 'there is no romance in modern war,'" Lewis writes. "That is absurd, I am sorry to have to
say" (*Blasting and Bombardiering*, 121). He then proceeds to trope war as a
form-making effect whose "romance" resides in refiguring what is seen as

what is felt. As an artillery officer, Lewis playfully refunctions the big guns as romantic artists: "Of course, it would be impossible to overstate the contribution of the guns to these great romantic effects. Even in such an essentially romantic context as war, they are startlingly 'romantic' accessories. . . . It is they who transform a smart little modern township, inside an hour, into a romantic ruin worthy of the great Robert himself, or of Claude Lorrain" (ibid., 122). The guns reproduce landscapes already assimilated to prior sublimations, like the romantically idealized landscapes of Hubert Robert, "Robert des Ruines." But when Lewis goes on to romanticize shell wounds—"they give the most romantic and spectacular wounds of all—a bullet wound, even a dum-dum, is child's play to a wound inflicted by a shell-splinter" (ibid.)—he sardonically demystifies the romance of war as nostalgia for a repressed and disavowed algolagnia, a secret and denied enjoyment of destruction and suffering.

Lewis's satirical inveighing against "the romance of war," which repeats the premodernist attacks on Romanticism in the work of T. E. Hulme, prepares the way for clarifying the formal and affective hardness of modernism. The sadism of his gestures—the "rational violence" of cruelty in the service of the machine and reason—serves the production of the "vortex" well, by transforming his intelligence and his writing into an energetic instrument of aggression without affect or malice. *Blast*, better than *Blasting and Bombardiering*, stages the formal implications of an epistemology that he himself implies as equivalent to the sculptural form that defines his paintings even more than his writings: "Give me the *outside* of things, I am a fanatic for the externality of all things" (*Blasting and Bombardiering*, 9). In Henri Gaudier-Brzeska's *Blast* piece, "VORTEX GAUDIER-BRZESKA (Written from the Trenches)," the double violence of sculpture—externalizing and disavowing what is inside or felt—becomes visible as the modernist aesthetics of war. Gaudier gives Lewis's fetishized obsession with externality or form the displaced logic of the objective correlative: "I SHALL DERIVE MY EMOTIONS SOLELY FROM THE *ARRANGEMENT OF SURFACES*, I shall present my emotions by the ARRANGEMENT OF MY SURFACES, THE PLANES AND LINES BY WHICH THEY ARE DEFINED" (34). Gaudier's formalistic epistemology allows him to cast the war into the hard angularity of one of his own sculptures. "THE BURSTING SHELLS, the volleys, wire entanglements, projectors, motors, the chaos of battle DO NOT ALTER IN THE LEAST, the outlines of the hill we are besieging" (33). This description could virtually double as a historical referent for the Great War, in which unprecedented firepower failed over the course of a year to produce significant alteration in the trench lines, or in the relative strength of the combatants. However, Gaudier extends the sculptural trope of the war to the shape of its army population as well: "HUMAN MASSES teem and move, are destroyed and crop up again" (33). The war becomes for him the dynamic stasis of a Nietz-schean eternal return of the same, which he internalizes as his own sculptural view: "DOGS wander, are destroyed, and others come along. . . . *MY VIEWS ON SCULPTURE* REMAIN ABSOLUTELY *THE SAME*" (33).

The figure of Gaudier's war writing is his carving of the enemy gun, a stolen German Mauser, into *objet trouvé* art: "I broke the butt off and with my knife I carved in it a design, through which I tried to express a gentler order of feeling, which I preferred. BUT I WILL EMPHASIZE that MY DESIGN *got its effect* (just as the gun had) FROM A VERY SIMPLE COM-POSITION OF LINES AND PLANES" (34). Gaudier clearly intended his contribution to the 1915 war issue of *Blast* to function as a piece of verbal vorticist sculpture on the war—an intention emphasized, and foregrounded, by the journal's exile of the historical referent culminating in Gaudier's death to a prefatory note and an appended and boxed obituary coda. Gaudier's sculptural effects depend not only on the suppression of the historical reference from his text but on the play of difference between the two. In a gesture borrowed from the ninth thesis of F. T. Marinetti's 1909 futurist manifesto ("We will glorify war—the world's only hygiene" [Apollonio, 22]), Gaudier's sculptural procedure abstracts the army's decimation as a prophylactic eugenics, "THIS PALTRY MECHANISM, WHICH SERVES AS A PURGE TO OVERNUMEROUS HUMANITY. / THIS WAR IS A GREAT REMEDY" (33). In contrast, the historical preface at the beginning of the piece restores to Gaudier's war service the particularity of time and narra-tive—"In September he was one of a patrolling party of twelve, seven of his companions fell in the fight over the roadway" (33)—and the boxed obitu-ary at the end completes the historical factualism. In his sculptural text, Gaudier strips soldiering of all symbolic social or cultural reference ("IN THE INDIVIDUAL IT KILLS ARROGANCE, SELF-ESTEEM, PRIDE" (33); yet the preface and obituary restore his institutional context.

Thus the most provocative portion of the piece is the paratext Gaudier couldn't and didn't write: "Henri Gaudier-Brzeska: after months of fighting and two promotions for gallantry Henri Gaudier-Brzeska was killed in a charge at Neauville St. Vaast, on June 5th, 1915" (34). A modernist response was now required to explore the parataxis of Gaudier's own aesthetic, in which the mass dead are figured as "NUMBERS UPON NUMBERS OF UN-IMPORTANT UNITS" (Lewis, *Blast,* 33) juxtaposed with his material death. John Tytell writes, "News of Gaudier's death shocked Pound into an awareness of the closeness of the war. Gaudier had become for Pound a personal totem of the artist, a symbolic figure who had been sacrificed in a conflict that would prove nothing" (119). In "Hugh Selwyn Mauberley," Pound, in fact, both preserves the parataxis and sublates the loss of the artist into the loss of art. Poem IV preserves the insignificance of the mass dead who fought in the weak necessity and indeterminacy of "in any case" (a slippage from "in any cause") by investing their identity in a fragmentation and reduction of the proper noun that might have signed them into significance. The Somme, now become lowercase, slips into the pronominal obliquity and indeterminacy of the "some":

> Some quick to arm,
> some for adventure,
> some from fear of weakness,
> some from fear of censure,
> some for love of slaughter, in imagination.
> (*Personae,* 190)

Although the "some" outrageously understates the casualties of the Somme, where 12,000 soldiers are said to have fallen within the first hour, Pound uses its anaphoric repetition to break up the mass of men into smaller clusters, thus performing an ideological diaeresis by rhetorical partition. But given the flaccid catalogue—anti-epic in its bland abstractions, anti-imagist in its appeal to cliché—Pound's Juvenalian protest (Crawford, 83) seems more likely aimed at trench poetry ("Died some, pro patria, non 'dulce' non 'et decor'" . . . "hysterias, trench confessions" [*Personae,* 190) or at the democratic Whitmanesque catalogue than at the decimations of war. In V, Pound restores both the numbers ("THERE died a myriad" [*Personae,* 191]) and the style, in honor of Gaudier-Brzeska: "And of the best, among them." In place of the scattered abstractions of jejeune motives (adventure, weakness, fear) he restores the bite of vulgar anger to his assault on the symbols of patriotism ("For an old bitch gone in the teeth, / For a botched civilization" [*Personae,* 191]), as he does again in Canto XVI ("And because that son of a bitch, Franz Josef of Austria . . ." [*Cantos,* 71]) and in Canto XXXVIII ("They began to kill 'em by millions / Because of a louse in Berlin / and a greasy basturd in Ausstria" [*Cantos*, 188]). Gaudier's quality as artist is conjured up in sharp economy as a good bite ("Charm, smiling at the good mouth" [*Personae*, 191]), an ability to sculpt words with the chisel of teeth.[9] And his death is invested in a double synecdoche, "Quick eyes gone under earth's lid" (*Personae*, 191), the sculptor's eye extinguished and enclosed in the closing eye of a grave figured as a sculpture, Gaudier disappearing into the art of one of his own sculptural heads.

In Canto XVI, Pound makes the doubling of the death of sculptor and sculpture explicit: "And Henri Gaudier went to it, / and they killed him, / And killed a good deal of sculpture" (*Cantos*, 71). The death of Gaudier posed a historical conundrum for Pound that he solved narratively by inserting social credit theory into his poetic history of World War I. The result, in the Cantos, is an excess of historical reference to arms and munitions manufacture and trade as the cause of a war recoded, after the death of Gaudier, as a war on art. In "Murder by Capital" Pound wrote, "I have blood lust because of what I have seen done to, and attempted against, the arts in my time" (*Selected Prose*, 229) and referred to "sin against the best art of its time" (228). The Cantos become dotted with allusions and references to Basil Zaharoff and Vickers, Ltd., and Krupp, Mitsui, Schneider-Creusot, and other armament firms and trades (Froula, 167):

> 500 to St Petersburg and 300 to Napoleon Barbiche
> from Creusot. At Sadowa
>> Austria had some Krupp cannon;
>> Prussia had some Krupp cannon.
> 'The Emperor ('68) is deeply in'erested in yr. catalogue
> and in yr. services to humanity'
>> (signed) Leboeuf
>> (Canto XXXVIII, *Cantos*, 191)

The guns that were romantic accessories to Lewis and objet d'art to Gaudier become obsessively quantifiable and enumerable commodities to the later Pound: "1885 / 1900 produced ten thousand cannon / to 1914, 34 thousand" (ibid.). The myriad mass dead—though now listed ("Liste officielle des morts 5,000,000" [Canto XVI, *Cantos*, 73])—nonetheless slide under guns and art as referent of anger and anguish in the narrative of economic cause and aesthetic effect in Pound's history of early modernity.

The Great War became for Pound a war on art not only because Gaudier and Hulme served as proxies for art in the trenches, thereby giving Gaudier what Tytell describes as his "totemic" function for Pound. The term's literal image—of a totem as a sculpture of primitive abstractness—is appropriate, because Gaudier carved himself, as he carved his trench experience and as he carved the German rifle, into a work of art, a sculptural text, like his piece in *Blast*. But Pound's later obsession with munitions manufacture makes it clear that he continues to narrativize the ideological relationship of the mass, violence, and form as an apologia for modernism's role in war's conduct. Pound's conception of mass psychology ("Lacking both perception and a basic curiosity about the workings of the world, the masses could only subside into 'abuleia'" [Chace, 44]) implicitly stressed the indiscrimination and indifference of the masses, whose intellectual and perceptual inanition makes them the enemy of art. The mass-produced guns serve as instruments of mass-produced death, whose killing of the true artists leaves mass-produced art ("For two gross of broken statues, / For a few thousand battered books" [*Personae*, 191]) victorious in the field. The problem with war, then, is not its violence but the failure of its violence to conform to its artistic projections in futurism and vorticism as "violence and precision." The sin of guns in their production of mass death resides not in the numbers of their victims but in their inability to function like art, their lack of discrimination, their failure to carve and cull the masses according to some formal principle that will reduce the formless mediocrity of populations while preserving an elite. Pound's selective mourning over the artist-casualties of the Great War—reckoning Rupert Brooke's death less as a loss to art than as the loss of a charming young man (Tytell, 120)—makes less facetious his mock-aggressive regret at military indiscrimination. Tytell reports Pound telling Harriet Monroe that "the real trouble with war was 'that it gives no one the chance to kill the right people'" (120). Lewis had no compunction, either, about wryly preferring artists to live or die on the basis of their politics and poetics: "Why should Gaudier die, and a 'Bloomsbury' live?" (*Blasting and Bombardiering*, 182). In this way and variously, the war's killing was textualized and valorized according to its repetition of the modernist poetic agenda.

War, Poetry, and Propagation

The notorious ninth thesis of the 1909 Marinetti manifesto programmatically links militarism to misogyny: "We will glorify war—the world's only hygiene—militarism, patriotism, the destructive gesture of freedom-bringers, beautiful ideas worth dying for, and scorn for woman" (Apollonio, 22). Lewis elaborates this ideological link in an analogy between munitions production and human reproduction by troping childbearing during the war years as the manufacture of cannon fodder: "Women's function, the manufacturing of children (even more important than cartridges and khaki suits) is only important from this point of view. . . . It takes the deft women we employ anything from twelve to sixteen years to fill and polish these little human cartridges, and they of course get fond of them in the process" (*Blast,* 16). Lewis takes the sentimental icon of the soldier's mother—whose form in Great War literature invariably figures her as a moribund Pietà, knitting socks for the boys at the front—and mechanizes and desentimentalizes her by restoring her to "the crowd" and the masses. His equation of the crowd with the inertia and mindlessness of Pound's "abuleia" makes it a figure for death—"Death is, however, only a form of Crowd" (*Blast,* 94)—which by the logic of a misogynistic algebra is deciphered as woman: "The Married Man is the Symbol of the Crowd: his function is to set it going. At the altar he embraces Death" (ibid.). The fruition of this logic can be found in Ford Madox Ford's "From 'Antwerp'" (Silkin, 145–46), in which a series of paratactical translations—"There is a great crowd"; "that is a dead woman—a dead mother"; "That is another dead mother, and there is another and another and another"; "These are the women of Flanders"; "They await the lost that shall never again come by the train"—fill Charing Cross with the masses of the Flemish dead, "the lost who lie dead in trench and barrier and foss." The poem enacts an oneiric montage of time as well as place—return become departure, Flanders become England—in order to figure the war dead as an overlay of losses, absences, waitings and failures to appear, misappearances and disappearances, prolepses and deferrals, apparitions and unrealities. The final statement of pure affect—"There is so much pain"—has been put, in a sense, under erasure.

Lewis's Nietzschean derision of "the crowd"[10] in *Blast* was widely echoed in modernist representations of patriotic enthusiasm and the blind obedience of massed armies and the mass casualties they produced. But in *Blast* Lewis doubly politicizes the crowd by naming its desire as suffrage ("Their attitude is as though these universal crowds wanted some new vague Suffrage. Is this opposition correct? dramatic Suffragette analogy. [For these crowds are willing to be 'Furies' in the humorous male way]" [*Blast,* 94]).

This sentiment echoes Nietzsche's excoriation of woman suffrage movements as bids for "the political rights of voting cattle" (*Ecce Homo,* 76). Of Cantleman, his alter ego in *Blasting and Bombardiering,* running with the crowds at the Olympiad, Lewis writes, "He was very stupid. He was a suffragette" (70). This feminization of the crowd brings modernism's contradictory discourse of population control into sharper focus and exposes an ideological strategy that lodges control with art. The 1915 war issue of *Blast* blasts "Birth-Control" and blesses "War Babies" (92–93). The logic of the etymological play ("blast" as blight, "blastemas" as differentiating embryonic cells: the blighting of birth control as enabling the development of the embryo) makes better biological than political sense. What is one supposed to make of a polemic that simultaneously despises the crowd produced by overpopulation and yet inveighs against the contraception that would reduce its size and proliferation? The issue is clearly one of control, Lewis preferring the indiscriminate population control by war to the discriminate population control by democratic female suffrage because the violence of the war releases energy and creates a vortex while feminism is thought to empower the herd. These proto-fascist modernist ideologies ultimately institutionalized themselves as war's cultural counterpart to discipline the masses.

The modernist text that becomes most conspicuously identified with the contradictory effects of this project—Maud Ellmann says that "it stages the ritual of its own destruction" (109)—is, of course, T. S. Eliot's *Waste Land.* The historical reference of this work, canonized as the premier address to "the unprecedented death toll of the First World War" (Ellmann, 101), encloses the illogical nexus of martial and feminist discourses of population control in order to sublate them wholly to the mythology of sacral fertility. Upon the editorial pruning by Pound, the poem's opening introduces a montage of displaced historical codes for the outbreak and aftermath of World War I: the figure of an archduke careening downhill on a sled nearly out of control ("And when we were children, staying at the arch-duke's, / My cousin's, he took me out on a sled, / And I was frightened" [29:13]),[11] the postwar haunting of watering places by the dislocated German and Austrian aristocrats from Eastern Europe[12] ("Bin gar keine Russin, stamm' aus Litauen, echt deutsch" [29:12]), the ethnic chauvinisms and tensions of the Habsburg Empire displaced from the Balkans to the Baltic. The challenge of the poem may be sited in the insomniac reading of the baroness—"I read, much of the night, and go south in the winter" (29:18):

> Summer surprised us, coming over the Starnbergersee
> With a shower of rain; we stopped in the colonnade,
> And went on in sunlight, into the Hofgarten,
> And drank coffee, and talked for an hour.
> Bin gar keine Russin, stamm' aus Litauen, echt deutsch.
> And when we were children, staying at the arch-duke's,
> My cousin's, he took me out on a sled,
> And I was frightened. He said, Marie,
> Marie, hold on tight. And down we went.
> In the mountains, there you feel free.
> I read, much of the night, and go south in the winter.
> (29:8–18)

What does one read after the catastrophe of a war that murders sleep, and what writing replaces the peace foreclosed by historical nightmare? "Falling towers / Jerusalem Athens Alexandria / Vienna London" (44:374)—the fall and dispersal of the Austro-Hungarian Empire (Vienna) opens the text, and the deferred twilight of the British Empire (London), ingesting the religion of its colonies along with India's tea and spices, closes it in a cacophony of undigested and untranslated quotations that textually foreclose geopolitical peace. The poem's tacit attempt to reconstitute a third empire of polyglot and polymath culture—what Terry Eagleton describes as "an alternative text which is nothing less than the closed, coherent, authoritative discourse of the mythologies which frame it" (150)—becomes no more than another haunting, another invasion of the poem by the dead. "Eliot celebrates the voices of the dead, "Maud Ellmann writes, "but he comes to dread their verbal ambush in *The Waste Land*" (101).

Ellmann's elegant rhetorical summation of the poem's compulsive attempt to remember and resurrect the dead through a doomed prosopopoeia—"*The Waste Land* strives to give a face to death" (109)—endows the impossibility of representing the mass death and destruction of World War I with a compelling figure of poetic performativity. But one might argue that there are two kinds of dead trying to appear in the poem, and that they are not equal: the poetic dead voices of the literary tradition, whose eloquence is the louder for the fragmentariness of their utterance, and the voiceless war dead. Indeed, even the figure of the spared, the demobbed returning soldier who gives the poem its most direct and specific historical reference to the war, is not detachable from the repulsiveness of the mob; he is, as it were, *demobbed* (demobilized) in one sense, but not *de-mobbed,* in another:

> When Lil's husband got demobbed, I said—
> I didn't mince my words, I said to her myself,
> HURRY UP PLEASE ITS TIME
> Now Albert's coming back, make yourself a bit smart.
> He'll want to know what you done with that money he gave you
> To get yourself some teeth. He did, I was there.
> You have them all out, Lil, and get a nice set,
> He said, I swear, I can't bear to look at you.
> And no more can't I, I said . . .
>
> (34:139–46)

The demobbed veteran's wife, in fact, is given a face—or gives herself a face ("pulling a long face" [35:158])—but it is the face of an anti-Helen, the face that launched a thousand ships become the young version of Pound's "old bitch gone in the teeth." Lil is a young bitch gone in the teeth, the poem implies, whose toothless face creates universal aversion, "He said, I swear, I can't bear to look at you. / And no more can't I, I said" [34:146]. In attaching Lil's supreme ugliness to the unwholesomeness of her class, Eliot tracks highly specific causalities—the toothlessness of calcium deficiency from the multiparity of six pregnancies before the age of thirty-one ("You ought to be ashamed, I said, to look so antique. / (And her only thirty-one) [35:156]"— back to the pullulating breeding of the masses.

The poem reverses the flow of the war dead to return them, by way of London Bridge, to the teeming slums whence they came. Eliot, like Lewis, tropes the war as a bridge between home and front, between living and dead—"The bridge, you see, is *the war*" (*Blasting and Bombardiering,* 2)— and this bridge crosses, too, the discourses of population control that have cast their contradictory shadows upon other modernistic war writing. Reversing Gaudier's "good mouth," Lil's toothless head is carved into the barren landscape like a giant dead skull: "Dead mountain mouth of carious teeth that cannot spit" (42:339) to be traversed by "those hooded hordes swarming / Over endless plains, stumbling in cracked earth" (43:369). But in spite of the industrial and urban pollution ("The river sweats / Oil and tar" [39:266]) that the population produces along with the "White bodies naked on the low damp ground / And bones cast in a little low dry garret" (37:193), the poem blasts birth control for the masses as surely as did *Blast*: "You *are* a proper fool," Lil's interlocutor judges her crippling abortion. "The chemist said it would be all right, but I've never been the same" (35:161). As a form of population control, the war too was a crippling abortion—of the sort that reduced her progeny but left Lil ill, disfigured, and prematurely aged. World War I may have reduced some of Europe's unwanted masses, but at the price of leaving its countries weak, disfigured, and spiritually desiccated.

The conversation in the pub that retells the conversation with Lil is Eliot's Arnoldian demonstration that the discourse of the populace is impervious to poetry because it lacks the porosity of other parts of the poem that let quotation leak in. For discourse to become art like sculpture requires the scission of metaphoric teeth. "I didn't mince my words" (34:140), the speaker says, and her narrative is conspicuous in its seamless wholeness, unchopped by the parataxes that segment the poem's other speech. The masses produce a nearly perfect redundancy of citation ("I said," "she said," "he said"), the episode suggests—culture and tradition replaced by verbatim or unmasticated reproduction of earlier verbatim reproductions. This pullulation or regurgitation of trivial discourse—the speaker telling us what she told Lil Albert had said before he left—reproduces endless Heideggerean *Gerede* or idle talk deprived of teeth: "You have them all out, Lil, and get a nice set, / He said" (34:145). The conversation's twice-told and triangular structure, whose parenthetical asides "([She's had five already, and nearly died of young George]" [35:160]) make a confidante of the poem's addressee, restores the implied reader herself to the masses. It is among the poem's projects to break up this mindless abuleia of the masses ("'Are you alive, or not? Is there nothing in your head?'" [34:126]) by using the text's erudition to Babelize its readership, carving its homogeneous philistinism into polyglottal segments and cultural elites. By refusing to translate or reference many of its citations, the poem's cultivation creates borderlines of incommunication and minefields of incomprehension that recreate in the field of reading the conditions of geopolitical war and class revolution. The unified empire of culture the poem conjures up in its referenced appeal to the cosmopolitanism of Cambridge anthropology and the archetypalism of comparative religion becomes no more than a bogus sublation of the poem's politics into a myth of universal order that its own textual Babelization ritually destroys.

International Currents

Before the end of the twentieth century, an institutional armistice had settled over the World War I poetry wars, whose nadir was Wilfred Owen's exclusion from Yeats's anthology of modern verse in 1936. Jon Silkin's widely used anthology, *The Penguin Book of First World War Poetry,* secured in its 1981 second edition a relatively broad inclusivity based on aesthetic rather than didactic considerations: "I was in the end concerned with excellence, not the representation of extrinsic concerns. . . . So in the end I had to choose what I thought was good; and if I thought the poem good it was included" (74).[13] Even in the face of this modernist criterion of craft, trench poetry is explicitly canonized in Silkin's sophisticated critical introduction to this volume—a canonization consolidated a few years later by the publication of Pat Barker's stunning World War I fiction trilogy about the treatment of Siegfried Sassoon and Wilfred Owen by the remarkable Craiglockhart War Hospital psychiatrist William Rivers. Through three searing volumes Barker presses the war's destruction of art, speech, memory, dream, and sanity, to end her 1995 Booker Prize–winning *The Ghost Road* with the implied death of Wilfred Owen seven days before the Armistice ended the war on November 11, 1918. Owen, who saw only four of his poems published in his lifetime (Crawford, 174), is generously represented in Silkin's anthology. By stretching modernism's boundaries and diversifying its functions, Silkin also manages to internationalize World War I poetry, bringing together voices from various sides and corners of the martial divide and letting them speak to each other in a kind of institutional reenactment of Owen's "Strange Meeting." By offering English translations of the Continental poetry of German, French, Italian, and Russian war and prewar writers, the Silkin volume lets their formal dialogues, disputes, and agreements become audible in an anthological diplomatic summit that gestures much more dramatically to a universalizable peace than to war.[14] Two lone women, both Russian, intriguingly speak to the formal techniques and the religious voice of T. S. Eliot. Anna Akhmatova's "July 1914" conjures up a wasteland, "the fields have been parched since Easter" (Silkin, 263), and has a maimed pilgrim deliver dire prophecies: "'Beware of terrible times . . . the earth / opening for a crowd of corpses'" (Silkin, 263; Akhmatova's ellipsis); Marina Tsvetayeva uses an overdetermined figure of scarecrow or bayonet practice effigy to conjure up both hollow men and the trope of a crucified "Hanged-Man" ("On the sand, serried ranks of straw-stuffed forms as large as men, hang from some cross-beam" [Silkin, 266]). Among the fiercely avant-garde Germans, Georg Trakl's expressionism outstrips the modernists in despair—"the night embraces / Dying warriors, the wild lament / Of their broken mouths" ("Grodek," Silkin, 232). For Trakl—who suffered a possibly lethal breakdown after helplessly enduring a vigil over ninety heavily wounded men after the battle of Grodek—the "broken mouths" exceed Eliot's and Pound's concerns with precision in poetry to signify the end of all speech and articulation.

In keeping with Silkin's cosmopolitan gesture, a brief acknowledgment of the innovations of two German avant-gardists—the naturalist Wilhelm Klemm and the expressionist August Stramm—might provide a fitting closure to this discussion of World War I poetry. Wilhelm Klemm, a physician, like John McCrae, graphs the body more painfully than Owen, and August Stramm stands virtually incommunicable on a threshold at the end of language. Klemm's two "Clearing Station" poems reflect his experiences in makeshift emergency medical stations at the front: "Across the nocturnal vault of the church / Moans go drifting and choking words" (Silkin, 236). Klemm's relentless anatomizing of the injured body and its issue of fluids and odors ("There's a stench of blood, pus, shit and sweat" [ibid.]) tackles the daunting task of literalizing the outcome of battle as *slaughter* (the German words *Schlacht* [battle] and *schlachten* [to slaughter] have the same root) in a way that dramatizes the inhumane and dehumanizing effects of military violence without dehumanizing the bodies that are its victims. Like the Anglo-American avant-gardists, Klemm glosses his clearing station abattoir in the simile of art—"Naked wounded, as in old paintings" (237)—but immediately vivifies the scene by making the wounds come alive, making them sensate, as it were, rendering them mobile, vocal, and expressive:

> The curiously dark, mysterious head wounds.
> The quivering nose-wings of the chest wounds.
> . . . .
> The rhythmical groaning of those with a stomach wound.
> The terrified expression on dead faces.
> The ventriloquist voices of the tetanus cases.
> The frozen, agonized grinning, their wooden grimaces.
> . . . .
> The careful gait of the ones with broken arms and shoulders.
> The hopping of those with foot and calf wounds, the stiff stilting
> of those with buttock wounds; th crawling on all fours.

Intestines hang out. From a ripped saddle of flesh
the spleen and stomach have welled. A rump-bone gapes round an
    arse-hole.
On the amputated stump flesh foams into the air.
        ("Clearing Station," trans. David McDuff, in Silkin, 237–38)

The German avant-gardists created a poetics of counterassault that transformed Lewis's dramatic wounds and tropes of military romance ("the source
of light is within your own belly" [*Blasting and Bombardiering,* 122]) into
numbing taxonomies of martial pathology that turn the wounded body inside out and make language bleed:

Blut
Und
Bluten
Blut
Und
Bluten Bluten
(Adler and White, 63)

These lines from August Stramm's poem "Haidekampf"—

Blood
And
Bleeding
Blood
And
Bleeding bleeding—

are intended to imitate, iconically, the dripping of blood with increasing volume, as John White points out (ibid.). August Stramm even tries to articulate
with powerful syntactical deformations the intractable unrepresentability of
mass death in combat. In his poem "Battlefield," Stramm pluralizes unquan-
tifiable and indivisible substances ("bloods," "rusts," "fleshes") to transform
an algorithm of murder into the elemental ontology of the battlefield as a
mass subject:

> Yielding clod lulls iron off to sleep
> bloods clot the patches where they oozed
> rusts crumble
> fleshes slime
> sucking lusts around decay.
> Murder on murder
> blinks
> in childish eyes.
> (Trans. Michael Hamburger; Silkin, 239])

With the use of synecdoches severed from their referent, the agon on the scene of battle has lost altogether human, social, even martial form in its reduction to destroyed organic, metallic, atomic matter. The resulting chaos of language and logic [15] spells a supererogation of killing ("Murder on murder") without sense to the incomprehension of disembodied, blank ("childish") witness. Stramm's war poetry comes closest to performing the First World War as an end to the world.

3

THE NOVEL AS WAR
Lies and Truth in Hemingway's *A Farewell to Arms*

Reader Resistance and "Writing Truly"

THE WAR (IF YOU WILL) IN THE FIELD OF ENGLISH POETRY between the modernists and the trench poets was replayed in the field of fiction—with significant differences—eleven years after the First World War ended. The year 1929 saw two major war novels published on opposite sides of the war's geopolitical divide: the American Ernest Hemingway's *A Farewell to Arms* and the German Erich Maria Remarque's *All Quiet on the Western Front*. Their conflict, or contest, was tacit and dialogical rather than polemical, conjuring up dramatically different combat experiences in very different expressive modes, with the result that they seem two novels come back from different wars. Their authors had, in fact, come back from the First World War—albeit with vastly different durations and degrees of infernal experience behind them—and both felt the veteran's urgency to tell an untellable tale to home front audiences that seemed not yet to have fully grasped the enormity of horror that had occurred a decade before. This veteran's need to communicate required a strategy of poetic translation, the invention out of the experimental possibilities that had become available in both English and Continental writing during the 1920s of a fictional technique that could adequately narrate World War I. But besides the common narrative device of the voice of a first-person witness, *A Farewell to Arms* and

All Quiet on the Western Front addressed the problem of reception—how to
bend their tales to the different literary horizons of their implied readerships—in radically different ways that reflected the subtle differences between Anglo-American modernism and the Continental avant-garde traditions. Hemingway's path was highly self-reflexive, incorporating problems
of reception and reader resistance into the narrative performance of his
novel, while Remarque forged a highly inventive poetics of necrological representation and depopulation. I will explore these diverse strategies in turn,
in two consecutive chapters, beginning with Hemingway.

More than for any other modernist writer, *style* became an *ethic* for
Ernest Hemingway with a quasi-martial coloration: a proving ground of
manhood and courage achieved by discipline, economy, and, at times, aggression. New Criticism abetted this interpretation of Hemingway's form
and style. "It is the discipline of the code that makes man human, a sense
of style or good form," Robert Penn Warren wrote in his 1966 essay on Hemingway. "It is important because, ultimately, it is a moral achievement" (40).
In recent years, however, as New Historicists, among others, have begun to
interrogate the politics of modernism's aesthetics, Hemingway's style has
suffered an especially damaging translation into its ideological determinants.
Walter Benn Michaels, for example, reads the signature of simplicity ("nice,"
"good," "true") in Hemingway's miraculously clean prose as the transformation of racism ("breeding") into aesthetics (196). While revisionary skepticism has, of course, regularly followed praise of Hemingway throughout his
publication history, the current climate of challenge to modernism's aestheticism makes an interrogation of the ethics of style in Hemingway's war
writing particularly timely. Given *A Farewell to Arms*'s popularity as, arguably, *the* great American World War I novel, I bring my own revisionary
impulses to the novel while poised, at the same time, to challenge some of
the cruder political indictments of Hemingway as a masculinist poseur who
uses war as an existential arena for self-aggrandizement. Using chiefly tex-
tualist strategies that revisit the tensions between narrative unreliabilities
(which have traditionally been recognized) and their function to alert the
reader to their own power of rhetorical manipulation, I hope to demonstrate
in Hemingway's novelistic treatment of World War I a series of thoughtful
and shrewd maneuvers to challenge the desires and resistances that readers
bring to war novels. When we treat plotting and style, narrative and dialogue, as self-conscious exercises by which Hemingway recognizes (and
shows that he recognizes) that novelistic writing is inevitably enmeshed in

an ethical function (veracity, lying, self-deception, misdirection), Hemingway's textual practices lose some of their transparency and take on the self-reflexive sophistication more usually imputed to his modernist contemporaries. While this does not solve the problem of judging the residues of either authenticity or bad faith that survive in writing when the courage to tell the truth is transformed into the courage to betray that one is lying, the Hemingway who writes *A Farewell to Arms* can be shown to bring to his text an ethical sophistication that contrasts sharply with that of his character and narrator, Frederic Henry.[1]

In *A Farewell to Arms* the stakes of "writing truly" take on special seriousness as a fictive witness to the unknowabilities of war. The novel therefore provides an excellent opportunity for testing for patterns of self-reflection that reveal an authorial willingness to problematize the ethical status of modernistic poetics. What can be demonstrated, I believe, is that Hemingway inscribes attention to ethical discourse into speech acts within and outside the narrative—an inscription that relates discrepancies between *speaking truly* and *writing truly* to problems of reception that plague ideologically invested fiction—particularly novels of love and war. We can begin by noting in *A Farewell to Arms* a moment in which Hemingway appears to stage the obverse of Walter Benn Michaels's formulation, when he shows figures transforming aestheticism into racism. When Catherine Barkley produces the lovely Shakespearean locution "'Othello with his occupation gone'" (257), Frederic Henry transforms her poetry according to the modernistic poetic into the form of the short declarative sentence, whose valued simplicity is here a stark brutality: "'Othello was a nigger'" (257). But without attempting to separate Frederic's ugly sentiment from Hemingway's own demonstrable racism, we can read this dialogue with its poetic juxtapositions as a complex set of speech acts intended to foreground, rather than ignore or excuse, a hatefulness of character in the protagonist. Catherine's Shakespearean lines, intended as a tactful reference to the lassitude brought on by Frederic's desertion, inadvertently places him in a painfully embarrassing moral contrast to the courageous, victorious Moor. The vicious epithet with which he responds is meant to assault and negate the ground of contrast, but serves instead to foreground Frederic's cowardice, desertion, racism, and bad faith. But the dialogue supplements this tacit moral with a generic gloss that has, I believe, a wider implication for the ambiguous genre of the novel. Catherine's poetry textualizes Frederic and interpolates him into a Shakespearean play in which—as in *A Farewell to Arms* itself—the war story and the love story are peculiarly implicated in each other. The allusion complicates the generic question that has plagued the novel since its publication[2] by raising the possibility that Hemingway here, as elsewhere, makes a self-reflexive gesture to foreground the mutually seductive relationship of war and love stories that ultimately corrupts and perjures both. *Othello* and *A Farewell to Arms* are, of course, opposites: in the former a war story is used for seduction in love, in the latter a love story seduces readers into misreading and misprising a war story.

As I will argue in a moment, Hemingway produces, and uses, critical resistance to facing and censuring Frederic Henry's hatefulnesses in order to demonstrate reception's power to warp and suborn texts—especially fictions of love and war. He thereby has *A Farewell to Arms* perform, or stage, the lying about war induced by reception, by the desire of listeners or readers to evade its truths, which in earlier war texts he merely thematized. "Krebs found that to be listened to at all he had to lie," Hemingway wrote of the returning veteran in his sketch "Soldier's Home" (*Short Stories,* 243). In telling and writing his own war story, he faces a similar problem—namely, that in order to be listened to, in order to give the novel a popular reception, he feels he has to mask his war story as a love story.[3] He thereby subordinates his preferred style, the philosophical naturalism he tests in his sketch "A Natural History of the Dead," to that signature simplicity that seems to disavow rhetorical intentions by appearing to absorb rhetoric so completely into representation that what remains is a residue of guileless and "true" discourse. In "A Natural History of the Dead," published three years after *A Farewell to Arms* as a satirical disquisition in chapter 12 of *Death in the Afternoon,* Hemingway effectively demonstrates why he wrote *A Farewell to Arms* as he did. One is tempted to construe the essay's displacement, its being somewhat "out of place" in its textual homes (it was later included as a short story in *Winner Take Nothing*),[4] as symptomatic of its moral exile as an unwanted and transgressive text that should have found its proper place and function in Hemingway's World War I novel.

In its version in *Death in the Afternoon,*[5] which includes the comments of the *Old lady,* "A Natural History of the Dead" may be read as an allegory of modern reading that supplements the satirical treatment of the ideologies of eighteenth- and nineteenth-century naturalists and twentieth-century New Humanists, for which the essay is usually read (Beegel). In the mock dialogue with the *Old lady,* the mock Author sets out to shock her with increasingly horrific descriptions of the physiology of dead male and female bodies, of battlefield trauma, euthanasia, and sadistic doctors, under the guise of empirical objectivity and detachment ("war has been omitted as a field for the observations of the naturalist" [133]). This mock Socratic dialogue is figured as a combat of reciprocal violence between an author prepared to assault the reader's sensibility with brutal truths and little tact and a passively aggressive bourgeois reader whose complacency insulates her from being disturbed by his story's provocations. In this exteriorized truth telling of the hidden coercions and aggressions that govern the compact of narrative reception, the author presents a version of the true story of war as he would actually like to tell it, and dramatizes the responses that make it clear why he cannot: readers are less interested in the violence and cruelty that is the truth of war than in their own comfort and pleasure as readers. Thus the *Old lady* does not much like the title of "A Natural History of the Dead"—"You may very well not like any of it" (133), the Author retorts—or his justification for the graphic descriptions of body fragments he picked from the barbed wire around the exploded Milan munitions factory. To her "This is not amusing" the Author snaps, "Stop reading it then. Nobody makes you read it" (137). But in practice, *A Farewell to Arms* gives the *Old lady* exactly the war novel she desires: "I like it whenever you write about love" (138).

However urgent Hemingway's sense of war as requiring a special testimonial veracity—"It was one of the major subjects and certainly one of the hardest to write truly of" (*Green Hills of Africa* [70])—he perhaps promises less to write of war truly than to write truly about what makes it "one of the hardest to write truly of." The answer lies deeply embedded in the phenomenology of war itself, and in the essential disjunction between its discourses and its activity, its ideologies and its materiality, its justifications and its facts. "The essential structure of war, its juxtaposition of the extreme facts of body and voice, resides in the *relation* between its own largest parts, the relation between the collective casualties that occur *within* war, and the verbal issues (freedom, national sovereignty, the right to a disputed ground, the extra-territorial authority of a particular ideology) that stand *outside* war," Elaine Scarry writes (*Body in Pain,* 63). Hemingway, of course, seems to thematize just this point when he has his narrator, Frederic Henry, declare, "I was always embarrassed by the words sacred, glorious, and sacrifice. . . . I had seen nothing sacred, and the things that were glorious had no glory and the sacrifices were like the stockyards at Chicago if nothing was done with the meat except to bury it" (185). But we should be wary of trusting Frederic's demystification of patriotic cant, however seductive its allegiance to the hard, concrete words of the modernistic poetic ("Abstract words such as glory, honor, courage, or hallow were obscene beside the concrete names of villages, the numbers of roads, the names of rivers, the numbers of regiments and dates" [184–85]). For it fails as a warrant of the kind of truth telling we feel promised by the fiction of rhetorical self-identity associated with Hemingway's style ("The facts shall be so rightly ordered that they will speak for themselves" [Beach, 82]). For all the verbal purity it thematizes, *A Farewell to Arms* is riven with inconsistencies and ruptures that call attention to themselves—between words and actions, words and words (particularly those of Frederic Henry the character and Frederic Henry the narrator), genres and genres. These inconsistencies are designed, I believe, to test the reader's resistance to other hypocrisies, cant, and bad faith. This ethical focus on war as a rhetorical problem—as a site of contradictions and disjunctions between its language and its unadorned material "reality" as violence—shapes the specialized, and perhaps inevitably reductive, sense of the term "war" as I use it in this discussion. Insofar as it belongs to the rhetorical structure of war to mask and disavow its violence and cruelties with sentiment and idealism, the layering of the love story and the war story in *A Farewell to Arms* can be treated as an analogue to the duplicitous discourses of war itself. Looked at in this way, *A Farewell to Arms* becomes less a novel *about* war than a novel *as* war, a text whose own relationship between what is said (or not said) and what is shown (or not shown) is constructed on the model of war's own possibilities of bad faith.

In writing *A Farewell to Arms,* Hemingway achieved a double maneuver whose outcome is a deliberate, if deliberately ineffectual, textual self-betrayal. He will have it both ways, writing the war novel readers want (a love story that transforms war casualties into the more sentimental forms of maternal and infant mortality) while thematizing and dramatizing his "lying" in a way that both discloses and conceals the narrative perjury delivered in its testimony about the First World War. "How many had I killed?" Frederic Henry is asked about the Austrians. "I had not killed any but I was anxious to please—and I said I had killed plenty" (94). In fact, he kills (or partially kills) only one man—the Italian sergeant who refuses to help him move his truck. But the novel's narration of that act makes it very clear that this particular war casualty is produced by an act of cold-blooded murder.

Readerly resistance to accepting this point (and its larger ramification, that the violence of war permits and produces many such murders) was clearly understood not only by Hemingway but by F. Scott Fitzgerald as well. Fitzgerald patently had no compunction about pointing the narration of war in the direction of readerly reception and readerly desire:

> I had a long letter sent over by F. Scott Fitzgerald in which among other things he said I must *not* under any circumstance let Lt. Henry shoot the sergeant and suggesting that after Catherine dies Frederick [sic] Henry should go to the cafe and pick up a paper and read that the Marines were holding in Chateau Thierry. This, Scott said, would make the American public understand the book better. He also did not like the scene in the old Hotel Cavour in Milano and wanted changes to be made in other places "to make it more acceptable." (Hemingway to Charles Poore, Jan. 23, 1953, in *Selected Letters*, 800)

Fitzgerald was right: the shooting of the sergeant would require much tortured critical apology to keep Frederic Henry a hero, and critics of the 1980s were no more comfortable with the passage than Fitzgerald: "How we meet our fate is everything in Papa's world, and it is unlikely that he would have made his protagonist in this, one of his best novels, anything but honorable. Frederic Henry shoots the sergeant because, by the cold logic of war, that is what is required of him" (Nolan, 274).

Hemingway seems to have set up a double system of testimony in which his style determines its ethical value in a perverse test against readerly desire. Truth is less a fidelity to experience than an act of narrative aggression: a willingness to frustrate and disappoint readers by telling them not what they want to hear but what they don't want to hear. A story that would make Frederic Henry dishonorable is intolerable to a reader and critic like Charles J. Nolan Jr. But Papa's concern with how we meet our fate extends to readers as well as to soldiers. In his writing, therefore, the warrant of truth is not a historical referent, a fact, but the courage to inflict a cruelty (in the form of a cruel truth) that itself replicates the activity of war. Insofar as it embeds this cruel truth in an ideology that American soldiers must, at all costs, be portrayed as honorable, the novel also replicates the "cold" logic (which can mask murder as duty and honor) of war. That is why I say *A Farewell to Arms* is less a novel about war than (figuratively) a novel *as* war.

Verbal Economy and Lying

Because "writing truly" seemed to imply claims to historical accuracy, Hemingway's World War I experience has been consistently tested for its ethical reliability as a script to the novel—in spite of Hemingway's own disclaimers ("Remember Charlie in the first war all I did mostly was hear guys talk: especially in hospital and convalescing. Their experiences get to be more vivid than your own. You invent from your own and from all of theirs" [Hemingway to Poore, *Selected Letters*, 800]). Hemingway's stylistic ethic was thought to have placed a great burden on the discursive proportion and economy with which war experience is narrated (Beach, 82), because it has displaced the heroic from soldierly action onto writerly action, and situated heroism in the act of truth telling and veracious witness. James Nagel's 1989 "Hemingway and the Italian Legacy" is perhaps the most rigorous and convincing examination of this period of Hemingway's life, and his meticulous sifting of fact and fiction produces much precise information and correction of the biography and of biographical idolatry (see, for example, Kurt Singer and Jane Sherrod's 1963 *Ernest Hemingway, Man of Courage*). Nagel confirms that Hemingway was not a lieutenant in the Italian army ("Hemingway was in the Red Cross at all times, never in any army or combative position" [252]) and "Contrary to many people's impressions, Hemingway did not receive his injuries while serving as an ambulance driver" (22). He was, in fact, a *cantinier,* hit after only six days of canteen service while handing out chocolate to soldiers. Nagel treats as unverifiable Hemingway's account in his letter to his parents of August 18, 1918, that he carried a wounded Italian on his back while his legs were full of shrapnel ("The 227 wounds I got from the trench mortar didn't hurt a bit at the time. . . . They couldn't figure out how I had walked 150 yards with a load with both knees shot through and my right shoe punctured two big places. Also over 200 flesh wounds" [*Selected Letters*, 141). According to Nagel, "Ernest's suggestion that even after he was hit by machine-gun bullets he still assisted a wounded soldier, walking 150 yards, cannot be confirmed with certainty" (221).

Whether or not the wounded Hemingway carried the wounded soldier on his back, he clearly understood—in translating the story to fiction—the ambiguous ethical economy of the equivocal story. Heroism is not served by perjured testimony that fails to compel belief, and Hemingway decides to have Frederic Henry earn his moral credit by truth telling rather than by self-sacrifice[6]—"'They say if you can prove you did any heroic act you can get the silver. . . . Did you do any heroic act?' 'No,' I said. 'I was blown up while we were eating cheese'" (63). Frederic's candor earns his narrative a credulity that would serve the reader better by strain—particularly because his motives are themselves undecidable. For example, Frederic may have resisted fabricating false heroic tales because he feared skepticism of their implausibilities: "Gordini says you carried several people on your back but the medical major at the first post declares it is impossible" (63). In the end, in spite of his disclaimers ("'I didn't carry anybody. I couldn't move'" [631]), Frederic receives the undeserved decorations ("'Did you get the boxes with the medals?' . . . 'The boxes will come later'" [164]), and like Hemingway (who received his medal in the mail rather than from the hand of the Italian king or from General Diaz, as his brother Leicester claimed [Nagel, 253–54]), he wears the decorations[7] ("I opened my cape so he could see the two ribbons" [164]). Is wearing an unearned decoration a *lie?* If so, does the falsity of Frederic the character impugn the honesty of Frederic the narrator, to whose credibility we are subject as readers? The question is important because the text continually invites us to match Frederic's words, both as character and as narrator, with his experiences and his deeds, and the two are not always in accord.[8]

The critical tradition has long invested ethical value in Hemingway's stylistic strategy of verbal economy, whose quantitative calculus is one of reduction and subtraction, and whose qualitative form is one of containment and the prevention of excess or spillage.[9] Less is more, in the stylistic morality of the Hemingway discourse, and truth is invested in silence rather than speech. Unlike the voluble Italians in *A Farewell to Arms,* who always say too much and whose excess produces the inflation and the lie that damage credibility, the laconic Frederic practices a stoicism in which the suppression of truth and its investment in conspicuous silence are simultaneously equated with manly virtue. "We have heroes too," Catherine Barkley sniffs at the boasting Ettore Moretti. "But usually, darling, they're much quieter" (124). The problem this specific ethical coding of language creates in the text is that it privileges gaps and omissions as signs of candor and courage by denying their opposite functions as lies or deceptions. The modernistic poetic of simplicity depends on formal principles of selection that are not purely aesthetic and ethically neutral. They depend, indeed, on the rigorous rhetorical control of a variety of unaesthetic contents (pain, excessive feeling, erratic behaviors, filth and poverty, masses and crowds, etc.).[10] The equation of verbal form with moral control creates an ethical economy in which truth in the modernistic poetic is itself reckoned as a disfiguring addition—an excess, excrescence, and waste—that must be expelled from discourse and occluded. Hemingway chooses to have the text of *A Farewell to Arms* perform or act out the thematized relationship between containment and truth.

In the novel, the narrative describing Catherine's preparation of Frederic for surgery rigorously suppresses the procedure named in Hemingway's early sketch for the novel called "A Very Short Story" ("When they operated on him she prepared him for the operating table; and they had a joke about friend or enema" [239]). In describing this operation in *A Farewell to Arms,* Frederic the narrator obeys Catherine's injunction that Frederic the character censor his thoughts and words; yet Catherine's actions perversely reverse her words. While violating the containment of Frederic's bowels, she enjoins him not to violate his verbal containment: "And, darling, when you're going under the ether just think about something else—not us. Because people get very blabby under an anaesthetic" (103). Instead of describing the action, the enema he receives at Catherine's hands, Frederic doubles or repeats her interdiction: his censorship thus fronts itself with her censorship to shield the reader from an unaesthetic and unerotic image. This novelistic moment might be seen as paradigmatic of the novel as a whole, as the tightly controlled and contained love story—which articulates its own control and containment—is offered to shield the reader from unappealing and appalling images of war. The narration, like the text, enacts a euphemism—"Now you're all clean inside and out" (104); "I was clean inside and outside and waiting for the doctor" (105)—to avoid naming the figurative excrements, rapes, cowardices, desertions, and murders produced by war.

By juxtaposing dirty and clean with truth and lying, the text puts in place a tropology of discourse that constitutes the "clean" prose of modernism by expelling the dirty and embarrassing truths of love and war, and by expelling the realism of its more vulgar and obscene discourses ("they had a joke about friend or enema"). At the same time, the text does not lie as much as it performs or stages the logic and practice of lying. Thus the narration performs the lovers' discourse at the same time that it thematizes it as a compact of lying. When Catherine asks Frederic how many women he has had, he says, "None":

> "You're lying to me."
> "Yes."

> "It's all right. Keep right on lying to me. That's what I want you
> to do. . . ." (104)

Catherine, of course, wants a lie spoken that she herself does not believe,
and she asks Frederic to extend his lying to other discourses of love—between men and their prostitutes, for example: "'Does she say she loves him?
Tell me that.' . . . 'Yes. If he wants her to.'" The complicity of lying is extended
to the point where it turns back on itself and can no longer speak a truth.
When Catherine asks Frederic if he ever told other women that he loved
them, he, of course, lies about having lied to them:

> "But you never did? Really?"
> "No."
> "Not really. Tell me the truth."
> "No," I lied. (105)

The result of the compact of lying between Catherine and Frederic is that he
tells her lies that she knows, and desires, as lies.

The echoic structure of the novel's dialogues (like the mirrored structure of some of its incidents, as I will discuss later) makes discourse reciprocal on many textual levels: between the lovers, between the love story and
the war story, between the text and its readers as the text tells readers what
they want to hear and readers interpret the text as the narration prompts
them to interpret it. The structure borrows, as Hemingway is no doubt perfectly aware, from the narcissism of Romanticism, both in its Shelleyan versions of having lovers constructed as siblings, twins, or symmetrical types
and in its Victorian revisitations, most prominent in the passions of *Wuthering Heights* ("I am Heathcliff"), the novel that Catherine and Frederic, in
naming their unborn offspring "young Catherine," appear tacitly to claim as
their eponym.[11] By thematizing the lovers' narcissism as constructed on the
principle of the mirror and the echo—Catherine's "'I do anything you
want'" (106) and its dialogical version of "I say anything you want" in the
novel—Hemingway maps the politics of the male author onto the representations within the text. Female representation (and self-representation) is
thematically staged as a product of male desire constructed as a double mirror (men creating women as conforming themselves to male fantasies of
women). If Catherine, the character, is a male construction, a male lie about
what women say to men, she at least announces that she is a construction of

male desire, a product of doing, saying, and being whatever Frederic wants, or whatever she imagines Frederic wants "'I'll be a fine new and different girl for you'" (304). The precious quality of some of Catherine and Frederic's *love talk* results from the mirror-like quality of the reciprocity produced by the mandate to say what the other wants to hear. During their tryst in the Milan hotel room before Frederic is shipped back to the front, they engage in a dialogue in which his part consists largely of a catalogue of terms of endearment prompted by Catherine's need to avert a painful argument ("Oh, hell, I thought, do we have to argue now?" [152]) over her feeling of sexual degradation ("'I never felt like a whore before'" [152]). Her corrective— "'Come over, please. I'm a good girl again'" (152)—is repeated by Frederic ("'You're my good girl'" [153]) and elaborated throughout their talk with a set of aesthetic adjectival variations—"'You're a lovely girl' . . . 'You're a grand girl' . . . 'You're a fine simple girl'" (153)—which Catherine herself affirms at the end of the set, "'I am a simple girl'" (153). The product of this reductive and repetitive amorous taxonomy is to make Catherine an empty girl, a cipher (Millicent Bell calls her an "inflated rubber woman available at will to the onanistic dreamer" [141]). The text refuses to divulge or even imagine a "true" content for Catherine or to break the discursive containment that makes her a mere vessel for an imagined male desire. Her fate is virtually allegorical: to deliver only a dead male, a male form rather than the reincarnated version of her female self ("young Catherine") that she desired. Catherine dies as though her only rhetorical content or self had been spilled by her delivery, in a gesture cruelly figurative of her poetic status as male echo in this text.

But my purpose in exploring the mirrored and echo-like structures of the love story and its discourses here is less to judge its gender politics than to make visible the role discursive symmetries and reciprocities play in reception. The lovers are shown creating a set of scripts that textualize their situation, that turn their communications into a poetic dialogue geared to appease each other's sense of aesthetic pleasure, and each other's expectations of how lovers speak in love stories. The ethical issues of the novel's sexual politics are thereby located more interestingly in its manipulation of the reader and the novel's reception than in its role as either representation or behavioral model for the sexes. Furthermore, by focusing the crux of the love story on its effects as a *story*, I mean to argue that in thematizing itself as an instrument for producing and controlling readerly desire, it makes visible the far more obscure and disturbing politics of the *war story*'s narrative effects. In this way, the love story and the war story can be read against each other, as forming an interpretive system that opens alternatives and challenges to more traditional thematic and philosophical readings. Love, for example, in addition to being interpreted as the "separate peace" that permits escape and redemption in a world of war, or as entrapment and subjection to the malevolent fate that governs war, may also be seen as an experience that parallels war in its obligation to conform to the idealistic and aesthetic expectations of those to whom it is told. When love and war are treated as narrations by the same voice, the same figure and subjectivity, the reader can test the ideology and philosophy of one against the other, and thereby identify astounding contradictions, disjunctions, and hypocrisies that confound both sentimental and nihilistic readings of the novel's ending.

Love Stories in War Stories

Specifically, Frederic's narration offers us two intimate testimonies to the fact of death—the Italian sergeant's and Catherine's—that test both his logic and his ethics, his sense of conceptual order and his sense of responsibility and justice. Frederic's failure to acknowledge that both deaths (not only the one he suffers but also the one he inflicts) must be weighed as evidence in his philosophical meditations on fate and cosmic justice produces a corresponding refusal and resistance in the reader to deprivilege and demythify certain habits of reading and interpretation. The result is that the novel is read much as war itself is frequently read or understood: with philosophical and ideological rationalizations that deny and occlude both violence and responsibility. But before we compare the way Frederic acts with what he says in relation to the deaths that surround him, it is necessary to examine three episodes of the Caporetto retreat as tests of self-presentation and narrative consistency: the soldiers' encounter with the virgins, Frederic's killing of the sergeant, and his desertion in the face of execution.

By having the love story frame the Caporetto retreat, Hemingway surrounds the war story with the love story in a way that causes the conventions of one to contaminate and distort the conventions of the other. Readers interpret the war incidents through the filter of the love story, and submit both narratives to a moral ideology that conflates eros and agape to equate the lover, the man with the ability to love, with the goodness of the good man. But in *A Farewell to Arms,* this conventional pressure will warp the moral equation in such peculiar and sinister ways that one overlooks the lover's equivocal relation to wartime rape and unequivocal relation to wartime murder. Frederic's treatment of vulnerable women at the front participates in a brutal and ugly wartime occurrence: the endangerment of young girls by rape or traumatizing threats of rape. Frederic's narrative account of this incident gives the reader ample information to assess the extent to which the provincial pubescent sisters are being terrorized: "Every time he said the word the girl stiffened a little. Then sitting stiffly and looking at him she began to cry. I saw her lips working and then tears came down her plump cheeks. . . . The older one, who had been so fierce, began to sob" (196). Yet the text implicitly allows Frederic's tenderness to Catherine to carry over as a dubious warrant for their safety, as though he would let nothing happen to the girls. As a result we are barely prompted to remark Frederic's own threatening gestures toward the girls—"'All right,' I said and patted her knee. I felt her stiffen away when I touched her. . . . Aymo put his hand on the elder girl's thigh and she pushed it away. He laughed at her" (196). The text neither encourages us to notice Frederic's refusal to intervene, as commanding officer, in the menacing conduct of his men nor to remark the incriminating import of his sleepy thoughts: "Those were a couple of fine girls with Barto. A retreat was no place for two virgins. Real virgins. Probably very religious. If there were no war we would probably all be in bed. In bed I lay me down my head. Bed and board. Stiff as a board in bed. Catherine was in bed now" (197). "Stiff" had been used repeatedly by the narrator to describe the girls' fear and resistance to the men's vulgar verbal and manual aggressions. "Stiff as a board in bed" therefore alludes to Frederic's discomfort and fatigue without ceasing to serve as a code for a sexual erection and for the virgins' terrified resistance to what he knows they perceived as a threat of rape ("I felt her stiffen away when I touched her" [196]). The girls are saved neither by Frederic's chivalry nor by his authority as commanding officer, but by their own mistrustful and fearful instincts—"'Come on,' Aymo said to the girls. . . . The older sister shook her head. They were not going into any deserted house. 'They are difficult,' Aymo said" (200). Frederic, the character, never interferes with the designed rape, just as Frederic the narrator never disapproves. The love story has blotted out or erased the earlier Frederic who patently favored Catherine as a free whore ("This was better than going every evening to the house for officers where the girls climbed all over you" [30]), but brings him back, fleetingly, in his unguarded descent into sleep during the retreat. The narrative both disavows and affirms the legitimacy of Catherine's feelings about her ambiguous sexual status ("'I never felt like a whore before'" [152]) by leaving the unregenerate Frederic in place as a textual memory.

Hemingway further uses the moral credit as a loving and decent man that Frederic's love for Catherine earns him to work a complex double ethical maneuver in writing the episode of Frederic's killing of the Italian sergeant. Hemingway conjoins two narrative strategies—a detailed and virtually unambiguous description of the action with an utterly impersonal, objective narrative that betrays no emotion. This action without affect places the reader in a position of judgment without a clear moral compass, and with the necessity of judging both an action and an act of narration. Since this episode confronts readers with behavior that violates norms of decency and honor in their protagonist, they are placed under immense hermeneutical pressure to rationalize and justify that behavior if the story is to sustain itself as Fitzgerald's kind of war story: one in which our boys are heroic and gallant, and all the atrocities and cruelties are committed by the other side. Charles Nolan exemplifies this pressure, as he continually begs the question by taking as his premise the very point in dispute in the episode: "As a decent man and a man of honor" (272); "As a man of honor, Frederic will keep his commitments and do his duty"; "To make Frederic less than heroic is to undercut his character and diminish Hemingway's meaning" (273). The critical situation is thus one of double jeopardy: while the episode places readers under obligation to conduct a hermeneutical court-martial of Frederic's acts, readers are themselves placed on trial in a test of their ethics of reading. Hemingway's text works to act on his readers, prodding them into committing a series of interpretive outrages that allow them to transform A Farewell to Arms into an ideologically acceptable war story, but only at the price of colluding with the specific atrocities and hypocrisies in the narrative.

By designing the shooting of the sergeant to serve as the mirror image of Frederic's desertion, Hemingway places the reader in the excruciating hermeneutical position of recognizing, yet desperately wanting to resist, the troubling, silent countertext to the war story and the love story that we have come to expect and want. With the killing of the sergeant, the novel splits into the two novels adumbrated by the epigraph from Christopher Marlowe's Jew of Malta—"Thou hast committed— / Fornication—but that was in another country; and besides, the wench is dead." Hemingway, who titled the short stories prefatory to the novel "In Another Country" and "In Another Country—Two" (a late title for "Now I Lay Me"), can be seen as having inscribed two versions of the same novel within *A Farewell to Arms*. The love story invites us to assimilate Frederic's killing to itself, as an alternate example of the soldier's honor—perhaps the unspecified thing that Krebs in "Soldier's Home" calls "the only thing for a man to do, easily and naturally" (244)—some sort of traditional test of his intestinal fortitude to be able to kill in war when he must. But Frederic's shooting of the sergeant can (and, I would argue, ultimately must) also be read and named as the transgression—*murder*—committed in another moral country than that of the ideologically ingratiating version of the novel that has, chiefly, been canonized. If one has no brief for exonerating Frederic, every element of the incident can be discerned as carefully chosen to make Frederic's shooting of the sergeant indefensible. The victim is an Italian, an ally, not an enemy soldier. He is an engineer rather than a warrior. He has no military connection to Frederic's small troop, to which he is attached accidentally, temporarily, involuntarily, to hitch a ride during the retreat. He in no way threatens Frederic or any of the soldiers or civilians in his charge, and there is no indication in the narrative that the sergeant is even armed. He is shot in the back while walking, then running, away. The killing is not done in panic, or without premeditation: when the sergeant is not dead, Frederic gives Bonello his gun to finish him off, and when it fails to fire, tells him how to cock it to make it shoot. Although the retreat certainly makes it perilous and stressful, the situation is neither combat nor self-defense nor a life-and-death crisis: Hemingway contrives it to resemble as much as possible a civilian traffic jam ("Still traffic could tie up in cities in which everyone was awake" [197]) in which the sergeant is an ungrateful hitchhiker who refuses, in a stressful road emergency, to help the people who gave him a ride. Frederic quite simply shoots in the back a soldier who wants to leave an ad hoc situation that has come to seem to him very dangerous.

The Killing of the Sergeant

There is no ambiguity in the text about the existential "facts" of the killing of the sergeant. What makes the shooting troubling for the reader is the incident's relation to the speech act in which it is embedded. Since neither the Frederic of the action nor the Frederic of the narration attempts to interpret the killing or draw it into a symbolic or moral order, the text fails to identify its significance. The "facts" are cold—embedded in the silence of an emotional and cognitive vacuum that makes it impossible to apply even

WRITING WAR IN THE TWENTIETH CENTURY

Hemingway's hedonistic morality, "what is moral is what you feel good after and what is immoral is what you feel bad after" (*Death in the Afternoon*, 4). There is no indication of remorse, regret, pleasure, satisfaction, or even memory past the point of narration in the narrative discourse, and Nolan infers that "to his credit, his action makes him feel bad" (274) purely from Frederic's indecipherable refusal to laugh with Bonello about the killing. The narrative account of the killing stops at an empirical level, giving evidence but no witness, no testimony of the self's vision or feeling that could endow the incident with significance or meaning in the story. Meaning emerges elsewhere—in the text's dialogical manipulation of the plot that obliges readers to adjudicate similarities and differences between two incidents with a sharply reciprocal structure: Frederic's shooting of the Italian and the Italians' threat to shoot him. The second incident provides us with feelings and principles of action and judgment that can be applied retrospectively to the first. The exercise becomes a textual court-martial of Frederic's good faith as excuse is matched against excuse, outrage against outrage, transgression against transgression.

Hemingway addresses the most compelling justification for the killing of the sergeant, that Frederic lawfully executed a deserter under military law or code, through its narrative reflection in the act of the carabinieri "executing officers of the rank of major or above who were separated from their troops" (224). Frederic's jurisdiction over the two Italian sergeants is no clearer than the battle police's right to discipline him. The sergeant's desertion is as questionable as Frederic's; the sergeant too may have been merely attempting to rejoin his unit as surely as Frederic was attempting to rejoin his at Pordenone. Nor does Frederic's action receive ready extratextual support. Although military law in most Western nations provides for summary as well as judicial punishment of soldiers,[12] such discipline is left to the commanding officers of military units ("In the majority of countries, summary penalties can be inflicted only by officers not lower than the rank of captain" [*Encyclopaedia Britannica*, 12:195]). Even in cases of the most serious breaches of discipline on the battlefield, "mortal punishment" has historically required some sort of tribunal, like the "drumhead court" invoked by analogy in Melville's *Billy Budd*. Indeed, Hemingway ensures that if Frederic mistakenly thought he had an obligation to shoot a deserter under some mysterious military code,[13] his action becomes arbitrary and inconsistent when—even before his mistreatment by the carabinieri—he decides not to report the desertion of Bonello. The judicial and transgressive situation of

Bonello is much clearer than that of the sergeant: Bonello is formally under Frederic's command, and Bonello explicitly deserts in order to give himself up to the enemy. Piani further makes it clear that in pleading for Bonello, he recognizes that he is asking Frederic to abrogate a military responsibility: "'Can't you just put him down as taken prisoner?' 'I don't know.' 'You see if the war went on they would make bad trouble for his family.' . . . 'I won't make a report that will make trouble for his family,' I went on with our conversation" (219). This conversation raises the possibility of a troublesome gap in the narrative logic: namely, that Frederic agrees to hush up the desertion of Bonello because he is afraid that Piani (and Bonello) could in turn report him for shooting the sergeant.

The reader is blinded to the ethical perversities of Frederic's acts by the ethical warrant seemingly bestowed on the narration by his silence. Frederic's silence appears to guarantee both courage (lack of justification, defense, apology, or contrition) and truth (lack of self-serving feeling or explanation) while averting other possibilities, such as blind fear and panic. When Frederic is captured by the carabinieri, he loses his cool both as a character ("'Why isn't there somebody here to stop them?' I said. 'Why haven't they blown the bridge up? Why aren't there machine-guns along this embankment?'" [211]) and as narrator ("I was very angry" [211]). Frederic is also very frightened: beneath the mock-officiousness of his protest he can't control his voice ("'What's the meaning of this?' I tried to shout but my voice was not very loud" [222]). His appeal to military protocol ("'Don't you know you can't touch an officer?'" [222] precisely mirrors the sergeant's earlier appeal to him ("'You can't order us. You're not our officer'" [204]), just as the carabinieri's rationale for killing ("'*A basso gli ufficiali!* Down with the officers!'" [219]) precisely mirrors Bonello's rationale for killing the sergeant ("'all my life I've wanted to kill a sergeant' " [207]). In his bitter judgment of the carabinieri, Frederic the narrator delivers—without irony or recognition—a perfect if inadvertent indictment of his own comportment in shooting the sergeant: "The questioners had all the efficiency, coldness and command of themselves of Italians who are firing and are not being fired on" (223).

Frederic's narration does not explicitly lie, but its factualism riddles it with holes and blindnesses. For example, his mourning of the desertion of Bonello is marked by a significant oversight that he catches neither at the time of his rumination nor during its reportage: "It seemed so silly for Bonello to have decided to be taken prisoner. There was no danger. We had walked through two armies without incident. If Aymo had not been killed there would never have seemed to be any danger. No one had bothered us when we were in plain sight along the railway. The killing came suddenly and unreasonably" (218). There was no danger? For the Italian sergeant he and Bonello killed there was surely quite mortal danger, and to the sergeant the killing must have come as suddenly and unreasonably as the killing of Aymo. Frederic's erasure of this shooting in his thinking about the war and about death persists throughout his subsequent narration. When we track how Frederic processes his experiences philosophically, this erasure or amnesia about the shooting becomes visible as a problem of reading, as Frederic's refusal to assimilate this incident to the remaining text of his war experience. His "separate peace" depends on a reading protocol of his experience that permits him an unruffled self-righteousness. In constructing the critical register of his narrative, Frederic banishes his shooting of the sergeant from the categories of senseless deaths (Catherine's, Aymo's) that become the philosophical "evidence" for his famous stoical fatalism.

The peculiar and suspect philosophical outcome of this selectively mutilated reading process is the nihilism that assigns war and death to a motiveless cosmic malignancy: "Now Catherine would die. That was what you did. You died. You did not know what it was about. You never had time to learn. They threw you in and told you the rules and the first time they caught you off base they killed you. Or they killed you gratuitously like Aymo" (327). The syntactic peculiarities of Frederic's language—the shift from passive to active construction ("You died . . . they killed you") with its unreferenced pronominal agent—are marked, by the preceding novelistic events, with the silent echo of the grammar of the now perjured truth of agency ("You died" [*you were killed*]; "they killed you" [*I killed him*]; "they killed you gratuitously like Aymo" [*I killed the sergeant gratuitously*]). Frederic's thoughts are textually haunted by the ghost of the counternarrative from another ethical country whose story tells him (and us) that he committed murder, and that, besides, the man is dead. At the end of the novel, the reader becomes witness to the witness, and catches the witness in a perversion of logic that amounts to a lie about the truth of war. Frederic knows, as the reader knows from Frederic's own account, that the killing of war is not done by an agentless, will-less corporate machine—a deific, irresponsible, unresponsive "they" stripped of purpose, necessity, reason, or heart. The killing of war was done, at least in this instance, without purpose, necessity, reason, or heart by the American soldier Frederic Henry.

The philosophical climax of the novel, Frederic Henry's theological parable about the ants on the burning log, invokes a patently false analogy that uses two modes of dying to illustrate two modes of inadvertence in the killing of people in wartime. The fire represents combat death, with soldiers like ants incapable of directing their movements toward a place of safety where there is no danger. The water Frederic tossed on the log (not to save the ants but to rinse his whiskey cup) deftly figures his aquatic desertions, alone and with Catherine, his attempts to escape the fires of war by water only to have Catherine "steamed" to death, as it were—the fire of war coloring, or heating, her own fate to die in the rain ("I'm afraid of the rain because sometimes I see me dead in it" [126]). Frederic's parable is designed to neutralize agency by absorbing the deaths war produces, or encompasses, into inevitability, inadvertency, and indifference. The novel's philosophical conclusion summarizes the novel's final generic self-contradiction. *A Farewell to Arms* ends as a love story masking and protecting a war story from the truth of its own violence and its own lies. If from classical times literature reflects how war lies about itself—as Wilfred Owen claimed of Horace—then Hemingway's own separate peace with his resistant readership is to give us a novel that textually performs just this function of war.

4

THE NOVEL OF DEPOPULATION
Remarque's *All Quiet on the Western Front*

The Effect of an Extraordinary Reception

BEGINNING A 1998 *NEW YORKER* REVIEW OF STEVEN SPIEL-berg's film *Saving Private Ryan,* Hendrik Hertzberg writes:

> At the age of twelve or thirteen, I read Erich Maria Remarque's "All Quiet on the Western Front," the great novel of the First World War, published in 1928 [*sic*]. One passage made an especially powerful impression. . . . The narrator, a young German soldier, glances over his shoulder and sees that a lance corporal running next to him has just had his head sheared off by a shell. But the man does not fall, not right away. "He runs a few steps more while the blood spouts from his neck like a fountain." This terrible image disturbed my sleep and my calm for days, and for many years afterward that headless, running, spouting man often flashed into my mind's eye. (30)

The power of Erich Maria Remarque's *All Quiet on the Western Front* to haunt and disturb literally millions of readers makes it unique in the field of twentieth-century war writing. Remarque's novel wrote in advance, and in large format, what Hemingway in "A Natural History of the Dead" tacitly argued could not be achieved: a graphically and brutally *realistic* portrayal of the First World War that became an event "unprecedented in the entire history of publishing" (Eksteins, 276); a book acclaimed as "the greatest best-selling novel of all time" (Barker and Last, 2). Within the first year of its publication in 1929, *Im Westen nichts Neues* had sold nearly a million copies in Germany, another million in Britain, France, and the United States together, and "had been translated into about twenty languages, including Chinese and Esperanto" (ibid.). By the 1970s Wilhelm Schwarz could report that "*Im Westen nichts Neues* has meanwhile reached a circulation of eight million and is still the greatest European best-seller of the twentieth century" (13). But the book's remarkable popularity has not been matched by serious critical attention, and C. R. Owen's querulous 1984 *Erich Maria Remarque* opens with the complaint "that 50 years after the publication of the all-time best-selling novel *All Quiet on the Western Front* no reliable nor exhaustive study on this work existed, nor for that matter, was there a valid biography of Erich Maria Remarque to be had on the market" (1). Since the publication of Owen's study, Modris Eksteins's 1989 *Rites of Spring* has included a serious discussion of the critical controversies generated by Remarque's novel. But Eksteins resolutely treats the work as a *postwar* work significant chiefly for its illumination of Remarque's postwar frame of mind—"*All Quiet,* contrary to the claims of many of its enthusiastic readers, was not 'the truth about the war'; it was, first and foremost, the truth about Erich Maria Remarque in 1928" (298).

I intend my discussion of *All Quiet on the Western Front* to make much larger claims than Eksteins's, but without disputing many of his disavowals. I find Remarque's novel the most successful representation of Edith Wyschogrod's "death world," whose genesis she locates ("arbitrarily," she concedes [15]) in World War I. I will argue that in spite of his strategic use of "vignettes" or representative figures of soldiers, Remarque writes his story of the First World War as a compelling novel of *depopulation*—and that he does so not by techniques of "realism" that convey the "reality" of the trenches but by poetic techniques that are themselves coeval with cultural and aesthetic technologies—montage, X rays, filmic surrealism—that emerge at the time of the First World War. It does not matter that "a man with his legs or his head blown off could not continue to run," as Remarque's critics protested (Eksteins, 282), and that the image of the headless running soldier that haunted Hendrik Hertzberg these many years might be a fiction with no physical basis in reality. Remarque's novel is better read as a poetic allegory of modern manmade mass death depicted in images whose power is structural and deconstructive—spatial and temporal fragmentations and disjunctions of the human body, porous and trangressed boundaries between the living and the dead, supererogations and superimpositions of the dead upon the dead. Remarque invented in *All Quiet on the Western Front* a necrological poetics capable of illuminating not only the phenomenology of the "death world" but also its profound ontological effect on the subject steeped in killing and dying. A focus on Remarque's generic and rhetorical strategies in animating the fate of the body in battle allows me to penetrate innovations for which the term "irony" may finally be too coarse and imprecise.

Samuel Hynes reads the fragmentary and paratactic structure of the novel chiefly as *ironic* with the purpose of illustrating the inherently ironic character of war—"This war-world, with its butterflies and skulls, its quiet fronts on which men die violently, is ironic in its essential nature. War has disturbed the familiar world of values and meanings, leaving only contradictions, denials, conflicts, tensions, incoherences" (426). But while conceding that all war is ironic ("Every war is ironic because every war is worse than expected"), Paul Fussell privileges the First World War as "more ironic than any before or since" (7–8). This sense certainly prevails in light of the revisionary interpretations that had taken hold by the time Remarque's novel was held to have reported the "truth about the war":

> But what was this "truth" to which almost all referred? That the war had been a nihilistic slaughter without rationale? That its frontline protagonists and chief victims had no sense of purpose? That, in short, the war had been in vain? Few said so outright, but the liberal left and moderate socialists throughout Europe, and even here and there in America and the dominions, were now inclined to view the war as, in the end, a tragic and futile civil conflict in Europe, one that need not have occurred. (Eksteins, 286)

This growing sense of the World War's violent disjunction between unclear political objectives pursued with utterly concrete material means and effects certainly prepared the ground for *All Quiet on the Western Front*'s overwhelming reception. The "truths" of war are not only political, as Eksteins suggests, but also material, psychological, and finally ontological.

At the same time, the political moment of the publication of Remarque's novel cannot be reduced to the seemingly homogeneous response of its enthusiastic reception. In Germany, particularly, the fractured political response to the war with its crippling Versailles Treaty was reflected in a fractured literary response that made Erich Maria Remarque's success controversial, embattled, and anguished. Wilhelm Schwarz reduces these fractures to two currents that he terms, admittedly roughly, the militaristic and the pacifistic.[1] These camps operated in dynamic interaction, and Remarque, while working for the glossy sports magazine *Sport im Bild,* reviewed a series of war novels that Eksteins characterizes as "[Ernst] Jünger's exuberant, intoxicating vitalism and brutal grandeur, [Franz] Schauwecker's breathless, mystical nationalism, and [Georg] von der Vring's lyrical simplicity" (280)—military and militaristic novels that might have inspired Remarque's animated reaction.[2] Germany's factioned politics mirrored itself in attacks on his novel by both left and right after its publication: the communists derided it as bourgeois sentimentality, the fascists as degenerate art. C. R. Owen quotes a review by the Marxist Adolf Grabowsky, published in *Die Tat* in 1929: "The West thinks privately, it no longer experiences collective fates, it has sunk deep into its petty bourgeoisie and Remarque is the best symbol for it. Remarque is the symbol for the decay of the Western world, the most beautiful proof for the correctness of the Spenglerian thesis" (151–52). The fascist denunciations of *All Quiet on the Western Front* took more violent forms in the 1930s. Joseph Goebbels arranged for the disruption and banning of the American film version of *All Quiet on the Western Front* (directed by Lewis Milestone for Universal Studios) in 1930 (Barker and Last, 41); the novel was ritually burned in the Opernplatz in Berlin on May 10, 1933, with the formal sentence: "As a protest against the literary betrayal of the soldiers of the Great War, and on behalf of the education of our people in the spirit of truth, I consign to the flames the writings of Erich Maria Remarque" (Barker and Last, 32–33). More seriously, Remarque was stripped of his German citizenship in 1938, and his youngest sister, Elfriede, was beheaded by the Nazis in 1943—"it was generally assumed that Elfriede's death was, in part at least, a result of Nazi antipathy towards her brother" (Barker and Last, 22). For a book that Remarque himself described as "unpolitical," *All Quiet on the Western Front* certainly unleashed a huge number of political consequences upon the author.

The contentious political scene into which *All Quiet on the Western Front* made its debut created conditions that subjected Remarque to intense scrutiny with respect to his military service, and eventually made him vulnerable to controversy and criticism. The novel's publishers erroneously elevated his rank to lieutenant in their advertisements (Owen, 12) and cited medals whose legitimacy had been questioned after the war. Remarque had claimed that a Council for Workers and Soldiers (*Arbeiter- und Soldatenrat*) had voted to give him the Iron Cross, yet apparently he was reprimanded by the city of Osnabrück in 1919 for wearing unearned medals. But there is little dispute that Remarque did serve in combat in the First World War; he was probably drafted (some say he enlisted, and there is some question about his age, which was probably around eighteen), received basic training, and served in a trench unit "based somewhere between Thourout and the forest of Houthult" (Barker and Last, 8)—that is, probably not as far as the actual front line. A number of his comrades appear to have served as models for the troops in *All Quiet on the Western Front,* including Theo Trotske, the probable precursor of Kat: "Trotske was badly wounded by grenade splinters in July 1917 and Remarque carried him back behind the line of fire; but Trotske later died in hospital of head wounds which at first passed unnoticed. . . . Rabe suggests that this incident formed the basis of the fate which befell Kat in Remarque's novel" (Barker and Last, 8). Remarque told Frédéric Lefèvre about a different combat trauma in a 1930 interview for *The Living Age:* "I saw my best friend lying in the mud, his abdomen torn open" (Owen, 11–12). Owen finds the traumatic sight compulsively repeated in Remarque's works: "Every one of Remarque's books dealing with war contains battle scenes in which both soldiers and animals are depicted with their intestines laid bare" (Owen, 12). Remarque himself was wounded during the Battle of Flanders in 1917 (Barker and Last, 8–9) and hospitalized for a time. Although this outline might seem to bear considerable similarity to Hemingway's military experience, Remarque's tour of duty was clearly more traumatic than Hemingway's six days in action as a volunteer food dispenser, and there is wide agreement that he suffered serious post-traumatic depression until the therapy of writing *All Quiet on the Western Front.*[3]

This sketchy and sketchily documented information on Remarque's war experience needs to be kept in focus if Remarque's status as a *survivor* is not to be distorted and negated by his and his novel's subsequent celebrity. For both novel and man, fame seems to have undermined and deferred serious consideration. For Remarque, perhaps even more than for Hemingway, his postnovel celebrity cast an aura of glamour that so thoroughly externalized his persona as to occlude the private self the writer jealously guarded and concealed from publicity.[4] Remarque's exceptional good looks (Marlene

Dietrich is said to have called him the most attractive man in the world [Barker and Last, 23]), sartorial elegance, and European worldliness (he was a connoisseur of exotic cocktails, Oriental rugs, and tropical fish, as well as an art collector) were enhanced by his association with the world's most glamorous women—Dietrich and Garbo during his years in Hollywood from 1939 to 1942, and later his wife, the actress Paulette Goddard. But the cosmopolitanism of living in Switzerland, Hollywood, New York, Rome, of traveling several times on the *Queen Mary,* and of moving in celebrity circles occludes the perils and inconveniences of émigré life and the governmental pressures and threats that necessitated several of his removals. In 1932 Remarque was obliged to remarry his divorced first wife, Ilse Zambona, in order to secure a Swiss visa for her and prevent her deportation to Germany. His own visa problems as a "stateless refugee" (Owen, 229) without a valid national passport required detours through Panama and Mexico, and caused many bureaucratic complications. Remarque's postwar success and affluence neither compromise nor negate the complexity of his historical existence, including the combat experiences that transformed him into a survivor of trauma imbued with credibility as a witness and a writer of fictional testimonial.

Samuel Hynes divides war narratives into two basic forms, the autobiographical and the historical, and he claims *All Quiet on the Western Front* as the "great example of the autobiographical mode in war fiction" (425). Although I concur with Hynes's assessment of its greatness, I would reformulate the novel's autobiographical form in ways that rescue it from the limitations of the "personal" rather than the "general" and the "small picture" rather than the "large." (425). I would argue rather that Remarque's construction of the soldier's voice in his novel serves a rhetorically innovative attempt to recreate a kind of discursive no-man's land—a space where speech that is impossible both socially and psychologically can take place. The voice of Paul Bäumer turns his narratee into an ideal interlocutor of the humane, who will hear what the soldier cannot tell his family or his townspeople. "I realize he does not know that a man cannot talk of such things," Paul explains of his father's distressing curiosity about his combat experience. "I would do it willingly, but it is too dangerous for me to put these things into words. I am afraid they might then become gigantic and I be no longer able to master them" (165). The first-person story of *All Quiet on the Western Front* is this hypothetical outpouring—gigantic and unmasterable—that can be produced only as a fiction since even in the therapeutic confession ("This book is to be neither an accusation nor a confession") its form would be maimed by blanks, signs, symptoms, and traumatic performativity. If the voice of trauma is released through the wound, as Cathy Caruth suggests (2), then the narrative voice of Remarque's novel must be seen as a clinical impossibility, a voice not maimed or scarred by the horror of its war experience. Paul Bäumer's voice speaks in a soldier's language of desire, speaks in the way soldiers wish they could speak of what they saw and lived through. Besides enacting a seeming clinical impossibility, the narrative voice of *All Quiet on the Western Front* enacts a seeming moral impossibility as well, for Paul retains a fundamental innocence that allows his voice to enact the closing lines of August Stramm's "Battlefield"—"Murder on murder / blinks / in childish eyes" (Silkin, 239). This moral quality of the voice creates a problematical polemical situation for the novel, since its blamelessness (in two senses of the word—"This book is neither an accusation nor a confession") compromises the novel's realism in the interest of magnifying and intensifying the sensation of loss at the novel's end. The benign tone and sentiment of the voice make it a fragile humanitarian outpost in the novel's war world—the discursive equivalent to the function of the pastoral in English Great War poetry and fiction. Paul's extinction at the novel's end is therefore an ethically apocalyptic moment, the death not just of a boy but of innocence, of decency, of civility, of civilization. This character of the book can be construed as its sentimentality, a depiction of war as resolutely external to the men who fight it, as relatively uninternalized and without power to corrupt. Remarque's decision to empty his protagonists of aggression and violence may have been motivated by his desire to resist the martial adventuring and soldiers' blood lust celebrated in Ernst Jünger's *In Stahlgewittern*. But it may also have reflected a little-known phenomenon that Gwynne Dyer discusses in *War*—namely, that soldiers who are unobserved will generally not kill, even if they are in danger of being shot. After the Second World War a U.S. Army colonel named S. L. A. Marshall conducted interviews with over four hundred infantry companies and discovered "that on average only 15 percent of trained combat riflemen fired their weapons at all in battle. The rest did not flee, but they would not kill—even when their own position was under attack and their lives were in immediate danger" (118). Dyer concludes from this evidence that "men will kill under compulsion—men will do almost anything if they know it is expected of them and they are under strong social pressure to comply—but the vast majority of men are not born killers" (119).[5] The innocence of

Remarque's soldiers may be less a sentimentality than a truth counter to the passionate celebration of violence Klaus Theweleit found in the *Freikorps* literature.

A further challenge that the convention of the autobiographical voice poses to Remarque's project is the problem of transforming its experience into a transindividualized phenomenon that will allow it to speak for the entire world of the trenches and its soldiers. Remarque announces the novel's intention to speak for the death world—that is, to speak for "a generation of men who, even though they may have escaped shells, were destroyed by the war" (n.p.)—and, according to both his critics and his detractors, he succeeded. Bruno Frank is said to have praised Remarque for representing not only the suffering of an individual but the cacophonous howling woe of a hundred million people driven together into hell by an idiotic politics ("*Nicht das Leid eines einzelnen, sondern das ineinanderheulende Leid von hundert Millionen Menschen, die von idiotischer Politik in die Hölle zusammengetrieben wurden*" [Antkowiak, 27]). Conversely, Remarque's conservative and fascist critics excoriated just this ontological state—the protagonist's consciousness of himself as immersed in a world of massed men, "a grain of sand in an endless desert," Schwarz says (25)—in which his experience is the experience of the fluid, borderless sea of soldiers poured into the trenches in waves. In the German political right's campaign to neutralize the novel's popularity, the antiheroic mass mentality of the novel— Paul Bäumer as a *Massenmensch*, a man governed only by animal drives, materiality, and the absence of spirit (Antkowiak, 23)—becomes a repeated target of "ethical" attack. Soon after the book's publication, government officials and civil servants became literary critics to excoriate *Im Westen nichts Neues* to boys' clubs and youth groups (ibid.). They were guided by precisely the ideology Klaus Theweleit reports embedded in the fascist fantasies of the *Freikorps* culture he explores in *Male Fantasies*—"Alongside his capacity to mobilize great masses of human beings, there exists within the fascist a simultaneous contempt for the masses; while he addresses himself to them, he feels himself at the same time to be raised above them, one of an elite standing against the lowly 'man-of-the-masses'" (3).

Remarque appears to achieve this transindividuation of Paul Bäumer into the aggregate of unknown soldiers in spite of a technique that at first may seem to rely merely on the use of vignettes. The novel initially assembles an *imaginable* homogeneous community of homosocial camaraderie around Paul, and sets it against the background of an army that is an *unimaginable* community in its fragmentation, displacement, and jumbling together of men in alien territories, engaged in unnatural activities, thrown together more by chance and accident (*"aus Zufallserlebnissen zusammengewürfelte Gruppe"* [Antkowiak, 12]) than by the logic of a socially ordered society. To the novel's small kernel of school friends, bearing the last vestiges of social and institutional bonds amid the chaos and arbitrariness that reigns in the field, their military function, their role in strategy and tactical logic, is invisible and unimaginable, a matter of agnostic faith. The criticism of ahistoricism leveled against the novel by critics on both the left and the right took a particularly curious form when it argued that *All Quiet on the Western Front* delivers merely the protocol of the war experience (*"das Protokoll des Kriegserlebnisses"* [Antkowiak 29]), which strips it of strategic, military, or historical interpretability. The word "protocol"—suggesting the programmatic scripting of rules, plans, and goals—seems provocatively inappropriate to describe the world of Remarque's trenches. One might argue rather that the inability of military protocol to be translated into an intelligible sense of function and instrumentality, into a map of strategy and tactic in the field, virtually prevents the soldiers from entering into history, from being able to imagine themselves as actors in a historical process. In *All Quiet on the Western Front* the autobiographical mode confounds the historical mode in Samuel Hynes's sense of the categories of those terms. By superimposing the individual voice, the small group, and the fluid and indeterminate waves of bodies, Remarque overlaps the various population scales in their progress toward the same end of violent decimation and annihilation. Remarque gives the "lost generation" an actuarial as well as a spiritual meaning, as he blunts the modernist nostalgia, cynicism, and posturing with which the Anglo-American literati imbued the term, by making the war's survivors a species of the living dead.

The Calculus of Death

Remarque's war novel begins, rhetorically, with an antiphrasis—a moment of profound peace: "We are at rest five miles behind the front. Yesterday we were relieved, and now our bellies are full of beef and haricot beans. We are satisfied and at peace" (1). This moment must be translated into a Darwinian allegory of war in which census taking is interpreted according to a Malthusian arithmetic:

> Fourteen days ago we had to go up and relieve the front line. It was
> fairly quiet on our sector, so the quartermaster who remained in the
> rear had requisitioned the usual quantity of rations and provided
> for the full company of one hundred and fifty men. But on the last
> day an astonishing number of English heavies opened up on us with
> high-explosive, drumming ceaselessly on our position, so that we
> suffered severely and came back only eighty strong. (2)

Paul Bäumer's Second Company is turned into a population whose competition for scarce resources is alleviated by the decimation of half its numbers.
The novel opens with an ironic image of war as effective population control
whose activity of depopulation will produce peace and prosperity according
to Malthusian principles. Each man lost represents a ration gained, and the
soldiers have internalized this ironic economy to the point where calculation
of gain replaces the calculation of loss, which, in its affective version, would
(and *will*, later in the text) function as mourning: "'What a bean-feast! That's
all for us. Each man gets—wait a bit—yes, practically two issues'" (5). In a
communion with a highly displaced logic, the soldiers ingest or introject
their dead comrades as a second ration, eating in their place as though each
living man were inhabited by a ghostly double of a slain counterpart who
has a right to be fed. Remarque literalizes here the antiphrastic economy of
much war ideology that translates loss into gain, the indeterminate transformation of the death of one part of the population into tangible benefit and
enhanced life for the other part. With this opening gambit Remarque explores the structural logic of war by allegorical rather than polemical means,
not by direct address to the specific political and ideological discourses of
Prussian militarism but by analyzing the hidden and devious logic that relates the fate of the human body in war to war's presumed political effects.

Remarque has Paul Bäumer produce a narrative of subtraction and frac-
tionation that depopulates his thrown-together little group of a dozen or so
men, by reducing their number not only one by one (like the children's
game, with its genocidal thematic, of "Ten Little Indians"), but sometimes
part by part, an eye here, a foot there, now a mind, and so on. He further
collapses the boundaries between the living and dead by having them assume each other's features, showing the living inhabited by death while
the dead body is animated and vivified—forbidden stasis, rest, and freedom
from violence. These narrative and poetic devices serve less the ends of

realism (although many of the violent scenes and images are empirically referential) than the expressive challenge of conjuring an unimaginable ontological space where human being becomes virtually unrecognizable to itself because it is forced to inhabit what Elaine Scarry has termed an "unmade world." These devices require analytical elucidation if the charge of unproductive exhibitionism leveled against the novel by the German revolutionary left—Johannes Becher, for example, characterized its reading as voyeuristic leafing through a horror album (Antkowiak, 31)—is to be answered. I hope that my reading of Remarque's strategies does more than merely revisit the text's disturbing scenes and grisly sights, but explicates their allegorical and rhetorical mechanisms and functions to express the supererogation of the First World War's mechanized violence and its effects on the soldier's body and soul. This expression, I hope to show, was influenced and inflected by the innovations of modernistic poetry and avant-garde art—the habits of parataxis, disconnection, antiphrasis, and surreality that were themselves coeval with the twentieth century's creative and destructive technologies. The affinities of avant-garde imaging to the psychoanalytic devices of hallucination and nightmare further equip Remarque with updated versions of the Gothic for representing the destruction of the reality sense in the scene of combat.

One of Remarque's most powerful strategies for showing the sign of the death world in the trenches entails a series of narratives and images of *twice-killing* whose most spectacular instance—which I will explore a bit later—is the graveyard shelling in which the buried dead are shelled and killed again. But hard upon the novel's pastoral opening, in which bumblebees drone out the distant thunder of the guns to preserve the undisturbed opulence of the windfall of double rations, Remarque invents a variant figure of the death world as a permeable divide between living and dying, which in the case of Franz Kemmerich, one of Paul's not-yet-dead companions, fails to defer death and lets it invade the still living. Remarque uses the infant technologies of experimental photography (particularly the photomontage, already operative in avant-garde art and cinematography) and X-ray machines to represent death announcing and preceding itself in the moribund figure of what had been a blooming nineteen-year-old whose hair used to fly in his face like silk during gymnastics on the parallel bars. "Death is working through from within. It already has command in the eyes. . . . He it is still and yet it is not he any longer. His features have become uncertain and faint, like a photographic plate from which two pictures have been taken" (14).

On a second visit to Kemmerich's hospital bed, the double exposure resolves itself into the clearer outlines of impending death: "His lips have fallen away, his mouth has become larger, the teeth stick out and look as though they were made of chalk. The flesh melts, the forehead bulges more prominently, the cheekbones protrude. The skeleton is working itself through" (28). Remarque here figures fictionally one of the most powerful and terrible literal iconographies that the Holocaust incised on the bodies of its victims, familiar from pictures of victims of famine: their transformation while living into the skeletal forms of a merely deferred death. The narrative eye has X-ray vision that produces a spatial image to represent the temporal transition from living to death.

Kemmerich's subtraction from Paul's cadre is not the first—although, like Joseph Behm, who was the first of the school friends to fall, he dies in pieces. Behm is the first of the twice-killed figures in the novel—shot in the eye and left for dead, only to be shelled and shot again when he regains consciousness ("Because he could not see, and was mad with pain, he failed to keep under cover, and so was shot down before anyone could go and fetch him in" [12]). Remarque's technique of fragmentation and metonymic loss intensifies the death-world effect by factoring each man's death into multiple mutilations and losses, and by particularizing the body in order to multiply and specify its vulnerabilities. This strategy serves as a rhetorical antidote to the Prussian militaristic tropology by which the soldierly body, both individual and collective, is figured with insentient hardness and impassability as a living armor, as—in Kantorek's phrase—the "Iron Youth" (19).[6] Remarque uses metonymies not only to picture Kemmerich as disappearing piece by piece—his watch stolen, his foot amputated, his boots taken away—but also to make the ironic point that the boy's accoutrements, such as the fine boots that he gives to Müller and that eventually circulate throughout the Second Company upon the death of each subsequent owner, are more durable than the fragile bodies of the men. Eventually Kemmerich—whose dying issues in alternate versions for the reader ("He is entirely alone now with his little life of nineteen years, and cries because it leaves him" [31]) and for his mother ("I invent a story" [181])—becomes folded into the census taking that tracks the Second Company's depopulation: "Kemmerich is dead, Haie Westhus is dying, they will have a job with Hans Kramer's body at the Judgment day, piecing it together after a direct hit; Martens has no legs anymore, Meyer is dead, Max is dead, Beyer is dead, Hämmerling is dead" (139). By the time Kemmerich's mother asks for a report of her son's dying, Paul is out of patience with her monadic assumptions. "When a man has seen so many dead he cannot understand any longer why there should be so much anguish over a single individual" (181).

Remarque supplements the visual montage to figure the death world with forms of temporal montage, the neural disjunction at the moment of death that can confuse and rupture the boundary between quickness and death to make the dismembered body mobile, the impossibly dismembered body appear still living, in a ghastly parody of live locomotion. If Remarque's images here depict a medical impossibility, they nonetheless powerfully express combat's premature and abrupt dispossession of life by death:

> Beside me a lance-corporal has his head torn off. He runs a few steps more while the blood spouts from his neck like a fountain. (115)

> We see men living with their skulls blown open; we see soldiers run with their two feet cut off, they stagger on their splintered stumps into the next shell-hole; a lance-corporal crawls a mile and a half on his hands dragging his smashed knee after him; another goes to the dressing station and over his clasped hands bulge his intestines; we see men without mouths, without jaws, without faces; we find one man who has held the artery of his arm in his teeth for two hours in order not to bleed to death. (134)

In a reverse formation, the corpse continues to "speak" and grow and move like a live thing: "Many have their bellies swollen up like balloons. They hiss, belch, and make movements. The gases in them make noises" (126). Eventually the body of the soldier is deployed like a sign of the death world's invasion of nature itself. Paul perceives the dead men hanging in trees like a sign that must be deciphered—"What can that mean?" (208)—and must be given an instrumental explanation: "If a mortar gets you it blows you clean out of your clothes. It's the concussion that does it" (208). But the image of trees burgeoning with parts of dead men is powerfully contrasted with the blooming cherry tree that overwhelms the farmer Detering with Chekhovian longing ("It had no leaves, but was one white mass of blossom" [275]) and drives him to madness, desertion, and probable execution. In contrast, Paul sees that "a naked soldier is squatting in the fork of a tree, he still has his helmet on, otherwise he is entirely unclad. There is only half of him sitting up there, the top half, the legs are missing" (207–8). Juxtaposed, these trees form a powerful montage of the vegetation of the death world of war, burgeoning with partial corpses in place of the cherry blossoms of a lost, prelapsarian eastern front.

The decimation of the Second Company after the offensive transforms the survivors themselves into a body part, a synecdoche of a once whole corps, or corpus, which is now only a "handful"—"a dreadfully small handful, and a dreadfully small remnant" (135). Behind this rhetorical figuration is its statistical counterpart: Paul's company is reduced from 150 men to 32 in a matter of a few months (they count off "'One—two—three—four—' and cease at thirty-two" [136]). Paul's little group of comrades dwindles apace: "We count up: out of twenty, seven are dead, four wounded, one in a mad-house. That makes twelve" (84). This more precise census taking calibrates degrees of population reduction to strategic military success or failure, which in the trench warfare of World War I was calculated in limited topologies of measurable ground, like those contested in sports: "Still the little piece of convulsed earth in which we lie is held. We have yielded no more than a few hundred yards of it as a prize to the enemy. But on every yard there lies a dead man" (135). Paul Bäumer's observation is paradigmatic for the whole of World War I, whose 10 million dead and 20 million wounded were deployed by all sides largely for a strategic impetus early transformed from the conquest of territory into the endlessly frustrated aim to achieve mere mobility, to "break through" and "move on" to destinations whose objects and value had already become a species of fantasy ("They argue about what we ought to annex. The head-master with the steel watch-chain wants to have at least the whole of Belgium, the coal-areas of France, and a slice of Russia. He produces reasons why we must have them and is quite inflexible until at last the others give in to him" [166]). Paul Fussell notes, "From the winter of 1914 until the spring of 1918 the trench system was fixed, moving here and there a few hundred yards, moving on great occasions as much as a few miles" (36). The "movement" of this line that is itself a geometrical and political abstraction is figured like a writing or a penning whose ink is blood—like the blood of Leer, who loses the power of movement when his hip is opened. "Leer groans as he supports himself on his arm, he bleeds quickly, no one can help him. Like an emptying tube, after a couple of minutes he collapses" (284).

Remarque uses the slipping signification of ground, earth, or land, in its relation to soldiers and death, to interrogate and confound the teleological and instrumental logic by which military strategy makes the injury and

death of populations the means of pursuing a species of power most frequently figured in relation to a topos. Tjaden, the peat cutter in the Second
Company, plays with the figure of a country as its topology by rendering the
facile personification of nation as "country" or "land" absurd ("A mountain
in Germany cannot offend a mountain in France. Or a river, or a wood, or a
field of wheat" [204]). The soldier does not politicize the earth, as Paul's
rapturous embrace of her (*die Erde* is feminine in German) articulates a more
primal if no less figural relation to the earth as security and shelter: "To no
man does the earth mean so much as to the soldier . . . when he buries his
face and his limbs deep in her from the fear of death by shell-fire, then she
is his only friend, his brother, his mother; he stifles his terror and his cries
in her silence and her security" (55). But his eulogy is antiphrastic: the earth
is also transformed by shells into grave and into lethal weapon ("It was winter when I came up, and when the shells exploded the frozen clods of earth
were just as dangerous as the fragments" [271]). The shells bury the dead
("We cannot fetch them all in, if we did we should not know what to do with
them. The shells will bury them" [126]), and unbury them again when a
cemetery with freshly dug graves is badly shelled, only to rebury them again
thereafter ("Two of our dead lie in the upturned graves. We merely throw
the earth in on them" [73]).

Even the dead are not safe or removed from war, and their coffins are
ripped from the earth and shattered to become missile and weapon ("The
coffin has hit the fourth man in our hole on his outstretched arm" [69]). In
a ghastly reversal and prophecy, the corpse-filled coffin becomes shelter for
the living: "I merely crawl still farther under the coffin, it shall protect me,
though Death himself lies in it" (67). Remarque's aim here is clearly to desig-
nify cultural mortuary semiology in order to break death out of its symbolic
confines in the culture of the life world and depict it as the contaminant of
all systems in the death world of the trenches. At some moments on the
battlefield the entire earth becomes a vast grave, psychologically ("We sit as
if in our graves waiting only to be closed in" [110]) and literally, when mines
excavate the earth ("The whole region where they go up becomes one grave"
[106]) and transform it into an abattoir ("we stumble over slippery lumps of
flesh, over yielding bodies; I fall into an open belly" [117]). Paul Fussell
writes, "The idea of mass graves seems to pertain especially to the twentieth
century," and goes on to produce a paradigmatic image of the material reality
that underlies the monadic assumptions that are culturally imputed to the

military cemetery: "There are 2500 British war cemeteries in France and Belgium. The sophisticated observer of the rows of headstones will do well to suspect that very often the bodies below are buried in mass graves, with the headstones disposed in rows to convey the illusion that each soldier has his individual place" (6).

The Killer and the Killed

Remarque uses the event of Paul's being thrown into a dead man's coffin and replacing the corpse in the grave during the shelling to figure the serial replacements of dead soldiers, the waves of recruits taking the place of dead predecessors in a proleptic position that announces their own destiny. Paul's tour of duty enfolds within it a passing of generations, as the ages of man— and particularly childhood and adolescence—are annihilated in an extreme compression of experience that forecloses development, learning, and maturation. Alfred Antkowiak characterizes the novels of the lost generation of sad young men ("*die Bücher der 'traurigen' jungen Männer*" [40]) as though they were anti-*Bildungsromane* in which character is static, condemned to immobility, to passive and impotent reaction to event and power, incapable of change or maturation, like a blighted bud. Remarque gives this condition both figurative and narrative play. By juxtaposing Paul's Second Company with the recruits who are their reinforcements ("infants," Kropp calls the boys who are only two years younger than himself), he produces a distorted generational structure ("We are forlorn like children, and experienced like old men, we are crude and sorrowful and superficial—I believe we are lost" [123]) in which, at twenty, one is old without ever having been young, and in which the recruits seem younger, greener, and smaller with each wave ("For most of them the uniform is far too big, it hangs on their limbs, their shoulders are too narrow, their bodies too slight; no uniform was ever made to these childish measurements" [130]) until they turn, upon their first combat, into spiritual and literal dead children ("Their sharp, downy, dead faces have the awful expressionlessness of dead children" [130]). Remarque reverses the mythology of war as a moral rite of passage for young men that made Ernst Jünger's *Storm of Steel* (*In Stahlgewittern*) the model of the fascist premise of war as testing ground for human greatness, and soldierly virtue and masculinity as the model of civic value (Antkowiak, 21). The concept of *Bildung* is particularly negated in *All Quiet on the Western Front* as the culture and art that shape cultivation in the *Bildungsroman*. Paul Bäumer's play "Saul," with its suggestion of the dramatic conversion and growth into greatness of his apostolic eponym, remains unwritten and unfulfilled. Remarque puts several types of education[7] into dialogue—for example, the utterly useless book learning of school ("'When was the battle of Zana?'" . . . "'What offices did Lycurgus consider the most important for the state?'" [85]) and the equally useless, if more sadistic, training in military drill. The semiology of the death world becomes the only worthwhile and viable course of study:

> They get killed simply because they hardly can tell shrapnel from high-explosive, they are mown down because they are listening anxiously to the roar of the big coal-boxes falling in the rear, and miss the light, piping whistle of the low spreading daisy-cutters. They flock together like sheep instead of scattering, and even the wounded are shot down like hares by the airmen. (130)

Even this education is more in evidence by its negation than by its practice: "A surprise gas-attack carries off a lot of them. They have not yet learned what to do. We found one dug-out full of them, with blue heads and black lips. Some of them in a shell hole took off their masks too soon; they did not know that the gas lies longest in the hollows" (131). The death world has its own curriculum and educational system, whose grisly skills ("it is best to stick a bayonet in the belly because there it doesn't get jammed, as it does in the ribs" [85]) form the anti-*Bildung* needed, in Elaine Scarry's terms, to unmake the world.

Wilhelm Schwarz argues that for Remarque one great redemptive value emerges from the death world of the trenches, and that is *comradeship* (25). Comradeship is indeed the most intense and driving social force of the trenches, but the violence of combat utterly routs comradeship's power to protect and save. The impotence, helplessness, and futility of compassion mock and defile the last vestiges of humaneness in the field of the death world, and removed from its efficacy to aid and ameliorate, compassion boomerangs and becomes an instrument of torture to those afflicted by it. Remarque carefully structures a complex narrative around Paul's tangential encounter with a very young recruit as an allegory of the evisceration and frustration of compassion. Paul encounters the young recruit in such a fragmented way during a rocket shelling that neither his name nor his face is ever clearly apprehended by either Paul or the reader. He is recognizable only by partial features, his fair hair visible because he "has buried his face in his hands, his helmet has fallen off," his youth signaled by the gestures and movements of a terrified child: "I fish hold of it and try to put it back on his head. He looks up, pushes the helmet off and like a child creeps under my arm, his head close to my breast. The little shoulders heave" (61). The infantilic portrait is intensified when the boy's fright causes him to soil his pants; later, when Paul slits up the trouser leg of a soldier with a splintered hip joint to tear a bandage from the underpants, he recognizes the fair-haired recruit by their absence. Between the onset of the rocket attack and its end, when the boy will be taken off on a stretcher to end his remaining few days as "one screaming bundle of intolerable pain" (72), Remarque introduces the harrowing night of the screaming horses,[8] when the men are driven nearly insane by their cries: "The cries continued. It is not men, they could not cry so terribly. 'Wounded horses,' says Kat. It's unendurable. It is the moaning of the world, it is the martyred creation, wild with anguish, filled with terror, and groaning. We are pale. Detering stands up. 'God! For God's sake! Shoot them'" (62). Whether realistic or not, the screaming animals signify to the narrator, as to the farmer Detering, a murder of the innocents ("Like to know what harm they've done. . . . I tell you it is the vilest baseness to use horses in the war" [64]), a cruelty visited on the nonideological body whose injury, if instrumental, is nonetheless unjustifiable. It is a symbolism readily transferred to the terrified young recruit, who will be deprived of the mercy of Paul and Kat's compassion when in anguish at his certain fate ("Every day that he can live will be a howling torture" [72]) they would take a revolver and put him out of his misery. The small mercy of euthanasia for horses ("The soldier runs up and shoots it. Slowly, humbly, it sinks to the ground. We take our hands from our ears" [64]) is denied to the fair-haired recruit, and the mercy of its delivery is denied to Paul and Kat.

Compassion and empathy are sources of suffering in Remarque's novel that are defeated not by transformation into coldness or cruelty but by being made inoperative when the soldiers' double command to kill and to survive collapses into a single animalistic, instinctual activity exempt from reason: "We have become wild beasts. We do not fight, we defend ourselves against annihilation. It is not against men that we fling bombs, what do we know of men in this moment when Death is hunting us down" (113). It is precisely such personifications as this, when the particularity of the nationalized physiognomy of the enemy (the Frenchman's "dark pointed beard and . . . strange eyes" [113]) is shown as erased in their figuration as Death itself, that we can see Remarque's much criticized intention to erase all political, historical, and military features of the war in order to let it emerge as a brute power of nature that overwhelms the individual like a fate (Antkowiak, 29). The enemy in the trenches is not French or English or Russian, but war itself. At the same time I would argue that Remarque carefully removes his death-world rhetoric from significations of universalism and transcendence by complicating the question of agency in systemic, if not historical, terms. While making of Paul's poignant vigil with the dying Frenchman he has stabbed a scene of painfully unmotivated killing, Remarque is careful to stress both the deindividuated techniques of mass killing and its deindividuated character as a strategic phenomenon in battle.

Before the offensive, Paul's Second Company see hundreds of new, freshly built coffins ("They still smell of resin, and pine, and the forest" [99]) leaning against a schoolhouse in readiness for their own casualties: "The coffins are really for us. The organization surpasses itself in that kind of thing" (100). The combat deaths of the company are fully premeditated and industrially anticipated by the military establishment: the agency that makes an individual German soldier like Paul Bäumer kill an individual French soldier like Gérard Duval has been absorbed even before the event into a statistical calculation, a theoretical and hypothetical figure that strategic planning intends to produce. In warfare, only the individual victims—not their aggregate numbers—appear to be products of chance ("Over us, Chance hovers. . . . In a bomb-proof dug-out I may be smashed to atoms and in the open may survive ten hours' bombardment unscathed" [101]). But Paul understands the laws of probability that turn chance into fate: "No soldier outlives a thousand chances" (101). The sense of war as a brute natural force is inscribed in the text less as an ideological agenda than as a psychological figure: an internalization of the bureaucratic calculation and technological delivery of manmade mass death as the certainty of a fate.

When Remarque does renationalize the enemy in the novel, he has Paul's imagination domesticate them, and recontextualize them back into the "made" worlds that produced them and preceded their degradation by war and imprisonment. He describes the Russian prisoners of war as "big fellows with beards—they look like meek, scolded, St. Bernard dogs" (189), and is distressed by their starved and diseased condition: "They have dysentery; furtively many of them display the blood-stained tails of their shirts. Their backs, their necks are bent, their knees sag, their heads droop as they stretch out their hands and beg in the few words of German that they know—beg with those soft, deep, musical voices, that are like warm stoves and cosy rooms at home" (190). The sentimentalized stereotyping of the rural Russians, their glowing cigarette ends reminding Paul of "little windows in dark village cottages saying that behind them are rooms full of peace" (194), refuses to foreshadow "the failure of the Allies to release the German prisoners of war" after the war's end (Schwarz, 7) and the cruel conditions of their unjustifiable and prolonged postwar internment ("Of the 300,000 Austrian troops taken prisoner at the beginning of November 1918, as many as 30,000 had died in captivity by the autumn of 1919" [Gilbert, 520]). A decade later, Remarque would have known these facts, but he nonetheless resolutely depoliticizes the renationalized enemy. When Paul Bäumer kills the Frenchman in the shell hole, he likewise constructs a domestic persona from the evidence of his effects—Gérard Duval, a printer or compositor, with a wife and a little girl "against an ivy-clad wall . . . they are clearly not rich people" (224–25). The enemy is refunctioned into a peacetime civic identity, stripped of the political overlay of the war's issues.

Paul Bäumer's vigil with the dying, and then dead, French printer serves, like many of the narrative moments and tropes of the novel, a hypothetical function, a moral fantasy that one could maintain in the midst of mechanized warfare enough humanity to experience the death of the enemy, the death of another, as a mortal moral wound to the self—"every gasp lays my heart bare" (221). The moment also twists a literal traumatic experience that Allyson Booth notes when she writes, "The extremely restricted space within which trench warfare was fought . . . ensured that Great War soldiers would live with the corpses of their friends" (21). This was, quite literally, the cause of Wilfred Owen's breakdown. Fred Crawford writes of Owen, "By January 1917 he was in the trenches, and in April, after spending some days in a shell hole with fragments of a fellow officer, he developed neurasthenia and went to Craiglockhart" (174). Remarque uses the intimacy of the encounter between unwilling killer and his victim to reprieve the mechanized, impersonal, dehumanized nature of the war's slaughter into a moment of subjective and humane recognition of the *corpsefulness* (to twist Booth's neologism of *corpselessness*) of the trenches: "I prop the dead man up again so that he lies comfortably, although he feels nothing any more" (221). The scene is significant for the reader, who becomes witness to a double murder—the killing of the French printer doubled by the killing of a great heart, war as perpetrator not only of the death of bodies but also of the murder of moral man, the murder of humanity, empathy, civility, and compassion.

Paul's final words express a life that has already been emptied of life: "Let the months and years come, they can take nothing from me, they can take nothing more. I am so alone and so without hope that I can confront them without fear" (295). And yet even though the novel elides the violence that marks the transition between Paul's life and death, the rupture between his solitary, hopeless voice—the last humane voice on earth, we feel—and its replacement by the other voice of the epilogue announcing his death shortly before the Armistice ("He fell in October 1918" [n.p.]) still comes as a shock. "The publisher of *Im Westen nichts Neues* originally demanded that Paul Bäumer should live and survive the war to make possible the appearance of a sequel, but Remarque refused to comply with this request," Schwarz reports (25).[9] The epilogue's voice provides us with the comfort (or fiction) of Paul's painless death ("He had fallen forward and lay on the earth as though sleeping"); it even turns over his body to assure us that "turning him over one saw that he could not have suffered long" [n.p.]). The reader has become Paul Bäumer's grieving father, as it were, told that "his face had an expression of calm." Dare we remember that that is precisely the lie Paul told Kemmerich's grieving mother—"I will never tell her, she can make mincemeat out of me first. . . . I say rather impatiently: 'He died immediately. He felt absolutely nothing at all. His face was quite calm'" (181)? We have been transformed by the epilogue back into figures on the home front who need to be protected from the story of the death world, into which Paul Bäumer's voice has admitted us as a fictive witness to the witness. Paul's story is swallowed by the official army report with its dismissive telegraphic message "Im Westen nichts Neues," with its intimation that the death of one soldier, or ten, or a hundred, in the arena of that massive carnage that killed ten million, is nothing, not worth reporting. The novel's title at the outset places its narrative under erasure, as a story never actually told, a voice of the silences of the dead that never spoke, a voice that virtually acknowledges itself as a fiction pressing against the inability of those who suffer beyond comprehension to speak what they know but cannot tell.

5

UNMAKING AND REMAKING
A WORLD

Thomas Keneally's Book and Steven Spielberg's
Film of *Schindler's List*

Ethical and Aesthetic Problems

ORLD WAR I, IT HAS OFTEN BEEN SAID, WAS A QUIN-
tessentially *literary* war; World War II was *not*. In the early twentieth century, art responded to a great war so shattering that it
required new forms of expression and engendered theoretical and institutional controversies over the priorities of aesthetics and pity. But when
combat targeted civilians in World War II and regimes murdered entire populations of cities and communities, art—like the world itself—stood aghast.
Bafflement over *how* to speak this magnitude of manmade violence was overtaken by bafflement over *if* one can speak, or should speak, the unspeakable
at all. The artistic challenges posed by World War II were recognized as
foundational ethical challenges to the functions and prerogatives of art itself. By extension, a similar ethical challenge confronts the work of criticism,
and my own decisions—in shaping a field for the exploration of Second
World War writing—had to reflect this concern in my choice of texts and
topics. In a book focused specifically on military violence and activity, the
Holocaust could be considered an epiphenomenon of World War II, and
could therefore have been omitted. But the death world of the trenches became extended to civilian populations in World War II, and the Shoah has
become the most large-scale, visible, and troubling of its atrocities. Given

99

the significance of the literary controversies over its representation and their illumination of the difficult ethical terrain of World War II writing, Holocaust writing could not be omitted from this study. With the Holocaust, as with my following chapters on Hiroshima, my aim to ground the events historically prompted me to eschew fiction in favor of nonfiction, and to broaden my focus from aesthetics to more general explorations of the ethics of representation. Methodologically, I opted for an approach that includes a mimetic dimension—a reiteration of narrative and a repetition of representation—in order to have my critical writing serve a commemorative as well as an analytical function. My study of *Schindler's List*—and my treatment of Hiroshima in the ensuing chapters—will therefore interleave writing, testimony, history, and critical issues in order to disrupt the containment of critical discourse and create (imperfect) spaces for emotion and mourning.

Steven Spielberg's film of Thomas Keneally's book *Schindler's List* has had a curiously split critical reception—widely acclaimed by the mainstream press in the United States and Europe, yet sharply criticized in quarters of the academy, the more conservative press, and some parts of the international media. Claude Lanzmann, the maker of the documentary *Shoah,* objected to Spielberg's film on the ground that the Holocaust "is unique above all in that it surrounds itself with a ring of fire. . . . Fiction is a transgression, and it is my deepest conviction that every representation is prohibited" (176; my translation from the German). Lanzmann's own work produces what Geoffrey Hartman regards as a "radical and principled" nonfictional and nonarchival alternative to representation in his focus on human speech, testimony, and memory (132). But others find the interdiction against Holocaust representation worrisome and fear that, for some, it may spring from a touch taboo or contact phobia that masks itself as piety. Ruth Klüger also worries that repressing representation may produce a bracketing or ghettoization of memory (37). For better or worse, Keneally's nonfiction "novel" and Spielberg's film violated the taboo, and thereby engendered a series of significant debates that it is less important to adjudicate than to track and explore for their ethical and aesthetic gestures. My own insertion into these controversies will be to argue that *Schindler's List's* often cited flaws and failures—the lack of individualization of the victims, the occlusion of their perspective by a German perspective, and the misleading and unearned happy ending—serve paradoxically powerful functions for apprehending many important aspects of the Holocaust experience. This claim does not dispute the validity of much critical disapproval of the film even as it concedes the impossible ethical demands and artistic constraints that plague Holocaust writing.

In his superb introduction to *Writing Degree Zero,* John Whittier Treat, while careful to respect the tension found "in any attempt to describe the atrocities in Europe and those in Japan in the same language" (4), posits both the Holocaust and Hiroshima "as a *model* for contemporary knowledge" of "modern man's savage treatment of himself" rather than "as *an optional example*" (9) of some universal and ubiquitous human tendency toward evil. Put differently, both Holocaust and atomic bomb literature must negotiate the status of their event as a rhetorical figure for unimaginable manmade human suffering and relate this trope to the event's facticity as a historically and phenomenologically specific moment of the twentieth century.[1] The most difficult consequence of that negotiation is the recognition that these events are not detours or aberrations in the advancement of Western civilization but logical products of technological achievement disoriented by incommensurate, unrefunctioned, and broken moral compasses. This point is particularly important for historians and analysts of Hiroshima and Nagasaki who define the atomic bombings *as atrocity* by "scale, intention, and ruthless logic" (Treat, 8) but find this event nonetheless refused ethical recognition: "Germany lost the war, so its Final Solution is now understood as a criminal 'aberration' of Western civilization; but Hiroshima and Nagasaki, acts committed by the victor, 'have passed into our culture as rational strategic actions'" (Treat, 13). Semiotically, the Holocaust therefore bears not only its own historiographic and testimentary burdens, its needs to remember and represent itself, but also larger semiotic and rhetorical responsibilities for symbolizing its moral significance without either marginalizing itself or, conversely, subsuming all other World War II violence and thereby eclipsing or trivializing other military atrocities.[2]

The double burdens that press conflicting and perhaps irreconcilable demands upon Holocaust literature to sustain its own maimed condition while answering to the shock of a post-traumatic world place it, textually, in its own condition of post-traumatic stress. The clinical trope allows the limitations, incapacities, disproportions, and other problems that mark Holocaust writing to be read as symptoms of its impossibly overdetermined tasks. The mourning of Holocaust literature is always already doubled: a mourning for its victims and a mourning for itself, a rage at the unspeakability of the crimes, and a rage at the unspeakability of finding itself rendered mute by them. Holocaust writing suffers a despairing necessity to combat its despair in order both to effect and deliberately to frustrate its power to heal. The sin of intolerance that engendered the Holocaust has become transformed into the necessity for its rigorous critical opposite: the need of criticism both to recognize the incapacities of Holocaust writing and yet to tolerate their proliferation as a continually reinvented sum of textual symptoms. Even the obligation *to remember* is a complicated responsibility. While German critics warmly lauded the film, and German audiences saw the Spielberg film in overwhelming numbers, a survey sponsored by the American Jewish Committee determined that "52% of Germans are of the opinion that, now that Germany has been reunited, the Nazi past should be regarded as well and truly over" (Niven, 168). Some Israelis, on the other hand, find rememorative films superfluous for themselves: "People here live the Holocaust. . . . We can't escape the Holocaust; it sits on our shoulders" (Corliss, 110). Roger Gottlieb further textures that superfluity by discussing the Holocaust's power to overwhelm and obsess the individual to the point of absorbing and obliterating the post-Holocaust self (2).

A literature caught in a post-traumatic condition is caught in a postgeneric condition as well. There are effectively no genres available to Holocaust writing unless they are refunctioned in some significant way, and even then the pitfalls that attend all expressions of extreme human states and extreme affect—melodrama, grotesquerie, sentimentality, Gothicism—threaten its expressive efforts. Even such "authentic" documentary material as photographs and film footage is problematized insofar as it was produced by the Nazis themselves, and therefore reflects *their* eyes, perspective, and documentary agenda. Claude Lanzmann prefers the verbal over the visual mode of representation for this reason, among others, and uses testimonial performativity—the empty chair as Jan Karski initially bolts from the interview, for example—to function as a powerful objective correlative of painful emotion and memory (Louvish, 80). The autobiographical memoir likewise must be retooled, according to Lawrence Langer, because it risks benumbing and disorienting the reader "as though he were wandering in a wilderness of evil totally divorced from any time and place he has ever known" (75). Successful exceptions, like Elie Wiesel's *Night,* refunction a conventional genre, in this case the *Bildungsroman,* so that "the youthful protagonist becomes an initiate into death rather than life" (Langer, 75). The extraordinary popularity of *Anne Frank: The Diary of a Young Girl* highlights another form of generic difficulty with quite specific relevance for *Schindler's List.* The diary's humanistic and inspirational premises—"In spite of everything, I still think people are good at heart"—died pitilessly in the concentration camp and the memoirs they produced, as Langer points out (77). Cynthia Ozick further explores the extent to which the diary's idealistic aura may be an artifact of editing and translation. Dismayed that the diary of Anne Frank is treated as a Holocaust document, Ozick says "that is overridingly what it is not" (78).

Michael André Bernstein argues eloquently for the "untenability of any fixed categories for literature about the Shoah" (53) and against ethical prescriptions for Holocaust writing. But the generic difficulties that haunt written Holocaust texts are compounded in the format of drama, especially in the popular, widely disseminated form of cinema. While European auteurs have produced a range of strong films in the shadow of the classics—Marcel Ophuls's *The Sorrow and the Pity,* Alain Resnais's *Night and Fog,* and Claude Lanzmann's *Shoah*—these are generally marginalized as "art-house films with small audiences" (Schickel, 75). Steven Spielberg's attempt at the virtually oxymoronic project of making a serious popular film about the Holocaust obliged him to work with and against the genre of the narrative Hollywood film. The project generated a host of complaints. The film's commercial and entertainment aegis was derided even though Spielberg agreed in advance to donate his "blood money" (as he himself called it [Schickel, 77]) to Holocaust foundations. Stanley Kauffmann defended the film in the *New Republic* by writing, "If the opening credit had said Film Polski or Sacis or some other foreign brand name instead of Amblin Entertainment, it's a fair guess that fewer nerves would have been grated at the start" (24). Critics worldwide trivialized the film by association when they called *Schindler's List* "Spielberg's Holocaust Park" (in Israel's *Ha'aretz*) and "Indiana Jones in the Krakow Ghetto" (in *Die Welt*), or expressed condescending surprise at its maturity (Corliss, 110). Spielberg also had to work against a firmly entrenched tradition of Hollywood Holocaust kitsch that for decades has catered to the pornological and fetishistic fascination of "Nazi junkies" (as Pauline Kael called them) with the seamiest Nazi sadism (White, 55). Startlingly, Lanzmann still calls Spielberg's film "kitschy melodrama" (177) and Armond White does not exempt critics and admirers of Spielberg's *Schindler's List* from lurid interest: "A pornography of suffering—and revenge—that sneaks into movies on this subject can be read between the lines of the film's rapturous notices" (55). Yet conversely, White denounces Spielberg's documentary pretensions—"Kaminski's b&w,

a superlatively achieved combination of documentary style, natural light, and dramatic stylization, actually serves a banal, reverential function" (52)—calling it "a dream of the Holocaust" (51).

Yet, ironically, the indisputable craft that rigorously transforms Spielberg's *Schindler's List* from entertainment to art makes the film vulnerable to the charge of aestheticization: "It all has a terrible beauty, the cinematographer's seductive lure," Simon Louvish writes of the "glistening nocturnal lighting . . . the shimmering infernal fire of the crematorium chimney" (81). Janusz Kaminski, the film's Polish cinematographer, used the black-and-white pictures of Roman Vishniac's *A Vanished World* as his model. "Vishniac photographed Jewish settlements in the period between 1920 and 1939. I found inspiration in that book because this man, Roman Vishniac, had nothing—inferior equipment, inferior film stock and only available light—yet he managed to create really beautiful pictures with a timeless quality" (Erbach, 101). To counteract the polished luster and richness of the black and white—Richard Brown notes that "The photography literally becomes a character that is critical to the understanding of the film" (Wloszczyna, 110)—Spielberg insisted on shooting the film "in a very crude technical manner" that deliberately creates effects of imperfection and mistakes (Erbach, 105). Can film's aesthetic effects rise to the metaphysical standard that has been set for Holocaust poetry by the oscillations of silence and expression that Jacques Derrida tropes as the performative "cinders" in Paul Celan's work?

> I had at first imagined that cinders were there, not here but there, as a story to be told: cinder, this old gray word, this dusty theme of humanity, the immemorial image had decomposed from within, a metaphor or metonymy of itself, such is the destiny of every cinder, separated, consumed like a cinder of cinders. Who would still dare run the risk of a poem of the cinder? (*Cinders,* 31)

Spielberg figures "cinders" as well—cinders that are both literal and metaphorical in the form of the "snow" over Auschwitz, which in its ubiquity and uniformity symbolizes the millions of dead, a "snow" hot rather than cold, which in Cracow was soaked in hot blood and in Auschwitz cannot melt or dissolve because it is the literal substance of victims. Are Spielberg's "cinders" a poetic conceit or a powerful symbol of the extermination of Europe's Jews? Perhaps only an avant-garde art can hope to preserve the silences that

Holocaust writing must utter, and that conventional narrative, seeming to suture or close the gaps of what was not told or cannot be told, cannot. But avant-gardism is a poor vehicle for mass dissemination.

Perspective and Population

Steven Spielberg grew up hearing about the events of the Shoah: "My parents talked about the atrocities, without using that word. They didn't say 'the Holocaust,' either. But they talked about it all the time. . . . They would say, 'We're telling you so that it should never happen again'" (Guthmann, 52). How can "telling the Holocaust" be made a prophylactic enterprise, particularly when this "telling" is transferred to book or screen? If it is to be more than a nonproductive visual assault that inflicts a secondary or vicarious trauma on the reader or the viewer, then a didactic Holocaust presentation must both rouse moral indignation and wed the reflex of horror and pity excited by violent representations to a political understanding. The viewer must imagine the self implicated as both victim and perpetrator in the event—able to imagine, in whatever attenuated form, both the suffering of the victims and the fearsome possibility of being incriminated in its production. In contrast to the limited painful sensation of watching what magazine ratings called "Holocaust horrors" (Gourevitch, 49), the Jewish experience of the Holocaust becomes a life project of authentic thinking, remembering, and ethical responding (Gottlieb, 4). *Schindler's List,* in both book and film versions, aspires with humility, I believe, to convey a complex and detailed historical understanding infused with subjective feeling, meaning, and mourning to a global audience.

This task is bedeviled by the Holocaust's double extremity of violence and scale, the Jewish genocide as a population cataclysm that exceeds, qualitatively, the vast quantitative sum of individual sufferings and deaths. Edith Wyschogrod characterizes the concentration camp as "the creation of a new social form, a death-world made up of mini-cosmoi of the living dead embedded in larger societies" (2), and argues that we cannot comprehend its ontology by picturing a collection of individual experiences because the numbers themselves qualitatively alter the phenomenon experienced. *Schindler's List,* both book and film, gesture toward the ontology of Wyschogrod's kingdom of death, but without releasing their hold on the factual specificity that situates the Holocaust on the border between history and testimony.

Spielberg remembers that when Sidney Sheinberg, president of MCA, first brought a review of Keneally's novel to his attention, he said, "It'll make a helluva story. Is it true?" (Thompson, 66). In spite of Michael André Bernstein's caution not to assume "that *only* the gathering of facts has ethical validity" (53), Spielberg's reflexive remark shows that it *matters* whether Holocaust stories are true. Since the publication of the work of Arthur R. Butz (*The Hoax of the Twentieth Century,* 1976) and Paul Rassinier (*Debunking the Genocide Myth,* 1978), Holocaust denial or revisionism has become a "growth industry," according to Elinor Brecher (xx). The resulting pressure to document and compile monumental facts and statistics makes magisterial histories like Raul Hilberg's three-volume work *The Destruction of the European Jews* both awesome and forbidding. Spielberg's decision to anchor his popular film in the historical ballast of Thomas Keneally's copiously researched nonfictional reportage underwrites his film's ethical power. Ironically, the wealth of historical fact earned Keneally as much criticism and faint praise as credibility: Michael André Bernstein lumps it with "mediocre" and "clumsy fictionalizations" of the Holocaust (51), Simon Louvish calls it a "worthy but dull non-fiction book" (79), and Philip Gourevitch praises it as a "clunky but compelling novel" (50). Spielberg's own aspirations for documentary status for his film earned him even sharper and more ethically pointed criticism:

> In *Time* [Spielberg] is reported as having instructed his cast, "We're not making a film, we're making a document." This is perhaps the most pernicious notion that has become attached to *Schindler's List*—that it is somehow more than a movie, more than a simulation: that it is "the real thing." Yet to confuse any aesthetic representation with the object represented is either to participate, or to be lost, in a lie. (Gourevitch, 52)

Although he makes his criticism in the interest of praising the film's poetic and visionary expressivity, Armond White too derided Spielberg's documentary pretensions: "*Schindler's List* might have been an even stronger movie if it clarified itself as a *version* of history rather than a document of the real thing. . . . *Schindler's List* is best experienced as something other than a Holocaust history" (56).

Spielberg's film brought the perspectival difficulties of Keneally's discursive straddling of the story of a murderous regime and the story of its victims into even sharper relief. Although Geoffrey Hartman's nuanced criticism of the film's camera techniques concedes the viewer implication produced by the oscillations of long shots and close-ups, he worries that "uncomfortably but tellingly we sometimes see the action as if through the telescopic sights of Göth's murderous rifle. . . . the premium placed on visuality by such a film made me deeply uneasy. To see things that sharply, and from a privileged position, is to see them with the eyes of those who had the power of life and death" (128). But the *German* perspective is actually divided in the film between two kinds of panoptical vision: Göth's vantage of power, but also Schindler's resistant and troubled vantage of responsibility. The same might be said of the *Jewish* perspective, which—even though Philip Gourevitch complains that Spielberg's film is not "a 'Jewish' movie'" (51)—is not only the view from the despairing depths of camp, boxcar, or hiding place, but also Stern's savvy view of the economic and administrative Nazi systems he helps Schindler exploit for the Jews' benefit. I believe there is much to argue against Gourevitch's opinion that, as a population, the Jews in the film are treated with "the detachment of a National Geographic ethnographic documentary" that views them "either as a silent, cowering mob or as a shrieking, scampering mob" (Gourevitch, 52).

The Schindler story gave Keneally and Spielberg an innovative and powerful narrative device figured in two dramatic moments from the history of the transmission of the Schindler story. The first—which became available only retroactively, after Keneally's book had been published and the movie made—was a meeting reported by the Canadian journalist Herbert Steinhouse, who met Oskar Schindler through Itzhak Stern in 1948. After a party in January 1949 (documented by many photographs taken by Al Taylor), Steinhouse asked both Schindler and Stern to come to his office to tell their story together:

> We went back to square one and, jointly, they told the entire story, repeating most of what I already had on paper. When one of them forgot an incident or detail or a name, the other would supply it. Itzhak Stern had a fabulous memory, better than Schindler's, certainly better than mine. He kept providing prompts and Schindler would say, "Yes, yes, that's exactly how it happened." (Fensch, "Journalist," 16)

Steinhouse received, synchronically, a collaborative Holocaust narrative from a German and a Jew, one that blended the historical perspective of the political situation with the subjective testimony of witness. The story Stein-house produced in 1949 was never published, and languished in a drawer until December 1994, when—after reading the Keneally novel and seeing the Spielberg film—he was interviewed by Thomas Fensch. Fensch published Steinhouse's account in his collection of essays and reviews called *Oskar Schindler and His List* (1995). When Thomas Keneally was waiting for his credit card to clear after buying a briefcase from Paul Page (Leopold Pfefferberg) in his Beverly Hills luggage shop in 1980, this scene of narration was repeated—but in diachronic form. Schindler was now dead, and what Pfefferberg gave Keneally was another version of the collaborative telling Stern and Schindler had given Steinhouse—a layered narrative in which Page wrapped his memories around the German's story and convinced Keneally of the urgency of having it told. Because of its exceptional status, Lanzmann found both the thematization and this imaginative enactment of a narrative common cause between Jews and Germans historically mislead-ing and unethical (174).

Yet I believe that Schindler presented to Keneally and Spielberg a viable paradigm for prophylactic and didactic Holocaust telling. This telling re-quired a grasp of the historical emergency of the Jews on the *systemic* level, as embedded in a synchronic network of nonreciprocal relations of agency, power, ideology, and suffering organized into a diachronic movement to-ward genocide. *Schindler's List* gives Adolf Hitler virtually no role except that of a dramatic absence as on July 20, 1944, Schindler and his Jewish engineer Adam Garde listen to the radio coverage of the assassination attempt on Hit-ler's life. The point that Keneally imputes to Adam Garde, that "Hitler was more than a man: he was a *system* with ramifications" (Keneally, 269), con-trols the donnée of the lesson of the story. The historical Oskar Schindler possessed a view and grasp of the entire system—political, social, eco-nomic, and moral—that allowed him to turn an outraged and knowing eye on the panorama of *a total war against a civilian population:* "With people behaving like pigs, I felt the Jews were being destroyed. I had to help them" (Brecher, xxxiii). His very liminality both inside and outside the Nazi sys-tem—implicated by collaboration yet simultaneously critical and resis-tant—gave Schindler the systemic perspective that is indispensable to a his-torical understanding of the Holocaust, but in a form morally inoculated with the internalized sufferings of its victims. Schindler becomes a "seer" with double, intersected, and liminal vision—a modern-day Tiresias—who saw as a German yet with the eyes of a Jew, saw how the Jews saw the Nazis and therefore had to see himself through their eyes. Arguably, only witnesses should tell historical Holocaust stories. But if one were told by a nonvictim, Thomas Keneally's was a deeply understanding and highly qualified voice. Keneally's social activism springs from a capacity to internalize the trials of people remote from his life, like the aborigines of his 1972 *The Chant of Jimmie Blacksmith* or the African Eritreans in his 1989 *To Asmara*. An Australian author of more than twenty-five books and a former Catholic seminarian, Keneally has had experience that allows him to see moral questions as, "in a way, novels" (Ponce, 39).

The story of the *Schindlerjuden* further offered Keneally and Spielberg a way to tell the Holocaust as a *population story* that preserves a clear focus on the cruel role the *census* played in the bureaucratic administration of Jewish ghettoization, internment, and extermination—registrations, roll calls, identification papers, passes, lists, selections, tattoos—without letting the population lose its social identity. The Schindler story deals with an identifiable, if neither simple nor stable, population: the Jews of Polish Cracow, whose numbers remain large, loose, and identifiable enough to represent the larger population of European Jews without becoming an abstraction. Keneally, perhaps forgetting that Steven Spielberg had already made a profane film about Nazis and the Ark of the Covenant (*Raiders of the Lost Ark*), asked Spielberg why he didn't keep his book's original European title: *Schindler's Ark*. Spielberg's answer, that he planned to foreground *lists* (Ruth Klüger calls them a leitmotiv of the film [35]), instantly made sense to Keneally: "The whole film is full of recurrent lists; there are right lists and wrong lists. And every time you see a folding table and chair and an inkwell on the table in an open-air place, you get the shivers. You know people are going to be divided" (Takahama, 47). The lists point to the heart of the *intellectual* atrocity of the Nazi regime's invidious "sorting myths," as Edith Wyschogrod calls them (41). The film further embodies the lists as individuals whose story may be told in the aggregate, as a community or population, but who are nonetheless individualized, as in the opening registration scene. Depicting the influx of rural Jews into Cracow, Spielberg presents a population with "the sharp character faces of incidental actors—each a unique human being with his or her own manner of speech" (Klüger, 35; my translation). The cinematic structure allows Spielberg to handle the relation between population and identity in a way that elicits a politicized viewer engagement with the plight of the Jews. By refusing to individualize the *Schindlerjuden* until Schindler's list restores to them the names and identities of which the regime has robbed them, the film cinematically poses responsible activism as the challenge to reverse the normal order of empathy and caring, and to care first for a population *on principle*. Some symbolic entity like Benedict Anderson's "imagined community" is established both within the film and between the viewer and the represented Jews, in Anderson's sense of a "horizontal comradeship" that at least provisionally transcends inequalities and unfamiliarity to produce a sense of communion. By the time Schindler's list puts names to faces, we realize that we have "known" not only Itzhak Stern and Helen Hirsch all along, but also Leopold and Mila Pfefferberg, Rabbi Levartov, Mrs. Dresner and Danka, and the Rosner family, including little Olek, and many more—if not as individuals, then as members of a community to which we have vicariously and sympathetically bonded.

But because this imaginative bond with survivors can become a sentimental indulgence, *Schindler's List*—both book and film—confers a painful computational obligation to grasp that while the *Schindlerjuden* may be synecdochic or representative of other Holocaust victims in their suffering, they are wildly fractional and exceptional in their survival. Just as the term "survivor" is semantically the exception to death, so the term *Schindlerjuden* is the exception to Auschwitz, an exception even to Jews who survived without German protection. Even though the survivors of the story call themselves "Schindler Jews" in grateful and affectionate tribute to Oskar Schindler (Brecher, xxxvii), their collective story also redefines "survival" as a process active rather than passive, requiring, as Keneally points out, immense "cleverness, bravery, and native cunning" (Brecher, xiv). The survival of the *Schindlerjuden* was a collaborative process that involved a large and ragged cast of agents—including Schindler, Stern, and the Jews, as well as some strategic Germans and Nazi officials. Yet like all of Schindler's enterprises, which were obliged to mirror those of the Nazis, his "list," however benign (Stern echoes Keneally in the film in calling it "an absolute good"), was implicated in the harrowing arithmetical operations of selection, exclusion, and arbitrariness that kept collapsing into the omnicidal Nazi logic. The testimony of survivors is shadowed by the truer silence of those who died, or who survived unable to speak the experience, and the representation of survival in book and film risks denying the unrepresentability of the experience of failing to survive: "The actors cannot act this state of being which another Holocaust writer, the forgotten 'Katzetnik' (aka Yehiel Dinur), described as being on another planet" (Louvish, 79).

Ultimately, both Keneally's book and Spielberg's film may appear, prob-
lematically, to suture the wounds and gaps left by the dead and mute Jews of
Cracow, whose stories are only implied, but not shown. But what remains is
nonetheless a collaborative narrative operation that creates an illuminating
artifact of a population or community story. By the time of Keneally's writing, the Jews had to speak for Schindler as well as for themselves, and they
did so in considerable numbers, both in person and on record. Keneally interviewed fifty Schindler survivors (Keneally, 9) and consulted "the wide
and varied range of *Schindler* testimonies in Yad Vashem" (Brecher, xiii);
Spielberg consulted additional survivors during the filming (Thompson,
71–72). Since the event of book and film, further narrative testimony has
been produced, such as the stories collected by Elinor Brecher in *Schindler's
Legacy* (1994) and the Polish memoir of Stella Müller-Madej, translated into
German. These further accounts corroborate, intensify, and complicate the
historicity of both book and film, supplying some of the living signs of painful memory that make Lanzmann's documentary so powerful—the hesitations, stops, and tics and winces of remembered fear. The *Schindlerjuden*
testimonies filter into the story a level of detail, of authentic representation,
that bolsters the ethical function of the story by enhancing its credibility.[3]
To clarify the function of this testimonial contribution requires a careful
consideration of the problem of Holocaust *domestication*. In a moving tribute
to Elie Wiesel, whose Yale seminar inspired his work on atomic bomb literature, John Whittier Treat repeats Wiesel's caveat against domesticating atrocity: "Should our records of suffering ever become wholly familiar to us, they
will make sense of what we must let remain senseless" (Treat, xvii). The
ambiguity and tension within that "wholly" point to the untamable problem
of maintaining the integrity of the horror without thereby exiling the experience to realms of alienation or unreality. The version of "domestication"
that would hypothetically be needed to make even an attenuated Holocaust
experience subjectively and ethically available to the nonvictim requires a
familiarization that must nonetheless refuse to cater to audience comfort at
the expense of blunting representational painfulness.

Its affirmative outcome or "happy end," as the German critics call it, may
be attached by many viewers of *Schindler's List* to the cost of an attenuated,
vicarious viewer "survivor guilt." Spielberg makes this ambivalent feeling of
undeserved relief at having been spared atrocity productive by giving the
nonvictim viewer—both Gentile and Jew—emotional and ethical access to
the experience by "bringing it home" without the illusion that the imagined

experience is either comprehensive, exhaustive, or authentic. *Schindler's List* enacts, I believe, what Michael André Bernstein calls a "prosaic ethics," a writing that restores to Holocaust history the repressed "value of the quotidian, the counter-authenticity of the texture and rhythm of our daily routines and decisions" (121). It is precisely a high level of what we might call domestic detail that allows *Schindler's List* to infuse its population representation with an extraordinary degree of particularity without resorting to the device of the vignette, whose homogenized aura of suffering led Jonathan Alter to describe the 1978 NBC miniseries *Holocaust* as "just another sentimentalized disease-of-the-week show" (199). The testimonial specificity further preempts the kind of pious prescription for Holocaust representation that Philip Gourevitch invokes in criticizing the film: "And here are the Jews as the SS invade their apartments. Are they consoling their children? No, they are making them eat jewels wadded in balls of bread. Are they praying? No" (51). Yet Anne Thompson explains that Spielberg received this detail from Nuisa Horowitz, the smaller of the girls Schindler kissed on his birthday and thereby provoked his arrest ("Horowitz's story became the basis of a scene in which a family presses its diamonds into bread and then eats them during the liquidation of the ghetto" [Thompson, 70]). Gourevitch's preference could suppress the crucial role that money—especially money in its most durable and portable forms such as diamonds—played in the survival of the Cracow *Schindlerjuden*.[4] Pfefferberg, for example, tells how Marcel Goldberg extorted diamonds from people who wanted to be put on the list: "'Do you have any diamonds?' Goldberg asked Pfefferberg. 'Are you serious?' asked Poldek. 'For this list,' said Goldberg, a man of prodigious and accidental power, 'it takes diamonds'" (Keneally, 293). Keneally's book—more than Spielberg's film—tacitly makes the impious point that uncontrollable capitalism fueled Nazi totalitarianism while its power to corrupt could be turned into an antidote to ideological fanaticism. The perverse hero of the Schindler story was the same black market that plays such a sinister role in Carol Reed's postwar film *The Third Man*. But Spielberg uses the diamond-eating scene differently, as Ruth Klüger points out: "Even the stomach offered no hiding place from the Final Solution" (36; my translation).

The Unmaking of a World

Although both Keneally's book and Spielberg's film bring a systemic focus to their story of the Holocaust, they must rely on a hero of indecipherable motives—motives overdetermined because they were engendered by complex conditions. More significant than Schindler's motives was his vision, his panoramic and increasingly shocked view that the Nazi vision of glorious world-making required the most sordid and brutal activity of world-destroying. This vision makes Schindler a model of ethical reading—a proleptic exemplar for the reader of the book or the viewer of the film, who, following Schindler, feels obliged to transform the privilege of being a nonvictim into taking *responsibility* for what is learned and seen. But Schindler's ethical implement, like the reader's, is compromised by the position of power a historical overview inevitably confers. Industry becomes the unlikeliest source of rescue for a small fraction of the Cracow Jews because industry is also the instrument of their enslavement. Keneally is able to give a despairing twist to the conundrum of resistance[5] by showing that Schindler's tools of succor and rescue were fashioned from the very institutions of Jewish oppression, and were doubled and tweaked versions of Nazi instruments of enslavement, degradation, and destruction. Schindler replicated *with a difference* the Nazi slave-labor factories with Emalia, the Płaszów forced labor and concentration camp, with his own Emalia subcamp, and the Nazi sortings and selections with his own list of rescue. Wishful reader identification with Schindler's heroism cannot escape identification with his incrimination. In telling this story, Keneally provides an immense historical record, naming hundreds of names, providing a tacit month-by-month calendar, mapping the geography of Cracow, analyzing the byzantine Nazi administration, supplying cultural information. His tone of wry understatement is both the mark of the nonwitness and a warrant of credibility in its suppression of theatricality.

Yet cinema cannot forgo the theatrical, and even Keneally was daunted by the difficulty of translating the complex web of interlocking worlds he created on his pages into a dramatizable form. His own adaptation was "the length of a mini-series" (Ansen, 60), and Steven Spielberg eventually asked several screenwriters to try their hands, including Kurt Luedtke, who wrote the script for *Out of Africa,* and Martin Scorcese. Eventually Spielberg asked Steven Zaillian, the writer-director of the sensitive *Searching for Bobby Fischer,* to undertake the writing. Spielberg instructed Zaillian on what he wanted: "I wanted the story to be less vertical—less a character story of just Oskar Schindler, and more of a horizontal approach, taking in the Holocaust as the whole raison d'être for the project" (Schiff, 153). Violating few of Keneally's facts, Zaillian shaped a chronology for the story that foregrounds the major events in Jewish lives under Nazi rule in Cracow: the 1939 intensification of confiscations, disenfranchisements, and harassments of Jews under the Nazi *Gleichschaltung* (racial and political purification) directives; the 1941 consolidation of the Cracow ghetto and its March 1942 *Aktion* liquidation; the Płaszów labor camp; the detour through the Auschwitz-Birkenau extermination camp on the way to a haven in Brinnlitz, Czechoslovakia; and the liberation and coda of real-time survivors honoring Schindler's grave in Israel. Keneally's narrative is far more complex, with these stages less tidily demarcated, and layering and interpenetrating one another; there are several assaults, with varying degrees of intensity, on the Cracow ghetto, for example. Keneally's text is also stronger in its "prosaic ethic," to borrow Bernstein's term, its felt quotidian texture of innumerable incidents. But Zaillian's screenplay delineates more clearly the shocking structure of the Holocaust as built on the logic not just of war—where violence is reciprocal—but of the one-directional and progressive momentum of torture.

My invocation of *political torture* as the model of the Holocaust plot is intended not as a melodramatic trope but as a theoretical political analogue. Keneally's and Zaillian's careful avoidance of images of libidinal Nazi sadism (though they represent many wrenching incidents of cruelty and murder) allow them to avoid the hyperbolic pornologizing of Nazi practice that moves the understanding of German totalitarian policy unproductively into the realm of pure pathology. Instead, they illuminate operations of agency, autonomy, and power as constitutive aspects of totalitarianism that are generalizable for political understanding. Elaine Scarry's argument that *war* and *torture* are differentiated by the presence or absence of *assent*—that war is constituted by implicit assent of the populace (not to specific acts of violence, but to the enterprise as a whole) while the subject of torture does not assent—points to one feature of the uniqueness of Jewish suffering in the midst of the massive violence of World War II. Emil Fackenheim points out that "'Aryan' victims of the Third Reich, though robbed, enslaved, subjected to humiliation, torture, and murder, were not *singled out* unless they *chose* to *single themselves* out; Jews, in contrast, were *being* singled out *without choice of their own*" (Gottlieb, 227). Another point of Scarry's analysis—that torture works to objectify inflicted pain in order to transform it into an insignia of the regime's power (18)—helps explain the politically gratuitous nature of Nazi violence, since the Jews posed no plausible threat to the regime. Even if the motive was patently race hatred, the destruction of the

European Jews' world served as a symbolic instantiation, a proof or illustration, of the Third Reich's power. Edith Wyschogrod writes that "the driving force of the death-world is pure power" (75), and Elaine Scarry elaborates: "The direct equation, 'the larger the prisoner's pain, the larger the torturer's world' is mediated by the middle term, 'the prisoner's absence of world'" (37). Keneally and Zaillian both convey this relationship between pain and world in the dramatically shifting relationship between Jewish and German worlds from 1939 to 1945.

By grounding their representation of the Holocaust in a systemic political model, Keneally and Zaillian are no less damning of Germans than is Daniel Jonah Goldhagen in *Hitler's Willing Executioners*. But their historically textured narrative produces a far more nuanced range of German responses to the radically unsocializing effects of a sociopathic ideology and policy apparatus. Goldhagen's thesis, that the regime's ideology of virulent anti-Semitism produced a population of German men and women willing "to devote their bodies, souls, and ingenuity to the enterprise [of Jewish genocide]" (417), is perfectly plausible for explaining the actions of operators in the industrialized extermination camps, the special details of *Einsatztruppen, Sonderkommandos,* and other cadres of criminal extermination. But when applied to the wider range of Holocaust experiences beginning in 1939, Goldhagen's explanation for the motivational cause of the Holocaust homogenizes the texture of the violence and gives it a mechanical character less accommodating of specific time and circumstance. Keneally, in particular, names and details innumerable murderous incidents, but he also provides analysis of the relationship between policy and behavior—embedding Amon Göth's ability to rule by spontaneous violence in the local control of the labor camps, for example, and exploring the bureaucratic nuances that generated a surprising inventory of "good Germans" besides Oskar Schindler.[6] Zaillian's script strategically suppresses the wider gallery of "good Germans" because their foregrounding produces a moral distortion of German responsibility. "Now all at once there are ever more people who saved Jews. But if there were so many Righteous Gentiles who saved Jews, why were so many Jews annihilated?" Claude Lanzmann asks bitterly (177; my translation from the German translation).

Both Keneally and Spielberg articulate specific phases of the politico-military strategy with which the Germans waged war against the civilian population of the Jews. Keneally's account is much more complex and untidy than the film's, but Zaillian's script, by simplifying and compressing the historical narrative, constructs a smoother, more graspable outline. One characteristic of the Holocaust that emerges with particular clarity in *Schindler's List* is the Holocaust's function as a nexus between *older forms of violence* ("The new kind of society that the labor and death camps of the Nazis represent—namely twentieth century slavery, more ruthless and proficient than its predecessors—was also a variation of an older kind of society" [Treat, 14]) and the unprecedented *highly mechanized and industrialized* forms of extermination into which they transmogrified. This articulation is significant because it allows viewers to recognize in phases of the Holocaust imprecise but illuminating analogues to other historical moments in the history of the twentieth century that make meaningful discriminations among various manifestations of political and military violence possible. The *first phase* of the Holocaust experience socially and economically immobilized the European Jews through bureaucratic control of their movement and property. Many, though not all, of the operations of this process of registration, segregation, restriction, licensing, and confiscation authorized by the Nazi race edicts were mirrored in aspects of apartheid policies in South Africa, for example, which too used racial identification, segregation, restriction, and licensing to control the movements and economic access of South African blacks. The lethal potential of the *second phase* of ghettoization was initially masked because it was so historically familiar to the Jews. But almost immediately the constricted but still functional social life within its walls was horrifically disrupted by commando actions or *Aktionen* that mirror other military massacres of civilian populations, such as My Lai. Seymour Hersh's famous account of My Lai has uncanny similarities to Keneally's account of the ghetto liquidation:

> Haeberle noticed a man and two small children walking toward a group of GIs: "They just kept walking toward us . . . you could hear the little girl saying, 'No, no . . . 'All of a sudden the GIs opened up and cut them down." Later he watched a machine gunner suddenly open fire on a group of civilians—women, children and babies— who had been collected in a big circle. . . . He saw a GI with an M16 rifle fire at two young boys walking along a road. The older of the two—about seven or eight years old—fell over the first to protect him. The GIs kept on firing until both were dead. (55)

Only the specific phenomenology is comparable here. The scale and official status of this specific Vietnam War scandal and those of the virtually globally institutionalized forms of the Jewish ghetto massacres during World War II are, needless to say, incomparable. The *third phase* of the Holocaust experience, the forced labor and concentration camps, share similarities with other modern military imprisonments of civilian peoples—for example, the prison camps in which the Japanese interned foreign women and children in World War II. But the extermination camps of the *final phase,* with their combination of bureaucratic sorting and ingeniously devised technology for mass killing, are unique in the violent history of the twentieth century and bear no analogues—notwithstanding David Rieff's contention that "what took place in Rwanda exactly fit the typology of Hitler's Final Solution" (6). Unique too was the lethal synergism of these old and new forms of population oppression and annihilation. Zaillian's script perhaps too seamlessly constructs these phases into a willful German concatenation of stages in a genocidal program that, if arguably historically reductive,[7] nonetheless compellingly illustrates the Nazi project of *unmaking* the European Jewish world.

The Cracow Ghetto

The Holocaust enacted the phenomenology of war as an *unmaking of a world*—albeit an unmaking functionally conjoined to a making of another world. Robert-Jan Van Pelt describes how startled he was to find that Auschwitz was not an isolated place in a rural Polish wilderness but a camp adjacent to a populous and thriving town—"Auschwitz under the National Socialists was to become a district capital and the site of massive industrial activity. It became clear that the mythification of Auschwitz, to which I had contributed, had blinded me to a more complex reality in which two seemingly opposite things—the design for utopia and the reality of dystopia—existed side by side" (94). This economic and political cannibalism, this dependence of a new world of industrial and economic enterprise on the destruction of an old society, drives the Schindler story as well. But there was a twist in the robber baron plot of Schindler's entrepreneurial ambitions: on his way to becoming a millionaire, Schindler became distracted by efforts to salvage a small part of the smashed-up world of the Cracow Jews. Both Keneally and Zaillian had to manage the representational tension between these contradictory but conjoined plots of Jewish unmade and German newly made worlds, and skillfully hold together the dissonant affect of watching Schindler's exuberant and successful rise in conjunction with the progressive dispossession, demoralization, and degradation of the Jews. Pairing an attractive and heroic Schindler with an impoverished and diminished population carries aesthetic and ideological risks, and Lanzmann was disturbed by the attractive Nazis in their dashing uniforms in the film ("The Germans weren't like that" [175]). But the representational problem notwithstanding, the pairing of intersecting German and Jewish worlds produces an important political point—namely, that Schindler's individualism, attractivenenss, and moral privilege were as much political artifacts of Reich policies as was the Jews' systematic and deliberate *Deklassierung*.

Keneally is able to do what the film cannot—supply a precise chronology and geography of events to show with what disorienting swiftness the German occupation after the defeat of the Polish army at the beginning of September 1939 savaged the social landscape of the Polish Jews. By the time Schindler and Stern met in late October 1939—only a few weeks after German troops entered Cracow on September 6—Dr. Otto Wächter, the SS district governor for the Cracow area, had already put in place six restrictive edicts governing Jewish behavior, as well as sharply reduced rations and bans on kosher meat preparation. Between November 8 and November 24, all Cracow Jews had to register; the decree of November 23 forced Jews to wear the identifying star and denied them access to their bank accounts and safe deposit boxes, now placed in fixed trusts. December 4, 1939, saw the first *Aktion*—an illegal SS raid on private citizens in the Jewish quarter to loot apartments and rip furs and jewelry from their bodies ("A girl who would not give up her fur coat had her arm broken" [Keneally, 60]). The Nazi technique of externalizing Jewish identity was paired with economic immobilization and the first physical assaults. In just the first four months of the occupation the social conditions of Jewish life had become radically altered.

Zaillian's script skillfully compresses the opening events of the film to highlight the intersection of the Jews' rapid decline and Schindler's rapid rise. After the cacophonous opening registrations of spoken and typewritten Jewish names that begin to aggregate people and strip their individuations, we see an anonymous German stranger—who appears to have come to Cracow with only stylish clothes and much cash—set out to make a name and create an identity for himself. The extended scene in the elegant club is a fiction, but Zaillian uses it as shorthand for Schindler's style of bribery, bonhomie, and calculated hospitality, which attracted a large and lively circle of acquaintances and made him a *somebody* in their midst. In the course of that first symbolic evening, everyone's repeated queries of "Who is that man?" are triumphantly answered by the maître d's emphatic "That's Oskar Schindler!" In contrast to Schindler inventing an identity for himself, Itzhak Stern is coerced by Governor Frank's decree to introduce himself to Schindler with an announcement of race: "I have to tell you, sir, that I am a Jew" (Keneally, 44). In October 1939, Stern is forced to speak his Jewish identity; a month later his Jewishness is already reified in the silence of the visual star he must wear.

Zaillian must dramatize how the dramatic crossings between the Jews' and Schindler's fortunes are underwritten by moral ironies. Keneally points out that all businesses had been "Aryanized" by the time Schindler, in December 1939, filed an application to lease, with option to buy, a bankrupt enamelware plant called Rekord. In the ensuing months, the capital to put Schindler's plant into operation was raised by Abraham Bankier, Rekord's office manager,[8] from dispossessed Jewish businessmen (often "a man already in shock—his apartment gone and himself now an employee in his own business" [Keneally, 69]) willing to trade their reserves of now illicit currencies for more disposable and negotiable goods. Keneally's specificity connects many temporal and spatial factors that play important roles not only in the Schindler story but also in the Cracow history of this time. By July 1940 the newly renamed Deutsche Emailwaren Fabrik (also known as DEF, or Emalia) went into operation with forty-five workers—soon to be expanded by the lucrative defense contracts Schindler's well-oiled social machinery put in place. Its geography was important: the factory was located not in the city of Cracow but in a suburb called Zablocie, across the river. This location gave the Jews who worked there access to a space outside the Jewish ghetto and, later, outside the Płaszów labor camp. While the groundwork of Schindler's enterprise was being laid, the Jews of Cracow were massively on the move. In an effort to make Cracow *judenfrei,* the German governor general of Poland, Hans Frank, moved 23,000 Jews out of Cracow by November 1940. Evictions that were initially "voluntary" moves under pressure became mandatory, and on March 3, 1941, Edict Gen. Gub. 44/91 established a new Jewish ghetto on the models of those earlier established in Lódz and Warsaw. It was located in a different suburb called Podgórze, whose own geography, bounded by river, railway, and hills, made it both small (600 by 400 meters) and very crowded.[9] On March 20, 1941, the new

Jewish ghetto in Podgórze was sealed, ostensibly for the Jews' own safety and security, a rationale the Pfefferbergs and their friends are shown to mimic and mock in the film as they joke that at least "the walls keep *them* out." Their rueful declaration that "this is the bottom" becomes the shattering irony of the spiral of unstoppable suffering that ensues.[10]

Steven Zaillian uses a series of vividly contrasting scenes to represent the complex interrelationship between Schindler's rise and the Jews' fall. He shifts the first meeting between Stern and Schindler to the offices of the Jewish Council, or Judenrat, to depict the Jews' outrage at the new policies. Angry voices invoke the law against their evictions and confiscations, cite Article 24 of the Hague Convention, and threaten to refuse to comply. But the system of civil justice and redress is shown as visibly broken down. Against this backdrop of chaos and confusion, Schindler is shown approaching Stern about raising Jewish capital for his firm. Later we see him striking deals with Jewish financiers for which there are no contracts—only trust in a German's word and in Stern's instinct and judgment of character. Between these unraveling and newly consolidating legal and financial worlds operates the liminal economy of the black market, whose transactions provide Schindler with the rare luxury goods that serve as his premier currency of bribery. But Zaillian does more than evoke a new upside-down political and economic world in these contrasting scenes. A wealthy, middle-aged Jewish couple are shown dismantling their home under guard and trundling their valuables through an ugly gauntlet of jeering and mudslinging children. Back in their elegant, empty apartment a highly satisfied Schindler happily takes possession.[11] Schindler's rise is overtly and clearly incriminated in Jewish dispossession,

Schindler is surrounded by space, modernity, and new beginnings. His factory and office building was designed "in the style of Walter Gropius" (Keneally, 87), and in the film we see walls being painted and a novice factory force being trained. Again Schindler's rise to industrial baron is incriminated in the degradation of the Jews from professionals to unskilled labor. As Schindler's enterprise proceeds to make him rich, "the era of individuality was vanishing" (Keneally, 121) for young Jews like Poldek Pfefferberg, who is transformed from HIGH SCHOOL PROFESSOR into METALPOLISHER in order to get the indispensable blue worker's certificate, or *Blauschein*. Schindler learned how deadly the lack of a *Blauschein* could be when a group of his Emalia men, including Abraham Bankier (Itzhak Stern in the film), were nearly deported in a cattle car. Zaillian—perhaps to heighten the ghetto liquidation's effect on Schindler's shocked "conversion"—makes Schindler's rescue of Bankier-Stern the mercenary move of an angry businessman whose factory operation has been disrupted. But in Keneally's book, Schindler is shocked by this first sight of Jews packed into cattle cars—and by his fear, based on an invitation for bids he had seen in the *SS Bulletin of Budget and Construction,* that their destination would be a labor camp at Belżec in which crematoria were being built.[12] "Now, shocked by the sights of the Prokocim depot, he decided to go riding again" (121), Keneally reports, and taking his German mistress, Ingrid, with him, Schindler rode to a ridge above Rekawa Street in order to see what was happening in the Jewish ghetto below. What he saw was the *Aktion* in the Cracow ghetto that is depicted so horrifically in the film.

The shocking liquidation of the Cracow ghetto in the film was actually the culmination of a series of actions or *Aktionen* that began with the June 4, 1942, event that Schindler and Ingrid witnessed from the hilltop and ended on March 13, 1943, with the brutal final evacuation under Amon Göth's command. By compressing incidents of at least three *Aktionen* spread over nearly a year into a single day, Spielberg was able to use his frenetic handheld camera action to convey the overwhelming subjective experience of panic, derangement, terror, and mayhem in ways Keneally's highly focused attention to detail and reporting could not. Together, film and book create a compelling representation of dramatized history. Many poignant vignettes in the film are given names and contexts by Keneally—the miraculous pluck of little Genia in her red coat,[13] Mrs. Dresner shut out from her neighbor's hiding place, Dr. Rosalia Blau gunned down while trying to protect her scarlet fever patients. But if Keneally's historical specificity sacrifices the intensity of horror that comes with Spielberg's compression and abstraction, he recoups some of it by viewing the *Aktion* through Schindler's eyes and narrating Schindler's reaction. The visceral extremity of his response— "Schindler slipped from his horse, tripped, and found himself on his knees hugging the trunk of a pine tree. The urge to throw up his excellent breakfast was, he sensed, to be suppressed" (130)—reminds us that even though World War II had been two years in progress by the time of the June 1942 *Aktion,* Schindler had no combat experience and had never seen an actual killing until that day. Nor does Schindler appear to have become hardened by the accelerated brutality; Henry Rosner remembers that a little later, in Płaszów, Oskar saw Göth shooting two young female escapees seconds before they died by hanging: "Schindler vomited in front of everybody" (Brecher, xxxii).[14]

A long and broad tradition of cinematic violence has stripped viewers of the innocence of Oskar's first encounter with murder, and therefore obliges Spielberg to work against naturalized viewer familiarity with the conventions of filmic violence. But realistic depictions of massacres of civilian populations are rare even in film, and Spielberg carefully refused to reference even the best of these scenes, such as Sergei Eisenstein's famous Odessa steps sequence in *The Battleship Potemkin*.[15] Spielberg replaces Schindler's visceral response with Schindler's telescopic perspective, frantically alternating rapid long-range and close-up shots so that the viewer oversees the scene, sees it as an assault on the total population, and then sees it again from inside the mayhem of suffocatingly close encounter with explosive and unpredictable violence. Spielberg forgoes showing the killing of children—which Schindler not only saw, but with horrified eyes saw little Genia seeing (according to Keneally). Perhaps to avoid being perceived as emotionally manipulative, Spielberg transposes the killing of children, which so sickened Schindler and Pfefferberg, into the shooting of adults trying desperately to protect their young.[16] Keneally reports chiefly what Pfefferberg saw during the liquidation: a pile of sixty or seventy corpses in the hospital courtyard, some of whom Pfefferberg recognized, and the killing of a woman and her toddler. But Spielberg also represents the many random murders that could be inferred from the 4,000 ghetto inhabitants killed during the liquidation. His most chilling effect—because its initial quiet infects the viewer with the same false security with which it infects the ghetto dwellers—is the dramatization of the nocturnal cleanup of those in hiding. The eerie silence that opens this scene underlines the pathos of entire families forced to lurk in the holes and crannies of their homes and furniture like vermin, exterminated with as little conscience and humanity. The sorrow of the scene is amplified by the powerful subjective resonance from a Holocaust narrative elsewhere, the highly familiar diary of Anne Frank infusing the scattered vignettes of families routed from their hiding places with the Frank family's agonies of hope and fear.

Spielberg's compression of the *Aktionen* into a single, horrifically dramatic episode foregrounds the most physical terrors of the trauma. Keneally's less dramatic narration of the whole year of sporadic and unpredictable violence illuminates the psychological lacerations of trying to cope with an incoherent mass of frightening information, shocking sights and events, and misleading reassurances and rationalizations. Over and over, shocking new violence had to be recognized and accepted not as an aberration or exceptional pathology but as a new status quo, a new ongoing state of affairs. "What in June had been seen as a culminating horror had become by October a daily process" (Keneally, 142). The trusted Jewish Council or Judenrat, composed of liberal intellectuals, was almost immediately brutalized and marginalized—"*Untersturmführer* Brandt had *Judenrat* president Artur Rosenzweig around to Pomorska for a beating with the handle of a riding crop" (Keneally, 117). Its authority was transferred to its enforcement or police arm, the Jewish *Oberdienst* (its officials were called OD men), which had been formed in March 1941 with the sealing of the Cracow ghetto. Most OD men, who were eventually issued and ordered to use truncheons to control panic during *Aktionen,* were themselves terrorized into compliance by brutal OD leaders such as Symche Spira, who "settled in to a career of extortion and of making out for the SS lists of unsatisfactory or seditious ghetto dwellers" (Keneally, 99). One of the Müller family's most painful crises occurred when Symche Spira put Stella's father on a detail to hang six Poles the following day, causing Müller to effectively suffer a nervous breakdown (Müller-Madej, 68–69). Symche Spira and his family were themselves executed in Płaszów once the Cracow ghetto was dismantled in 1943 (Keneally, 255).

Given the danger to themselves of ghetto unrest and panic, the Jewish Council and the OD withheld distressing information and warnings of impending actions, thinking it was "better to let people hear wild rumors, decide they were exaggerated, fall back on hope" (Keneally, 135). As a result the ghetto community was continually deceived and placated by lies and broken promises—that luggage would be forwarded or children sent. A story Keneally does not report concerns the brutal clearing out of the ghetto children's day-care center, which Stella Müller-Madej, living across the street, describes in shocking detail: "They throw the children out of the windows onto the platforms of the trucks, sometimes they miss" (63; my translation from the German). When the mothers and fathers returned from work, they ran in and out of the building in howling despair, unable to grasp that the children were gone. Phyllis Karp, who worked in the uniform factory of the humane Julius Madritsch, tells that "when word reached him that

Amon Göth had slaughtered eight hundred Jewish children in the ghetto—after giving their Płaszów-bound parents his 'word of honor' that the children would follow—Julius Madritsch wept uncontrollably" (Brecher, 113). Keneally reports that during the October 1942 *Aktion* the German Czech sentry, or *Wachtmeister,* of the ghetto, Oswald Bosko, smuggled dozens of children out of the ghetto in cardboard boxes (138).

Spielberg's film—obliged to rigorously contain the sprawling plot of the story—omits the story of ghetto information and intelligence, including Schindler's dramatic 1942 trip to Budapest to brief Zionist rescue organization officials. By temperament, Schindler extended the intelligence-gathering skills he had sharpened as agent for military intelligence in the Abwehr to the grimly unfolding Nazi design for the European Jews. He maintained contact with old Abwehr friends and sympathetic policemen like Eberhard Gebauer and Herman Toffel, and received advance information and warning of impending actions from them. Information also flowed to Oskar from Itzhak Stern by way of the Jewish Combat Organization (ZOB), which brought underground newspapers, forged documents, and news from other ghettos into Cracow. Shortly after the *Aktion* of June 4, 1942, a young pharmacist named Bachner was shipped out of Cracow in a boxcar, along with other professionals without a *Blauschein.* Eight days later he returned to the ghetto—a man returning from hell. "He had seen the final horror, he said. He was mad-eyed, and in his brief absence his hair had silvered" (Keneally, 135). Bachner saw two days of gassings at the camp in Belzec, and escaped by lowering himself into the hole of a latrine and hiding for three days, "the human waste up to his neck" and his face "a hive of flies" (Keneally, 136).[17] Schindler verified Bachner's story from his own sources and, six months later, in December 1942, traveled to Budapest at the urging of an Austrian dentist, Dr. Sedlacek, to brief two members of a Zionist rescue organization. At the Hotel Pannonia, he gave them a comprehensive account of the plans for labor camps and extermination camps then in progress (154–55). According to Keneally, Schindler's vision and grasp of the cataclysmic horizon startled even the Resistance:

> One was asked to believe that in the midst of a desperate battle, the National Socialists would devote thousands of men, the resources of precious railroads, an enormous cubic footage of cargo space, expensive techniques of engineering, a fatal margin of their research-and-development scientists, a substantial bureaucracy, whole arsenals of

automatic weapons, whole magazines of ammunition, all to an extermination which had no military or economic meaning but merely a psychological one. (Keneally, 148)

Göth's Distopia and Schindler's "Relative Paradise"

Those Cracow Jews who survived either massacre or deportation in the liquidation *Aktion* of March 13, 1943, were transferred to the *Zwangsarbeitslager* or forced labor camp called Płaszów, which had been placed under Amon Göth's command a month before. Both Keneally's book and Spielberg's film chillingly convey the doubleness of that world: its wildly ruptured and dissonant significance as a gold mine for the German military and industrial leadership—a site of lively entertainment, gracious living, and flourishing business—and as a domain of terror for its brutalized prison population. The Germans envisioned Płaszów as a sprawling industrial complex the size of a city, encompassing "the clothing workshops of Madritsch, the enamel factory of Schindler, a proposed metal plant, a brush factory" (Keneally, 164), and dozens of other enterprises.[18] Powerful incentives—free rent, factory maintenance, proximity of their labor force, and administrative autonomy—were offered to the industrialists to persuade them to move their factories into the camp, and Madritsch and Schindler faced an agonizing decision on how best to protect their workers ("Madritsch . . . wanted to be inside Płaszów with them . . . Schindler . . . wanted to have his with him in Emalia" [Keneally, 165]). Appalled by his first sight of teams of women forced to haul trolleys full of limestone along tracks with cables, like slaves building pyramids (Keneally, 166), and shocked by hearing of the murder of the architect Diana Reiter, Schindler decided to stay out. He met with Göth over a bottle of brandy and, by invoking industrial expediency and implicitly promising lavish bribes, bargained to keep Emalia where it was. Emalia eventually became an alternative to Göth's dystopia, an official subcamp in back of his plant at No. 4 Lipowa Street in Zablocie, which Emalia workers called a paradise—or at any rate "a relative paradise, a heaven by contrast with Płaszów" (Keneally, 203).

The Płaszów camp had two phases in its eighteen-month history: designated for roughly half of its existence (from March 1943 to January 1944) as a *Zwangsarbeitslager,* or forced labor camp, and during the other half (from January 1944 to October 1944) as a *Konzentrationslager,* or concentration camp.[19] The difference in these phases offers little to dramatization, and therefore plays little role in Spielberg's film. In Keneally's account, however, the shift sheds important light on the politics and policies of the Jewish camps that significantly conditioned the subjective lives of the prisoners within them. Amon Göth, under the lax control of local police chiefs, appeared to enjoy virtually absolute power over the camp's population during the forced labor phase. When the camp was transformed into a concentration camp, conditions worsened in many respects as, for example, high-voltage wires now segregated the men's and women's barracks. But Amon Göth was now under the command of the headquarters for central concentration camp administration in Oranienburg, from which "every aspect of prison life and death was regulated" (Keneally, 242). The summary executions that were Göth's chief instrument of terror were prohibited by Department W directives—chiefly to avert claims for compensation from industry disrupted and left short-handed when the workforce was decimated. Göth continued to murder on a smaller scale, but he now had to produce justifications—sabotage or sedition—and fill out a mountain of paperwork for every execution. By foregrounding chiefly the first phase of Płaszów in the film, Spielberg is able to dramatize much more compellingly the subjective ambience of Göth's terrifying force. Spielberg further reinforces the transfer of prisoner suspense and agony to the viewer by blunting Oskar Schindler's humanistic activism during this phase. Zaillian's script depicts Schindler (much more than does Keneally's book) as a sharp businessman with ambiguous and suspect motives—a strategy designed, I believe, to abort premature viewer security in his saving function. Arguably that security should be no part of a Holocaust representation at all. But Zaillian's writing at least tries to defer it in order to represent the prisoners' own lack of reason to hope. According to Stella Müller-Madej's memoir, Płaszów prisoners not employed at Emalia knew Schindler's kindness only as a rumor and were wary of trusting him. Zaillian emphasizes Göth's murderous excess as the compelling motive for Schindler's growing resolve to turn his factory into a Jewish sanctuary.

Sited on Cracow's Jewish cemetery, Płaszów had roads paved with headstones from old Jewish graves as a macabre symbol of its industrial ingestion of Jewish culture and Jewish lives. Even with a population of between 20,000 and 35,000, the camp was theatrically overseeable and accessible to snipers' rifles from its watchtowers and Amon Göth's raised villa with its elevated balcony. But while Spielberg's camera most effectively depicts the power enabled by this panoptical geography, Keneally's more specific detail of Göth's practice conveys the insidious psychological eviscerations of Płaszów life. The infractions for which Göth meted out domestic discipline to his personal servants, for example—beating Helen Hirsch for preparing food for his mistress without his express permission, or killing young Lisiek because he had harnessed a horse and buggy for Bosch without checking with Göth[20]—illustrate Göth's determination to stamp out every illusion of even the smallest and most inadvertent autonomies. Elinor Brecher's metaphor for Göth's arbitrary shootings—his "favorite recreation was using Jews for target practice" (xxix)—inadvertently misrepresents Göth's ruthless logic for maintaining absolute control in the camp. The extinction of the psychological space of inmate will or action served as guarantor of Göth's absolute power. His rare mercies were contemptibly self-indulgent; Helen Rosenzweig (one of the two Helens compressed into the figure of Helen Hirsch in the film) gives a complex account of Göth that is both extremely bitter and very scrupulous in commenting on his depiction in the film: "He treated us not even like human beings. . . . The way he was touching her hair, it made me sick. He never did that, not to me!" (Brecher, 65). There were in Płaszów no rational rules for inmate behavior. "You can't say to yourself, If I follow *these* rules, I'll be safe" (28), Helen Hirsch tells Schindler early in Keneally's book.

The ideological character of the Nazi camps worked to place the population as a whole, rather than the individual, under collective discipline. Just as in political torture the body itself is transformed into an instrument of pain, so in the Nazi camps the population or community was used to inflict pain on the individual and vice versa. The Płaszów camp especially became a composite of Foucauldian archaic and modern systems of punishment and discipline: physical pain and psychological terror, public spectacle and hidden executions, panoptical surveillance and physical confinement, all worked in synchrony to produce an effect of virtually absolute control. Although a fearsome knoll with an old Austrian fortification called Chujowa Gorka served as a killing ground for hidden group executions, public gallows were erected in the center of the camp to be visible to inmates lined up on the *Appellplatz,* or parade ground. The daily roll call on the parade ground served as instrument of collective discipline, since punishment for infractions or escapes by single persons were frequently visited on entire barracks groups or arbitrary groups of individuals, chosen from capriciously formed "lines." Müller-Madej's account of being forced to stand for a whole day and night, forced to urinate in her pants, her legs numb, her shoes sinking in the mud, hit in the face when she spoke, hearing beating and cries around her, recreates the intolerable misery and anguish of these exercises more powerfully than either book or film (110–13). Keneally tells how Göth once purged half the girls in the administrative office because of an illegal bacon rind (235), and Zaillian includes a Keneally scene in which men in a line are arbitrarily shot because no one will inform on a transgressor. Manci Rosner, who served as a barracks elder or *Blockälteste,* was once held responsible for a missing woman who had escaped; "Manci Rosner paid for her disobedience with twenty-five lashes on the bare buttocks. . . . 'Luckily, it was an OD man who did it, so he slapped once the boot, once me'" (Brecher, 5). Mrs. Rosner's point, that a Jewish OD man was obliged to flog her, suggests at least one of the possible reason why the film eschews the more horrific Płaszów punishments that Brecher finds missing:

> There were no hangings in *Schindler's List.* No Jews dangled from iron rings in Amon Goeth's office. The dogs wore muzzles. . . . Spielberg's storm troopers refrained from swinging infants by their feet into brick walls. . . . He spared audiences Goeth's theoretically non-lethal punishment of choice. Every one of the *Schindlerjuden* to whom I spoke had either undergone it or witnessed it at sickeningly close range; twenty-five strokes of a lead-tipped leather whip on the bare buttocks. (Brecher, xix)

Manci Rosner's account and Keneally's make it clear that Jews, Ukrainians, Latvians, and others were widely used by the SS to flog, hang, and shoot prisoners. Spielberg was clearly sensitive to the misleading confusion of representing this practice—and, indeed, Lanzmann complained that showing OD men attacking Jews in the ghetto created the impression that the Jews participated in their own annihilation (174). Neither Keneally's book nor Spielberg's film can adequately convey the layered anguish of those implicated in provoking or delivering brutalities on others. Even the film, with its greater power to show and produce a vicarious viewer witness, greatly understated the miseries of the Płaszów camp. As some of the *Schindlerjuden* told Brecher, "But they couldn't show these things; nobody could watch it" (xix). Spielberg appears to have made a principled decision to sacrifice some verisimilitude to suppress violence that might be unbearable, traumatizing, or productive of inappropriate responses.

Zaillian's script contrasts the arbitrariness and caprice of Göth's murderousness with Schindler's opposite practice of targeting specifically vulnerable and imperiled individuals or family groups for rescue. Rabbi Levartov, concealed as a refunctioned hingemaker, was taken into Emalia, with his family, after he narrowly escaped execution when Göth's revolver malfunctioned. Elinor Brecher credits Schindler with this remarkable accomplishment: "families emerged intact" (xix); "That was the thing about Schindler," Celina Karp Biniaz, a survivor, concurs, "he saved families" (Brecher, 115). Schindler's efforts to preserve Jews as a community were, of course, enabled by the Nazis' having delivered them to him as a community. Keneally tells the bureaucratic narrative of how the mechanisms for rescue were constructed out of the oppressive institutional structures. An early instance of Płaszów's practice of collective punishment—the flogging of an entire barracks for a stolen potato (Keneally. 193), prompted Julius Madritsch to phone Schindler and urge that they both complain. Schindler decided he needed to figure out how to keep Emalia workers on his own premises, where he might have better control over their welfare. The argument suggested by Madritsch—that prisoner discipline interfered with productivity ("shifts would arrive hours late at the Madritsch clothing factory. . . . They would arrive shocked, too, unable to concentrate" [Keneally, 193])—was refined to make a case for establishing Schindler's own official subcamp behind his Emalia plant. Not long after the establishment of Płaszów, Schindler bought additional adjacent land, obtained signatures from neighboring businesses, and secured administrative permissions to expand his original two barracks to six, with enough room to house 1,200 people. According to Keneally, Göth probably agreed to this subcamp because he could withhold budgeted rations and supplies for his own black market transactions, and count on Schindler to supply them from Emalia profits.

Schindler's entrepreneurial impulse and vision had become transformed over only a year or two into a humanitarian project that increasingly perverted traditional industrial logic and its inverted ethics. Productivity and profits—traditional rationales for oppressive working conditions—became Schindler's deceptive discourse to covertly purchase humane working conditions and some semblance of a cultural and social life for Emalia's Jewish workers. Emalia was a relative paradise only: "By Schindler, we were hungry but not starving. We were cold, but not freezing. We had fear, but we were not beaten" (Brecher, xviii); but Keneally imputes to Emalia workers gratitude for a year of living as they faced the abolition of their haven: "Emalia has given us a year's rest, a year's soup, a year's sanity" (276). Julius Madritsch and his manager, Raimund Titsch, appear to have provided similar welfare for their workers, and Betty Sternlicht Schagrin admits that she was relatively spoiled working for Madritsch. When she was offered soup on the first day of the women's detour to Auschwitz, "I said 'I wouldn't touch it!' I had it that good in Płaszów. Later on, I ate it, because I was starving" (Brecher, 70). Zaillian's emphasis on the terrors and miseries of Płaszów over the relative security and ameliorated conditions of Emalia helps to keep the highly exceptional nature of Emalia as a Holocaust experience in clearer focus. But the reader and viewer of film and book are still required to adjust their perceptions to seeing the *Schindlerjuden* experience as the positive template, the obverse, of what was everywhere else a negative norm of extremity.

Perversely, Płaszów's transformation from forced labor to concentration camp in 1944 brought some provisional improvements, notably an abatement in Göth's spontaneous shootings and peremptory executions. The structural shift and the corresponding changes in Göth's camp practices and policies reflected Germany's rapidly deteriorating military fortunes on the Russian front. While Spielberg highlights two highly traumatic moments during this phase—the burning of the corpses and the medical selection—Keneally also sketches in the political sea-change that engulfed the camp during 1944. For Göth, the change in the camp's status produced a major panoptical shift, with himself and Płaszów now uncomfortably subjected to the surveillance, supervision, and discipline of a higher German administration. As the Russians approached and began to discover evidence of the Jewish extermination camps, the Third Reich's regime saw its own actions proleptically scrutinized and condemned by a wider world. Schindler himself never lost sight of an external moral eye outside the regime, and collusion with the exploitive practices of the camp and factory system always troubled men like Schindler and Madritsch: "Both Oskar and Madritsch were uneasy about [not paying wages to their Jewish workers], for they knew the war would end and the slaveholders, just as in America, would be shamed and stripped naked" (Keneally, 88). Long before the shift in Płaszów's status Schindler had tried to temper Göth's excesses by appealing to his moral vanity and to the danger of future reprisal. But Göth appears to have responded only when the threat became official. Once under central Berlin administration, Göth—concerned about Jews who could implicate him in black market activity and various economic swindles—created bizarre plots in order to justify official executions, where earlier he would simply have lifted his revolver. He entrapped Wilek Chilowicz, his Jewish chief of camp police, into attempting an escape with his entire family and then claimed sedition to justify their execution.[21] It did no good. In September 1944, about a month before the closing of Płaszów, Amon Göth was arrested on charges of embezzlement and black-marketeering—ironic white-collar crimes of which virtually no one in his milieu, including Schindler, was guiltless.

But before Göth's removal from Płaszów, two dramatic events occurred that reflected the changing course of the war and emblematized in figural form the final phase of the Final Solution. As the Russians drove west, the Germans began to close the Polish extermination camps and obliterate the evidence. Thousands of murdered bodies produced by the ghetto *Aktionen* and Göth's camp executions had been dumped in the woodlands behind Płaszów during 1943. In 1944 Göth was ordered to exhume and burn them in order to destroy their evidence. The implication that no Jews would survive to bear witness was unstated and frightening. Moses Goldberg, assigned to an exhumation detail, bribed a Polish guard to reassign him: "This was the most horrible job, and they didn't keep you afterward. They got rid of you, too" (Brecher, 340). This moment in the history of the Cracow Jews served as a terrible reprise of the innumerable murderous instances of the past three years—the various ghetto *Aktionen* with their thousands of dead, the repeated group executions on Chujowa Gorka, the frequent shootings and hangings in the *Appellplatz*. The eight to ten thousand dead from all these actions were synchronically reassembled in their varying states of decay into an entire macabre population, an entire horrible city of the dead. This historical material moment presents itself as a literal emblem of the Holocaust. Both Keneally and Spielberg introduce a synecdochic gesture of remembering the individuality of the dead by using the device of Schindler's sight and recognition: in Keneally's book, Schindler imagines the executed families of Symche Spira and David Gutter (254–55); in Spielberg's film he is stricken to see the little red coat of Genia, whose death Zaillian transposes from Auschwitz to Płaszów. It seems as though both Spielberg and Zaillian, creators of tender cinematic images of children, cannot bear to represent the murder of a small child except as an ellipsis and a synecdochic sign.

Even though the burning of the corpses in Płaszów and the *Gesundheit-saktion,* or medical selection, of May 1944 were not related, their juxta-position in Zaillian's script effectively adumbrates the horrific images of the crematoria that had been operating in Bełżek and Auschwitz since 1942. Keneally gives the background for the medical selection. Göth was asked to house 7,000 Hungarian Jews destined for an armament factory in Auschwitz, but, since Płaszów was already overcrowded, he asked if he could either clear the camp of "the unproductive element" (259) or double-bunk his inmates. The second option was denied because of fear of typhus; the first was sanctioned. The public medical selection Göth ordered was unusual and frightening even by Płaszów standards. Spielberg's filming of the scene's bizarre, discordant atmosphere of happy popular music, comic songs, children's tunes, and gay banners, set to the terrified stripping and running of naked people trying to dissemble their ravages, conveys the atmosphere of chaos and panic various *Schindlerjuden* remember. This medical selection and the roundup and transportation of the children were among the most traumatic events remembered by *Schindlerjuden.* Lew Fagen (Feigenbaum) tells that on that day machine guns were set up all around the *Appellplatz.* "We figured this was the end of it; they were going to shoot us all. . . . All of a sudden, the first truck came in with the children, and there was such an outcry, and everybody started running. They were shooting over our heads" (Brecher, 265). Stella Müller-Madej remembers a terrifying cacophony of sound: "The whole *Appellplatz* wails out loud, the whips crack down, the dogs bark. . . . The women throw themselves on the ground, rip at their clothes, tear their hair out, scratch their faces, some crawl toward the lectern where Amon Göth is sitting" (137; my translation from the German). "You can imagine how I felt," Fagen told Elinor Brecher, "and I can't forget how the mothers felt. Some ran after the trucks" (265). Fagen believes that one of his cousins—a girl, now living in New Jersey—was among the children hiding in the latrine (265); Stella Müller-Madej remembers that it was two boys, Jerzyk Spira and Julus Cinz (139). Keneally reports that the unnamed boy who lowered himself into the latrine found ten other children hiding in the sewage (263). According to Mietek Pemper, Göth found the yield of 1,668 adults and children from the *Gesundheitsaktion* disappointingly low, given the number of spaces he needed in Płaszów. But Keneally reckons the event's results in a calculus that underlines how numerically disproportionate Schindler's efforts seem in the context of Holocaust casualties when he points out that Göth "would in a day abolish as many lives as Oskar

Schindler was, by wit and reckless spending, harboring in Emalia" (259). Spielberg uses the scene of the medical selection to underline the logical malice behind the Nazi "sorting myths," as Edith Wyschogrod calls them, which used invidious *lists* to perpetrate a *lie of rationality*—a ghastly pretense that Jews were selected for extermination on some rational principle. Wyschogrod writes, "The criteria used for sorting—ideology, race, and so on—become the bearers of the logical paradigm which itself remains invisible. The myth when it first appears must be so powerful that all considerations of fact are swept aside . . . to continue the process of division, to sort without end" (41).

Schindler's List

Like every other aspect of his wartime enterprise, Oskar Schindler's list was a mirror or double of the Nazi enterprise, and thereby suffered some of its moral contaminations. But if every aspect of Schindler's project shared characteristics of Nazi projects—if Emalia used slave labor just as I. G. Farben used slave labor, for example—it did so *with a difference.* "The truth is, though, that no one collapsed and died of overwork, beatings, or hunger in Emalia. Whereas at I. G. Farben's Buna plant alone, 25,000 prisoners out of a work force of 35,000 would perish at their labor" (Keneally, 203). Unlike other Nazi lists, Schindler's was neither arbitrary nor, strictly speaking, principled except insofar as its principle was *social:* Oskar *knew the people he knew.* Leon Leyson credits Schindler with the social "memory of an elephant" (Brecher, 83) and claims Schindler could pick an Emalia worker out of a deportation line on sight. The genesis of Schindler's list was an order transmitted in the summer of 1944—not long after the medical selection—telling him that along with Concentration Camp Płaszów, his Emalia plant was being disbanded, and his workers were to be "relocated" to Auschwitz and Gröss-Rosen. By 1944 the euphemism was transparent to everyone. Fortunately, two factors conspired to give Schindler a plan: he had early on bargained to get Emalia a munitions contract, and he had been obliged by Płaszów's shift to concentration camp status to contact and ingratiate himself with a sympathetic and extremely highly placed German official in Berlin named Erich Lange.[22] Upon receiving the order to disband, Schindler decided to use his munitions contract to negotiate Emalia's relocation to a remote village near his home in Czechoslovakia, a place in Moravia called Brinnlitz. He pressed Madritsch to join him, hoping that together they could get 4,000 Jews out. But in spite of the strenuous support of Raimund Titsch, Madritsch's plant manager, Madritsch declined after much anguished consideration, convinced—Keneally suggests—that the plan wouldn't work (291). Titsch worked feverishly to get Madritsch Jews onto the list, and appears to have appended around seventy. Getting the move to Brinnlitz approved required Oskar to "negotiate" with a whole new cast of characters in a region where people actively resisted any move to bring a thousand Jews into their rural hamlet. Keneally reports that many *Schindlerjuden* found Oskar's estimate, that it cost nearly $40,000 "to grease the transfer to Brinnlitz," much too low (289).

In Spielberg's film the compiling of the list is depicted with moral simplicity as a heroic collaboration between Stern and Schindler. Keneally believes the list took on mythological proportions even at the time: "The list is an absolute good. The list is life," Stern tells Schindler in the film. Keneally adds, "It was a *List*. It was a sweet chariot which might swing low" (277). But from deeper within Keneally's and Elinor Brecher's accounts, the list emerges as deconstructed as a postmodern text, its content disputed and disrupted by iterations and inconsistent versions, its authorship fragmented, its constitution corrupt, and even its aim uncertain and overdetermined. Peter Körte in the *Frankfurter Rundschau* (Mar. 1, 1994) complains that it should be called Stern's List (Weiss, 96), whereas Elinor Brecher insists, "In reality, it was Marcel Goldberg who controlled the list, not Stern or even Schindler" (xxxv). Keneally clarifies some of the confusion by pointing out that Schindler began thinking of the list as soon as he had decided on the Brinnlitz plan after getting the order to disband Emalia in August 1944— and that Amon Göth agreed to have the list drawn up if Schindler could get the necessary approvals from the Evacuation Committee and other boards and authorities. According to Keneally, Schindler's blackjack game with Göth for Helen Hirsch's inclusion on the list occurred that same evening, making Helen Hirsch the first name on the list. After Amon Göth was arrested on September 13, 1944, Płaszów's new commandant, Arnold Büscher, became responsible for the list. Because Büscher didn't care who was on the list as long as it didn't substantially exceed the designated number of 1,100, he let his corrupt personnel clerk, Marcel Goldberg, compile the names.

There was never any question that Itzhak Stern would be on the list (Keneally, 293), or that Schindler or Stern dictated the bulk of its names, although there are some discrepancies in Keneally's and Brecher's accounts of the list's makeup. Keneally reports that Emalia workers were indeed returned to Płaszów when the plant was disbanded in August 1944—but not that 700 were deported, as Brecher insists.[23] He claims that Schindler's preparatory list contained more than 1,000 names, "the names of all the prisoners of the backyard prison camp of Emalia, as well as new names" (290), and that "in spite of Goldberg, Oskar got for the most part the people he had asked for" (298). Brecher, however, maintains that "the October list" used to actually ship people on their way to Brinnlitz "consisted of three hundred original Emalia workers and seven hundred replacements for those shipped out in August" (xxx). Keneally tells that all the *Schindlerjuden* from the earliest days were on it—the Rosners, the Jereths, the Perlmans, the Levartovs—though some had to pay Marcel Goldberg for inclusion, and Goldberg crossed some of Schindler's Emalia workers off the list. The Dresners claim they paid (Keneally, 292), and the jeweler Mordecai Wulcan and his family, and the Horowitzes. Of course, Marcel Goldberg and his family were on the list. Stella Müller-Madej describes how her family, who were not Emalia workers, fearfully debated whether to try to get on the list, uncertain whether Schindler could be trusted or whether the plan was a trap (174). Keneally tells of one Emalia worker who was crossed off the list and barely survived Mauthausen, and in 1963 angrily complained about Schindler to the Martin Buber Society; but given the incredible administrative and logistical problems of the move, Schindler "could not police Goldberg by the hour" (296).[24]

The list itself was never a single list. Keneally reports that the list was "finalized" at a final Płaszów party attended by all of Schindler's SS friends as well as Madritsch and Titsch. It was at this party that Titsch and Schindler typed in, from memory, the names of seventy Madritsch workers, including young Janka Feigenbaum, who suffered from terminal cancer. Titsch woke up next morning "damning himself because one [name] had come to him too late" (Keneally, 291). The transport was required to have the men from Płaszów pass through the concentration camp at Gröss-Rosen and the women to pass through Auschwitz. At Gröss-Rosen it was discovered that the list had not been sent from Płaszów, and Marcel Goldberg, obliged to reconstruct it from memory, was "surrounded by a spate of final pleas for inclusion" and began fiddling with the list yet once again (Keneally, 301). Near the end of the time at Brinnlitz, as Schindler was preparing his escape, another list, cataloguing the people at Brinnlitz, was compiled—and it is

WRITING WAR IN THE TWENTIETH CENTURY

apparently this April 18, 1945, list that is the "final" list "currently circulating" (Brecher, xxxi). Keneally does not say which version of the list is preserved in the archives of the Yad Vashem (290). Brecher has studied the April 18, 1945, list and says:

> The April 18 list is a jumble of inaccuracies: phony birth dates—some off by decades—and altered identities. Some mistakes are intentional; others resulted from confusion or disinformation, or simple typos. There are German spellings, Polish spellings, and Hebrew transliterations into both languages. . . . Abraham Bankier, the enamelware plant's original owner, appears twice, and some people who unquestionably were at Brinnlitz don't appear at all. (xxxi)

In addition to saving lives, Schindler's list dramatically confers or restores identity in Spielberg's film, as dozens of figures viewers have tracked visually are at last formally given their names.

The detour that took the Płaszów men to the concentration camp at Gröss-Rosen on October 15, 1944, and the women to Auschwitz a week later, on October 22, posed the most dangerous narrative challenge to both Keneally and Spielberg. The affect produced by the suspense of a cliffhanger could so easily have trivialized the desperately serious and dark significance of this sojourn that ended in death for so many. Here is drawn, more starkly than during their time in Płaszów, the fragile line of bureaucratic, historical, volitional, and accidental intervention that separated those who survived and those who perished. The mythopoeia of this travel as a journey into the underworld was underwritten in both film and book by the naturalistic condition of Poland in October and November 1944 as a hell of mud and cold. The men's three-day journey and processing at Gröss-Rosen, miserable like all such journeys, was made painfully stressful by the need to reconstitute the missing Schindler list, and the worry whether all 800 would be sorted from the thousand other Płaszów prisoners going to other camps, and allowed to proceed. But for the men disaster was deferred until shortly after they arrived in the haven of Brinnlitz, when Oskar Schindler was arrested for the third time on the dangerous charge of complicity with Amon Göth's financial irregularities. During Schindler's absence, the SS searched the plant for illicit children and deported ten boys and their fathers, including Olek Rosner and Richard Horowitz. Ironically, on a railroad track this small group of men and boys briefly met their wives, mothers, and sisters, who had just been released from Auschwitz and were on their way to Brinnlitz. The women's delay for three weeks in Auschwitz was technically highly dangerous, according to Keneally, because Birkenau was then in its last week of selections for gassing inmates; the last selection occurred on October 30 — eight days after the Cracow women arrived.

Without stripping them of their significance as signs of depersonalization and mutilation, Keneally complicates two of the most shocking visual symbols of Auschwitz, the infamous tattoos and the shaved heads. There is some question whether Płaszów inmates were tattooed. Keneally's text seems to suggest they were not, though several survivors claim they were. Both Leon Leyson and Rena Fagen say they received tattoos at Emalia, but sucked them out right after inscription in order to obliterate them (Brecher, 89, 261). Some *Schindlerfrauen* were certainly tattooed at Auschwitz, although Keneally explains that at Auschwitz tattoos were given chiefly to inmates destined for labor camps, and therefore functioned, ironically, as signs of hope and reprieve: "The SS tattooed your arm if they wanted to use you. . . . With a tattoo, you could leave Birkenau and go to one of the Auschwitz labor camps, where there was at least a chance" (Keneally, 306). Not only the women's hair was cropped or shaved, but also their underarms and pubic hair—although the purpose appears to have been less disfiguration and humiliation than a critical prophylaxis against typhus (the disease that killed Anne Frank at Bergen-Belsen), since the typhus microorganism is transmitted by louse bites. Since the film could so little convey the miseries of Auschwitz, it was important for the Spielberg film to emphasize the effects of defacement and dehumanization in the shaving scene.

Uncertain of their fate, living in physical conditions much worse than Płaszów, subjected to frequent puzzling selections and moves, the women were miserable and terrified in Auschwitz, according to Keneally. The more isolated began to contemplate suicide and to petrify into catatonia. As the days became weeks, and their quarters were moved ever closer to the crematoria, the women became more and more frightened and dispirited, unsure "if they were to go to the showers or the chambers" (Keneally, 310). Spielberg received considerable criticism for what some critics saw as a stock horror-film "fake-out"—the horrific suspense of the naked women in the shower room expecting the worst and blessedly relieved by the spraying water. Edith Wertheim claims it happened as it was filmed: "They took us to a shower. We thought we were going already to the gas. We had to undress, and they pushed [us] in naked. We thought it was the last moment of our lives. Like a miracle, we felt water coming" (Brecher, 387). Ruth Klüger described her paradoxical anguish as the scene approached: that the gas chamber must not be shown, yet must not be left out. She notes that the scene strikes at the core of the aesthetic difficulties of Holocaust material, and she feels satisfied with the scene's function: "Spielberg has made the attempt to solve a genuine dilemma: namely to substitute fear of the gas chamber for the gas chamber, to adumbrate it without making the mistake of representing it" (37; my translation). The cinematic handling of the scene relies for its power, as does much of *Schindler's List,* on the viewer's ability to supplement what is shown with what is known but not shown. Spielberg's shower scene further recreates the anguish of encompassing paranoia—the imaginative suspense of living as condemned that becomes as compelling as the actuality. Keneally dramatizes this condition as a way of life even at Płaszów: Josef Blau, convinced he was being hunted for having visited his fiancée in the women's camp, and Mietek Pemper, convinced Göth was saving a space on a list of condemned insurgents for him, lived in terror only to find it was other men who were being hunted or slated for execution. The arbitrariness of selections and punishments collapsed the borders between threat and pain or killing, between peril and actual violence, and placed a psychological anticipation, a shadow of terror, before every disaster.

Spielberg simplified Schindler's rescue of the women at Auschwitz by eliding the role of a female emissary, either a secretary or family friend sent to bribe and negotiate their release, whose errand quickly became erotically glamorized as an act of sexual sacrifice that Keneally disputes.[25] Zaillian, who had muted Schindler's early activism in his script, accelerates it in the latter part of the story by showing Schindler at Auschwitz forcefully (if ludicrously) arguing for the release of the little girls as munitions workers. In fact, Schindler did not negotiate in the women's presence, and they were uncertain they were saved until they saw him, wearing an absurdly jaunty Tyrolean hat, at the Brinnlitz train depot when they arrived. In the interest of economy, Spielberg's film was edited to reduce the Brinnlitz episode of the *Schindlerjuden*'s journey to a relatively uneventful denouement—omitting a last apparition from something close to the final, frozen circle of hell: the arrival of prisoners from the Goleszów quarry who became known as "the frozen transport." Two freight cars, their doors frozen from the near-zero temperatures, arrived at the Brinnlitz depot, loaded with over a hundred critically frostbitten men and sixteen corpses frozen into grotesque postures. Abandoned by the disintegrating system, they had gone without food or

water for ten days. "They were abandoned on sidings, reattached to loco-
motives, dragged for 50 miles, uncoupled again. They were shunted to the
gates of camps, whose commanders refused them" (Keneally, 355).[26] Justifying taking in a hundred men patently useless for industry required Oskar's
most ingenious argumentation. The frozen transport functions as a trope for
yet another twist to the horror of the camps. Although it is a travesty to call
them "homes," the fate of the frozen transport nonetheless makes visible the
even greater emergency of the inmates' homelessness at war's end, when
thousands of Jews were expelled from the closed camps and taken on lethal
forced marches.

The Brinnlitz camp, built on the site of an abandoned textile mill, was
under control of an ideological SS man not easily bribed to stay away. It was
therefore plagued from the first by unannounced inspections of the sort that
caught the boys during Schindler's arrest. These inspections were so nerve-
racking and perilous that Schindler and his wife, Emilie—with whom he
was living now that he had finally returned to his home region—moved into
the factory to be with its inmates. The gesture was significant because it
joined the Schindlers in community with the Jews and consolidated the constitution of the Brinnlitz munitions factory as a "home" in which the chief
products were not munitions but invalid care, domestic life, and community
culture. "The uncertified industries of Brinnlitz were the ones that counted.
The women knitted clothing with wool looted from Hoffman's left behind
bags" (Keneally, 335). During this period, Schindler's provision extended
beyond necessities to encompass the Jews' cultural and spiritual needs as
well. He recovered the priceless violin—"a Guadagnini crafted in 1890 in
Turin" (Brecher, 13)—that had been taken from Henry Rosner at Gröss-
Rosen. "The Rosners never learned how much that particular transaction
cost" (Brecher, 14). According to Cantor Moshe Taubé, Schindler secured "a
single tefilla—the one worn on the forehead—for Mr. Jereth, the extremely
religious and wealthy lumber dealer who sacrificed a gold tooth for Schindler's ring" (Brecher, 212). Emilie Schindler made a trip to Cracow to get a
pair of eyeglasses for Lew Fagen after he broke his—a kindness she could
not remember when Fagen reminded her of it many years later (Brecher,
267). At some peril, Schindler maintained the industrial activity of the camp
as a front only; black-marketeering became his chief occupation for funding
the housing, feeding, and medicating of his thousand-plus workers. Schindler's efforts paid off. Only three men of the frozen transport failed to respond to the frostbite ointments and sulfa drugs procured by Emilie, who

herself spooned bucketfuls of farina, a nourishing and digestible wheat pap, into the starved men. But perhaps the most compelling sign of the remade world of the Brinnlitz camp was the treatment of its dead. Janka Feigenbaum, already dying of cancer when she was evacuated from Płaszów, and old Mrs. Hofstatter were granted the grace of a nonviolent death in Brinnlitz. In deference to the family's religious sensibilities, Schindler refused to cremate them in the factory furnace. Instead, he bought land for a small cemetery from the Catholic church in order to make Orthodox burial possible. These unprofitable but significant gestures marked efforts to create a covert civic normality at Brinnlitz, with Oskar and Emilie's care tendered as no more than the responsibility that went with their fortuitous opportunity to provide it.

Brinnlitz, in existence for only six months, dissolved with the end of the war and the liberation of the remaining Nazi camps by the Russians in May 1945. Even before the liberation, a secret Brinnlitz underground of Jews within the camp was supplied with weapons through the Czech resistance. The April 18, 1945, list was compiled, Sol Urbach believed (Brecher, xxxiv), in order to protect the Schindlers upon their flight from Brinnlitz—a fitting reversal of its lifesaving function. Although Keneally presents Schindler's departure speech (transcribed by two women who were present) to the workers and SS guards, the film's scene of Schindler's sobbing collapse was a Spielberg or Zaillian invention, much criticized for maudlin sentimentality. John Gross in his highly favorable review of the film calls it "heavy-handed" and "positively stagey" (16). The formal factory speech, according to Keneally, served the risky and urgent necessity of preventing his departure from triggering a final eruption of violence between the SS guards and the Jews, and between the Jews and the unfriendly villagers. Schindler's speech was almost entirely successful, since the SS largely deserted the camp; but some of the Jewish men did lynch a German guard. Keneally claims the guard came from Gröss-Rosen—"It was the first homicide of the peace, which many Brinnlitz people would forever abhor" (Keneally, 376)—but Victor Lewis reports that he came with the Goleszów transport: "We hanged him on a pipe" (Brecher, 224). The film's tearful Schindler farewell has an important metadramatic function, however. It allows Spielberg—before breaking the film's frame and restoring the story to the memory of a present historical time—to mount an extravagant moment of mourning for the countless dead outside the margins of the list, whose stories could not be told. Having the film's Schindler mourn them rather than the *Schindlerjuden* may be judged appropriative only if one disputes Schindler's right, after having bound himself to the Jews in risk and community, to grieve. Herbert Steinhouse described Schindler a few years after the war, in 1949, when he was forty-one years old: "His frank, gray-blue eyes smile too, except when they tighten in distressed memory as he talks of the past. Then his whole jaw juts out belligerently and his great fists are clenched and pounded in slow anger" (Fensch, "Journalist," 35). But on another level, Schindler's grief at the exclusivity of his list, its failure to embrace and save more Jews, the impossibility of saving all Jews, may be thought to stand in for the film's grief at its own failure to tell the stories of the dead, to embrace all the dead, the entire Holocaust rather than merely its small fraction of an exceptional, alloyed, and imperfect saving.

Spielberg's coda, when he cracks the film's frame and shows actual *Schindlerjuden* pass Schindler's grave to place a stone, opens the story and reveals its porosity, that as their stories flowed into *Schindler's List*, book and film now release their stories. But, of course, as Shoshana Felman and Dori Laub remind us in *Testimony*, the "complete witnesses" of the Holocaust, as Primo Levi called them, are the failed or silent witnesses, the ones who did not return or returned mute, the witnesses destroyed as witnesses. Among *Schindlerjuden* who were asked for their stories, Brecher reports agitations and hesitations:

> In some cases, survivors couldn't tolerate more than a few hours of discussion. In other cases, I returned several times. . . . Some are introspective and revelatory. Others preferred discussing events rather than feelings. . . . Some didn't want to be found. Others . . . didn't mind being found, but didn't want to go public. . . . A few have written, or want to write, their own books. Some didn't want to be interviewed because they can't tolerate the stress. (Brecher, xxiv)

By working sensitively to retain the survivors' own voices, accents, and idioms in her narration of their stories, Elinor Brecher succeeds in representing them as a community in all its diversity.[27] In style, emphasis, and detail—though, significantly, not often in substance—*Schindlerjuden* accounts of the fate of the Cracow Jews can differ from those of Keneally, of Spielberg, and of each other. Brecher's book tacitly complicates a response like that of Cordelia Edvardson, who said that "Spielberg's Holocaust is not *my* Holocaust" (266; my translation). The effect of Keneally's book and Spielberg's film is less a consolidation of the hegemony of a single version of the

Holocaust than a provisional displacement or aggregation of many accounts and supplementary versions. Elinor J. Brecher's collection of *Schindlerjuden* stories, Stella Müller-Madej's Polish *Oczami dziecka* (published in German as *Das Mädchen von der Schindler-Liste*), and other accounts of Cracow and Płaszów that have or will be written will corroborate, complicate, texture, and sometimes dispute Keneally's book and Spielberg's film (and each other) in ways that augment and fortify their aggregate authenticity. In his foreword to Brecher's book, Thomas Keneally expressed relief that *Schindler's List*, both book and film, appear to have stimulated rather than inhibited survivor stories:

> A number of Holocaust survivors have stated that the book and, more broadly, the film of *Schindler's List* have catalyzed them into speaking. When the film was first released, there were newspaper articles about survivors needing counseling as a result of having watched it, and I feared that it might have a disorienting and painful effect on some. But if widespread anecdotal evidence can be believed, the film and the book have somehow, through the benign muses that drove both myself and Spielberg, acted as a catalyst to memory and to partial healing. (xv)

The final appearance of the elderly *Schindlerjuden* at the film's end makes a complex gesture of pointing both to the film's mimesis—that it *was a movie*, and even *just a movie*, but a movie that attempted to imitate with rigorous veracity and attention to verifiable detail a historical or "real" experience. Retrospectively, the paired *Schindlerjuden* and their actors point to a parallel verbal pairing of Keneally's nonfiction history of events and Spielberg's dramatization, as though book and film too could walk hand in hand past Schindler's grave.

6

DIVIDING THE INDIVISIBLE
The Fissured Story of the Manhattan Project

Narratives in Dispute

JOHN HERSEY'S *HIROSHIMA* — THE AMERICAN TEXT I HOPE TO put into dialogue with Japanese accounts of the World War II atomic bomb attack—begins on the morning of August 6, 1945. The story is thereby truncated, severed from its origins in other narratives, its historical grounding in the complex vectors of World War II in general, and its specific genesis in the complicated, intertwined developments of U.S. science, military strategy, policy, and wartime geopolitics. This historical amputation undergirded Mary McCarthy's harsh criticism of Hersey's account, that he "actually minimized the atomic bombing by treating it like an earthquake or hurricane or some other natural disaster" and thereby turned the event into a human interest story for the *New Yorker,* "'familiar and safe, and so, in the final sense, boring'" (Lifton and Mitchell, 89). Without concurring entirely with this sentiment, I nonetheless find it necessary to reattach and rearticulate Hiroshima to U.S. history, and particularly to U.S. historical discourse and narrative, if the writing and memorializing of the event is to be given an ethical exploration. That such an ethical exploration is necessary seemed urgently demonstrated by the troubling symptom of the 1995 cancellation of the Smithsonian Institution's planned exhibition accompanying the display of the *Enola Gay,* the plane that dropped the first atomic bomb on

Hiroshima. Robert Lifton and Greg Mitchell make large claims for this therapeutic necessity when they write, "You cannot understand the twentieth century without Hiroshima. . . . There is no historical event Americans are more sensitive about. Hiroshima remains a raw nerve" (xi).

The canceled Smithsonian exhibit effectively demonstrated history as the inevitably conflictual discourse that the philosopher Jean-François Lyotard calls "phrases in dispute" (*Differend*). The exhibit, designed as an evenhanded moderation of conflicting interpretations, would nonetheless have celebrated this military anniversary with an unusually complex and sober review. By translating the academic debates over the deployment of the atomic bomb into a display for public consumption, the Smithsonian exhibit would have brought an amalgam of official and revisionary histories to public perception and popular understanding, and thereby produced for the war's ending an ambiguous and troubled historical sense, like that afflicting the Vietnam War. Its cancellation under protest from the American Legion, the Air Force Association, and members of Congress has been denounced as a political abuse of history and lamented as a sadly lost pedagogical opportunity. As a result of the cancellation, the Stanford historian Barton Bernstein writes, "The 'official' version of what might be called the Hiroshima narrative easily carried the day: The bombs had been necessary to end the war quickly and avoid the dread invasions with many American casualties; there were no likely alternatives to using the bomb; and the use of the bomb on enemy cities had been necessary, patriotic and just" (132). Philip Nobile contended that the planned exhibit's meticulous and copious historical documentation ("a steady stream of diaries, memoirs, interviews and declassified documents has moved revisionism solidly into the mainstream") would have collapsed ("like a bad alibi") the official justification that the atomic bomb was needed to save "a million American boys from being slaughtered in an invasion" (xix). Instead, he lamented, its cancellation stimulated an outpouring of "bipartisan nostalgia for the bombings" (xiv). There are, then, two official stories with functions as *master narratives* or *legitimation narratives* that are worth dilating before we look at accounts of Hiroshima—the story of science, centered on the Manhattan Project, and the story of policy, which has taken form as the "strange myth of half a million American lives saved," as Rufus E. Miles Jr. calls it. I will explore this latter story in my prelude to discussing specific Hiroshima narratives in chapter 7.

But first I wish to reconfigure the master narrative attached to the scientific enterprise of the Manhattan Project, which built the first atomic bombs at Los Alamos, New Mexico. Its brilliant success contributed to the mythological character of the sign of the atomic bomb in the popular imagination. E. L. Doctorow asked, in a 1995 issue of the *Nation*, "What is the mythic reference for such an event? Shiva? Prometheus? The Tree of Knowledge? None is sufficient. Participating cross-mythically in cultures that encompass the globe, the nuclear explosion must itself become a primary myth in the postnuclear world to come. It will become a scriptural text" (171). The mythic aura of the Manhattan Project was stoked by the familiar rhetoric of superlatives—Secretary of War Henry Stimson was said to have described it as "the greatest project in the history of the world" (Easlea, 86)— which borrowed figures from classical epic and mythology for its corporate labor, and phrases from sacral writing and theology for the apocalyptic spectacle of its brilliant success. Revisionary language has borrowed equally familiar (if erroneous) tropes of monstrously deific science: "We built one Frankenstein," David Lilienthal quotes a scientist protesting the planned hydrogen bomb at an Atomic Energy Commission meeting (Reid, 272). But the aspect of this mythologizing of the Manhattan Project that will serve as my starting point is a metonymy rather than a metaphor: the way Los Alamos came to stand symbolically for the entire Manhattan Project and the way J. Robert Oppenheimer became its most mythologized figure, embedded in a classical narrative that cast him as tragic hero and martyr. In the most morally poignant moment of the narrative, Oppenheimer became the conscience of the Manhattan Project as, in an epiphanic moment of anagnorisis, he took a scientist's responsibility for his creation, accepted the blood on the hands of science, and identified himself with its effects through the powerful prosopopoeia from the Bhagavad Gita: "I am become Death, the destroyer of worlds" (Reid, 185). When Oppenheimer was prematurely stripped of his security clearance in 1954 at an inquisitorial hearing before the Personnel Security Board of the Atomic Energy Commission, the perception emerged that he was punished not only for his reluctance to support production of the hydrogen bomb but also for his perceived recantations of the success of the Manhattan Project. Thus martyrdom was added to the glance of this "saint of science" (Wyden, 349) into the heart of darkness.

The seeds for the demythification of Los Alamos and Robert Oppenheimer lie submerged in the suppressed residue of such adulatory documentaries on Robert Oppenheimer as Jon Else's *The Day after Trinity,* which was widely aired on the fiftieth anniversary of Hiroshima, and which gave some voice to scientific protest and anxiety but without building it into a strong narrative to counter the project's mythology. My strategy is to fissure this master narrative by splitting it and doubling it into a historical dialogue between atomic technology and policy that will take the form of a historical retelling in which I embed an analysis of the story's (or stories') ideological stakes. By foregrounding in his dedication one of the foundational figures of the Manhattan Project's revisionary history—"This book is for Leo Szilard who tried to stop the bomb in 1945"—Philip Nobile provided me with an oblique historical and political link between my previous chapter on the Holocaust and my next chapter on Hiroshima. As an émigré from fascist Germany, Leo Szilard transformed his fear of Germany's atomic research capabilities into a political activism that simultaneously helped inaugurate U.S. atomic weapons research without being able to halt or control its outcome.[1] Thus the political fallout from Europe's population cataclysm became transformed, however obliquely, into the instrumentality for Asia's nuclear disaster, and into the major technical resource of the Cold War in the second half of the twentieth century.

The story of the Manhattan Project eventually fulfilled the etymological paradox of its effort—the splitting of the Greek word *atomos,* meaning undivided or indivisible, and implying something that can't be split—by exploding into the fissured revisionary histories of the 1970s and 1980s. Like theirs, my own aim in demythifying the familiar heroic symbolisms of the Manhattan Project is less to demean or domesticate Robert Oppenheimer's stature than to track what ideological functions have been served by having one version of the Manhattan Project story occlude another. Revisiting two oscillating perspectives on atomic history elucidates the subtle differences between two laboratories, two physicists, and two visions of scientific responsibility as it illuminates the sociological textures of institutions and policies that supported, modified, and utilized atomic research during World War II. When we compare Robert Oppenheimer's and Leo Szilard's participation in the project, the situations of Los Alamos and the Chicago "Met Lab," and the different political cultures of the U.S. physicists and the European émigrés who provided the scientific research and experimentation, the problem of scientific agency, power, and responsibility assumes sharper focus. By tracking the story of activism and protest within the atomic scientific community, one can see how its diversion, neutralization, and silencing served the ends not only of Cold War political agendas for atomic energy but of the scientific discipline and its institutionalization in the academy as well. The myth of the Manhattan Project's seamless blending of scientific and governmental cooperation—what Robert Reid called "the face of unity and brotherhood which [the scientists] had once presented to the world as the untroubled image of science itself" (278)—was needed to make it serve as model for the organization of postwar civilian science in the United States. I intend my revisitation of the Manhattan Project to complicate Dwight Macdonald's early powerful argument in his 1945 *Politics* editorials and essays, in which he decried the absorption of scientific agency into "that perfect automatism, that absolute lack of human consciousness or aims" (149), which made the dropping of the bomb such a strangely mechanical act. Within the political machine that absorbed them, the scientists who made the bomb "appear not as creators but as raw material, to be hauled about and exploited like uranium ore" (149).

Dividing the Manhattan Project story into two narratives—of which one overtakes the other—highlights the different ways the atomic scientific community saw not only the instrumentality of the bomb but also their own instrumentality as its creators. In these differences, the role of nationalism plays at least an oblique role in the larger problem of academic participation in matters of politics and policy. Richard Rhodes, in *The Making of the Atomic Bomb,* averred that "at the outset . . . scientists were summarily denied a voice in deciding the political and military uses of the weapons they were proposing to build" (46)—a statement with assumptions (that scientists had a right to intervene in policy) McGeorge Bundy sharply disputes: "The choice of the word *usurpation* is striking, suggesting as it does that scientists had a basic political right to a share in these decisions. Rhodes is here reflecting and representing a widely held feeling, strongest among such men as Leo Szilard, that they did indeed have a right to share in any decision about what they had made possible" (46). Szilard's assumption of such rights must be traced back to the impetus of the U.S. atomic bomb project in the prewar European nexus of science and politics, which drove Continental physicists to the States during the 1930s in flight from Hitler. For Leo Szilard, Albert Einstein, James Franck, and many others who emigrated from Europe as racist Nazi policies ousted Jews from the German scientific academy, science and policy were inseparable spheres of concern that mandated action and a voice in policy making. "Many of us are inclined to say that individual Germans share the guilt for the acts which Germany committed during this war because they did not raise their voices in protest against those acts," Szilard argues in the letter that accompanied his 1945 petition to the president (Szilard, 210). That responsibility, he goes on to point out, is much greater in a democracy, where protest incurs less risk.

The extent to which the activist émigrés failed to make (or succeeded in making) themselves heard was conditioned by their political marginalization as foreign nationals and newly naturalized citizens by a wartime bureaucracy wary of foreigners and unsympathetic to their imperfect mastery of American conventions of political communication and procedure. The émigrés who worked at the Metallurgical Laboratory in Chicago became better positioned to focus on the big political picture and avoid the engrossing fascination with the scientific and engineering problems that captivated the Los Alamos scientists. Chicago's cultural ethos as a cosmopolitan, urban academic environment differed greatly from the military frontier life of Los Alamos, isolated in the wilderness of the American West. Oppenheimer's greater comfort with military collaboration, his fuller integration into the governmental decision-making process, his stake in the successful outcome of the project's blatantly military objectives conspired to produce a very different sense of scientific responsibility. By attaching the Los Alamos–Oppenheimer scientific commitment—rather than Chicago émigré opposition—to the story of the Manhattan Project and its military outcome, the historical narrative of U.S. deployment of the atomic bomb remained a story of U.S. scientific achievement rather than a tale of heroic resistance by the foreigners, whom General Leslie Groves in his Interim Committee report called "scientists of doubtful discretion and uncertain loyalty" (Stoff et al., 118).

The Early Phase

The sociological texture of the development of the atomic bomb is clearly revealed in the events of two pivotal summers when significant decisions were made and actions taken: those of 1939 and 1945. Nineteen-thirty-nine was a landmark year in atomic physics, which culminated in a large migration of leading European physicists to England and the United States. Although McGeorge Bundy is right to point out that "it is a fundamental error to suppose that the rise of American physics toward the front rank had to await the great migration after Hitler" (30), the European émigrés did bring with them not only critical scientific intelligence but also a sense of acute political emergency. It was one of those physicists, Leo Szilard, who, together with Eugene Wigner (who was to win the Nobel Prize in physics in

1963), drafted a letter announcing the possibility of making an atomic bomb and persuaded Albert Einstein to sign it and help them transmit it to President Franklin D. Roosevelt. Leo Szilard was a forty-one-year-old Hungarian Jew who left Germany in 1933 for London, and found himself in New York in the late 1930s. McGeorge Bundy described him as "one of nature's born irregulars. In a borrowed laboratory at Columbia he performed a brilliant experiment with radium that he rented with a borrowed two thousand dollars" (33). The letter to Einstein was prompted by Szilard's alarm in January 1939, when two radiochemists at the Kaiser-Wilhelm-Institut in Berlin, Otto Hahn and Fritz Strassmann, published their finding that uranium nuclei "burst asunder under neutron bombardment" (Easlea, 74). The other part of the Berlin research team, the Jewish Austrian-born Lise Meitner and her nephew Otto Frisch, had left Germany for Sweden at the time of the annexation of Austria. They announced in early 1939 the principle of atomic *fission*, which supplied the "detonator" for atomic explosion, the chain reaction producing an enormous release of energy in an impossibly compressed instant of time. The news traveled with lightning speed. By the end of January 1939, the experiment was being discussed at a seminar in Berkeley. "I do not recall ever seeing Oppie so stimulated and so full of ideas," Glenn Seaborg, the discoverer of plutonium, reported of Robert Oppenheimer's reaction (Oppenheimer, 207).

Leo Szilard, much alarmed by the possible ramifications of this research for German weapons development, began to urge secrecy to the Paris researchers Irène Curie and Frédéric Joliot-Curie to contain the findings that moved atomic research closer to military application. When Szilard sent his own finding that neutrons were released during the fission of uranium to the *Physical Review* in February 1939, he asked the journal to delay publication for the time being. He then persuaded a reluctant Enrico Fermi to adopt the same strategy. But the Paris team went ahead and published their finding in *Nature* on March 18, 1939. Within six weeks, two former colleagues of the Cambridge physicist Ernest Rutherford—Paul Hartek and Wilhelm Groth—informed the Nazi War Office in Berlin "how the newest developments in nuclear physics had made possible, in their opinion, an explosive many orders of magnitude more powerful than any hitherto used" (Easlea, 57). Szilard—whom McGeorge Bundy described as "always a jump ahead in his political perceptions" (33)—began to worry about the possibility of Germany's getting its hands on the large supplies of uranium under Belgian control in the Congo, and he pressed Einstein to alert Belgium to secure this material. After various attempts to find a suitable intermediary with access to the White House,[2] Szilard and Wigner had their draft of Einstein's letter of August 2, 1995, transmitted to President Roosevelt by the economist Alexander Sachs, a delivery not made until October. The letter warned Roosevelt that "Germany has stopped the sale of uranium. That she should have taken such early action might perhaps be understood on the ground that the son of the German Under-Secretary of State, von Weizäcker, is attached to the Kaiser-Wilhelm-Institute in Berlin where some of the American work on uranium is now being repeated" (Nobile, 25).

Six summers later, in July 1945, Leo Szilard was once more desperately trying to have a letter delivered to the president of the United States, this time urging him strongly *not* to drop the atomic bomb on cities in Japan. But this time there was a different president and a different chain of command, and the letter was never delivered. Szilard's seeming inconsistency—promoting the development of the bomb and then excoriating its use—is underwritten by a deeper consistency whose logic illuminates the later ideological fissures within the Manhattan Project. Like the motives of many of his émigré colleagues whose activism was inspired directly by fear of a Nazi military victory, Szilard's were highly specific and pointedly defensive. A U.S. atomic bomb had to be built to enable the nation to counter a German nuclear first-strike capability. By this logic, the bomb became irrelevant as soon as Germany surrendered: "We, the undersigned scientists, have been working in the field of atomic power. Until recently we have had to fear that the United States might be attacked by atomic bombs during this war and that her only defense might lie in a counterattack by the same means. Today, with the defeat of Germany, this danger is averted" (Szilard, 211). Conversely, although Roosevelt did respond to Szilard's 1939 petition by appointing a commission to explore the exigencies of building an atomic weapon, U.S. policy makers did not take energetic action to conceptualize, fund, organize, and administer the enterprise until 1940–41, when attention was much captivated by the war in the Pacific.

While Szilard and many of the other émigrés focused their political commitments on defense against Germany, the U.S. scientists generally supported the U.S. war effort in a much more comprehensive, diffuse, and unfocused way. No doubt different configurations of victim identification infused different emotional responses to the European and Asian war theaters. While the émigrés identified with the victims of Germany, the Americans increasingly identified with those of Japan—especially late in the war, after such horrors as Bataan prompted a disinclination to protest even the most aggressive U.S. military policies. The émigrés, accustomed to a politicized academic environment and suspicious of government, wanted a voice in policy that the most highly credentialed among them could command. Nobel laureates, such as James Franck, could make political expression a condition for their cooperation. "When Franck agreed to join the bomb project in 1942, he received from Arthur Compton a promise that, when the bomb was near completion, and if no other nation had it, Franck might present his views about use of the weapon to policymakers," Barton Bernstein writes (*Atomic Bomb,* 25). The émigrés also had a keener sense that scientists (especially in a democracy with freedom of expression) would be held accountable for the effects of their creation. "I have no doubt in my own mind that from a point of view of the standing of the scientists in the eyes of the general public one or two years from now it is a good thing that a minority of scientists should have gone on record in favor of giving greater weight to moral arguments," Szilard wrote to the physicist Ed Creutz at Los Alamos in July 1945 (213). But many other physicists did not anticipate being assigned responsibility; "The reaction to the suffering inflicted on the inhabitants of Hiroshima and Nagasaki was inevitable. What surprised scientists, however, was . . . that the finger of guilt should have been pointed at science" (Reid, 217).

Szilard, Wigner, and Einstein may have set the spark that ignited U.S. government sponsorship of atomic weapons research, but it took the clout and administrative know-how of two U.S. scientific moguls to transform Szilard's idea into a brilliantly conceived and effective $2 billion project. The architect of this model of governmental-scientific collaboration was the MIT-educated engineer Vannevar Bush, who, while heading the Carnegie Institution of Washington before World War II, became friends with Harry Hopkins, President Roosevelt's close friend and adviser.

> In 1940, he obtained authorization directly from President Roosevelt himself to form a committee operating at the very highest levels of government with nearly unlimited authority to oversee scientific research during the impending conflict. Rather than founding a large number of new government-run research laboratories, Bush made the brilliant and parsimonious decision to utilize the research institutions already in place, especially those that had been established at innumerable American universities. (Seaborg, 10)

The vision of Vannevar Bush—which created the model for federally sponsored civilian science that has perdured in the academy since World War II—was translated into its first administrative structure in 1941, when the National Defense Research Committee (NDRC) was formed and authorized to contract projects with American research universities. Eventually the chairmanship of the NDRC was passed from Bush to Harvard University's president, James B. Conant, a chemist who served as a White House science adviser during 1940. Vannevar Bush then headed the newly established Office of Scientific Research and Development (OSRD), which had specific responsibility for the mobilization of physics for defense purposes. The key committee of the OSRD—the Section on Uranium—became known as the S-1 Section.

The alliance of government, industry, the military, and the academy that Bush forged for wartime atomic research was governed by a complex set of assumptions about the functions and interactions of the various sectors that arose out of the specific exigencies of the project. The scientists were granted autonomy to define their research needs, which industry, military procurement, and government funding would supply; in return, the laboratories were obliged to operate under extensive security restrictions. In their initial seminars and theoretical discussions, the S-1 scientists addressed the major technical difficulty that arose in the construction of an atomic weapon—obtaining sufficient fissionable material. Time pressures mandated the costly decision that all four known methods of uranium isotope separation would need to be developed—thermal diffusion, the diffusion of gases through a porous barrier, centrifugal separation, and electromagnetic separation. In addition, a further problem—vexed by the uncertainties of the science—was to find a way to produce large quantities of plutonium, or element 94, which had been discovered by Glenn Seaborg of the University of California at Berkeley. The critical role that material production played in atomic research shaped the massive direct involvement of the military, which alone had the procurement capabilities and wartime production priorities to supply the scientists with their raw materials and the means of processing them. Kenneth D. Nichols, the chief district engineer for the Manhattan Project—who as Major General K. D. Nichols, U.S.A. (Ret.), published a valuable managerial and materials history of the project in 1987—estimated that "ultimately, over 90 percent of the cost of the Manhattan Project went into building the plants and producing the fissionable materials, and less than 10 percent was applied to the development and production of the weapons" (34).

Faced with the need to build a series of multimillion-dollar plants, Bush and Conant decided that "they would have to transfer the gigantic task of design and construction to the Army" (Hewlett and Anderson, 71). Building an atomic weapon required a coordinated effort integrating theoretical and experimental physics, engineering design, plant construction, and industrial management. In the summer of 1942, the newly promoted Brigadier General Leslie R. Groves was appointed to oversee the enterprise to build the bomb. On August 11, 1942, the Manhattan Engineering District, with its main office in New York City, was formed, its name serving as an incidental decoy: "Giving the project that name would focus attention away from the actual site of the plants" (Nichols, 40). Groves moved quickly to set up the needed plants and laboratories, which eventually included the Hanford Engineer Works in Washington State for plutonium-239 production; the Clinton Engineer Works in Oak Ridge, Tennessee, which produced both uranium-235 and plutonium-239; the laboratory of the Argonne Forest Preserve, connected to the Metallurgical Laboratory ("Met Lab") at the University of Chicago, which was specifically built to manufacture plutonium; and the Los Alamos Laboratory in New Mexico. At Los Alamos, which in spite of its location was (and still is) contracted to the University of California, the first bombs were assembled and tested. The procurement of the rare materials graphite and uranium began. Ken Nichols, despairing of finding large quantities of relatively pure uranium in Canada and Colorado, surprisingly hit the mother lode in New York City. Leo Szilard's anxious schemes to get the Belgians to protect their African uranium ore from the Germans were realized by other means: by 1942 Union Minière had shipped 1,200 tons of high-grade uranium ore from the Belgian Congo and stored it in a warehouse on Staten Island. Nichols was then able to buy it for the Chicago Met Lab (Nichols, 43).

In the political ecology of the Manhattan Project's various components, Los Alamos eventually overshadowed the sharply argumentative and critical culture of the Chicago Met Lab, as Oppenheimer eclipsed Szilard. The Manhattan Project mobilized U.S. physics into the psychological structure of a military campaign. Los Alamos, formally a military outpost, absorbed the military ethos far more thoroughly than the Met Lab. The Chicago plutonium lab remained urban, and its physical, intellectual, and psychological connections to the University of Chicago gave it a more civilian and cosmopolitan mind-set than that of Los Alamos, whose geographically remote connection to its academic affiliate remained largely bureaucratic. The Chicago

Met Lab came under the direction of Arthur Holly Compton, who had won the Nobel Prize for physics in 1927 and had chaired a committee of the National Academy of Sciences on the military uses of uranium before the outbreak of the war. At the Met Lab he oversaw the building of a nuclear reactor that could be used for the production of plutonium. Desperately dangerous, the experiments and tests of the Met Lab nonetheless seemed domesticated by the urban collegiate setting. In November 1942 Compton authorized Enrico Fermi's experiment to test the possibility of a nuclear chain reaction in the squash court under the west stands of Stagg Athletic Field, the University of Chicago's football stadium. "After all," Compton wrote in justifying the elaborate safety precautions, "the experiment would be performed in the midst of a great city" (137).

The big-city, big-university character of the Met Lab was intensified by the active citizenship of the many émigrés, who chafed at the operating conditions governing the lab. Eugene Wigner, responsible for designing the first water-cooled graphite pile, was uncomfortable working with engineers from the Du Pont company, under contract to the Met Lab. He and many of his colleagues also hated the military compartmentalization of information designed to protect the project from spies and from the loose lips of scientists ("Each should stick to his own job and keep quiet" [Wyden, 66]). They also wanted a voice in how the project was run. Throughout 1944, Szilard prepared a series of detailed and cantankerous reports for Vannevar Bush, airing a list of complaints about the operation of the Met Lab. His reports include such headings as "Du Pont Not Able to Utilize Our Staff," "Rule by Directives," "Lack of Permanent Board of Experts," "The Scientists Without Representation," and "Psychological Situation of the Scientists," in which he complained of discrimination against the foreign-born scientists (Szilard, 164–79). Szilard's contentiousness and brashness had earned him such an instant reputation as a troublemaker that as early as August 1942 General Groves wrote out an arrest order addressed to the U.S. attorney general, claiming that Szilard was an "enemy alien" who should be "interned for the duration of the war" (Rhodes, 503). Terrified that his émigrés would all jump ship if Szilard was manhandled, Compton sent a frantic telegram to stay his hand. Groves, grudgingly persuaded that Szilard had set the whole U.S. atomic project in motion and that his brilliance was indispensable to the science, was forced to content himself with putting Szilard under surveillance ("Subject is of Jewish extraction, has a fondness for delicacies and frequently makes purchases in delicatessen stores" [Rhodes, 506]). Szilard's project directors liked him little better, and Conant bluntly branded him an opportunist, saying, "I think Szilard is interested primarily in building a record on the basis of which to make a 'stink' after the war is over" (Hershberg, 195). By and large, Szilard's complaints were sidetracked—although his colleague Irving Lowen was eventually able to convey the concerns of the Chicago group to FDR (ibid.). Compton was repeatedly in the uncomfortable position of having to represent fairly a mutinous laboratory with whose contentious outlook and back-channel tactics he was seldom in sympathy.

In contrast, few of these problems plagued Los Alamos. Sometime in August 1942, General Groves appointed the thirty-eight-year-old Berkeley physicist Robert Oppenheimer to plan and direct a new separate laboratory for the building, assembly, and testing of the bomb. The selection of Oppenheimer was not self-evident. He had not, in fact, published widely in the field ("Of the nearly one hundred papers on topics related to fission that appeared prior to the scientists' self-imposed ban on publication, none bears Oppenheimer's name" [Oppenheimer, 222]) and had limited administrative experience ("He had never even chaired a physics department" (Oppenheimer, 261). The task of getting him a security clearance turned into a major headache. Like Szilard, Oppenheimer had an ideologically sensitive temperament, although his political education was more remote, passive, and romantic than that of Szilard. By 1934, Oppenheimer was pledging 3 percent of his salary to a fund organized by Eugene Wigner and Rudolf Ladenburg to assist Jewish physicists displaced from their universities by the Nazis (Oppenheimer, 173). By 1937, he was helping his aunt and other German Jewish relatives resettle in Berkeley. In his response to the 1954 Personnel Security Board hearing that deprived him of his clearance, Oppenheimer grounded his political awareness in his "continuing, smoldering fury about the treatment of Jews in Germany," his concern about his students during the Depression ("through them, I began to understand how deeply political and economic events could affect men's lives"), and his support of the Loyalists in Spain (*In the Matter*, 8). He did not remember having responded to a government security questionnaire that he had "probably belonged to every Communist-front organization on the west coast" but was certain that if he did, "it was a half-jocular overstatement" (*In the Matter*, 9). In spite of these red security flags, distinguished people vouched for Oppenheimer; he impressed Army officials immensely ("He's a genius," Groves is said to have said [Rhodes, 448]), and so was appointed to head Los Alamos.

Groves and Oppenheimer agreed on the need for an isolated, secure, centralized bomb laboratory in the wilderness with room for test sites and proving grounds. The choice of the Los Alamos Ranch School, some twenty miles from Santa Fe, New Mexico, met the essential requirements as well as giving Oppenheimer—whose family had owned a vacation home in New Mexico—a sentimental satisfaction. "My two great loves are physics and desert country," Oppenheimer once told a friend; at Los Alamos, he was able to combine the two (Rhodes, 451). From October 1942 to April 1943, an entire frontier community was created from scratch in the New Mexico mountains. The country's top physicists and engineers were recruited, laboratories were built and supplied with highly specialized scientific equipment, and an entire scientific and civilian infrastructure was put in place. "Room is being provided for a laundry; each house will have its washtub; and we shall be able to send laundry to Santa Fe regularly," Oppenheimer wrote to Hans and Rose Bethe, in reply to Rose Bethe's inquiries about the domestic arrangements (Oppenheimer, 244). But the raison d'être of Los Alamos's isolation—security and control—required its thorough militarization. Worries over security obsessed James Conant, who, the year before Los Alamos was built, sent an Army security officer "to infiltrate Berkeley undercover and snoop on the physicists there" (Hershberg, 157). He subsequently ordered a secret meeting at which the atomic scientists were officially dressed down for speaking loosely about their research. In spite of the chafing of Met Lab scientists against the hated compartmentalization policies in Chicago, Conant wanted a fully militarized lab at Los Alamos. Oppenheimer did not object, but two distinguished recruits, I. I. Rabi and Robert Bacher, refused to join up under these conditions. A compromise was achieved: the lab would be under civilian administration during the experimental stage of research, but the physicists would be expected to become commissioned officers when the critical trials began. That stipulation was never put into effect. Nonetheless, the security apparatus, which began innocuously enough ("Oppy just wrote a letter on University of California stationery to serve as a pass" [Serber, xxxiii]), soon became quite military.

Its official history describes Los Alamos as "a military reservation. The community, fenced and guarded, was made an army post" (Oppenheimer, 249). Oppenheimer recalled: "Telephone calls were monitored, mail was censored, and personnel who left the area—something permitted only for the clearest of causes—knew that their movements might be under surveillance" (*In the Matter*, 12). As at the Met Lab, the foreign nationals caused some of the greatest security problems. Oppenheimer had to remind his most distinguished physicists to refrain from speaking German and Italian with their families when they were in public (Oppenheimer, 263). Eventually false names were supplied to scientists and their families for travel, including absurdly anglicized ones for the foreigners: Enrico Fermi became Henry Farmer, Niels Bohr became Nicholas Baker, and Eugene Wigner became Mr. Wagner. The ad hoc establishment of Los Alamos from scratch combined the adventure of frontier living, the esprit de corps of combat ("There was also an exhilarating sense of mission and of comradeship" [Oppenheimer, 253]), occasional depression and loneliness ("Kitty Oppenheimer responded to the stress of living at isolated Los Alamos by drinking heavily" [Rhodes, 571]), and illusions of grandeur ("One evening the Oppenheimers gave a party. Edward U. Condon picked up a copy of *The Tempest* and sat in a corner reading aloud passages appropriate to intellectuals in exotic isolation" [Oppenheimer, 253]).

Testing and Targets

During the spring of 1945, with Allied victory within reach both in Europe and in the Pacific, the ideological divergences between the Chicago Met Lab and Los Alamos sharpened. For many Met Lab scientists, once Hitler was defeated, the urgency for developing an atomic bomb was over, and they wanted its testing and deployment set aside in favor of addressing and debating its long-range implications. Frustrated by "his continuing exile from the high councils of government" (Rhodes, 635), Leo Szilard circumvented channels to have Einstein, through Eleanor Roosevelt, help him set up an appointment with FDR for May 8, 1945. The meeting, however, was aborted by the president's death on April 12. Meanwhile, those "high councils of government"—the Interim Committee, appointed by Secretary of War Stimson, and "its *Doppelgänger,* the Target Committee" (Rhodes, 630)—were busily meeting to discuss the use of the atom bomb, a discussion in which Robert Oppenheimer was centrally involved. Los Alamos hosted the Target Committee, which met in Oppenheimer's office on May 10 and 11, within days after Germany's surrender, and selected the following Japanese cities as targets for the first atomic bomb drop: Kyoto, Hiroshima, Yokohama, Kokura Arsenal, and Nigata (Stoff et al., 101).

The two laboratories—Los Alamos and the Chicago Met Lab—were ideologically moving in opposite directions. On May 25, Szilard had figured out a way to approach the new president, Harry Truman. He did not speak to Truman directly but was sent to South Carolina to speak to the director of war mobilization, James F. Byrnes, who would soon be appointed as secretary of state. Byrnes dismayed Szilard by expressing interest in the bomb chiefly as a means of intimidating and controlling Russia (Rhodes, 638)—a point he tried to drive home with an unsuccessful appeal to Szilard's nationalism: "Well, you come from Hungary—you would not want Russia to stay in Hungary indefinitely" (Szilard, 184). Szilard's response was that "I was concerned at this point that by demonstrating the bomb and using it in the war against Japan, we might start an atomic arms race between America and Russia which might end with the destruction of both countries. I was not disposed at this point to worry about what would happen to Hungary" (Szilard, 184). On the same day, unbeknownst to Szilard, the Target Committee met again, this time joined by Colonel Paul Tibbets, who would in little more than two months fly the *Enola Gay* over Hiroshima. Szilard was still in Washington, getting ready to return to Chicago, when Oppenheimer arrived there to attend a meeting of the Interim Committee, which had decided to add a scientific panel consisting of Oppenheimer, Compton, Fermi, and Lawrence. The two physicists intersected and spoke briefly. Szilard remembered that Oppenheimer started the conversation by saying, "'The atomic bomb is shit.' 'What do you mean by that?' I asked him. He said, 'Well, this is a weapon which has no military significance. It will make a big bang—a very big bang—but it is not a weapon which is useful in war'" (Szilard, 185).[3] Oppenheimer also dismayed Szilard by touting the bomb chiefly as a diplomatic tool—although, unlike Byrnes, Oppenheimer urged the Interim Committee to promote sharing scientific information with Russia rather than exacerbating tensions.

Since he attended both the Target Committee meeting on May 10 and 11 and the Interim Committee meeting on May 31, Oppenheimer was fully aware that the United States intended to drop the bomb on Japanese cities. Szilard and the activist Met Lab scientists were, in fact, working against the grain of a policy machinery that had neutralized their agency in advance. Even those scientists who had a voice—Oppenheimer and his Scientific Panel—were expected to give technical information, not policy advice, and they ultimately undercut the efforts of their most engaged colleagues. The policy makers thus missed a monumental opportunity by ignoring scientists with the vision to imagine new political paradigms to attend their paradigmatically new invention. The Met Lab physicists felt strongly that demonstrated restraint with regard to the bomb was an absolute precondition for guaranteeing the scientific cooperation and international control required to avert a disastrous postwar nuclear arms race. Compton came to the May 31, 1945, Interim Committee meeting briefed on the ideas that James Franck had been discussing with his colleagues in Chicago. These included the radical proposals that Franck's committee on "political and social problems" eventually wrote up as the Franck report and tried to send to the second Interim Committee meeting, in mid-June. The Franck report would strongly urge a diplomatic use for the bomb as an alternative to a lethal atomic assault on a large city, proposing instead that *"a demonstration of the new weapon might best be made, before the eyes of representatives of all the United Nations, on the desert or a barren island"* (Stoff et al., 144). Ironically, the concerns of the Met Lab scientists, the technical expertise of Oppenheimer's Scientific Panel, and the military objectives of the Target and Interim committees could have productively converged in a technical demonstration. The Target Committee decided on May 10 that the atomic bomb was not needed to increase the physical devastation of Japan, but that "psychological factors in the target selection were of great importance" (Stoff et al., 102) A nonlethal demonstration could have served to make "the initial use sufficiently spectacular for the importance of the weapon to be internationally recognized when publicity on it is released" (ibid.). Oppenheimer assured the Interim Committee that the atomic bomb would indeed produce the "big bang" he had mentioned to Szilard. "Dr. Oppenheimer stated that the visual effect of an atomic bombing would be tremendous. It would be accompanied by a brilliant luminescence which would rise to a height of 10,000 to 20,000 feet" (Stoff et al., 117). Indeed, the Target Committee's choice of Kyoto as the premier target was based not on tactical grounds—the migration of industry from other bombed urban areas—but on its history as the ancient cultural and intellectual center of Japan: "From the psychological point of view there is the advantage that Kyoto is an intellectual center of Japan and the people there are more apt to appreciate the significance of such a weapon as the gadget" (Stoff et al., 100). Oppenheimer's information about the bomb's "big bang" provided crucial assurance that its effects would be distinguishable from those of previous massive air strikes.

Throughout the discussions of the Target and Interim committees, the value of the bomb as *spectacle,* as a visible sign of unimaginable power, significantly influenced a number of policy decisions.[4] The cities chosen would have to be previously unbombed in order to inscribe the bomb's power unambiguously on the landscape ("Hiroshima . . . is such a size that a large part of the city could be extensively damaged" [Stoff et al., 100]).[5] The decision was made to "request reservations" (Stoff et al., 101)—exemption from fire bombing—for these virgin targets. Indeed, Stimson used this argument in the following weeks to persuade President Truman to rein in the Air Force's strategic bombing: "I was a little fearful that before we could get ready, the Air Force might have Japan so thoroughly bombed out that the new weapon would not have a fair background to show its strength" (quoted in Rhodes, 650). Oppenheimer concurred that several simultaneous atomic bomb strikes would be feasible (Stoff et al., 117), but Groves feared that "the effect would not be sufficiently distinct from our regular Air Force bombing program" (Stoff et al., 118). Throughout these deliberations, the production of spectacle, drama, and difference in the bomb's effects outstripped any tactical or utilitarian goals. The aim was not to disable specific Japanese military or industrial installations or otherwise physically cripple its fighting capability. The targets were arbitrary except as surfaces for inscription, semiological fields capable of registering the unmistakable mark or sign of the United States' absolute power.

The technical demonstration the Met Lab scientists were proposing could have achieved this goal with nonlethal means, and the first atomic bomb blast at Alamogordo in New Mexico on July 16, 1945, could have served as proof of the power of a demonstration. The technical demonstration appealed to the scientists' academic tradition of persuasion by experiment and intellectual respect for the rhetorical power of evidence. In all respects but one, the technical demonstration would have served the Target Committee's commitment to the bomb's psychological instrumentality. But the policy deliberations were conducted amid conventions of military logic so deeply committed to injury as the proper activity of war that a new paradigm for the psychological rather than the physical use of the new weapon was treated as inconceivable. The Target Committee went in bizarre search for a city of intellectual victims instead of considering the technical demonstration's potential for making an immense political impact without the necessity of killing. Arthur Compton—aware that military convention would prevail—brought up the Met Lab's benign alternative only informally at the May 31 Interim Committee lunch. "I asked the Secretary whether it might not be possible to arrange a nonmilitary demonstration of the bomb in such a manner that the Japanese would be so impressed that they would see the uselessness of continuing the war" (Compton, 238). The idea was dismissed after only ten minutes of discussion (Hewlett and Anderson, 358), though on what grounds remains conflicted. Compton recalled three: the possibility that a demonstration might fail technically ("We could not afford the chance that one of them might be a dud" [239]), the doubt that the fanatical Japanese military leadership would be impressed, and the reluctance to yield the advantage of shock and surprise, without which the Japanese could interfere with an atomic attack. Reid mentions more fantastic elaborations, such as the fear that the Japanese would drag Allied prisoners into the demonstration area as a "sacrifice" (202). In his famous 1947 *Harper's* piece, "The Decision to Use the Atomic Bomb," Stimson reiterated the technical reason, the danger that the only two available bombs might have been duds. Szilard called this "a completely invalid argument . . . it would not have been necessary to wait for very long before we would have had enough bombs to eliminate the risk that they were all duds" (Szilard, 185).

The members of the Scientific Panel were permitted to tell their laboratories about the May 31, 1945, Interim Committee meeting ("The identity of the members of the Committee should not be divulged" [Stoff et al., 120]). The disparate responses of Los Alamos and the Chicago Met Lab reflected the different exigencies and tempos of their scientific moment as well as their different sociological temperaments. The Met Lab's most critical research contribution—refining the processes for recovering fissionable material and testing nuclear chain reactions—had occurred in the project's early phase, in 1942 and 1943. By 1945, the Met Lab's heyday had passed, and in response Groves reduced the Chicago research program, diverting resources and attention to Los Alamos. Los Alamos's own concentration on the project's later phase of weapons design, production, and testing accelerated throughout 1944 and 1945. After the May 31 Interim Committee meeting, the work at Los Alamos intensified to a feverish pitch, greatly inspired by Oppenheimer's own commitment to the use of the bomb and desire to see it work. Szilard had estimated Oppenheimer accurately—"Oppenheimer, we thought, would not oppose the using of the bomb which he had tried so hard to make" (Szilard, 186). Los Alamos thus accelerated its schedule with fifteen-/ to eighteen-hour days in the summer of 1945, and its scientists later recalled that they surrendered to what Bernard Feld called "a mesmeric quality about the bomb," with little thought to its immediate purpose; "nobody stopped and said, 'We are not at war with the Germans any longer, do we have to stop and think?'" (Easlea, 84).[6] Robert Wilson had tried in 1944 to provoke a formal discussion on "the impact of the gadget on civilization" but was "disappointed at the unimaginative level of discussion" (Reid, 178). By the summer of 1945 there was little time or inclination to debate the subject further.

In Chicago, Arthur Compton briefed the Met Lab scientists three days after the Interim Committee meeting on June 2, 1945. His information mobilized the Chicago scientists, who within hours formed themselves into a series of committees, including James Franck's Committee on Political and Social Problems. The Franck committee's memorandum was finished on June 11, and Arthur Compton forwarded it to the secretary of war a day later, along with a statement that his own preference was not for a technical demonstration but for a "military demonstration" (Stoff et al., 138). The Franck report, however, was never forwarded to the Interim Committee and instead was routed to the Scientific Panel for comment. Four days later, on June 16, 1945, the Scientific Panel—consisting of Compton, Lawrence, Oppenheimer, and Fermi—undercut the Met Lab scientists totally with the extraordinary move of abdicating for scientists any policy role in the use of atomic power: "We have, however, no claim to special competence in solving the political, social, and military problems which are presented by the advent of atomic power" (Stoff et al., 150). They also set themselves firmly against the Met Lab's proposal for a technical rather than a military demonstration: "We can propose no technical demonstration likely to bring an end to the war; we see no acceptable alternative to direct military use" (ibid.). Szilard's suspicions of both the Interim Committee and its Scientific Panel turned out to be well founded. As he saw so clearly, the Interim Committee was stacked with people who "had a vested interest that the bomb be used. You see, we had spent two billion dollars. Bush and Conant felt a responsibility for having spent two billion dollars and they would, I think, have very much regretted not to have something to show for it" (Szilard, 185). He respected his colleagues on the Scientific Panel as good men but noted that "they were men who could be expected to play ball on this occasion" (186).

Deducing from a new ban on phone calls to Los Alamos in late June and early July that an atomic bomb test was imminent, Szilard frantically developed new tactics and launched a new round of protest activity. He did not know that he had been effectively neutralized in advance. Although the technical demonstration so many of the scientists had urged never reached the agenda of the Interim Committee's May 31 meeting, Leo Szilard did. Under item "IX. Handling of Undesirable Scientists," Groves brought up the Met Lab activists, and although it was decided that nothing could be done until the bomb was tested and used, it was decided that steps would then be taken "to sever these scientists from the program" (Stoff et al., 118). Szilard knew by summer that proposals for a technical demonstration—which eventually found isolated supporters outside the scientific community as well (Wyden, 153)—had been defeated: "What we did not discuss enough was that Japan was defeated; the war could be ended by political means and need not be ended by military means" (Szilard, 186).

The Franck committee's efforts had failed. "While the Franck report argued the case on the ground of expediency, I thought that the time had come for the scientists to go on record against the use of the bomb against the cities of Japan, on moral grounds" (Szilard, 187). Consequently, Szilard drafted a petition, initially proposing that *"the United States shall not, in the present phase of the war, resort to the use of atomic bombs"* (210). After revising the petition to urge more narrowly that Japan be given warning and opportunity to surrender before the bomb was dropped, Szilard collected about sixty-seven signatures, including those of all the leading physicists at the Met Lab and many of the leading biologists. Only the chemists refused to sign, citing the argument for preemptive violence ("what we must determine was solely whether more lives would be saved by using the bomb" [187]). Szilard was unmoved by this "utilitarian argument with which I was very familiar through my previous experiences in Germany" (187). Failing to stop the petition on security grounds ("The right to petition is anchored in the Constitution," Szilard maintained [187]), Groves urged Compton to reduce its impact by conducting polls and stimulating counterpetitions. Edward Teller, who later regretted having declined to sign it, reported that Oppenheimer refused to circulate Szilard's petition at Los Alamos on the grounds that it was "improper for a scientist to use his prestige as a platform for political pronouncement" (Reid, 208). Peter Wyden speculates that the security file that would get Oppenheimer in trouble in the 1950s may already have been doing its job in 1945 by providing the "convenient hold Groves possessed on Oppie to insure his good behavior" (148).

Compton produced a poll with strong support for a "military demonstration" (though not outright use of the bomb on cities) and a sentimental anecdote about a young Los Alamos scientist who pleaded that the bomb be used to save his buddies who had fought at Iwo Jima. "Tears came to his eyes. 'If one of these men should be killed because we didn't let them use the bombs, I would have failed them'" (Compton, 243). The moral calculus informing the "humanitarian justification" for Hiroshima, with its thinly veiled nationalistic agenda, was already in the process of consolidation. Compton eventually sent Szilard's petition on to Nichols, who forwarded it to Stimson with the recommendation that it be passed on to the president "with proper comments" (Nichols, 190). Nichols's own comments made it clear that the petition's main utility was to keep control of the subversive Met Lab scientists ("the various scientists who have ideas regarding the political and social implications concerning use of the weapon" [190]). Szilard had been right in distrusting the chain of command; James Franck, who had insisted on staying within approved channels, had been wrong: the petition never reached the president.

The Szilard petition was dated July 17, 1945—the day after "Trinity," the code name for the first test of an atomic weapon, conducted on July 16, 1945, at Alamogordo, New Mexico—300 miles south of Los Alamos. Historically, Szilard was finished; his efforts to ban the bomb were doomed, displaced by the event that became the scientific apotheosis of the Manhattan Project. Trinity became the sublime, benign, aesthetic fulfillment of the science—as yet uncorrupted by cruelty and mass murder—that verified theory, proved hypotheses, justified design decisions, and *worked*. The event was self-mythologizing, beginning with its deific, erudite name, derived from John Donne, as Oppenheimer later remembered:

> There is a poem of John Donne, written just before his death, which I know and love. From it a quotation:
> . . . As West and East
> In all flatt Maps—and I am one—are one,
> So death doth touch the Resurrection.
> That still does not make Trinity; but in another, better known devotional poem Donne opens, 'Batter my heart, three person'd God'. (Oppenheimer, 290)

In this telling interpretive moment, Oppenheimer alludes to a wish for an erasure of radical difference through rhetorical rather than violent means. But the world into which Trinity was inserted was not a metaphorical map but a political space in which the global contiguity of East and West had been savagely shattered and the religious contiguity of death and resurrection had become a cruel fable. Had Trinity been the end of the Manhattan Project, the technical demonstration urged by the pacifists, then the Donne poem might have become prophecy rather than painful irony.

The drama of the explosion at Alamogordo made the event a magnet for rhetorical excess, for stretching the limits of exalted representation. It is useful to compare Trinity to the equally dangerous test of the first nuclear chain reaction, conducted at the Chicago Met Lab on December 2, 1942. Arthur Compton's account tries to make it as dramatic as possible, describing in minute detail each event, the drama of the "suicide squad," ready "to throw buckets of cadmium solution over the pile" if the reaction could not be stopped, and the look in Crawford Greenewalt's eyes as though "he had seen a miracle" (Compton, 142, 144). But in fact the first nuclear chain reaction produced no spectacle beyond a rattling radioactivity counter and the rising stylus of a galvanometer. Trinity's dramatic setting in a remote desert was infused with the danger of Enrico Fermi's bet that the detonation could ignite the atmosphere, destroying not only New Mexico but the entire world (Groueff, 352). The delaying rain and possibility of storm created further danger both at the site ("The steel tower stood like a lightning rod in the middle of the desert") and for the surrounding areas ("rain and wind could bring dangerous radioactive fallout over populated areas" [ibid.]).[7] Highly dangerous last-minute repairs had to be made to the protective nickel coating on the plutonium hemispheres, which had inexplicably blistered. But when the bomb was detonated, it produced a visual spectacle so extraordinary that, according to Brigadier General Farrell,

> the lighting effects beggared description. The whole country was lighted by a searing light with the intensity of many times that of the midday sun. It was golden, purple, violet, gray and blue. It lighted every peak, crevasse and ridge of the nearby mountain range with a clarity and beauty that cannot be described but must be seen to be imagined. It was that beauty the great poets dream about but describe most poorly and inadequately. (Groueff, 355)

Farrell's phrase "many times that of the midday sun" was quickly translated from the quantitative to the apocalyptic metaphor "several suns at midday" (ibid.), although General Groves's version, "Brighter than two stars!" in reference to his expected promotion to three-star general after Trinity, brought the celestial rhetoric back down to earth (Wyden, 213). Farrell's eloquence greatly outstripped that of William Laurence, the *New York Times* journalist on the Manhattan Project payroll, handpicked by General Groves to produce official coverage for Trinity and Hiroshima. Laurence served up a mess of purple metaphysical prose:

It was like the grand finale of a mighty symphony of the ele-
ments . . . full of great promise and great foreboding. . . . On that
moment hung eternity. Time stood still. Space contracted to a
pinpoint. . . . One felt as though he had been privileged to witness
the birth of the world—to be present at the moment of Creation
when the Lord said, 'Let there be light.'" (Groueff, 355)

Laurence later was cleared to fly on the instrument plane that accompanied
the bombers over Nagasaki, and filed a dispatch ("It is a thing of beauty
to behold" [Wyden, 212]) for which he won a Pulitzer Prize—presumably
for his scoop rather than for his style. Laurence, described by Peter Wyden
as "a valuable government propagandist . . . [who] displayed no reservations about anything he saw or heard," virtually worshiped the bomb
(Wyden, 212).[8]

The Aftermath

Oppenheimer's own sacred language at the moment of Trinity—"I am
become death, the shatterer of worlds!" (in Wyden's translation, 212)—has
become the poignant punch line to the Manhattan Project story. Like his
other melodramatic utterances after Hiroshima—when he told Truman,
"Mr. President, I have blood on my hands," and an MIT audience that "the
physicists have known sin" (Wyden, 349)—it fails to fit his actions on the
Interim Committee or his demeanor when he heard news of Hiroshima.
Three weeks after Trinity, on August 6, 1945, the atomic bomb the Manhattan Project built was dropped not on Kyoto, which Secretary of War Stimson
exempted on account of its ancient cultural heritage and sacred temples, but
on Hiroshima, which would in time count 130,000 of its 350,000 inhabitants
dead from the single bomb blast. The event fissured the sociology of the
scientists and principals of the Manhattan Project profoundly and visibly
along the fault lines that had been widening between the labs and among the
participants since its inception. Los Alamos was largely jubilant, its jubila-
tion reported in the tropes of sport and athletic victories. "'The place went
up like we'd won the Army-Navy game,'" Robert Wilson remembered, and
Oppenheimer later walked into the auditorium of clapping, yelling, foot-
stomping scientists and "clasped his hands together overhead in the classic
boxer's salute" (Wyden, 289, 290). Oppenheimer's confessions of incarnate

death, bloody hands, and sin appear to display a turn for melodramatic language ("He often spoke in riddles and was addicted to dark sayings" [Wyden, 217]) rather than remorse.[9] As late as the year before his death, he is said to have written to a friend, "What I have never done is to express regret for doing what I did and could at Los Alamos" (Wyden, 354). Yet such is the power of drama and rhetoric that historically Oppenheimer's eloquent confessions, whatever their sincerity, have displaced Szilard's feverish efforts to serve as the Manhattan Project's conscience.

Los Alamos and the Met Lab had, of course, dramatically different responses to news of Hiroshima and the later bombing of Nagasaki on August 9. The work of Los Alamos was effectively finished after Trinity, and Otto Frisch remembers that on August 6, 1945, "somebody opened my door and shouted 'Hiroshima has been destroyed!'; about a hundred thousand people were thought to have been killed. I still remember the feeling of unease, indeed nausea, when I saw how many of my friends were rushing to the telephone to book tables at the La Fonda Hotel in Santa Fe, in order to celebrate" (Frisch, 176). In contrast, Eugene Rabinowitch walked into the Met Lab on August 9, 1945, and "saw from the faces of the research workers there that something was wrong. The news was broken to him that Nagasaki had been devastated, and like the rest who had signed the Franck report . . . he was shocked and bitter" (Reid, 215). Leo Szilard was anguished and horrified when he heard of Hiroshima, but even before the shock had worn off he resumed his activism with respect to the new situation. Two days after the bombing of Nagasaki, Szilard wrote the minister of the Rockefeller Memorial Chapel of the University of Chicago, requesting that if a V-J Day service were held, it should include "a special prayer to be said for the dead of Hiroshima and Nagasaki" (*Szilard,* 230). It was not an empty gesture. Szilard was already foreseeing the massive relief effort the destroyed Japanese cities would require: "I also wondered whether it would be possible to arrange for an offering at the end of the service for the survivors of Hiroshima and Nagasaki . . . donations for this purpose [could] be sent to the Swiss Legation in Washington, D.C., for transmittal" (Szilard, 230).

On August 13, 1945, Szilard drafted another petition to the president to be signed by outraged scientists, stating: "We, the undersigned scientists engaged in war research at Chicago, believe that further bombings of the civilian population of Japan would be a flagrant violation of our own moral standards" (Szilard, 231). Since Japan surrendered the next day, the petition was never sent. The day after Hiroshima, Szilard also asked to have his first petition to the president declassified and made public, a move that was countered by an overt threat from the military to charge him with treason. After it was made clear to him that the Manhattan Project had legal authority to prevent him from declassifying material, Szilard was reminded that "any information considered 'secret' by the highest authority which you divulge to persons unauthorized to receive it will be in violation of the above agreements and of the Espionage Act" (Szilard, 218). Delivered in a climate that would see Julius and Ethel Rosenberg executed a few years later, the threat was not idle. General Groves also saw to it that Szilard was threatened with termination of his contract with the University of Chicago, and he secretly vetoed Szilard's nomination for a "Certificate of Appreciation for Civilian War Service" (Wyden, 347). A few years later, Leo Szilard left the field of physics altogether and returned to an early love, biology. He left physics just as the political and ideological views of physicists were becoming respectable, according to Samuel Allison: "Suddenly physicists were exhibited as lions at Washington tea-parties, were invited to conventions of social scientists, where their opinions on society were respectfully listened to by life-long experts in the field" (quoted in Reid, 261). But as Evelyn Fox Keller writes of the shift of interest from physics to biology after the war, "The technological prowess that underwrote the authority of physicists after World War II was perhaps too much in evidence, and too worrisome, to need or want to [sic] mention. The attraction of a science of life over a science of death was palpable" (108).

If the historical suppression of Szilard and Met Lab protest was intensified by Cold War U.S. nationalism and the need to salvage a heroic vision of scientific wartime cooperation, the coercive tactics of Groves and the military reflected their larger difficulties in containing the post-Hiroshima public relations disaster. Church leaders pronounced the atomic bomb drop immoral, and the military editor of the New York Times, not on Groves's payroll as Laurence had been, made dark pronouncements ("We have sowed the whirlwind" [Wyden, 317]). Groves was unaccountably unprepared for the panic created by news of the effects of radiation. The reasons are difficult to fathom, since Groves had had to contend with safety regulations and insurance coverage in the hazardous labs, and there had been at least two deaths by runaway reactions and other laboratory accidents (Frisch, 160). But the effects of radiation surfaced rarely in the scientific and political discourse of the Manhattan Project. The Interim Committee dealt with it only briefly with respect to the safety of the bomber pilots, and Oppenheimer's brief report on "the radiological effects of the gadget" makes no allusion to the victims of the blast.

As a result, the disturbing reports from Tokyo about "uncanny effects" observed in the aftermath of the bombing upset General Groves, who phoned a physician at Oak Ridge—Lieutenant Colonel Rea—to ask him about the news items people had been hearing: "Radio Tokyo described Hiroshima as a city of death. . . . 'Now it is peopled by ghost parade [sic], the living doomed to die of radioactivity burns'" (Stoff et al., 258). The transcript of the telephone conversation (omitted from Groves's memoir, *Now It Can Be Told*) goes on to report Rea's response:

> R: . . . I would say this: I think it's good propaganda. The thing is these people got good and burned—good thermal burns.
> G: That's the feeling I have. Let me go on here and give you the rest of the picture. "So painful are these injuries that sufferers plead: 'Please kill me,' the broadcast said. No one can ever completely recover." (Memorandum of telephone conversation between Gen. Groves and Lt. Col. Rea, Oak Ridge Hospital, 9:00 A.M., Aug. 25, 1945, in *Stoff et al.,* 258)

Rea dismissed the slowly mounting death toll—30,000 three days after the bomb drop, 80,000 two weeks later—as the result of "the delayed action of the burn" (Stoff et al., 259). Rea further belittled reports of dramatic drops in the red and white blood counts of construction workers at bomb sites with the remark, "There's something hookum [sic] about that" (ibid.). Groves, relieved, chimed in with "Of course, we are getting a good dose of propaganda, due to the idiotic performance of the scientists," and got General Farrell to announce at a press conference in Hiroshima that the delayed deaths were due to the incompetence of Japanese doctors (Wyden, 325).[10]

In the aftermath of Hiroshima and Nagasaki, Groves devised a protocol of U.S. military information management designed to publicize the Army's destructive technological power while minimizing and denying the magnitude of its violence to human populations. Concern that the overwhelming U.S. approval rating for the bomb drop might decline if "too much graphic detail about the suffering of burned and irradiated victims" (Wyden, 326–27) became available, the armed forces muzzled documentary filmmakers and confiscated their film. According to Peter Wyden, "in 1982, an Air Force archivist confirmed that 95,000 feet of color film shot by an Air Force film crew in Hiroshima and Nagasaki . . . [was] 'buried' because of the 'medical aspects, the horror, the devastation it showed'" (327). As a result, General Groves was able to tell the U.S. Senate Special Committee on Atomic Energy in November 1945 that radiation deaths, according to doctors, occurred relatively quickly and painlessly: "In fact, they say it is a very pleasant way to die" (Wyden, 345). With this public relations strategy, Groves was laying the groundwork for future use of nuclear weapons—particularly Edward Teller's hydrogen bomb, a weapon with a destructive potential 1,000 times that of "Little Boy," the bomb dropped on Hiroshima. In 1952, Ken Nichols, who had been the Manhattan Project's chief engineer and Groves's right-hand man, was asked in his capacity as deputy director of guided missiles for the Defense Department to prepare a memorandum for the Eisenhower administration on the political and military implications of the hydrogen bomb. He unhesitatingly urged its immediate use in Korea. To ensure a pretext, he suggested staging a series of provocations such as withdrawing U.S. troops to a line in the rear, and then "if the Communist forces make any offensive move to proceed beyond the present front lines, each day such a move continues atomic weapons will be dropped on both North Korean and Chinese targets" (Nichols, 11). The wider objective, Nichols conceded, was to start World War III—"precipitate a major war at a time when we have greatest potential for winning it with minimum damage to the U.S.A" (12).

Groves's management of the public relations problem inherent in Hiroshima was recapitulated when Air Force pressure forced the cancellation of the Smithsonian's exhibition on the *Enola Gay* in the summer of 1995. My aim here has been to suggest that the Manhattan Project, like Hiroshima itself, has had an "official story." It is the narrative of an epic corporate alliance between government, science, and the military to produce a monumental technical achievement, made poignant by the fall of Robert Oppenheimer, its brilliant and charismatic leader, to McCarthy-era witch-hunting. Daniel Ellsberg played on this perception of the epic and multidimensional unity of the Manhattan Project when he named his nuclear disarmament enterprise for Physicians for Social Responsibility "Manhattan Project II": "giving the tasks of ending proliferation and eliminating the threat of nuclear war the same urgency and priority from 1993 to 1995—and beyond—as marked the original Manhattan Project, which built the world's first atomic weapons between 1943 and 1945" (brochure for Manhattan Project II). This image of monumental cooperation allowed the Manhattan Project to continue to serve as the model for the national organization of postwar civilian science. Vannevar Bush outlined this scheme—even before the bomb was dropped on Hiroshima—in his famous presidential report of July 1945 titled "Science, the Endless Frontier," in which he recommended the foundation of a "National Research Foundation." The resulting "Vannevar Bush social contract" has supplied federal funding for autonomous scientific research in U.S. universities for more than half a century. Erasing the ideological and sociological fissures within the Manhattan Project—thereby silencing and occluding the specter of scientific responsibility as the partner of scientific autonomy—has effectively preserved the aura of scientific innocence and moral neutrality in the wake of Hiroshima.

A moment recorded in the journals of Glenn Seaborg—the leading chemist at the Chicago Met Lab, who discovered plutonium—functions as a miniature allegory of the ethos enveloping postwar U.S. science. On August 11, 1945, Seaborg wrote in his journal, "Helen, Clayton Sheldon, and I played golf at Rio Honda Golf Club. Today's paper is full of hope for peace. It also reports that 30 percent of Nagasaki was destroyed" (746). Three months later, on Armistice Day, November 11, 1945, Seaborg—who signed the Franck report—appeared on the popular ABC radio program called *Quiz Kids* to promote arms control. The transcript of the show has been preserved and contains such dialogue as "All right, children, fire away. Let's start with five-year-old Sheila. Sheila, what would you like to know about the atomic bomb?" When ringleted five-year-old Sheila asks, "How big is an atomic bomb and how big a piece will it take to blow up this big building that we're in now? (Laughter)," the answer tropes the quantity of uranium in a harmless sports analogy: "A chunk about as big as a football" (Seaborg, 784). One wishes an Asian voice could have penetrated the radio waves transmitting *Quiz Kids* to U.S. families on Armistice Day 1945 and uttered a ghostly accompaniment to Seaborg's benign answers:

> The house had burned completely. All our household goods, so carefully piled up for evacuation, and some rationed food we'd accumulated were still burning. So were the corpses of my children. When I approached, I saw a line of buttons from my son's white shirt. Akiko, my girl, was curled up next to Takeo. Flames were still licking up from them. I couldn't walk anymore. Pieces of the house were imbedded in my back. (Cook and Cook, 390)

7

WRITING THE APOCALYPSE
OF HIROSHIMA

Discursive Violence

BEGIN THIS CHAPTER ON HIROSHIMA AS I ENDED THE LAST
one on the Manhattan Project: with a U.S. entertainment program. Many
things had changed between the *Quiz Kids* radio program of Armistice Day,
November 11, 1945, with the plutonium physicist Glenn Seaborg as guest,
and the broadcast of Ralph Edwards's popular television show *This Is Your
Life* on May 5, 1955. The surprised guest of honor was the Reverend Kiyoshi
Tanimoto, one of the *hibakusha,* or atomic bomb survivors, who had been
featured in John Hersey's *Hiroshima.* Television had replaced radio in popularity, and fascination with the science of the atomic bomb had given way,
with increasing Cold War tensions, to morbid fear and anxiety about its destructive effects. Norman Cousins, the editor of the *Saturday Review of Literature,* saw an opportunity to use television to promote one of his many
peace projects. In his 1985 "Aftermath" to a new edition of *Hiroshima,* John
Hersey presents an acerbic account of what he saw as the shameless commercial exploitation of atomic bomb victims on *This Is Your Life:*

> "*This* is Hiroshima," Edwards said as a mushroom cloud grew on
> the viewers' screens, "and in that fateful second on August 6, 1945,

a new concept of life and death was given its baptism. And tonight's principal subject—you, Reverend Tanimoto!—were an unsuspecting part of that concept. . . . We will pick up the threads of your life in a moment, Reverend Tanimoto, after this word from Bob Warren, our announcer, who has something very special to say to the girls in the audience." (144)

Since the Reverend Tanimoto was in the United States to raise money for plastic surgery for the scarred "Keloid Girls" or "Hiroshima Maidens"— young women who as schoolgirls clearing firebreaks in the streets had been dreadfully burned and disfigured by the blast—the show's sponsorship by Hazel Bishop cosmetics was particularly ironic. It explains, moreover, why the disfigured young women were veiled. "Next, two of the Maidens, Toyoko Minowa and Tadako Emori, were presented in silhouette behind a translucent screen" (146). The sponsors clearly did not want their nail polish and cosmetic commercials intersected by the mutilated faces of the Keloid Girls.

But the show held even more vulgar surprises in store for Reverend Tanimoto:

Next came the shocker. In walked a tall, fattish American man, whom Edwards introduced as Captain Robert Lewis, copilot of the *Enola Gay* on the Hiroshima mission. In a shaky voice, Lewis told about the flight. Tanimoto sat there with a face of wood. At one point, Lewis broke off, closed his eyes, and rubbed his forehead, and forty million watchers across the land must have thought he was crying. (He was not. He had been drinking. . . . It seemed that he had expected to be given a fat check for appearing on the show, and when he learned that he would not, he had gone out bar crawling.) (Hersey, 145)

As Hersey presents it, the moment culminates the brutal tactlessness of the show's producers, Cousins's exploitation of his Japanese peace movement colleague, and Tanimoto's painful indignity as an involuntary entertainment spectacle ("He sat there, torpid, sweating, and tongue-tied" [145]). Lewis was apparently not too befuddled to give what Hersey patently implies was a cynical performance. Asked what he wrote in his log after dropping the bomb, Lewis told Ralph Edwards, "I wrote down the words, 'My God, what have we done?'" (146).[1] But even if the levels of sincerity and cynicism in the show remain undecidable, *This Is Your Life*'s premise and format for celebrating a successful life had no way to accommodate or remember what Tanimoto had seen on August 6, 1945:

> Soon he found a good-sized pleasure punt drawn up on the bank, but in and around it was an awful tableau—five dead men, nearly naked, badly burned, who must have expired more or less all at once. . . . Mr. Tanimoto lifted them away from the boat, and as he did so, he experienced such horror at disturbing the dead—preventing them, he momentarily felt, from launching their craft and going on their ghostly way—that he said out loud, "Please forgive me for taking this boat. I must use it for others, who are alive." (Hersey, 37)

The dead of the atomic bomb blast are the moral keloids of Hiroshima's history that resist the abrasion of memory, the suture of repentance or forgiveness, the sublation to narrative and art. When Mary McCarthy disrupted the highly respectful reception accorded John Hersey's *Hiroshima* by implicitly challenging him in the November 1946 issue of *Politics* to interview the dead, her gesture dilated the ethical problem of human apprehension, articulation, and communication posed by manmade mass killing. When John Hersey's *Hiroshima* is interleaved with other sophisticated and compassionate Japanese and U.S. testimonies,[2] the more subtle ethical difficulties that haunt perception and expression of this "death world" come to the fore. When these stories—reportage, memoirs, medical journals, and the like— are used as a narrative and moral compass, the conditions of death and living death they describe oblige us to read them against their inspirational and meliorative grain. Unlike Robert Lifton, who turns a therapeutic focus on survivor writings in his monumental psychological study, *Death in Life*, I try to expose and explore the different ideological and rhetorical agendas that U.S. and Japanese accounts of the event serve, however humane and compassionate their intentions. Their differences were partly conditioned by Occupation control of *hibakusha* testimony in the immediate postwar period through U.S. censorship designed to consolidate the legitimacy of atomic weapons during the nuclear arms race of the early Cold War. By setting Hiroshima writing against its historical legacies of rhetorical constraint, distortion, and violence, we can address Hiroshima's amputation from history even if we cannot remedy it.

John Hersey's *Hiroshima* begins, as many such accounts do, at or about the moment of the flash: "At exactly fifteen minutes past eight in the morning, on August 6, 1945, Japanese time, at the moment when the atomic bomb flashed above Hiroshima . . ." (1). Such openings themselves represent a narrative rupture with significant implications for constituting Hiroshima as a historical and moral event, for they begin the story in medias res, by confounding the ending of a story (the dropping of the atomic bomb, the ending of the Second World War) with a beginning (the survivor memoir, the creation of *hibakusha*, the story of Japan's postwar recovery). When the story of the atomic bomb is told without diachronic or historical continuity, it fractures into a variety of disparate and incommensurate discourses that allow us to compartmentalize them into such discrete and unconnected disciplinary monads as military history, atomic research, political analysis, medical history, and memoirs. Hersey's *Hiroshima*—like other Hiroshima diaries and memoirs—is entombed within the silence of the *why: why* did this happen, and *how* could it happen? The partial answer given in chapter 6, on the Manhattan Project, supplies a technical and political causality whose ethical link to the apocalyptic medical and social emergency produced by the bomb needs to be reforged in this chapter. It is the moral connective tissue between the science of weapons development, the politics of policy decisions, and the lethal effect of population destruction whose logic remains, more than half a century later, porous, unconvincing, and assailable by revisionary historiography. John Dower reports that in urging the cancellation of the *Enola Gay* exhibit, "the chief historian of the U.S. Air Force publicly asked how the Smithsonian could have blundered so badly on such a 'morally unambiguous' subject'" (Dower, "Foreword," in Hachiya, vii). It is ironic that those most certain of the justice of using the bomb need most urgently to censor pictures and stories of its cruel impact. The problem both for apologists for use of the bomb and for chroniclers of its damage lies in the severed logical and moral connections between the event's causes and effects. Hiroshima memoirs that begin on August 6, 1945, remain dehistoricized and detached from the larger political discourse to which they belong.[3]

The justifications for dropping the atomic bomb are multiple, overdetermined, and, according to revisionary historians, doubled and devious: documents of the reasons that informed the decision and the reasons given in subsequent memoirs, biographies, and histories are not identical. As I've noted previously, *the* official version, *the* premier legitimation for the use of atomic bombs against Japan is the humanitarian argument: "For nearly four decades, the belief that the Hiroshima and Nagasaki bombs averted hundreds of thousands of American deaths—far more than those bombs inflicted on the Japanese—has been a part of accepted history" (Miles, 140). Rufus E. Miles Jr., a former thirty-year U.S. government career official and senior fellow of Princeton's Woodrow Wilson School, notes that this argument "was neither needed nor used by President Truman in the weeks immediately following the obliteration of Hiroshima . . . since the public overwhelmingly approved of the action" (121). But by 1947, when word of the horror on the ground provoked questions about the necessity of dropping the bomb, Secretary of War Henry L. Stimson argued, in a famous *Harper's* article, that without the bomb a massive invasion of Japan would have been necessary to end the war at a cost of over a million casualties to U.S. forces alone. In 1953 Winston Churchill repeated this argument with a vastly inflated estimate of a million U.S. deaths,[4] and in 1955 Truman reiterated Stimson's argument in his biography. Thus what Miles calls "the strange myth of half a million American lives saved" entered into history. Rufus Miles was prompted to question the official estimates of proleptic lives lost when he noticed the discrepancy in the figures of Henry Stimson (who projected a million U.S. casualties) and Winston Churchill (who projected a million U.S. deaths)—a discrepancy occasioned by "the careless and imprecise use" of the terms "casualties" (which includes those injured and missing in action) and "deaths" (Miles, 123–24).

Eventually the humanitarian justification included Japanese lives as well, arguing that the massive casualties of Hiroshima and Nagasaki had the benign net effect of saving millions of Japanese who might have perished had the war continued. Although the peculiar moral calculus equating actual persons killed with hypothetical numbers of dead makes the humanitarian argument vulnerable on epistemological grounds, revisionary historians have attacked not its theoretical premises but its documentary evidence and strategic logic. Rufus Miles gives a detailed account of the minutes of the June 18, 1945, meeting between Truman and the Joint Chiefs of Staff, and insists that only OLYMPIC, the plan for the invasion of Kyushu, at the southern tip of Japan, was discussed and authorized: "Neither then nor at any other time did the Joint Chiefs discuss with Truman a plan for the invasion of Honshu" (134).[5] The cost they estimated for such an operation was comparable to the losses at Luzon, "31,000 casualties, 7,000 – 8,000 deaths" (135)—and at most 20,000 deaths, if a worst-case scenario is calculated (Miles, 135). Furthermore, an invasion of Japan was by no means a "necessity" for ending the war, the only option available to the United States. The administration's own Strategic Bomb Survey, established by Secretary of War Stimson after the war to interview numerous Japanese military and political leaders and review vast numbers of Japanese documents, produced the following conclusion:

> Based on a detailed investigation of all the facts and supported by the testimony of the surviving Japanese leaders involved, it is the Survey's opinion that certainly prior to 31 December 1945, and in all probability prior to 1 November 1945, Japan would have surrendered even if the atomic bombs had not been dropped, even if Russia had not entered the war, and even if no invasion had been planned or contemplated." (Quoted in Miles, 131)

Since this report was available to Stimson, Churchill, and Truman when they wrote their memoirs, their humanitarian argument was at best misleading and at worst a retroactive invention. The survey's findings also provided strong evidence that even if there had been an invasion of Japan, the Japanese military would scarcely have been capable of inflicting a half-million deaths, or for that matter a half-million casualties, on the United States. This finding undermines one of the chief assumptions of the humanitarian argument: "that such a devastated and thoroughly beaten nation, whose armies in the Pacific had taken losses of 22 times as many deaths as they had inflicted on General MacArthur's forces during their march toward Japan in 1944 and 1945, could have inflicted some 500,000 deaths—*70 percent more than the 292,000 the United States armed forces lost in all of World War II*— on the world's best-equipped army, navy, and air force" (Miles, 136). Given how palpably near to total collapse Japan was by the summer of 1945, it would have been strategic insanity and political suicide for Truman to authorize an action that was anticipated to produce a half-million American deaths, Miles argues. The humanitarian justification fails to hold up under scrutiny—convincing neither as the historical basis for governmental decision making in 1945 nor as a contemporary moral argument. Its effect, however, has been enduring and powerful. The unverifiable "statistic" of *a half-million U.S. deaths prevented* has invested the decision with the aura of rationality and authority that clings to mathematical and scientific thinking without the need to validate its accuracy or legitimacy. It also fabricates an ethical symmetry, lives saved for lives lost—indeed, an ethical surplus—in which hypothetical lives with no existential reality accrue greater virtue and value than historical material lives with documented sufferings and fearsome mortality rates. This symmetry at the core of the humanitarian justification conceals the oblique, fractured, and convoluted logic of the actual historical determinants of the decision: the diplomatic difficulties created by the different cultural valences assigned to unconditional surrender (Miles), the pressures of domestic politics engorged by fantasies of revenge and racism against the Japanese (Dower), and, above all, the rapidly shifting foreign politics that made the intimidation of the Soviet Union an increasing urgency as the war drew to an end.

The deviousness of the official justification for the use of atomic weaponry against Japanese cities has exceedingly malignant implications for the *hibakusha* because it doubles their trauma (as the traumas of rape victims have tended to be doubled) with a spiral of psychological violence. This becomes particularly visible when the argument that the inhumanity of Hiroshima represented a humane act is extended to include the Japanese. When U.S. authorities insist that countless Japanese as well as American lives were saved by the action, they pressure *hibakusha* to recode their sufferings as a necessary sacrifice for whose opportunity they should be grateful. The perversity of this transaction becomes painfully visible in the account given by the Manhattan Project administrator, Arthur Holly Compton, of his 1954 visit to Japan. Holly, interviewed by the Japanese press, was surprised and upset that journalists were angered by his contention that "'in spite of the great human damage that it would cause, we hoped and believed that [the use of the bomb] would result in the net saving of many lives, probably millions of lives, both Japanese and American.' This was not at all the answer the newsmen wanted. . . . Apparently no answer would have been well received except that I was sorry that we had used the bomb" (Compton, 260). Compton quickly learns to turn the tables on the Japanese. When he asks a reporter if he would have preferred the war to run its course, the newsman humbly apologizes for his blindness. "'I am sorry that I asked you that question,' he said. 'Had it not been for the bomb, the fighting would have continued'" (Compton, 261). Not only does Compton refuse to apologize for Hiroshima and Nagasaki, he insists, in effect, on being thanked by the Japanese.

A sincere, deeply religious, and yet ethically obtuse man, Compton has no sense for diplomatic subtleties such as the possibility that Japan might have surrendered in July if the United States had allowed the nation to retain the institution of the emperor—a condition that was, in fact, granted a month later. The United States' public refusal to apologize, to express regret, deferred and complicated the psychological process of reconciliation and healing for *hibakusha* and other postwar Japanese, as Robert Lifton has noted (334). Furthermore, when the mass deaths of Hiroshima and Nagasaki are sublated into the moral arena of sacrifice to save the lives of others, the *hibakusha* are pressured to embrace their condition as a martyrdom. But volition to suffer, the willing consent of the sufferer, is the essence of martyrdom; in its absence martyrdom reverts to simple torture. Elaine Scarry refers specifically to the issue of consent ("the very nature of the weapon eliminates the possibility that those injured can have consented to contribute their bodies to the substantiation process" [150]) in her distinction between conventional war and nuclear war. The impossibility of even tacit consent structures nuclear war on the model of torture: "Because the populations of the disputing countries cannot be consulted when the moment comes to fire the missiles, nuclear war has all the scale of conventional war (rather than the two-person structure of torture) but conforms in all its new massiveness to the model of torture rather than that of conventional war" (151).

The accounts and memoirs of Hiroshima are thus enfolded, at the outset, in the secondary discursive and psychological violence of this historiographic antiphrasis (expression by opposite, calling a dwarf a giant) that turns the event rhetorically into its opposite, an inhumane act called a humanitarian gesture, a shocking destruction of life named an extravagant rescue. The deviousness of this logic was already structurally built into the earlier logic for extending precision bombing of military personnel and installations to strategic bombing of civilian targets and ultimately civilian populations. The same humane argument—that destroying an enemy's morale by destroying its civilian population ends bloody and costly wars more quickly—masks the concealed origin of strategic bombing in the technical failure of precision bombing. "The slide from precision bombing attacks on industry to general attacks on cities followed less from political decisions than from inadequate technology," Richard Rhodes writes (469). Bomber Command's failure to hit military targets during nighttime raids more than a third of the time led to the creation of increasingly broader targets, and area bombing "was invented to give bombers targets they could hit" (Rhodes,

470). This devious slippage of justification—the masking of political, technical, and strategic rationales with psychological and ethical explanations—thus paved the logical ground for the atomic bombing of Hiroshima and Nagasaki. If the atomic bomb was dropped on Japanese cities chiefly to impress the Soviet Union—as many historians now believe—then the horror on the ground did indeed function chiefly as a "scientific demonstration," a technical display. In this case, the status of the Japanese victims is that of theatrical props, their fate a pure representation, a message, a writing, a sign. "In torture," Elaine Scarry writes, "it is in part the obsessive display of agency that permits one person's body to be translated into another person's voice, that allows real human pain to be converted into a regime's fiction of power" (*Body in Pain,* 18). In bombing Hiroshima and Nagasaki, the United States—like a torturer—converted human pain into the narrative of its power. William Lawrence of the *New York Times* (a war reporter not to be confused with William Laurence, the *Times* science writer on the Manhattan Project payroll) conceded as much when, according to Japanese reporters, "he 'extolled the obvious superiority of the bomb's potential' and [said] that 'its victims interested him only as proof of that might'" (Wyden, 320).

Science and Anger

Elaine Scarry opens *The Body in Pain* by announcing the three subjects that make up the book's single subject: "*first,* the difficulty of expressing physical pain; *second,* the political and perceptual complications that arise as a result of that difficulty; *third,* the nature of both material and verbal expressibility. . . . Physical pain has no voice, but when it at last finds a voice, it begins to tell a story, and the story that it tells is about the inseparability of these three subjects" (3). This brilliant thesis reminds us that, given the fracture between pain and its expression, it is a wonder we have any Hiroshima writing or Holocaust writing at all. We must therefore begin looking at atomic bomb literature as a speaking or writing in the face of violence not only to the body, the city, the landscape, the culture, but to language and expressibility itself. In the case of Hiroshima, the violence *to* expressibility took several forms that differed greatly for U.S. and Japanese writers. Deferring for a moment the interiorized difficulties of retrieval in *hibakusha* writing, I plan first to consider the ethical and psycho-political problems posed by exteriorized silencings, the U.S. Army's censorship of Japanese writing about Hiroshima.

Two books of Japanese accounts of Hiroshima published or reprinted in translation in the 1990s—Richard Minear's collection of the artistic memoirs and poetry of Tamiki Hara, Yōko Ōta, and Sankichi Tōge, and Dr. Michihiko Hachiya's *Hiroshima Diary*—remind us of the literal suppression of Japanese eyewitness accounts of the bombing by U.S. Army censorship during its occupation of Japan after the war. Peter Wyden explains:

> General MacArthur found it convenient to treat all aftereffects of the bomb as if they did not exist. After warning the Japanese press against publishing "inflammable" headlines and "needling" articles, he temporarily suspended two leading dailies, *Asahi* and *Nippon Times,* and on September 19 imposed a prior censorship on all media. As part of a new press code, the publication or broadcasting of all reports on A-bomb damage, including those on medical treatment, were unconditionally prohibited. (326)

Yōko Ōta was ordered by a U.S. Occupation intelligence officer ("a tall white American in his thirties" [Ōta, 138]) to eradicate her memories of the bombing: "I want you to forget your memories of the atomic bomb. America won't use the atomic bomb again, so I want you to forget the events in Hiroshima" (Ōta, 141). It was an absurd command: the memories of the blast were incised in the script of scars and keloids on the bodies of survivors, in their anemic and leukemic blood, and in their psyches. But the American may correctly have reckoned that writing of Hiroshima would survive the survivors. In his poem "August 6," Sankichi Tōge has the Hiroshima dead plead for remembrance with the survivors: "The stillness that reigned over the city of 300,000: / who can forget it? / In that hush / the white eyes of dead women and children / sent us / a soul-rending appeal: / who can forget it?" (306–7).

The U.S. interdiction of postwar Japanese testimony institutionalized a specific feature of the physical pain of torture—its shattering of language. The *hibakusha* were, in effect, deprived of voice twice: muted by the pain and trauma of the experience, they were then refused permission to speak of it. The disavowal of its effects is constitutive of the logic of war, according to Scarry: "While the central activity of war is injuring and the central goal in war is to out-injure the opponent, the fact of injuring tends to be absent from strategic and political descriptions of war" (12). While 70 to 80 percent of the U.S. public approved of the bombing of Hiroshima and Nagasaki, the material reality of those acts, the fact of injuring, was rigorously concealed and suppressed. Would the *Fortune* poll conducted in December 1945, which found 22.7 percent of respondents wishing that the United States had had the opportunity to drop "many more of them [atomic bombs] before Japan had a chance to surrender" (Dower, 54), have produced the same results if films and photos of burned bodies and the suffering dying had been presented to the U.S. public? The day after the first bomb was dropped, B-29s roared over the city, terrifying survivors, who were certain they were about to be strafed, only to learn much later from the newspapers (Ōta in Minear, 202) that the massive U.S. photographing, documenting, and data collecting had begun. Yet the nearly 100,000 feet of color film shot by Air Force film crews were classified "top secret" and buried in vaults for a quarter century because of "the medical aspects, the horror, the devastation it showed" (Wyden, 327).[6] For the benefit of the approving U.S. public, the government glorified the agency of the atomic bomb and rigidly disavowed and suppressed its material effects. In the process, Japanese suffering was denied voice and representation.

John Hersey was fortunate in his freedom: "He was at liberty to report what he saw in any way he might choose" (Sanders, *Hersey*, 41). His decision to opt for objective and factual journalistic writing was a professional decision that nonetheless reflected psychological and ideological pressures that set U.S. and Japanese accounts of the Hiroshima bombing apart, even when they corroborated the phenomenological details of what occurred on August 6, 1945. I link these pressures to what Elaine Scarry refers to as "the political and perceptual complications" (3) that result from the difficulty of expressing physical pain, and that in the case of U.S. and Japanese accounts of Hiroshima cluster around the nexus of agency and affect. Stated broadly, the nation's strong investment in a humanitarian self-image mandated strategies of reporting whose objectivity created the illusion of unsentimental rationality while deflecting tacit accusations (including self-accusations) of brutality. U.S. accounts had to resist perceived guilt for an act whose cruel impact, however politically rationalized, they were substantiating and documenting. Reports such as John Hersey's and Averill Liebow's enabled U.S. readers to defer confrontation with the emotions of Japanese survivors of the atomic bomb until the psychiatrist Robert Lifton's monumental study of *hibakusha* interviews, *Death in Life,* was published in 1967.

For Americans, John Hersey's clear-eyed objectivity and detached reportorial tone in *Hiroshima* possessed a twofold virtue and utility. It refused to manipulate readers' pity and guilt, and its objective tendency (which Hersey abandoned in his "Aftermath") belonged to a broader postwar U.S. strategy to assimilate Hiroshima quickly to a factitious orientation of "rational" policy and scientific research. However engaging, urbane, and humane ("When we saw the pitifully crippled and maimed we felt both guilt and shame" [Liebow, 208]), Averill Liebow's memoir, *Encounter with Disaster,* documents the instant and seamless transposition of the atomic bomb from one U.S. research project into another. "This unique opportunity may not again be offered until another world war," Colonel Ashley Oughterson wrote in the memo that initiated U.S. postwar research into radiation effects (Liebow, 36). Without missing a beat, the United States within weeks moved from using the atomic bomb to sending in scientific and medical teams to conduct massive research. Its initial aegis was the Joint Commission for the Investigation of the Effects of the Atomic Bomb in Japan (which for a time included a group from the Manhattan Project); later the Atomic Bomb Casualty Commission, or ABCC, took over the research (Lifton, 345).

The title of Liebow's memoir, *Encounter with Disaster,* announces how completely the violence of the U.S. act, the deliberate intention to destroy as much of a city and as many of its inhabitants in an instant of time as possible, was occluded by imagery of Hiroshima as a natural disaster like an earthquake, or a medical emergency like a plague. The language of Hiroshima dramatizes the fact that we have no word in English for a cataclysm (a "personal or public upheaval of unparalleled violence" [*Random House Dictionary*]) that is manmade and the product of human will and intention to injure and kill innumerable human bodies. It is as though the language itself had been unable to imagine such acts. As a result, a benign memoir like Liebow's medical diary of postwar U.S. research seems shocking in its unreflective hypocrisy as an "innocent" scientific project when put into dialogue with the suppressed anger of *hibakusha,* who felt they were used as guinea pigs. After suffering the mutilation of their bodies and psyches by the bomb, they were subjected to the secondary violence of ABCC invasiveness to draw blood, extract semen, measure keloids, photograph facial disfigurement, and dissect corpses.

There were early rumors that the findings of the ABCC would be used in further atomic weapons research: "*Habakusha* [*sic*] found it all too easy to look upon the entire effort as having the dual purpose of 'keeping secret' the nefarious things America had done while learning everything possible about

the effects of atomic bombs in order to prepare for future nuclear warfare"
(Lifton, 344). Sankichi Tōge's poem "Season of Flames" juxtaposes Hiroshima victims with the test animals of the 1946 atomic bomb test on Bikini:

> (Ah,
> we aren't fish,
> so we can't float silently, belly-up.
> The tens of thousands of tons of seawater
> that spouted into the air at Bikini
> were mirrored in the vacant eyes—eyes—eyes
> of the animals used in the test:
> pigs—
> sheep—
> monkeys.)
>
> (Tōge, 329)

Robert Lifton found *hibakusha* bitterness against the ABCC rife with imagery
of necrophilic desecration ("a morbid lust for corpses" [347]), accusations
of racism, and feelings of sexual violation and rape.[7] Sankichi Tōge contrasts
the castration of the *hibakusha* with the fecundity of the opulent ABCC,
which represents the city's prostitution, in his poem "Night":

> Ah, Hiroshima!
> Your night, whose erection the atomic bomb rendered sterile.
> My sperm lose their tails,
> don't reach the woman's womb.
> The lighted arch of the ABCC building,
> pregnant beneath the trees of Hijiyama Park
> on its glittering leasehold in the middle of Hiroshima—
> the taillights of the limousines that leave its womb,
> the rhythms of the New Mexican desert that fill the air—
>
> (350)

Hersey's "Aftermath" confirms *hibakusha's* feelings of sexual violation when
he reports how Reverend Tanimoto's young daughter Koko was placed on a
brightly lit stage at the ABCC clinic, was told to disrobe, and was then discussed by Japanese and U.S. medical personnel she could not see beyond the

lights: "Koko was so frightened and hurt by this experience that she was unable to tell anyone about it for twenty-five years" (149).

"A more persistent focus of resentment, bearing directly upon guinea pig imagery, has been the ABCC's policy of research without treatment," Lifton wrote in *Death in Life* (345). In a climate of desperate need for medical care and treatment in the immediate aftermath of the blast, U.S. researchers offered no treatment for atomic injuries even though they were dismayed by Japanese medical insufficiencies: "To us the treatment seemed deficient. . . . Transfusions in our sense were almost nonexistent. . . . The Japanese pharmaceutical industry had successfully reached the sulfapyridine production stage, but even this material was apparently not used in large quantities" [Liebow, 109]. Yōko Ōta desperately wished for medicines and food in the weeks after the blast, though none arrived: "Methods of treatment were determined, but then the stock of those medicines and injections immediately disappeared, even in doctors' offices. . . . Had huge trucks—loaded with medicine, injections, the equipment for various experiments, and nourishing food—come racing to us . . . Oh, how I hoped that well-meaning shipments would arrive at one village after another" (177).[8] Instead, *hibakusha* were coerced or pressured by Japanese authorities into offering their injured bodies and the corpses of their dead family members for U.S. research and autopsy:

> It is remarkable that the police control of the population is still firm. To obtain any given number of persons from any particular locality it has only been necessary to speak to the police chief, who obtains precisely what is requested at precisely the right time. The people who appear have been entirely docile, submit readily to questioning and examination, and seem grateful for the vitamin pills which are doled out after the examination. (Liebow, 138)

Liebow smugly explains that the multivitamin pills were used to give research subjects the illusion that they were receiving "treatment" for their injuries after examination: "We had been advised by our Japanese colleagues that custom required the physician to give every patient some type of treatment after examining him. . . . The vitamin pills were good-looking, would be entirely acceptable to the patients, and could certainly do them no harm" (Liebow, 70). Inmates at Hiroshima prison were obliged to produce semen samples and, like children, were rewarded with chocolate: "Colonel Mason had brought along a supply of chocolate bars, which were used as a reward for the men who cooperated" (Liebow, 168). The U.S. medical establishment's infantilization of *hibakusha,* bribing them with candy and placebos while refusing to address the monumental catastrophe of their care, belongs to a much larger U.S. adjustment in attitude toward the Japanese during the abrupt turning point between war and defeat marked by the atomic bombings. John Dower's impressive study of the role of racism, propaganda, and cruelty on both sides of the Pacific conflict notes that for Americans "the shrill racial rhetoric of the early 1940s revealed itself to be surprisingly adaptable" for domesticating demonic and demeaning prewar stereotypes of the Japanese after the war: "To the victors, the simian became a pet, the child a pupil, the madman a patient" (13). With memories of Japanese atrocities still vivid in memory, Americans like Liebow and Hersey who were suddenly obliged to work with the Japanese in some professional intimacy made rapid, complex, and flawed adjustments in attitude.

Even before he encounters Hiroshima on October 12, 1945, Averill Liebow—palpably afraid of Japanese anger and vengefulness—is comforted by encountering and translating a German eyewitness account by a Father Siemes called *Jesuit Report to the Holy See.* This document became an ur-text or pre-text with significant ideological ramifications for Averill Liebow's memoir and for the shape of John Hersey's entire project, since it inspired him to seek *hibakusha* interviewees in the Jesuit mission in Tokyo. The Jesuit report—speaking with the double authority of men of God who were themselves *hibakusha*—resolved the ethics of using nuclear weapons against civilians by blaming Japanese militarism for the disaster: "It seems logical that he who supports total war in principle cannot complain of a war against civilians" (Hersey, 90; Liebow, 83). Father Siemes then extrapolates an interpretation of Japanese behavior from this logic: "None of us in those days heard a single outburst against the Americans on the part of the Japanese, nor was there any evidence of a vengeful spirit. The Japanese suffered this terrible blow as part of the fortunes of war—something to be borne without complaint" (Liebow, 83). Both Liebow and Hersey might have been shocked to hear such feeling as Sankichi Tōge's troping of Japanese hatred with the intensity, heat, and immensity of the atomic bomb blast itself: "After that concentrated moment / of the explosion, / pure incandescent hatred / spreads out, boundless" (Tōge, "Flames," 311).

Hersey may reasonably have expected that the *hibakusha* friends and wards of the Jesuits would embody a similar apolitical view of their plight. He consequently represented the blast survivors he found through the Jesuit mission in Tokyo as largely deracinated—dehistoricized, without culture, without ideas or political views, chiefly materialist in their behavior and pursuits as they try to survive. Reverend Tanimoto's heroism remains so unconnected to his Christian principles or to any other ideology that when Hersey finally lets him speak for himself through a quoted letter at the end of the text, the effect is startling and dissonant. As he reports case after case of atomic bomb victims who died offering banzai to the emperor and singing patriotic anthems, a set of suppressed politicized stories strangely absent from Hersey's account break through Tanimoto's previously one-dimensional representation. The minister's account is now complicated with a conservative politics: "Yes, people of Hiroshima died manly in the atomic bombing, believing that it was for Emperor's sake" (Hersey, 89). Yōko Ōta, in contrast, interweaves a narrative of political thinking throughout her account, picturing her young self in secret rebellion against military ideology with her friend Ayako Saeki ("She was more of a romantic than I, but she criticized the war with a cool eye" [209]). Her picture of two young feminists resisting the fanatical patriotism of their world is unimaginable in Hersey's picture of Japan. Ōta's sublation of the war into an apotheosized "cosmic phenomenon . . . with truly fearsome power, with truly fearsome sadism" (211) is not escapism but a sardonic mock-alibi: "And this huge war itself— perhaps it wasn't something that some human beings had started against other human beings? Otherwise it was too tragic, too horrifying" (211).

Liebow's and Hersey's experiences with *hibakusha* generally confirmed Father Siemes's assertion of Japanese fatalism and passivity, and Liebow especially was relieved to find that even those horribly burned "seemed entirely docile and showed no evidence of hostility, but rather a submissive courteousness." (109). Yōko Ōta could have illuminated for him the profound abjection that monumental injury, disfigurement, and material dispossession confers on victims. In turn, she notes, an intuitive superiority accrues to nonvictims: "From the first, the average person treated the injured, from whom he differed only in not being injured, almost as if they had always been dirty beggars. . . . I could not help being struck both by this psychology and also by the psychology whereby victims as victims became absolutely servile, as if they had always been pathetic creatures" (217). Hersey, too, reports largely passive and accepting Japanese attitudes: "A surprising number of the people of Hiroshima remained more or less indifferent about the ethics of using the bomb" (89). He quotes Mrs. Nakamura as saying, "It was war and we had to expect it" (89), and Dr. Fujii as telling the Jesuit Father Kleinsorge, "*Da ist nichts zu machen.* There's nothing to be done about it'" (89). But Hersey concedes that many people also shared Dr. Sasaki's hatred: "'I see . . . that they are holding a trial for war criminals in Tokyo just now. I think they ought to try the men who decided to use the bomb and they should hang them all'" [89]).

Liebow and Hersey credit neither the habits of self-censorship bred by the suppressions of the wartime regime ("We had reached the point of wearing stiff masks over our ears, our eyes, our mouths; we had lost completely the ability to hear, to see, to speak," Ōta writes [210]) nor the politicized social constraints that muzzled *hibakusha*'s fury toward Americans. "The fact is that when Japanese open their mouths to communicate with foreigners, they are at a loss for words," Yōko Ōta writes. "When two parties do not understand each other, how can you expect the other party to understand either silence or offensive candor?" (257). If and when *hibakusha* speak, through small apertures that permit "the dark crying out with one voice: / resentment, regret, rage, curses, hatred, pleas, wails" (Tōge, "Landscape," 355), the effect is a flood of affect: "a pinprick, and it would all come gushing out— / the emotions!" (Tōge, "In the Streets," 352). Sankichi Tōge's own poetic anger achieves rhetorical urgency through the device of iterated questions: "Why must you suffer like this? / *Why must you suffer like this?* / For what reason? / *For what reason?* / You girls don't know how desperate your condition, / how far transformed from the human" (Tōge, "In the Makeshift Aid Station," 315).

The answers Americans gave these questions in newspaper interviews did not give *hibakusha* a satisfactory response. Yōko Ōta quotes Colonel Oughterson's equipoised two-wrongs-make-a-right argument: "Pearl Harbor was an unexpected tragedy for the United States. The atomic bombs on Hiroshima and Nagasaki were unexpected tragedies for Japan. It began in unforeseen tragedy and ended in unforeseen tragedy. I hope that we all cooperate from now on so that unforeseen tragedies do not arise for either side" (260). In his long, complex poem "When Will That Day Come?" Tōge has the poetic voice teach the corpse of a young girl the history behind her fate, a political etiology she could not have known and that has nothing to do with her ("There was so little time / between July 16—the test in New Mexico— / and the day of the Soviet entry!" [360]). Richard Minear notes that

"Tōge never once writes 'United States' or 'America' or 'American'" in his *Poems of the Atomic Bomb;* "Yet the United States is the unspoken subtext of virtually every poem in the collection" (295). Tōge is especially angry that Americans, in their fascination with the scientific effects of radiation—for example, the roses burned onto the back of a young woman through the pattern of her dress (Liebow, 155)—are insensitive to the searing pain of the flesh beneath. He therefore has the same radiation rays ignite a cosmic auto-da-fé:

> The hot rays of uranium
> that shouldered the sun aside
> burn onto a girl's back
> the flowered pattern of thin silk,
> set instantaneously ablaze
> the black garb of the priest—
> August 6, 1945:
> that midday midnight
> man burned the gods
> at the stake.
> (Tōge, "Flames," 312)

Testimony

The strength of U.S. and Japanese accounts of Hiroshima, when taken together, is their corroboration of the phenomenological details of the event in a way that makes the "facts" of the cataclysm indisputable. In his foreword to the 1995 edition of Dr. Michihiko Hachiya's *Hiroshima Diary,* John Dower collects a list of phenomena that he calls "the familiar iconography of the immediate aftermath of the atomic bombing":

The stunning flash (*pika*) of the bomb, followed by a colossal blast (*don*) that shattered buildings kilometers away. Nakedness or seminakedness, from the blast stripping clothing away. Eerie silence. People walking in lines with their hands outstretched and skin peeling off—like automatons, dream-walkers, scarecrows, a line of ants. Corpses "frozen by death while in the full action of flight." A dead man on a bicycle. A burned and blinded horse. Survivors in crowded ruined buildings, lying in vomit, urine, and feces. (viii)

U.S. and Japanese accounts converge not only on the pictorial content of the images but on a discontinuous and ruptured perceptual mode as well. Yet the vignettes or episodic narratives of their testimonies are conditioned by important psychological and ideological differences that are worth dilating. These differences flow from—and exceed—the crude divisions between first- and secondhand reporting, journalism and personal memoir, linear and retrospective narration, survival epic and social critique, to reveal the "perceptual and political complications" of speaking pain that Elaine Scarry announces.

In *Hiroshima* Hersey does not infantilize his Japanese protagonists, although he domesticates them in other ways for the benefit of his American readership. His decision to create six character vignettes—a method of reporting he had developed for his war correspondence—was reinforced by his reading of Thornton Wilder's *Bridge of San Luis Rey* just before he arrived in Hiroshima. The survivors he met through the Tokyo Jesuit mission were peculiarly homogeneous with respect to class and culture—bourgeois, respectable, several with Western and Christian orientations that were comfortable and familiar to John Hersey, who had grown up in China in a missionary family. American readers would have little trouble identifying with Father Kleinsorge, the German Jesuit missionary; Reverend Tanimoto, the pastor of Hiroshima Methodist Church, who was educated at Emory University in Atlanta; Dr. Fujii, who within the year after the bombing hung out his new shingle "in English, in honor of the conquerors" (78); and the entrepreneurial Dr. Sasaki, who prospered into a rich man after the war ("His life was insured for a hundred million yen; he was insured against malpractice for three hundred million yen; he drove a white BMW" (108). Following gender typologies congenial to U.S. 1940s culture, Hersey portrays these professional men as heroically active, while the two female protagonists, Miss Sasaki, an unmarried secretary, and Mrs. Nakamura, the destitute widowed mother, are passive victims in need of care. Both in material condition and in the subjective preoccupations imputed to them, Hersey's survivors hark back to prototypes of early generic realism: the enterprising survivors of shipwrecks, plagues, and other tides of fortune that people the writings of Hersey's journalistic predecessor, Daniel Defoe. Like Defoe, who made *homo economicus* the protagonist of the realistic novel, Hersey portrays his figures as having a "practical turn of mind," like the shrewd Jesuits who sent an ill and traumatized Father Kleinsorge to the police station to file a property damage claim within twenty-four hours of the bomb drop (54). Yōko Ōta, on the other hand, tells of the cringing social shame of accepting papers that certified her family for relief aid: "As if branding us definitively with the mark of victims of the atomic bomb, these small, thin sheets of paper seared our hearts; they made us miserable" (218). In an even more cruel instance, the Korean Bok-Su Shin, her husband and children killed, is denied compensation because, she is told, "'We cannot give anything to Koreans.' . . . My husband and two children had died because we were Japanese. Who had suddenly decided we were aliens?" (Cook and Cook, 391). Victimization had many cultural valences for *hibakusha*.

For both U.S. and Japanese reports, the complex set of overdetermined—and sometimes conflicting—conditions that contour the shape of the writing also influenced the philosophical reflections it enabled. Not surprisingly, U.S. and Japanese testimonies served both the ideological and the aesthetic expectations and needs of their readerships. Hersey's factualism not only underwrote the United States' ongoing treatment of Hiroshima as a scientific and military event with material and logistical disruptions as the predominant interest; it also earned political credibility and literary legitimation by allying itself with genres of writing (journalism) and modes of poetics (modernism) that themselves had formed a powerful alliance in early twentieth-century literature. While Hersey's account produced the most vivid and powerful representations of the blast's physical impact and destructiveness, the revealing subjectivity of Japanese testimonies (with characteristics of such Japanese fictional forms as the "I-novel" [Lifton, 399]) evoke much more profoundly Hiroshima's psychological and spiritual devastation. Hersey, who begins by positioning his figures as they were moments before the blast, dramatizes how an explosion reduces human bodies to stark matter, to be violently hurled about and damaged like a thing. He tells how "something picked [Mrs. Nakamura] up and she seemed to fly into the next room over the raised sleeping platform, pursued by parts of her house" (8). Dr. Sasaki, on his way to the lab with a blood specimen for a Wasserman test for syphilis, is stripped of his accoutrements: "The glasses he was wearing flew off his face; the bottle of blood crashed against one wall; his Japanese slippers zipped out from under his feet" (14). But Tamiki Hara, writing a requiem in 1949—two years before his suicide—metaphorically extends the material damage of the atomic blast into a realm of the soul: "Humanity is all like glass shattered into smithereens. . . . The world is broken. . . . Always inside me there is the sound of something exploding" (33). Yōko Ōta, desperate to flee the riverbed on which survivors began gathering right after the blast, explains, "I did not want my soul damaged more than it already had been by seeing the dismal spectacle of the city of corpses. If for some time I were to watch the city as it putrefied street by street, my heart might be injured, my very soul ruined" (208). Hersey too represents spiritual damage, but he does so in the form of the "objective correlative" borrowed from modernistic poetry: "He began at once to behave like an old man; two months later his hair was white" (34).

Hersey's most famous description of a painful inundation of the body by crushing material achieves its ironic effect for what it suppresses—the ambiguously overwritten materiality of books: "The bookcases right behind her swooped forward and the contents threw her down, with her left leg horribly twisted and breaking underneath her. There, in the tin factory, in the first moment of the atomic age, a human being was crushed by books" (16). Books are rigorously reduced to injurious and lethal material matter here; no connection is permitted to a later description of the convalescent Miss Sasaki reading Western fiction, a Japanese translation of Maupassant (69). Indeed, although at least two of Hersey's survivors are reading when they are struck by the blast—Dr. Fujii is reading the Osaka *Asahi* (newspaper) and Father Kleinsorge the Jesuit journal *Stimmen der Zeit* (*Voices of the Time*)—we are not told what they read or how they read. Hersey thereby depoliticizes the figures and denatures them culturally while consolidating them into a more generic and flat character. In contrast, the first-person memoirs of the Japanese poets Tamiki Hara and Yōko Ōta invoke Western writing in ways that stimulate reflections on the function of literary genre in *hibakusha* testimony. Hersey's rigorous suppression of the conventions of the Gothic in his reportage is highlighted by Hara's spontaneous allusion to the nightmare world of Poe: "Each time I entered the room that looked out onto the garden, there had come floating into my mind, unbidden, the words, 'The Fall of the House of Usher'" (48). The ruined materiality of a city in which nature has been stripped of the cultural associations that gave it "charm" (48) makes nature paradoxically unnatural: Gothic, morbid, cold, leached of vitality and living warmth. The very materiality that anchors Hersey's narrative represents to Hara one of the city's ontological wounds, its stripping, by the damage, of the cultural and human endowments that transformed it into a city, a home. Yōko Ōta makes literary allusion to the politicized naturalism of Maxim Gorky when she invokes lines ("I am cast out, with no home; / my clothes are all in tatters" [155]) that inject powerful tropes of class into her material dispossession by the blast ("I came back, a beggar, to this village that was once mine, where I no longer have a home of my own" [154]). She further tropes as a personal violence, a rapelike assault, the way the blast literally sheared from her back her silk white-on-blue nightdress, fastened with an obi: "Those clothes had all been sliced through in back as if by a sharp knife" (155).

Hersey's account was commissioned by the *New Yorker* as journalism, not art, although in the wake of Ernest Hemingway's transformation of the objective, stripped style of journalism into clean, dry, hard modernistic prose, the boundary between journalism and art had begun to blur. War journalism later in the twentieth century abandoned cold objectivity in the interest of reproducing in the style of narration itself the psychological atmosphere of combat; Michael Herr's agitated, hallucinogenic voice reporting on Vietnam for *Esquire* in the 1960s is a premier example. But Hersey's *Hiroshima,* removed in time, space, language, and culture from the destruction—written a year later, from the accounts of others filtered through translation—leaches emotional atmosphere and psychological affect twice from the story: first by removing it from description and again by removing it from narrative voice. The result is a flattening of experience into the dimensions of verbal diorama:

> He was the only person making his way into the city; he met hundreds and hundreds who were fleeing, and every one of them seemed to be hurt in some way. The eyebrows of some were burned off and skin hung from their faces and hands. . . . Some were vomiting as they walked. Many were naked or in shreds of clothing. On some undressed bodies, the burns had made patterns—of undershirt straps and suspenders and, on the skin of some women (since white repelled the heat from the bomb and dark clothes absorbed it and conducted it to the skin) the shapes of flowers they had had on their kimonos. (29)

Hersey's details are corroborated by other *hibakusha* accounts. But the curious slowing of the description to explain the thermal science of the "masks" or patterned burn marks betrays his own fascination with the physics of the damage. At the same time, Hersey's allusions to being hurt and in pain ("because of the pain") are given no voice in this passage, and he evokes one of the iconic symptoms of *hibakusha,* the "expressionless face" of survivors—"Almost all had their heads bowed, looked straight ahead, were silent, and showed no expression whatever" (29)—without being able to account for its interiority.

Tamiki Hara's description of his first walk through the city after the blast gives oblique but poignant voice to the effects of the devastation both in the reproduction of voices he hears and in his own paralyzed inability to respond to what he hears:

> Then we hurried briskly down the center of the road. From the other side of a flattened building came a voice crying, "Mister, please!" We turned, and a girl whose face was bloody came walking toward us; she was crying. Looking absolutely horror-stricken, she followed us for all she was worth, calling, "Help!" We went on a while and met an old woman standing squarely in our way in the road, weeping like a child: "The house is burning! The house is burning!" (48)

Hara's disjointed telling of a journey filled with ghostly apparitions that appear and recede without making a connection reflects his early writing of childhood fairy tales ("Japanese critics use the German term *Märchen*" [26]). But he also evokes, quite deliberately, the dreamlike juxtapositions of surrealism. Instead of giving us the realism we find in Hersey, Hara precisely recreates the feeling of unreality that permeated the event. *Hibakusha* accounts also try to restore an interiorized subjectivity—how it felt to be seeing, and how it felt to be seen—to some of Hersey's other iconic sights. The "expressionless face" Hersey alludes to is discussed by both Hara and Ōta, although both enliven the face with other expressive signs. Hara first saw this face on a middle-aged woman squatting, slumped over, next to some shrubs: "Wholly devoid of life, her face seemed even as I watched to become infected with something. This was my first encounter with such a face. But thereafter I was to see countless faces more grotesque still" (48). Ōta diagnoses the infection of this "expressionless face," which she uses both literally and as a trope throughout her memoir: "It is not, I think, something that develops after one contracts radiation sickness; it has been in evidence ever since August 6," she writes. She then delves inside to give it the etiology of trauma, to describe it as "a state of mind" that resulted when "the shadow of death crossed before our very eyes, returned, passed on." The "expression-less face" is the face of a dead self that accompanies and at times occludes the living self of the *hibakusha*: "Alongside one's live self stood one's dead self. There are no words to describe it" (253).[9]

The iconic image of nakedness is another picture that *hibakusha* attempt to humanize and endow with subjectivity. The blast literally blew clothes off people's bodies: "To my surprise I discovered that I was completely naked. How odd! Where were my drawers and undershirt?" (Hachiya, 1). The recognition produces an immediate sense of social vulnerability. As Dr. Hachiya resumes his hospital rounds in "dirty pants, patched shirt, and looking worse than the chief of a hobo village," he realizes that his clothed state embarrasses his unclothed patients: "Here was an old lady, on the verge of death, in nothing but an undershirt, and a horribly burned young man, lying completely naked on a pallet" (Hachiya, 52). In "When Will That Day Come?" Sankichi Tōge explores the ontological dimension of nakedness, the dehumanization of the naked corpses and the naked wounded, by transforming the reflexive gesture of abashment, the averted eye and averted word, into its exact opposite: the painfully and sharply focused stare. As the poet's stare penetrates both the body and heart of the dead young girl, it also penetrates the heart of the implied observer and implied reader.

The girl in Tōge's poem is one of the unlucky schoolgirls clearing the streets for firebreaks. But unlike the Keloid Girls or Hiroshima Maidens who became Norman Cousins's poster children, this young girl lies dead and forgotten. "There is no one to cover over the shame of your burned pants. / And of course no one to wipe away the mark of your agony clinging there" (363). In a deliberately perverse maneuver that allows his text to perform the violating effect of the blast, Tōge first gives the girl an intact body and the dignity of clothes:

> The other corpses are all naked and raw red;
> why is it that you alone are clothed,
> even have one shoe on?
> Above a cheek that is slightly sooty, your hair is full,
> and neither burns nor blood are to be seen—

Then he tears away the back of her pants and shows her body humiliated by the blast—all the while having the gentle address redress her with dignity and compassion:

except that the back of your cotton culottes, only the back,
is burned clear through,
exposing your round bottom;
forced out in your death agonies, a bit of excrement
sticks there, dried;
with shade nonexistent, the rays of the midday sun pick it out.

(358)

The sun's spotlight on the spot of excrement becomes the poet's brutal focus on what will not be talked about, what will not be faced, in order to discompose, to restore embarrassment and painful emotion to this restored, modern city branded with the names of its conquerors. Those stupidly useless firebreaks the schoolgirls were forced to clear ("Your beloved home was pulled down by the ropes of the firebreak-clearers, / and you four rented a hut in the eastern part of town" [Tōge, 359]) unwittingly prepared the fine bouvelard MacArthur named for himself ("And could you have thought / that the street leading to this square in our beloved Hiroshima would be widened out, / renamed MacArthur Boulevard?" [362]).

Nakedness is a transitory vulnerability, but survivors of the atomic bomb's radiation lived, and continue to live, in a permanent vulnerability. Yōko Ōta's ontological trope of the *hibakusha* as a living self always walking with a dead self serves as a figure for radiation sickness and radiation's residual effects. Survivors had to internalize the weapon, to enfold it into their bodies where it would interminably make their lives unsafe, and mock their putative survival. The bomb's colossal power first *injured* and then *insulted* with a horrific psychic betrayal. Tamiki Hara celebrates the tremendous relief of survival: "I felt, despite everything, that I was now safe. What had hung over our heads for so long, what in time surely had to come, had come. There was nothing left to fear: I myself had survived" (Hara, 49). But the horizon is already filled with the black rain that becomes the symbol of radiation's poisoning of the population. The insidious nature of the bomb continues its warfare against civilians long after military surrender and the return of peace. The atomic bomb dilates the concept of total warfare by extending its lethal range to civilians *temporally* into their futures and *intimately* into the most personal recesses of their postwar bodies, their sexuality, their family lives. In this sense, the atomic bomb becomes paradigmatic for materially exposing the great fiction that war is stoppable and announcing what has always been true—for veterans, for trauma victims, for war widows and orphans—that the effects of war are *unstoppable*.

Within weeks of the blast its uncanny aftereffects were felt. An uninjured husband discovers that he too has the radiation sickness that already afflicts his wife, and realizes they will die about the same time: "War has finally begun to kill us off in pairs, husbands and wives." Within a week he is dead and his wife "died quietly two days later" (Ōta, 163–64). The figures on radiation sickness are disputed and possibly indeterminable, and Peter Wyden notes that "the controversy over what constitutes realistic radiation tolerances still rages today" (326). Wyden characterizes as "conservative" the estimates of Stuart Finch, director of research at the Radiation Effects Research Foundation in Hiroshima, who claimed 20,000 deaths from radiation at the time of the blast, followed by another 20,000 radiation injuries (Wyden, 326). Both Dr. Hachiya and Yōko Ōta reported a shocking epidemic of fatal radiation sickness in the months after the blast. "And it was after August 24 that people listed as slightly injured, who had only scratches, and people wholly without either cuts or burns began to die one after the other. Even in my small village, three or four people died each day" (Ōta, 170). The illness began with mild flulike symptoms for many, and for many transmogrified into gruesome death. Dr. Hachiya's diary contains anguished observations: "Miss Kobayashi had died with massive hemorrhage in her abdominal cavity and Mr. Onomi with profuse bleeding from nose and rectum. Had hemorrhage also caused the sudden death of Mrs. Chodo and the death of Miss Nishii?" (139). The macabre deaths inspired terror in survivors as they uncovered symptoms in their own bodies. Ōta reports the derangement of one of Dr. S.'s patients when he discovers red spots on her arm: "She let out a shriek. Then she collapsed against him. Frantic she asked, 'When will I die? Doctor, tell me, when will I die? . . . Everyone dies—every last person who was in Hiroshima that day will die, all of them'" [Ōta, 161]). The reassurances Dr. S. gives the girl are a lie: she died within a week from massive hemmorrhage.[10]

The temporal interminability of radiation warfare has a profound effect on the temporality of *hibakusha* narrative. Like Holocaust survivors, *hibakusha* are marked by what Robert Lifton calls "the death imprint"—a psychic inability to expel the presence of death's macabre actuality, which gives survivors a "lifelong sense of vulnerability to the same grotesque death" (481).[11] Yōko Ōta tells that she wrote her memoir in the frenzy of an imagined death sentence:

I wrote *City of Corpses* between August 1945 and the end of November 1945. I was living at the time on a razor's edge between death and life, never knowing from moment to moment when death would drag me over to its side. After August 15 . . . alarming symptoms of atomic bomb sickness suddenly began to appear among those who had survived August 6, and people died one after the other. I hurried to finish *City of Corpses*. If like the others I too was dying, then I had to hurry to finish it. (147)

Ōta gives the painfully subjective obverse of the Joint Commission's checklist for radiation effect symptoms: "Nausea; Vomiting; Cramps; Diarrhea; Malaise; Anorexia; Gingivitis; Pharyngitis; Purpura; Epilation; Skin Pigmentation; Absence of sweating; Menstruation" (Liebow, 72). Checking for symptoms becomes for *hibakusha* "the discovery of a new hell"—an obsessive tugging at the hair to count the strands that come out, a fearsome feeling for loose teeth, a terrified search for the dreaded red spots or petechiae on the skin and mucous membranes. "Terrified of the spots that may appear suddenly, at any moment, I examine the skin of my arms and legs dozens of times, squinting with the effort," Ōta writes. "Small red mosquito bites I mark with ink; when, with time, the red bites fade, I am relieved they were bites and not spots" (153). *Hibakusha* are forced to become amateur doctors and scientists to cope with their contaminated bodies. Yōko Ōta obsessively collects and records scientific and medical information on radiation sickness, carefully copying the list of "standard symptoms" out of the *Chūgoku Shimbun* and transcribing the interim reports of internists from Kyushu University Medical School (158–59). Ōta's unease never disappeared. When Robert Lifton interviewed her fifteen months before her death of heart failure at the age of 60, "she quickly told me that she had just had a tooth pulled and 'since I experienced the atomic bomb, there is always a danger that the bleeding will not stop and that leukemia might develop'" (402). Even in late middle age, Ōta feared that the atomic bomb might kill her yet.[12]

The Poetics of Pain

The objectivity of Hersey's *Hiroshima* gave it solid credibility with a U.S. readership positioned to accept the facts if they put little rhetorical pressure on its conscience. In the United States, the reception of *Hiroshima* became an event, a sensation. "Albert Einstein was reported to have ordered a thousand copies and Bernard Baruch five hundred. The Book-of-the-Month Club sent free copies to its members" (Sanders, *Hersey Revisited,* 19). But the U.S. Army of Occupation effectively kept Hersey's *Hiroshima* from being distributed in Japan. Even though Hersey's book was in some sense a ventriloquism, a speaking *for* the *hibakusha* rather than letting them speak for themselves, its postwar censorship in Japan still deprived atomic survivors of a mirror in which they might have seen their suffering acknowledged. Hersey introduces a literal image with ironic implications for troping his own narrative: Dr. Sasaki, his glasses blown off his face by the blast, borrows an ill-focused pair from a wounded nurse for a month (25). Hersey's second-hand memoir could be figured as a depiction of Hiroshima through glasses borrowed from the wounded.[13] It illustrates the inverse relationship between *seeing* and *speaking* that governs the writing of trauma. Hersey was able to write more readily because he did *not see;* those who *saw* were afflicted with spiritually traumatized eyes—the psychic counterpart of *hibakusha* literally blinded by looking at the sky at the moment of the blast. External and internal obstacles conspired to mutilate and destroy speech of the experience. Yōko Ōta describes how "I hadn't even a single sheet of paper, not one pencil. . . . I got yellowed paper, peeled from the *shōji* of the house I was staying in . . . toilet paper, two or three pencils" (147). Yet even when she had supplied herself with writing implements, the exercise of writing itself made Ōta ill. "I have to call up from memory in order to write, and I become ill; I become nauseated; my stomach starts to throb with pain" (150). Some *hibakusha,* especially those who were children at the time of the blast, were unwilling or unable to remember, their amnesia and silence become a symptomatic language. Yasuko Kimura, who was nine years old in August 1945, refused to think or talk about her experience for thirty years: "I abhorred the word *Hiroshima.* If it came up, I wouldn't mention that I had family members who'd died there. On August 6 I refused to watch television and never read the newspapers" (Cook and Cook, 398). The poet Sankichi Tōge dramatizes this mutism in the trope of bodies mutilated in their expressive and affective organs:

> You girls—
> weeping even though there is no place for tears to come from;
> crying out even though you have no lips to shape the words;

> reaching out even though there is no skin on your fingers to
>   grasp with—
> you girls.
>
> (Tōge, "At the Makeshift Aid Station," 315)

A poignant reversal of the traumatic relationship between *seeing* and *speaking* occurred to Yoshito Matsushige, a photographer for the Hiroshima daily newspaper *Chūgoku Shimbun,* who had his camera with him as he wandered unhurt through the streets of the city after the blast. Torn between a professional impulse to photograph and a humane prohibition against exploiting the victims' dreadful exposure and pain, Matsushige was literally incapable of shooting much of what he saw. The five famous photographs he took are eerily chaste—the angles of the shot veiling faces, occluding expression, avoiding wounds. Yet in explaining why he could not photograph, he can tell what he saw: "People's bodies were all swollen up. Their skin, burst open, was hanging down in rags. . . . I put my hand on my camera, but it was such a hellish apparition that I couldn't press the shutter" (Cook and Cook, 392). He saw a skeletal trolley car full of naked burned bodies near the epicenter of the blast. "I thought about taking a picture. I even put my hand on the camera. But it was so hideous I couldn't do it" (Cook and Cook, 394). When he does take one of his five photographs of that day, "the viewfinder of the camera was clouded with my tears" (Cook and Cook, 393). Yōko Ōta tells how *hibakusha* must split their *eyes,* their vision, in two in order to be able to *speak.* Walking through the city of corpses, Ōta is criticized by her sister: "You're really looking at them—how can you? I can't stand and look at corpses." Ōta retorts, "I'm looking with two sets of eyes—the eyes of a human being and the eyes of a writer" (205). The *hibakusha* writer must *speak* what *is not fit* for human beings to *see.* Her doubled vision with one flinching and one unflinching eye carries the emotional and ethical risk that *hibakusha* writing will intensify rather than meliorate the pain of the experience. Confronting survivors with mirrors of their suffering and disfigurement can magnify rather than alleviate their heartsickness. Looking together into a mirror to see their faces for the first time after the blast, Ōta blurts out to her sister, "'What a face! All puffed up and ghastly!'" (237). Her sister is shocked and hurt. The ghastliness Ōta describes—more powerful than Hersey's in its emotional and psychic dilation—has arguably troubled her reception by both Japanese and Western readers and critics.[14]

But Ōta's decision not to flinch lets her participate in an extraordinary poetic maneuver that is rare in U.S. reports though frequent in *hibakusha* language: she describes atomic bomb burn injuries in culinary tropes, in images of roasting or grilled vegetables, baked goods, foods. Sister's "ghastly" face is "swollen up like a pumpkin" (183) and "puffed up like a round loaf of bread" (193). She calls the "eerie color" of Gin-chan, ill with radiation sickness, "opaque like that of roasted eggplant" (158), and she describes the "broil-like burns" "peeling off in strips, like the skins of roasted potatoes" (199, 188). The images of grilled flesh are naturalistically reinforced by survivors who remember making their first meals after the flash from squashes and cucumbers roasted naturally in the ground or on the vine by the heat of the blast. The blast occurred in August, at harvesttime, and Hersey tells how Father Kleinsorge "noticed a pumpkin roasted on the vine. He and Father Cieslik tasted it and it was good" (40). Other *hibakusha* use Ōta's culinary tropes to even more shocking effect. Dr. Hachiya heard reports that some fire reservoirs were found "filled to the brim with dead people who looked as though they had been boiled alive" (19). The photographer Yoshito Matsushige uses culinary language literally rather than figuratively—"they were still burning from below and the fat of the bodies was bubbling up and sputtering as it burned. That was the only time I've seen humans roasting" (Cook and Cook, 393). The troping of burned bodies as roasted vegetables or meat evokes a powerful image that transposes the atomic bomb from its antiseptic genesis as a product of rational calculation and science into a horrific and primitive cannibalism that transforms the U.S. military into a colossal and sadistic maw cooking and roasting its human victims. The Japanese victims implicitly imagine the Americans not as cerebral physicists in white lab coats but as cruel man-eaters roasting their live victims: "They had all been burned in precisely the same way, as if the men who bake *sembei* had roasted them all in those iron ovens" (Ōta, 188).

However justified by the appearance of the burn victims and burned corpses, their description as grilled or cooked food is itself a discursive violence that afflicts both victims and observers. Observers of blast victims were terrorized by the sight of humans who appeared organic rather than human. The swelling of injured bodies made them lose their anthropomorphic shapes and look inflated effigies of themselves, rubber dolls ("Eyes and mouths all swollen shut and limbs, too, as swollen as they could possibly be, they looked like huge ugly rubber dolls" [Ōta, 205]) or wooden dolls ("Those young men were wooden dolls wrapped in rags; only their faces showed any life" [227]). An even more frightening product of the burns was the sloughing of sheets or "rags" of skin as though bodies had suddenly doubled, were growing a second body or form, like the molting of reptiles or the shedding of human clothing. Reverend Tanimoto's most violent revulsion occurred when he "reached down and took a woman by the hands, but her skin slipped off in huge, glovelike pieces" (Hersey, 45). Hersey reports that Tanimoto "was so sickened by this that he had to sit down for a moment" (45). The swelling and shedding of dead, dying, and living bodies produced a horrible sensation of their duplicating or multiplying matter, as though they threatened to clog the element of the *other* living.

Observers of the bomb's immediate effects are implicated doubly in the dehumanization of the dead and dying, and of the living who are no longer recognizably human. First they are assaulted and terrorized by the inhuman vision of persons stripped of their human morphology and invested, literally, in a monstrous form. By writing that "one might have thought one was in the world of surrealistic paintings" (58), Tamiki Hara grasps precisely the ontological violence of the formal hybridities that transgress species or orders of being in surrealist art.[15] But eventually the violent ontological distortions produced by the Hiroshima blast are transferred onto the perceptions of the observer: in failing to recognize injured victims as human, the viewer of the destruction constructs them as monsters or hybrids. A particular form of this hybridity makes human form undecidable and makes injured and dead bodies indistinguishable with respect to gender. "You couldn't tell men from women," Bok-Su Shin remembers. "If there were breasts, that was a woman" (Cook and Cook, 390). Tamiki Hara reports a similar need to refer to secondary sex characteristics—long hair, for example—to determine the gender of some survivors (52). Yōko Ōta reports an early newspaper casualty count that lists as dead 21,125 males, 21,277 females, and 3,773 bodies labeled "gender unknown" (169).

Even when gender is not blurred by injuries, specific identity often is, and Sankichi Tōge uses unrecognizability ("so transformed that even your wife and children would not have known you" [339]) to evoke the dehumanization of victims: "a group of schoolgirls . . . / bellies swollen like drums . . . / skin half-gone, hairless, impossible to tell one from the other" (306). Survivors report that the disfigurement of burn victims was so severe that "at a glance you couldn't tell whether you were looking at them from in front or in back" (quoted in Lifton, 27). Michiko Yamaoka, one of Norman Cousins's Hiroshima Maidens, reports the shock of first realizing that she herself was unrecognizable: "I called her name, but she didn't respond. My face was so swollen she couldn't tell who I was. Finally, she recognized my voice. She said, 'Miss Yamaoka, you look like a monster!' That's the first time I heard that word" (Cook and Cook, 386). Yamaoka's agony of disfigurement does not end with her physical healing. "Keloids covered my face, my neck. . . . One eye was hanging down. I was unable to control my drooling because my lip had been burned off. . . . People threw stones at me and called me Monster" (ibid.). Her mother, who had searched for her in the city's rubble and rescued her with a stretcher, later confessed to her daughter that she had tried to kill her: "Once she told me she tried to choke me to death. If a girl has terrible scars, a face you couldn't be born with, I understand that even a mother could want to kill her child" (ibid.).

The dysmorphized condition of the dead and injured ruptures one of the most intimate intersubjectivities of social bonding: the recognition of one's own, of one's kind. Memoirs abound with quests to find loved ones that end in metonymy—the finding only of a material sign. Tamiki Hara describes "an encounter beyond tears" when his brother, taking a cartful of household goods through the West Parade Ground on the way to Nigitsu, spotted an unrecognizable corpse wearing a familiar pair of yellow shorts that were fastened with "an unmistakable belt. The body was that of my nephew Fumihiko" (57). Bok-Su Shin and her husband were given bones that they realized could not possibly belong to their children: "We were given two yellow envelopes. When we opened them, my husband said, 'These are from the backbones of adults.' Our kids were seven and four. So we released those bones into the river" (Cook and Cook, 390). Elsewhere Hara tells "the story of the man who, searching for his wife, lifted up the corpses of several hundred women in order to examine their faces; not a single one still had a wristwatch on" (77). This story achieves mythical resonance as the man—like Orpheus seeking his wife in the underworld—harrows hell in search of his wife. When her skeleton is not at the school where she taught, he checks every corpse on the road between his house and the school, and every burn ward in the area. The wristwatch that might have identified her does not turn up, since all wristwatches were blown off. The man's quest becomes Sisyphean and circular. "Then, having spent three days and three nights examining corpses and burn victims to the point of utter revulsion, N. started all over again, going once more to the charred ruins of the girls' school at which his wife had taught" (Hara, 60). Many families found the belongings of their loved ones, but no trace of their bodies, and the Hiroshima Peace Museum exhibits a collection of artifacts—bags, note-books, wristwatches, purses—that survived, severed from their owners, who were never found.

The best material sign that identifies the disfigured or dysmorphized body as human, as alive, and as individual is its voice. Many *hibakusha* accounts report the eerie silence of the hours after the blast, when it seemed that victims were deprived of voice except in its most visceral expression ("Those with burns vomited continually, and the sound was nerve-wracking" [Ōta, 189]). Sometimes voice itself was horrifically dysmorphized, like "the mad midnight singing" of a crazed young girl whose "screams were piercing, something like a night bird's," as she roared a weird song into the night:

> The moon's all alone;
> I'm all alone too.
> The moon's all alone;
> I'm all alone too.
> The moon's all alone;
> I'm all . . .
> (Ōta, 214–15)

When voice fails, the victim's humanity can still be expressed minimally by the eye. The speaker of Sankichi Tōge's poem "Eyes" harrows a burn ward "in search of the one who only this morning was my younger sister" and finds her when an unrecognizable "death mask" spills a tear and "from torn lips / red-flecked teeth / groans out my name" (318). As Tōge's speaker moves through the burn ward, the eyes of the voiceless, inert, unrecognizable objects on the cement floor become increasingly focused, alert, and demanding, "watching my every step. / Eyes fastened to my back, fixed on my shoulder, my arm. / Why do they look at me like this? / After me, after me, from all sides, thin white beams coming at me: / eyes, *eyes,* EYES—" (317). In this room of dysmorphized figures, an inversion has occurred, and the speaker's intact, unblemished, erect body has become the anomaly, the monstrous spectacle. Those eyes have become the norming faculty, and their gaze becomes concretely real, "eyes materialize, *materialize,* do not fade . . . fixed forever on me" (317).

The humanity of the dead, who have neither voice nor eye and often no face, no identity, is most difficult to convey in *hibakusha* accounts. Although

Hersey's interlocutors conjure up countless figures of the dead, he gives identity chiefly to the living. But *hibakusha* felt grave responsibility toward the dead and the establishment of their identities, and experienced great guilt at their irremediably dishonored state. Yōko Ōta is tormented by her experience with a fourteen-, fifteen-year-old boy from Sōtoku Middle School who dies ("I'm dying. I think I'm dying. It's horrible") without anyone asking his name. "My conscience troubled me for a long time thereafter. I had learned that he came from Miyajima. Why hadn't I asked his name so I could let his family know where he died?" (198–99). Hersey reports in his "Aftermath" that Dr. Sasaki's most haunting regret was that "it had not been possible, beyond a certain point, to keep track of the identities of those whose corpses were dragged out to the mass cremations, with the result that nameless souls might still, all these years later, be hovering there, unattended and dissatisfied" (109). Conversely, Yōko Ōta is reduced to sobs by the sight of a father who lovingly prepared the corpse of his dead twelve- or thirteen-year-old daughter for burial in an air raid trench: "A white cloth covered her. Beside her pillow had been placed a small red bowl holding a ball of white rice. An incense stick with a point of red flame was sending up smoke. New clogs had been put on her feet and fastened with thin thongs" (219). As crematoria overflowed, the dead were burned around the clock on the riverbanks, and Dr. Hachiya, asked to attend one of the many nightly cremations at his hospital, prayed: "One must excuse the perfunctoriness of this cremation by remembering that so many had died that the ritual normally accorded the dead was an impossible luxury." But in his heart "the fact there was not a priest to say a prayer for this departed soul disturbed me" (61).

The desecrations of the dead continued into the postwar years as the ABCC requested bodies of *hibakusha* for autopsy. A day laborer's wife told Lifton, "On the day of the funeral . . . a jeep from ABCC came and asked us if they could dissect the body. They said it would be for the good of society as a whole." Spurred by the image of her dead father's voice urging her to "stand up strongly," she resists turning him over to the Americans' "war-smelling hands" because she worries: "Based upon my father's body, would they make further discoveries for bigger atomic and hydrogen bombs?" (Lifton, 346–47). But although many *hibakusha* believe, like Yasuko Kimura, that "you can talk about your own experience, but you can't speak for others" (Cook and Cook, 398), many survivors and atomic bomb writers believe that they must speak—even when they cannot—for the voiceless dead, and the agony of their dying. In his poem "Dying," Sankichi Tōge does all that can be done, what little can be done, by expressing the *pikadon* with a punctuation mark (!) and the panic, pain, and disorientation it caused through chaotic images of chaotic perceptions:

> Wires, boards, nails, glass,
> a rippling wall of tiles.
> Fingernails burn;
> heels—gone;
> plastered to my back: a sheet of molten lead.
> "Owww!"
>
> (308)

The cry of pain returns ("Ah! Why?") at the end, as both poetic voice and poem die with a question:

> Why?
> Why here
> by the side of the road
> cut off, dear, from you;
> why
> must
> I
> die
> ?
>
> (310)

MODERNISM AND VIETNAM
Francis Ford Coppola's *Apocalypse Now*

Mythology and Quest

JOHN HERSEY SHARED WITH ERNEST HEMINGWAY THE INFLU-
ence of journalism in giving his war writing its modernistic cast. But
Hersey's report, written in the immediate aftermath of the bombing, yet
reflects little of the self-ironization that might have registered a sense of national implication in the narrative of the damage. However, his "Aftermath,"
added to the 1985 Vintage edition, restores *Hiroshima* to a Cold War history
of nuclear testing, a massive arms buildup, attempts to suppress the peace
movement, and suspicion that activist *hibakusha,* such as the Reverend Tanimoto, might be communist tools (146–47). The United States' incrimination in nuclear weapons policy and use is here restored. Tacitly Hersey's
"Aftermath" also gestures to the missing link between World War II and
Vietnam: the anti-Soviet fears that triggered the bomb's use later propelled
U.S. militarism into armed conflict in Korea and Southeast Asia in the 1950s,
1960s, and 1970s. In 1979 a highly popular Hollywood film, Francis Ford
Coppola's *Apocalypse Now,* restored U.S. responsibility for the violence in
Vietnam, and did so, curiously, by reaching back to the more ideologically
complex literary works of early twentieth-century modernism. Coppola's
film does not obviate the need for Vietnamese testimony; but in his dialogue

with Conrad's *Heart of Darkness,* he succeeds in making the case for U.S. self-incrimination in the horrors of the Vietnam War without recourse to dialogue with Asian voices.

Among its many surprises, Francis Ford Coppola's film of the Vietnam War, *Apocalypse Now,* shows the images of two key intertexts of high modernism "prominently displayed" (Zuker, 77–78) in Kurtz's compound: Jessie Weston's *From Ritual to Romance* and Sir James Frazer's *Golden Bough.*[1] These two texts on comparative mythology and religion—associated with the agnostic work of the Cambridge anthropologists of the early twentieth century—undergird the mythological framework of the premier poem of high modernism, T. S. Eliot's *Waste Land,* which is also considered the most significant poetic expression of World War I. Why did Coppola make a film about the Vietnam War that eschews historical verisimilitude and reference in favor of what T. S. Eliot called "the mythical method" (*Selected Prose,* 178)? Coppola's choice—to construct his film upon Joseph Conrad's novella *Heart of Darkness,* Eliot's *Waste Land* and other poetry, and the mythic quests and poetic pilgrimages they embody—seems especially eccentric for the treatment of the Vietnam War, which was not, like World War I, a literary war. Culturally, the Vietnam War was a video war, and aesthetically, a psychedelic war. Indeed, Coppola called *Apocalypse Now* "the first $30 million surrealist movie" ever made (Goodwin and Wise, 262). His comment recalls another strange anachronism in the recrudescence of early twentieth-century art forms to address mid- and late twentieth-century wars. However effectively modernism may have articulated World War I, it failed to serve as an expressive medium for representing World War II except in the reductive styles of journalism. Yet surrealism, its avant-garde contemporary, did belatedly serve to depict World War II in Volker Schlöndorff's cinematic translation of Günther Grass's *Tin Drum,* which shared the Palme d'Or for best film with *Apocalypse Now* at the 1979 Cannes Film Festival. The clue to the conundrum of Coppola's choice of modernism's mythical method may lie precisely in the problematic power of the surreal to express irrationality, absurdity, incoherence, fragmentation, and futility. *Apocalypse Now's* many surrealistic scenes and moments forcefully convey the war's incomprehensibility. But by themselves they do not produce an insight into or recognition of Vietnam's significance for the U.S. public, or a calculus for its damage to the United States' moral life. Like Eliot facing the modern world after World War I, Coppola in the aftermath of Vietnam required "a way of controlling, of ordering, of giving significance to the immense panorama of futility and anarchy which is contemporary history" (*Selected Prose*, 177). The "mythical method" served them both.

But the "mythical method" incurs the risk and cost of dehistoricizing—and thereby depoliticizing—its historical subject. An even greater danger lies in the use (or abuse) of the "mythical method" to idealize, apotheosize, occlude, or occult problematic ideologies embedded in the art. However subversive of Victorian pieties and hypocrisies, the work of Conrad, Eliot, Pound, Yeats, and Wyndham Lewis (among others) may be suspected of harboring its own moral darkness in compromised and sometimes incriminating relationships to colonialism, nationalism, class hatred, misogyny, and racism. We may ask, then, what ideological freight the experimentalism of modernism carried into its afterlife in late twentieth-century art. In the case of Coppola's use of Conrad and Eliot there may seem to be cause for worry—worry I hope nonetheless to allay by arguing that the ethical strategies he borrows from them *work* in his film. Although the impetus for framing Vietnam veterans' stories with Conrad's novella came from Coppola ("he made the crucial suggestion that Milius and Lucas write up the stories with Conrad's *Heart of Darkness* as the underlying structural agent" [Chown, 123]), the screenwriter John Milius initially interpreted Conrad through a war-mongering filter.[2] According to Jeffrey Chown's detailed analysis of Milius's original screenplay, the writer at first cast Conrad's Kurtz as the war's hypothetical savior—the man who "embraces the horror, and more specifically advocates it as the final solution for winning the Vietnam War" (130). Milius's Kurtz served as model and hero, rather than as nemesis or dark double, for the Army captain whose name somewhat anagramatically and palindromically deforms that of Conrad's Marlow: Willard. Milius's own 1982 explanation for the film's title confirms that the violent and right-wing sentiments infusing his scripts for *Magnum Force* and *Red Dawn* were fully engaged in his original conceptualization of Coppola's project:

> George Lucas and I were great connoisseurs of the Vietnam War. . . . George and I would talk about the battles all the time and what a great movie it would make. I had the title to call it, *Apocalypse Now*, because all the hippies at the time had these buttons that said 'Nirvana Now,' and I loved the idea of a guy having a button with a mushroom cloud on it that said 'Apocalypse Now,' you know, let's

bring it on, full nuke. Ever hear that Randy Newman song, 'Let's Drop the Big One Now'? That's the spirit that it started in right there. (Quoted in Chown, 123)

Coppola actually considered changing the title of the film back to *The Heart of Darkness* at one time (Chown, 130), and through the narration later added by Michael Herr he restored the darkly critical vision of Conrad's Marlow to Willard. I will argue that Coppola restored as well Conrad's genius for using both narration and narrative structure to create a textual performance of self-incrimination and moral implication that ultimately extends to the reader and the viewer.

The film's viewer is forced, like Conrad's Marlow and Conrad's reader, to choose between nightmares ("Ah! but it was something to have at least a choice of nightmares" (Conrad, 78). The nightmares represent forms of violence: the corporate, instrumentalized, ideologically rationalized, and morally deceptive violence of the military machine or the blatant, undisguised, ideologically stripped and frank barbarism that the renegade madman turns on the Vietnam War as the military's unvarnished mirror. In his 1979 interview with Greil Marcus for *Rolling Stone,* Coppola confirms this sense of his film: "I felt that in the end, the movie was always about choice" (quoted in Chown, 143). If Coppola grasped Conrad's strategy for criticizing colonial adventurism through a demonized double, then the continuities of *Apocalypse Now* and Coppola's *Godfather* films become clearly apparent. The *Godfather* series sets forth the same structure of immoral doubles: the overt brutality of the Mafia as product and humanized mirror of the more invisible but pervasive brutality of political institutions whose corruptible legislative, judicial, and police systems fail to protect its most vulnerable citizens. *Apocalypse Now* illustrates precisely the same point in what Jeffrey Chown calls the film's "puppy-sampan scene." The PBR boat's routine search of a peaceful sampan turns into a massacre less by inadvertence than from the pressure of the irrepressible violence built into the Army's sense of its mission. When Willard dispatches the wounded woman with a shot—as though euthanizing an animal—the military machine's brutality loses all hypocritical ideological cover and becomes narrativizable and visualizable as pure murder, a shadow of the historical My Lai massacre.[3] The sentimental rescue of the puppy allows the film to allude to the falsity of such public relations gambits as the pacification program to "win hearts and minds" in Vietnam:[4]

"It was a way we had over here of living with ourselves," Willard's voice-over narration comments upon his cold killing of the wounded Vietnamese woman. "We'd cut them in half with a machine gun and give 'em a Band-Aid. It was a lie, and the more I saw of them, the more I hated lies." There has been general contention that Coppola is not a political auteur ("He is more interested in the politics of family life and interpersonal relationships than in larger political issues" [Zuker, 33]) and an improbable political critic of the Vietnam War ("In pre-1974 interviews and film work, Coppola had never shown even a passing interest in the Vietnam War" [Chown, 122]). The cinematographer Vittorio Storaro, however, contended that Coppola "wanted to express the main idea of Joseph Conrad, which is the imposition of one culture on top of another culture" (Cowie, 133). By tracing how Coppola translated the philosophical modernism of Conrad (and its reso-nances in Eliot's poetic language) into the cinematic language of *Apocalypse Now,* I intend to dispute Joel Zuker's contention that in the film "the issue of American colonialism in a war we could never win are [*sic*] passed over" (Zuker, 31).

Procedurally, my plan is to explore Coppola's ideological and ethical critique of U.S. politics in Vietnam through its dialogue not only with Joseph Conrad's themes and scenes in *Apocalypse Now* but also with his structural strategies of mirroring and doubling, transposition and displacement, trans-lation and poetic commentary. Key scenes or moments in the film frequently function as responses to or translations of moments in *Heart of Darkness*—even when the parallel is indirect or initially obscure. I will therefore "read through" Conrad not only such obvious images as the severed head of Chef or the chaos at Do Lung bridge but also scenes that appear incongruent with Conrad's novella—the USO Playboy Playmate show, for instance—and fu-gitive images of seemingly little significance, such as the roast beef served in the Army COMSEC Intelligence Headquarters at Nha Trang. These scenes and images, I will argue, require acts of interpretation on the part of the viewer that gradually foreground the ethical and philosophical violence behind the military violence in Vietnam. In the second part of my analysis, I will turn to the film's sometimes audible, sometimes silent dialogue with T. S. Eliot's poetry to explore its meditation on art and culture in relation to colonialism, violence, and war. Any discussion of *Apocalypse Now* may ap-propriately end with questions about the film's own appropriative practices, from its uncredited ingestion of Conrad to criticisms of the production's underwriting of the corrupt regime of Ferdinand Marcos and its potentially harmful effects on the Philippine population.

Willard's Journey

Conrad's critique of colonialism is structured hermeneutically, as an interpretive quest and moral pilgrimage that operates through the telling and hearing of a story twice: an unnamed narrator tells of a story that Marlow once told aboard ship at anchor. Marlow's story thus becomes an education for a multiple audience in different time frames: immediately, for the unnamed narrator and other denizens of the ship *Nellie,* and, remotely, for the putative interlocutor or reader to whom the unnamed narrator repeats Marlow's story. The transmissibility of the story is crucial to its didactic function, which is to show Westerners the horrors that underwrite colonial empire and to argue that even silent or ignorant assent or benefit spells complicity with colonialism. Conrad's "frame" narrative in *Heart of Darkness* allows him to position the reader as a moral double to the unnamed narrator aboard the *Nellie,* anchored in the Thames, an affable and ingenuous jingoist who opens the story with a paean to the "great knights-errant of the sea"—"the *Golden Hind* returning with her round flanks full of treasure . . . the *Erebus* and *Terror,* bound on other conquests. . . . What greatness had not floated on the ebb of that river into the mystery of an unknown earth! . . . The dreams of men, the seed of commonwealths, the germs of empires" (Conrad, 18). The narrator's peroration is sharply disrupted when Marlow punctures this imperialist romance with grim naturalism—"cold, fog, tempests, disease, exile, and death. . . . They must have been dying like flies here" (Conrad, 20)— before he proceeds to narrate his own education in the sordid truth of colonial enterprise. Besides setting up a dialogue between the glorification of colonial conquest and its exposé as criminal robbery and murder, the frame that makes Marlow's story a twice-told tale serves to establish the lesson's historical reapplicability. Marlow's experience with Belgian commercial exploitation of the Congo repeats the Roman conquest of Britain and, by silent implication, Britain's own more recent conquest of India. Colonialism is a movable horror prone to displacement and repetition.

Coppola abandoned the narrative frame that John Milius had originally written into the script of *Apocalypse Now* and replaced it with an ambiguous layering of nightmares about the various "missions" of his protagonist, Captain Willard. Instead of a patriotic paean to U.S. foreign policy, the film opens with an expression of frustrated military desire—"Saigon. Shit! I'm still only in Saigon. . . . I'm here a week now, waiting for a mission"—which is overtaken by a voice from a later moment in time to announce its fulfillment and Willard's education: "Everyone gets everything he wants. I wanted a mission, and for my sins, they gave me one. Brought it up to me like room service. . . . It was a real choice mission, and when it was over, I never wanted another." Coppola opens the film in the interior of Willard's spiritual and psychological heart of darkness expressed in visual images and techniques— the exploding jungle of nightmare or memory; the rhythmic sounds of heartbeat, ceiling fan, and helicopter blending into one another; Jim Morrison's eerie wail of "The End" ("Lost in a Roman wilderness of pain, / and all the chil-dren are insane");[5] Willard's face, upside down, signaling a reversed perspective on Vietnam, war stories, and war movies; and his emotional and mental breakdown expressed in the fractured image of his Orientalized movements and martial art gesturings as he crashes his hand through the mirror. The result is an effect of layered but productive trauma, of Willard, already agonized by pain and guilt, obliged to enact his nightmares over again, until, by the end of the film, we understand that his encounter with Kurtz allowed him to see himself and to confront his own acts and guilts. "There is no way to tell his story without telling my own. And if his story is really a confession, then so is mine." If Willard's moves before the mirror resemble the movements of tai chi—a form of what is sometimes called "internal martial arts"—then his internal journey into self-recognition is, like Kurtz's, an experience of going native, of an Eastern looking inward toward a self-enlightening anagnorisis.

The highly charged affect of Willard's expressionism in the opening sequence of the film is his semiotic equivalent to Kurtz's "the horror! the horror!" But this stunning psychological effect required Coppola's sacrifice of the fascinating political point John Milius's original frame might have brought to the film: "Milius framed the story with Willard on a boat in Washington's Potomac, telling the story to a female journalist" (Chown, 131). We can instantly imagine the dark resonance of Marlow's opening line in such a venue: "'And this also,' said Marlow suddenly, 'has been one of the dark places of the earth'" (Conrad, 19). The settling of the United States is as mythified as the narrator's England, glorified as "dreams of men" and "seed of commonwealths." In Milius's Potomac opening, the story of Vietnam narrated in the shadow of the U.S. capitol could have demythified, obliquely, the nation's genesis as a story of native genocide and cultivation by slavery.

The removal of this frame seems like a colossal lost opportunity for political comment until we recognize Coppola's intriguing displacement of the burden of its message onto the USO Playboy Playmate show in the middle of the film. Staged and hosted by the San Francisco rock concert impresario Bill Graham, the USO show, in which three Playboy bunnies dressed in cowboy and Indian costumes are ferried in by helicopter to entertain the troops, parodies a military institution that is itself already heavily ironized. USO shows, designed to prop up combat troops' morale by inspiring patriotism and reminding the boys of what they are fighting for, traditionally display to soldiers conflicting and confused icons of sexual desire fused with patriotic imagery.

In *Apocalypse Now* this fusion is intriguingly verbally and conceptually textured: the rock concert signaling the cultural moment of the 1960s set against the Cold War symbol of rockets as backdrop for the eroticized movements that update the Rockettes with a soft-porn inflection. More pointedly, democracy is signaled by the domestication of the United States' bloody genesis in its ludic and juvenile version as stylized play of cowboys and Indians, performed by Playboy bunnies posing as domesticated and softened versions of strippers. However, Coppola has the Playmates' ludic and lewd gunplay incite a frenzied violence in the mob of soldiers, who storm the stage in an epic gang rape. The women and their manager escape only by a dangerous helicopter airlift that gestures proleptically toward the final closing scenes of the Vietnam War with its images of frenzied, desperate, dangerous airlift escapes from the collapsing country. The USO show economically glosses the particular darkness embedded in Cold War inflections of U.S. democracy as the saving alternative to the communism whose threat prompted the United States' intervention in Vietnam. The exaltation of individual freedom and dignity, traditionally sacrificed in the military, is further undercut by the USO show's display of mindless male frenzy and violence. The young, sexualized women as indiscriminate victims of the grunts' corporate assault assimilated the dawning feminism of 1979 into the larger critique of oppressive colonial practices.[6]

Coppola further produces a critique of the U.S. mercenary mentality by setting the USO show in a locale housing a supply depot whose U.S. commercial and consumer excess was named in the original Milius script by a pun on the Vietnamese name Hau Phat (how fat) (Chown, 128). The panoply of noncombat consumer goods—the motorcycles, for example, which suggest a thriving black market—gloss U.S. democracy as it was generally

figured in communist depiction: as an ideology of unbridled greed, materi-
alism, and consumerism. Willard narratively comments over the eyes of
a Vietnamese watching U.S. opulence from behind the iron curtain of a
barbed-wire fence: "Charlie's idea of R&R was a dead rat and cold rice."
Though not a major Conradian theme in *Apocalypse Now,* war profiteer-
ing—the donnée of Carol Reed's 1949 *Third Man*—aligns the ideologies of
anticommunist war with those of colonialism. The revelation of black market traffic in penicillin in postwar Vienna in *The Third Man* may also provide
an interpretive frame for one of the most horrific narrations in *Apocalypse
Now:* Kurtz's story of the Viet Cong cutting off the arms of all children recently inoculated with polio vaccine by the U.S. Army in a Vietnamese village. The awe that the "strength" of this fanatical and brutal gesture inspires
in Kurtz misses its political character as a dramatic allegory of refusal of the
cultural and spiritual pollutions that contaminated the United States' campaign of calculated humanitarianism "to win hearts and minds" in Vietnam.
Coppola alludes to an ideological blindness (dramatized in Frances Fitzgerald's *Fire in the Lake*) that blocked Americans' comprehension of a culture
that might refuse motorcycles, surfing, and Playboy bunnies for the integrity
of dead rats, cold rice, and freedom from Western cultural inoculation.

This reference to U.S. cultural imperialism—the importation of Western values and habits into Eastern colonial contexts—glosses a crucial
theme in *Heart of Darkness.* Conrad sets up the trading company that em-
ploys Marlow as a mirror of the renegade Kurtz in order to show European
values as absurd and perverse when transposed to an African context, and
to contrast them with the more broadly drawn absurdity and perversity of
"going native." Conrad's most ludicrous figure of European maladaptation
to the African colonial situation is the Company's chief accountant, who, in
"high starched collar, white cuffs . . . snowy trousers, a clean necktie, and
varnished boots" (Conrad, 32), manages to keep his books "in apple-pie order," even when the groans of an invalided agent make it "difficult to guard
against clerical errors in this climate" (33). Coppola's version of the accountant is the flamboyant Lieutenant Colonel Kilgore, whose U.S. Cavalry hat
foreshadows the cowboys-and-Indians theme of the USO show. The Cavalry
hat also serves to underline the genocidal destructiveness that overlies the
U.S. Army's mythic role of chivalric rescue[7] as Kilgore's helicopters visit napalm and bullets on a Vietnamese school. But it is Kilgore's passion for surfing that imports a key figure from U.S. culture—the California *jouissance*
and affluence popularized by the Beach Boys in the 1960s—into a combat

context and makes its aggressive and obsessive hedonism as perverse as the obsessive scrupulosity of Conrad's accountant.

Kilgore's allegorical name points to a one-dimensionality with the philosophical significance of making him—in contrast to the brooding, introspective Kurtz—a Conradian and Eliotian "hollow man" with no interiority, no self-consciousness, no conscience, no powers of anagnorisis. His insanity is of a different order than that of Kurtz—who sees his own perversity as the interiorization of the perversity of the war—because it is marked by the absence of any humanity, the hollowness of feeling and lack of sympathetic sight that make him autotelic, driven purely by his own will, a Nietzschean *Übermensch*. His placement in the pantheon of evil that poses the film's nightmare choices is therefore ambiguous and troublesome. Kilgore is curiously exempted from the poetics of cruelty that hovers around Kurtz's prose and actions, and he presides over his own Conradian "grove of death" (Marlow's first sight of criminalized black workers miserably dying from the brutality of their condition) with a casualness that also marks Coppola's decision to eschew graphic images of atrocity and sadism. Unlike the historical abominations Michael Herr reports in *Dispatches*—soldiers wearing necklaces made of human ears and unspeakably desecrating the heads of the dead—Coppola has Kilgore dispense symbolic "death from above"—playing cards that mark the corpses as his victims and signify the pure arbitrariness and chance of his killing. Kilgore's use of the card deck exceeds in nihilism that of Eliot's Madame Sosostris, the *Waste Land* clairvoyant who degrades the sacred mysteries of the tarot by deploying its symbols for horoscopes. Unlike Kurtz, who steps into the ritualized universe of the primitive and becomes a species of mystic, Kilgore remains a flying cowboy, a connoisseur of experience and sensation ("I love the smell of napalm") whose flight is aptly characterized by the apotheosized barbarism of Wagner's "Flight of the Valkyries."[8]

Coppola attends to the way Joseph Conrad took the great philosophical themes of the modern—the arbitrariness, chance, and absurdity—and gave them a precise function and figuration in the critique of colonialism. Conrad's various images of absurd, objectless fighting and unproductive, futile labor are the first landmarks of Marlow's journey. He encounters a French man-of-war firing into an invisible and unresponsive jungle ("There wasn't even a shed there, and she was shelling the bush. . . . Nothing happened. Nothing could happen. There was a touch of insanity in the proceeding" [Conrad, 28]). At his first Company station, all manner of vague dynamitings and unclear construction projects are going on: "They were building a railway. The cliff was not in the way or anything; but this objectless blasting was all the work going on. . . . I avoided a vast artificial hole somebody had been digging on the slope, the purpose of which I found it impossible to divine" (Conrad, 30–31). Coppola transposes Conrad's Sysiphean vision of the futility of Company labor to the scene of chaos at the Do Lung bridge, the last U.S. Army outpost before Cambodia: "Every night the bridge is rebuilt, and the Vietcong blow it up again. Willard attempts to find the commanding offer. When he asks who is in command, a black soldier replies 'Ain't you?'" (Zuker, 64). By choosing a bridge as the site of utter confusion and anarchy, Coppola glosses the ironic contrast between his images of war and the chivalric military fantasy of leadership, discipline, sacrifice, and honor in David Lean's 1957 *Bridge on the River Kwai*. The folly both Conrad and Coppola underline in their criticism of colonial adventurism is the senseless brutality, waste, and destructiveness of enterprises with misguided and hypocritical goals and inept and ill-conceived strategies.

When he transfers the scenes of the man-of-war and the first station to Do Lung bridge, Coppola preserves a small detail from Marlow's account of the morbidity of the French man-of-war ("We gave her her letters [I heard the men in that lonely ship were dying of fever at the rate of three a day] and went on" [Conrad, 28]). In that unlikely place at the end of the earth ("You're in the asshole of the world") a soldier gives Willard the mail he has been holding for the patrol boat. As the boat heads into Cambodia, the men read their mail, and the home front—the life and values the men are ostensibly fighting for—intrudes its multiple and fractured voice into the boat. Lance hears from his friend Jim in California ("There could never be a place like Disneyland, or could there? Let me know"); Willard hears that his precursor, Colby, has defected to Kurtz with a vehement repudiation of home ("Sell the house. Sell the car. Sell the kids. Find someone else. I'm never coming home. Forget it"); someone has sent a clipping of the Manson murders ("Charles Miller Manson ordered the slaughter of all in the home anyway as a symbol of protest"); and Clean's cassette tape from his folks in the South Bronx poignantly evokes U.S. middle-class family values and devotion. The attack on the boat intermittently drowns out the voice of Clean's mother as she marshals the love of her extended African American family behind the teenager ("Even Aunt Jessie and Mama will come to celebrate your coming home"). At the very moment Clean is hit and killed, the maternal voice gathers familial resources ("Grandma and Dad are trying to get enough money to buy you a car. But don't tell them because that's our secret") and dreams ("Pretty soon—not too soon—but pretty soon, I'll have a lot of grandchildren to love and spoil"). The dead boy never hears her homely admonition, "Anyhow, do the right thing. Stay out of the way of the bullets. And bring your heiney home all in one piece because we love you very much."[9] The letter stands in sharp contrast not only to the brutal scrawled "divorce" Colby has sent to his wife but also to the confession Kurtz (in a letter cited earlier) sends to his son ("Dear son . . . I've been officially accused of murder by the army"). The military action in Vietnam is shown producing U.S. domestic casualties along with its military and Vietnamese casualties. Unlike Conrad, who concentrates colonialism's violence to the home country in the single, majestically deluded figure of Kurtz's Intended, Coppola disperses the Vietnam War's domestic devastations among a wide and diverse array of people.

Coppola further uses the crew of the PBR boat to revise and sophisticate the crude and problematic ethnography Conrad applies to the issue of race. Conrad's maneuver to hyperbolize the aboriginal character of the Africans as much as possible (making them casual rather than ritual cannibals, for example) is designed to heighten the remarkable in Marlow's sense of kinship with them: "They howled and leaped, and spun, and made horrid faces; but what thrilled you was just the thought of their humanity—like yours—the thought of your remote kinship with this wild and passionate uproar" (Conrad, 51). Marlow's Eurocentric condescension is shocking; imagine Willard similarly "thrilled" at the thought that the Vietnamese are human. But I believe Conrad ironized this condescension precisely to reverse the conventional moral valences of civilization and savagery. The civilized heart is shown to harbor the more horrifying darkness.[10] Coppola in *Apocalypse Now* makes the same point, but in a more highly nuanced and particularized way, by contrasting the biracialism of the Army with the military's racial response to the Vietnamese.[11] In a bold move, he locates a heavily veiled racism toward blacks in his protagonist, in a Willard perhaps unconscious of the way the derogatory "shit" creeps into his thoughts about Clean ("from some South Bronx shithole") and Chief ("it sure as shit was the Chief's boat"), or that his irritation with them might be racially inflected. Asking Chief how long Clean's been on the boat, Willard says, "He's really specializing in busting my balls." "It's very possible, Captain, he thinks the same of you," Chief responds, while Clean makes silent rude gestures behind Willard's back. This veiled antagonism between Willard and the black men on board is suspended in indeterminacy between the issue of race and the issue of authority. But it erupts in a final convulsion of violence when Chief, unlike Marlow's mute and passive helmsman, tries fiercely to impale Willard on the same spear that impales him.

Coppola contrasts Willard's separation from the boat's crew with their remarkable biracial solidarity. In scenes that disavow the racial and cultural tensions that were ideologically riving the home front in the 1960s and 1970s, tensions between North and South, black and white, old and young, East Coast and West Coast, rich and poor disappear as Coppola makes the Navy patrol boat a site of domestic and democratic utopia. This biracial boat evokes other craft in nineteenth-century U.S. fiction that the critic Leslie Fiedler identified as the topos of homosocial biracial romance—the ship in Melville's *Moby Dick,* for example, or the raft in *Huckleberry Finn.* During their quiet moments on the river journey, the young men play together like kids in a family, dancing, water-skiing, smoking dope. The black teenager from the South Bronx, the high-strung white culinary artist from New Orleans ("I was raised to be a great saucier"), the sober, disciplined African American "Chief" of the Navy patrol boat, and the callow, blond California surfer, Lance Johnson ("L. B. Johnson") meld into a fraternal community whose bonds emerge most visibly when they are savagely sundered. Chef throws himself on the body of Clean, sobbing not the nickname but the familiar name "Bubba, Bubba." Lance, who becomes progressively feminized in what may have been intended as a homosexual coding during the narrative, transfers his nurturance from the lost puppy ("Where's the dog! We've got to go back for the dog!") to the dead Chief. The Whitmanesque mood of the boat's crew culminates in Lance's anointing his dead Chief with his lipstick, enfolding him in an embrace like a Pietà, and bestowing a kiss before releasing him for burial into the river.

As Willard's attenuated racism toward Clean and Chief is submerged in irritation and separation, so Coppola submerges U.S. racism toward the Vietnamese into a broader coding of cultural difference in terms of social and ethical superiority. Categories of domestic refinement and social order are pressed into service as codes for "civilized" and "savage" in ways that heavily ironize U.S. assumptions of moral superiority. Army radio reports a request from the mayor of Saigon for GIs living off base to dry their laundry inside: "Keep Saigon Beautiful." But the Navy patrol boat gleefully sweeps Vietnamese washerwomen and their laundry off the riverbanks with the powerful wash of the boat's speeding action. The crew's shout of "Sayonara!" carries the racism of an earlier war from one Asian people to another. The violence to Vietnamese order and civility intensifies during Colonel Kilgore's helicopter raid on "Charlie's Point," which is shown to house a beautiful school with orderly uniformed children attending, and is populated by people going about the business of their lives. This tranquil scene is violently ruptured when Kilgore's choppers descend like Wagner's barbaric horde and blow the scene below to kingdom come. "Outstanding, team, outstanding. We'll get you a case of beer for that!" "The key cut in facilitating the ironic point of view is to the shot of Vietnamese school children dressed in white just before the violence begins. Thus later, when a Vietnamese woman, apparently one of the teachers, tosses a grenade into a helicopter picking up American wounded, we can feel the irony when Kilgore calls her a 'savage,' orders his pilot to 'put a skid up her ass,' and guns her down" (Chown 137). Categories are turned on their heads, as U.S. savagery is cruder and less reflective than the Vietnamese savagery Kurtz recognizes as the "genius" of disciplined and principled action in the hacking of inoculated children's arms.

Native savagery in *Heart of Darkness* is coded as cannibalism: "I had made up my mind that if my late helmsman was to be eaten, the fishes alone should have him" (Conrad, 67), Marlow tells his listeners. Coppola takes Conrad's metaphorical play with the ethnological differences between the raw and the cooked (to take liberties with Claude Lévi-Strauss's categories) [12] and elaborates them in *Apocalypse Now* to underline specific registers of moral hypocrisy and sentimentality that attend the encounter between the "civilized" and the "savage." The hyperbolized opposite of the "raw" is typologized in the refinement of cooking represented by Chef, the New Orleans saucier whose vocational route to the Escoffier School was disrupted by the military, a site of culinary violence where gorgeous marbled prime rib is boiled to sodden gray masses in industrialized kitchens. Chef's sensibility as a culinary artist spills into the realm of the erotic: "I'm walking through the jungle gathering mangoes and I meet Raquel Welch," he tells Willard, and proceeds to fantasize making a mango cream pudding to "spread around on us." His walk into the jungle to find mangoes becomes, in effect, a wet dream violently disrupted by the pounce of a real tiger, who nearly turns the tables and makes him a feline feast. The significance of this episode fans out into the film in two opposite but related directions. After meeting the tiger in the jungle, the traumatized Chef vows never to leave the boat again—a vow respected, in a sense, when Chief orders Chef to board and search the sampan for contraband weapons. The sampan turns out to be a licensed market stocked with barrels of bananas, fish, rice, and even mangoes—a small site of Vietnamese civilization annihilated in the drug-crazed massacre that follows.

But these ironic juxtapositions of the raw and the cooked, the savage and the civilized, are enfolded into the larger ethical frame of the film. When, near the film's beginning, Willard is taken to the Army COMSEC Intelligence Headquarters in Nha Trang, he is briefed on his mission during a civilized lunch. "Roast beef, and usually it's not bad," the general tells Willard as the camera lingers close up on the plate of rare meat and vegetables. This image becomes retrospectively laden with significance when the Montagnard tribesmen under Kurtz's command in Cambodia ritually butcher a water buffalo on the screen. The disturbing scene was not a cinematic simulacrum but an actual slaughter filmed at an Ifugao feast. The interpretive juxtaposition of the two scenes makes other hypocrisies and sentimentalities of killing painfully apparent. The civilized roast beef is produced by an occluded and unacknowledged animal slaughter that is itself a violence like the killing of the water ox. Coppola thus underlines the point of Willard's choice of nightmare: that Kurtz's savage atrocities in Cambodia are merely the visible and unconcealed variant of the military's far more pervasive, routinized, denatured butchery of the Vietnamese. Coppola's indirect allusion to the savagery that underlies civilized custom may be borrowed from one of Conrad's most powerful images: the massive, lacquered grand piano in the parlor of Kurtz's Intended—"with dark gleams on the flat surfaces like a sombre and polished sarcophagus" (90)—whose keys are, of course, made of the ivory whose rapacious acquisition required the carnage of African elephants and natives for Belgian profit.[13] Conrad's "the horror! the horror!" echoes silently and implicitly through the glories of a Beethoven or Mozart piano concerto.

The raw and the cooked, the savage and the civilized, the valences of these binaries become confused and trade places in *Apocalypse Now* as they did in *Heart of Darkness*. The choice of nightmares that faces Marlow and Willard confounds the rhetoric of Manichean morality uttered by the Intelligence Headquarters commander, who enlists Willard in a mission to mediate the "conflict in every human heart"—"Because there's a conflict in every human heart between the rational and the irrational, between good and evil. And good does not always triumph." In all probity and sincerity, the commander quotes Abraham Lincoln to depict Kurtz as a fallen man, "a good man, a humanitarian man"—"Sometimes the dark side overcomes what

Lincoln called the better angels of our nature." With seemingly genuine sadness, the general delivers the shocking news of Kurtz's ordered arrest for murder to Willard, who is himself criminally compromised by his assassination of a tax collector for the CIA in June 1968. "How many people had I already killed?" Willard asks himself after leaving the headquarters. "Those six people I know about for sure—close enough to blow their breath in my face." Willard's assassinations in the line of duty outnumber Kurtz's "official" assassinations by two. "Charging a man with murder in this war was like handing out speeding tickets at the Indy 500," he concedes. For Coppola, as for Conrad, it is the pious cant of institutions in the service of brutality that is the bête noire of Western civilization. Conrad puts this fatuity into the mouths of women—Marlow's aunt, who exhorts her nephew to pursue his quest into Africa as "an emissary of light, something like a lower sort of apostle": "She talked about 'weaning those ignorant millions from their horrid ways,' till, upon my word, she made me quite uncomfortable. I ventured to hint that the Company was run for profit" (26–27). In the tape of his voice to which Willard listens during his civilized lunch at Army COMSEC Intelligence, Kurtz makes it clear that madness and irrationality are products of military logic: "We must kill them, we must incinerate them, pig after pig, cow after cow . . . army after army. And they call me an assassin." The last memo Kurtz tapes for the Army, just before he is butchered by Willard, rearticulates the moral contradictions and absurdities of the enterprise: "You train your men to drop fire on people. But their commanders won't allow them to write 'Fuck' on their airplanes because it's obscene." Coppola follows the lead of Conrad in making Vietnam's moral agon not the battle of good and evil, the fight between angel and devil, but rather the choice of nightmares, devil against devil. Marlow puts it thus: "I've seen the devil of violence, and the devil of greed, and the devil of hot desire; but, by all the stars! these were strong, lusty, red-eyed devils, that swayed and drove men—men, I tell you. But as I stood on this hillside, I foresaw that in the blinding sunshine of that land I would become acquainted with a flabby, pretending, weak-eyed devil of a rapacious and pitiless folly" (Conrad, 30).

Kurtz's Kingdom of the Dead

Willard's journey up the river takes its spiritual form as the processing of information (briefings, dossiers, photos, data) and the shaping of knowledge and judgment about Kurtz's moral nature. Throughout the episodes of this processing—which is the heart of Willard's actual mission—the camera, and thereby the film's point of view, takes its place on the dark side of the military: secretive, occlusive, censoring, as Willard looks in shock at photographs we are not shown, shuffles others we only partly see, and refuses to give us a frank glimpse of Kurtz's paramilitary operations in the Vietnam War. These oscillations between invisibility and visibility articulate ethical species of violence in both Conrad and Coppola. The two texts use the figure of Kurtz to mirror the corporate violence of Belgian colonialism and U.S. militarism, respectively, and make him the monstrous double whose cruelty externalizes the veiled atrocities of governmentally approved campaigns against non-Western peoples. But the difference between the U.S. military and Kurtz is one of blindness and insight—and Kurtz's anagnorisis, his self-recognition of his own monstrosity—is implemented in *Apocalypse Now* through Kurtz's ingestion and internalization of literary modernism. By having his Kurtz, like Conrad's, see his own "horror," Coppola invests his film with the redemptive possibility of having the U.S. public—if not its military—see the heart of its own darkness in Vietnam. However, by having the moral vision of the film articulated by modernism—an art that polemically reserves itself for a classically educated elite—Coppola incurred the risks he may have voiced in Kurtz's opening words as the peril of a snail slithering on the edge of a straight razor.[14] I take that trope to serve as a corporeal version evocative of the painful peril implied by Marlow's ocular metaphor of looking into the abyss, and surviving (Conrad, 86–87). The price of Coppola's sacrifice of entertainment to art was spread across the film's damning reviews by some of the country's leading film critics.[15] Jeffrey Chown reports critics' reactions to the shot of copies of Frazer's *Golden Bough* and Weston's *From Ritual to Romance* in the film: "Reviewers howled about Coppola's pseudo-intellectualism, since few viewers would be familiar with these works or recognize their significance. This, and Brando's slurred reading of T. S. Eliot's 'The Hollow Men' seemed attempts to dress up a muddled conclusion" (Chown, 144–45).[16] But I would argue that with the film's poetic ending, Coppola achieves a triumph undreamed in the Arnoldian philosophy of T. S. Eliot: a movie bringing the cultural insights of the English poetic tradition to a mass audience to illuminate the moral folly of another war, in another moment of the twentieth century.

The film's ending departs from Conrad's narrative, for Conrad's Marlow does not kill Kurtz, but rather (as Kurtz's moral double) nearly dies himself after Kurtz's death. With Conrad no longer serving as a philosophical guide and John Milius's patriotic action-movie finish unacceptable to his moral ambitions for the film, Coppola turned to other literary devices. Coppola is reported to have told an interviewer that he drew his inspiration for the ending from Eliot's famous line in "The Hollow Men"—"Not with a bang, but a whimper" (Zuker, 171). And Peter Cowie quotes Coppola's debt to the Cambridge anthropologists:

> I was really on the spot. I had no ending. . . . I was dealing with moral issues, and I didn't want to have just the typical John Milius ending, when the NVA attack and there's a giant battle scene, and Kurtz and Willard are fighting side by side, and Kurtz gets killed, etc., etc. That's the way it was in the script. I wanted to explore the moral side, and in reading some of *The Golden Bough* and then *From Ritual to Romance* I found a lot concerning that theme. T. S. Eliot's *The Waste Land* also seemed so apt for the conclusion of the story. (Cowie, 189)

This narrative exhibits a strange blind spot overlapping a keen cultural sophistication both outside and inside the film. The disingenuousness inscripted in Cowie's undocumented quotation—as though Coppola were unaware that Frazer, Weston, and the myth of the Fisher King are prominently and famously incorporated into T. S. Eliot's notes to *The Waste Land*—is curiously transferred to the figure of Coppola's Colonel Walter Kurtz himself. Coppola's Kurtz appears improbably ignorant of his eponym, Conrad's Kurtz in *Heart of Darkness*. Since Coppola's Kurtz quotes the first verse of Eliot's "Hollow Men" verbatim, he scarcely could fail to have noticed that the poem's epigraph is the epitaph of the man who shares his name: "Mistah Kurtz—he dead" (Eliot, 56).[17] Conrad is as absent from the consciousness of Coppola's Kurtz as he is absent from the consciousness of the film, including its credits.[18] Joseph Conrad is the victim of a cultural violence, an artistic savagery, a cinematic cannibalism that precipitates him as the vital spirit, the avenging angel, a palpable ghost of the film, haunting Colonel Kurtz, haunting Willard, haunting Coppola, and, finally, possessing them. Coppola's Kurtz—educated at Harvard like T. S. Eliot himself—ingests the cooked with the raw, the cannibalized and masticated fragments of texts ingested by the poetry of high modernism. This textual cannibalism marks him, as it marks the film itself, as exemplar of high culture swallowed by savagery—

224

like Conrad's Kurtz, who was musician, painter, poet, orator, and philan-thropist before he had "taken a high seat amongst the devils of the land" (Conrad, 64).

Eliot's poetry infects not only Kurtz and the photojournalist (Dennis Hopper) who quotes him. It infects the perspective and images of the Kurtz sequence of the film to produce a nimbus of the sort that the narrator of Conrad's *Heart of Darkness* attributes to Marlow's story-telling technique: "To him the meaning of an episode was not inside like a kernel but outside, enveloping the tale which brought it out only as a glow brings out a haze, in the likeness of one of these misty halos that sometimes are made visible by the spectral illumination of moonshine" (Conrad, 219). One can fruitfully narrate the episode set in Kurtz's compound in the film as a sequence haunted by Eliot's poetry. As Willard and his decimated patrol boat crew glide into the ghostly harbor of Kurtz's temple compound, they are like souls crossing the river Styx into the underworld, the literal land of the dead. ("This is the dead land / This is cactus land / Here the stone images / Are raised, here they receive / The supplication of a dead man's hand" [Eliot, "The Hollow Men," 57]). Lance, his face masked in fantastic camouflage makeup, encounters Montagnards in white face and body paint, more fan-tastic and fabulous than he ("There will be time, there will be time / To prepare a face to meet the faces that you meet" [Eliot, "The Love Song of J. Alfred Prufrock," 4]). The scene is shrouded in fog ("Unreal City, / Under the brown fog of a winter dawn" [Eliot, *Waste Land,* 39]) and the strange silhouettes that appeared to be crosses and totems now take form as human bodies hanging from trees like ripe fruit, some half-naked, some upside down, silently gliding past the moving boat or floating in the water like fish as the boat enters a land whose vegetation is the dead.

"The place was full of bodies," Willard's narration comments; he lists them like varieties of fruit: "North Vietnamese, Viet Cong, Cambodians." Willard and his crew see heads buried in the earth like tubers ("'Stetson! / 'You who were with me in the ships at Mylae! / 'That corpse you planted last year in your garden, / 'Has it begun to sprout?'" [Eliot, *Waste Land,* 39]). The fertility rituals that shape and inform the myth of the Fisher King have be-come irredeemable in Coppola's Cambodia, where Nature is irretrievable from the Unnatural, and where the macabre and the morbid have gained dominion over creation, reproduction, and growth.[19] The only thing bred in Kurtz's kingdom is death. Willard's silent, stately, eerie entrance of the boat into Kurtz's underworldly kingdom is a departure from Marlow's approach to Kurtz in Conrad's novella. For Marlow, Kurtz's monstrosity comes into view with a brutal shock, a sudden and unprepared visual assault. Coppola opts instead for a quiet, virtually unremarked introduction to horror that appears to be ubiquitous and inescapable: dead bodies visually fill the screen, appearing at the top, at the bottom, as background, as a grisly "local color" of death that is represented as endemic, as having become the ontological condition of the war.

If the dreamlike and mythified scene of Willard's entry into the domain of Kurtz appears to dehistoricize—and therefore depoliticize—the film, a comparison of Coppola's narrative and cinematic choices with their textual alternatives provides a different view. Coppola uses the same icon of horror—the severed head—used by Conrad to represent Kurtz's barbarity. But Conrad resorts to a highly specific perspectival strategy that makes Kurtz's brutality visible almost casually, through an inadvertence or chance, a stray sight whose visual and emotional shock is mitigated by the distance and miniaturization provided by the telescope, as Marlow scans Kurtz's house, with its seemingly ornamented fence:

> And then I made a brusque movement, and one of the remaining posts of that vanished fence leaped up in the field of my glass. . . . Now I had suddenly a nearer view, and its first result was to make me throw my head back as if before a blow. Then I went carefully from post to post with my glass, and I saw my mistake. These round knobs were not ornamental but symbolic. . . . They would have been even more impressive, those heads on the stakes, if their faces had not been turned to the house. Only one, the first I had made out, was facing my way. (Conrad, 73)

In his Vietnam account, *Dispatches,* Michael Herr—who wrote Willard's narration for *Apocalypse Now*—borrowed the Conradian technique of making U.S. sadism representable by distancing and miniaturizing it, not through a telescope but through a camera, through the device of snapshots in pornographic photo albums: [20] "There were hundreds of these albums in Vietnam, thousands, and they all seemed to contain the same pictures: . . . the severed-head shot, the head often resting on the chest of the dead man or being held up by a smiling Marine, or a lot of heads, arranged in a row, with a burning cigarette in each of the mouths, the eyes open . . . (211).

But Coppola, like Kurtz, has *something special* planned for the viewer, involving a severed head. Like Coppola's Willard, we are momentarily put off our guard by meeting the long-anticipated, multifaceted, mysterious, eloquent Kurtz himself. This shadowy figure is disarmingly congenial and adept at friendly small talk: "'Where are you from, Willard?' 'I'm from Ohio, Sir' . . . 'How far are you from the river?' 'The Ohio River, Sir?' . . . 'I went down that river once, when I was a boy.'" Kurtz's question about the Ohio River, with its evocations of other U.S. literary river journeys, displays an exquisite aesthetic and symbolic sensibility. Just before he begins an ablution of his (figuratively bloody) hands and head, Kurtz remembers the innocence of his boyhood river journey on the Ohio as ending in a gardenia plantation that made him feel that heaven had fallen upon the earth ("Yet when we came back, late, from the Hyacinth garden, / Your arms full, and your hair wet, I could not / Speak, and my eyes failed" [Eliot, *Waste Land,* 38]). This idyllic river journey to a gardenia plantation that was heaven on earth fairly echoes its poetic antonym, Willard's nightmarish river journey to a Cambodia plantation that is hell on earth. When Kurtz turns the conversation to Willard's mission ("Did they say why they wanted to terminate my command?"), his tropes are no less eloquent:

> "Are you an assassin?"
> "I'm a soldier."
> "You're neither. You're an errand boy sent by grocery clerks to collect a bill."

Without transition—like the parataxis of modernist poetry—Willard is seen tied to the inside of a cage, being given water by the photojournalist, who promises ominously that "he's got plans for you." While he speaks, the plan commences as large shoes walk through the mire toward Chef on his boat, preparing to call in the emergency air strike. Kurtz, painted like a Montagnard, throws the bloody, open-eyed head of Chef into Willard's lap in his cage as Willard shrieks in morbid disgust and moral horror. ("There will be time, there will be time / To prepare a face to meet the faces that you meet; / There will be time to murder and create. / And time for all the works and days of hands / That lift and drop a question on your plate" [Eliot, "Prufrock," 4].)

The shock of this severed head—giant and close up, not miniaturized and distant—exceeds in horror that of Conrad. The horror is reminiscent of another such moment in a Coppola film: the Hollywood producer Jack Woltz finding the head of his prize racehorse, Khartoum, in his bed in *The Godfather*. On one level, Coppola's point is the same: to show gangsterism's violence transgressing into the realm of psychological terrorism and gratuitously ghoulish sadism. We are reminded of Marlow's understated observation that "I want you clearly to understand that there was nothing exactly profitable in these heads being there" (Conrad, 73). But the image also has a political texture that has been prepared by layers of incident and irony throughout the film. Chef ("All I ever wanted was to fucking cook!") has been repeatedly traumatized to the point where he is terrified to leave the boat ("Never leave the boat!") without realizing that his destiny will snag on "the boat" (the Navy) as sampan and patrol boat become sites of massacre, madness, and execution. But Chef gets more than the safety of the boat wrong: fearing tigers and Montagnards, he dies not even by U.S. "friendly" fire—by military inadvertence, perhaps the called-in air strike that might have killed him—but by a sinister version of the Special Forces, gruesomely and deliberately murdered by "one of our own guys," by U.S. evil ("I was always afraid that if I died in an evil place, my soul wouldn't make it to heaven"). "I ain't afraid of all them fucking skulls," he told Willard when they arrived in Kurtz's compound—shortly before becoming one of them himself. By proleptically glossing with Kurtz's severed heads the heaped-up piles of skulls that became the notorious emblem of Pol Pot's Khmer Rouge reign of terror in Cambodia, Coppola presciently semaphores *The Killing Fields'* explicit blame that the United States' destabilization and fracture of the region inflamed the extremism of Cambodian communism.[21]

Why does Coppola, who is known to dislike producing gory scenes in his films (Chown, 133–34), invent Kurtz's decapitation of Chef? The act exceeds narrative necessity. Chef could have been captured or secured to prevent his calling in the air strike, his threat to the Kurtz compound simply neutralized by an underling. I believe that the Gothic melodrama of Kurtz, in Montagnard war paint, carrying the bloody head in bloody hands is necessary to deromanticize the enigmatic and increasingly charismatic figure of Kurtz. The violent terrorizing of Willard is followed by an eerily quiet interlude of serenity, recuperation, and philosophy that stands in dramatic contrast to the congested scene of portentous officiousness, moral hypocrisy, and palpable lying during Willard's initial briefing at Army Intelligence Headquarters in Nha Trang. Willard is brought into the temple-like rooms of Kurtz, given water, offered rice, and allowed to rest while native guards eat and smoke and Kurtz recites "The Hollow Men." The psychedelic photo-journalist (played by Dennis Hopper) tries to translate Kurtz's meaning to Willard, as the young Harlequin figure of the Russian sailor does in Conrad's novella. His explanation of Kurtz's "simple dialectics . . . there's only love and hate" sounds disturbingly like the Army general using Kurtz's lawless-ness to imply the virtue and probity of the Army. Kurtz's bookshelf with its mythological texts and his photos of wife and son are scanned to review signs of a cultured, humane mind dismembered by some remembered hor-ror that is given a narrative, a set of images, as the tale of the inoculated children's severed arms. "I cried, I wept like some grandmother," Kurtz tells Willard, "I wanted to tear my teeth out." Images of mutilation and dismem-berment become highly overdetermined by the end of Coppola's film, as Kurtz is represented as a figure of mutilation. "I should have been a pair of ragged claws / Scuttling across the floors of silent seas" (Eliot, "Prufrock," 5), the photojournalist quotes Kurtz as quoting. As Willard tries to decide what to do, he reflects on Kurtz: "I've never seen a man so broken up, so ripped apart." Kurtz's brutal murder and desecration of Chef is needed to under-score the point that even if Kurtz represents to Willard (and us) the pre-ferred nightmare of an ugly and blatant truth, his is an abominable night-mare all the same.

"You have a right to kill me. You have no right to judge me," Kurtz tells Willard. But the entire last sequence of the film judges Kurtz amid his own complex, ambivalent, and urgent conditions for judgment. Militarily, Kurtz demands killing "without feeling, without passion, without judgment," and pronounces "judgment" as the Army's failure in Vietnam: "It's judgment that defeats us." Yet like Conrad's Kurtz and Shakespeare's Hamlet before him,[22] Coppola's Kurtz asks his surviving witness to report him and his cause aright: "I'm worried that my son might not understand what I tried to be. . . . I would want someone to go to my home. . . . There's nothing I detest more than lies. . . . If you understand me, Willard, you will do this for me." In *Heart of Darkness*, Kurtz's onerous request that he be given justice becomes the rack on which Marlow is excruciatingly tortured during his painful moral inquisition by Kurtz's Intended: "'And you admired him,' she said. 'It was impossible to know him and not to admire him. Was it?' 'He was a re-markable man,' I said unsteadily" (Conrad, 91). The Intended prods Marlow to sustain her illusions, to tell her what she wants to hear, while he squirms and prevaricates until he can no longer equivocate, until he corners himself into having to repeat Kurtz's last words to her: "'To the very end,' I said shakily. 'I heard his very last words . . .' I stopped in a fright" (Conrad, 93). In the end, Marlow lies to the Intended about Kurtz's last words, and thereby commits his gravest sin. Had Coppola followed Conrad's novella to this painful end—"He talked about shooting one last scene where Willard tells Kurtz's son the wrap-up, the statement of what it is all about. Then he dropped the idea . . ." [Coppola, 282])—we might have seen a figurative moral enactment of Kurtz's nightmare of a snail crawling on the edge of a straight razor and surviving. What would Willard have told Kurtz's son about the end of his father's life, his father's deeds, his father's character, his father's mission as a warrior? The problem allegorizes the relationship between the U.S. government and its representation of the Vietnam War to the U.S. public.

Whatever lies Marlow and Willard tell about Kurtz the first time, they tell their stories again, a second time, in the texts we read and hear in Conrad's novella and Coppola's film. This second telling conveys the greater truth behind Kurtz's truth: that Marlow and Willard, working for companies in the business of corporate cruelty and murder, have bloody feet and hands from walking in the bloody footsteps of colonialism and doing the bloody work of assassination, respectively. "If his story is really a confession, then so is mine," Willard intones while telling of his briefing about Kurtz at Army Intelligence Headquarters in Nha Trang. Willard is technically guiltier than Kurtz (admitting to six assassinations "close enough to blow their breath in my face"), who is formally charged with murder by the Army not for his atrocities in Cambodia but for the execution of four intelligence agents he identified—correctly, Willard surmises—as counterintelligence agents. Willard's invocation of the empty moral cliché "for my sins" ("I wanted a mission, and for my sins, they gave me one") is filled with truth and irony: that as an assassin for the CIA, he can be blackmailed to assassinate again, *with a difference*—"This time it was an American and an officer." The difference between their corporations and the Kurtzes is that the Kurtzes look into their own diseased souls ("But his soul was mad. . . . I had—for my sins, I suppose—to go through the ordeal of looking into it myself" [Conrad, 82]); the trade company and the Army refuse to look into theirs and acknowledge what Coppola's Kurtz calls "their lying morality." To judge Kurtz, Willard must judge the military ("They were going to make me a major for this, and I wasn't even in their fucking Army anymore") and himself. "What do you call it when the assassins accuse the assassins?" Kurtz asks in the tape played at Nha Trang. Willard is ordered to terminate Kurtz "with extreme prejudice," though his literal prejudice shifts, like Kurtz's, away from the Army's "lying morality" toward the renegade's brand of brutal candor and candid brutality. Is Willard's killing of Kurtz then an act of euthanasia, like his dispatch of the wounded woman on the sampan—"He just wanted to go out like a soldier—standing up"? Is it a form of assisted suicide, an accession that Kurtz must become one with his kingdom of the dead, because everyone wanted him dead, "him most of all"? "Even the jungle wanted him dead," Willard says of Kurtz. "That's who he took his orders from, after all." Does Willard, in killing Kurtz, too begin to obey the law of the jungle, to go native and throw off his military trappings and the Army's "lying morality," to perform his murderous deed as a savagery of unvarnished and gory relish? By film's end, all remaining members of the Army mission have assumed images of having gone native—Chef, shaded by a banana leaf, like a hatted tropical fruit; benign Lance, dressed in a loincloth, playing with the children and petting the sacrificial ox; possibly it is the renegade Colby who performs tai chi in the background as Kurtz discourses to Willard; and, of course, Kurtz, scrawling his version of Conrad's genocidal recommendation ("Drop the Bomb—Exterminate them All") on his memo to headquarters. Finally, Willard, having become Kurtz's double in savage war paint, rises from the water as though returning from the abyss to kill the unarmed Kurtz, not like a soldier in battle but brutally, like an ox at slaughter, with a machete or a bolo knife. What could Willard have told Kurtz's son about how his father died?

Willard's narrative in the film is his confession ("If his story is really a confession, then so is mine"), and with it he looks into the heart of his own darkness, ranging from his military assassinations ("six for sure") to his savage murder of Kurtz, from his barely concealed racism toward Clean and Chief to his icy dispatch of the wounded Vietnamese woman. Willard's "sins" are no mere rhetorical evocation, and, like Kurtz's extremism, they are product, effect, and confession of the U.S. corporate violence that was Vietnam. The self-reflection inscribed in the twice-told narrative of *Apocalypse Now* generates a spiral of extratextual self-reflection as well, both for the viewer obliged by the film to confront the U.S. citizenry's complicity with the making of the debacle of Vietnam and for the auteur, the filmmaker whose own troubled journey in making the film has often been metaphorized as his own *Heart of Darkness* and his own Vietnam. Coppola is reported to have told an interviewer at the 1979 Cannes Film Festival, "The film is not a movie; it's not about Vietnam. It *is* Vietnam. It's what it was really like; it was crazy" (Goodwin and Wise, 263). Eleanor Coppola gave the metaphor a twist during a time of crisis in the filming when she accused Francis in a telex of recreating on his set in the Philippines the United States' corruption of Vietnam: "He was setting up his own Vietnam with his supply lines of wine and steaks and air conditioners. Creating the very situation he went there to expose" (Coppola, 177). The film critic Maureen Orth, of *Newsweek,* accused him of corrupting the local Filipinos with the company's disproportionate spending: "Although the local wage was less than $10 a week, for nine months the company had been spending $100,000 a week" (Goodwin and Wise, 226). Jeffrey Chown voices the larger criticism leveled against the film: "In paying the Marcos government for use of its military equipment, Coppola was supporting a government possibly more repressive than the South Vietnamese government of Diem" (126). More intimately, Eleanor Coppola's journal relates her husband's nervous breakdown during the film. "I began to see more and more clearly the parallels between the film and Francis's life" (212), she writes. "The film he is making is a metaphor for a journey into the self. He has made that journey and is still making it. It is scary to watch someone you love go into the center of himself and confront his fears, fear of failure, fear of death, fear of going insane" (180). But Jeffrey Chown finally severs the parallels between film content and film production when he argues that "the final moral of this story is that Hollywood-in-the-Philippines is not Vietnam. . . . If Coppola went through moral anguish with the rigors of *Apocalypse Now,* he was eventually well paid for his nightmares" (127).

The more significant relationship between the film's narrative and its production may be the one inscribed by Coppola into the film itself. By having photojournalists play small but crucial roles in the narrative, he glosses the role that the media played in Vietnam, for good and ill. By transforming Conrad's young Russian Harlequin from a romantic landlocked sailor to a manic photojournalist, Coppola conjured Vietnam's fascination for the news media and the collusion that romantic fascination provoked. He is less successful in showing the reciprocal military fascination with being photographed and reported, which Michael Herr so vividly dramatizes in *Dispatches:* "This particular colonel loved to order the chopper in very low so that he could fire his .45 into the Cong, and he'd always wanted pictures of it" (213). Coppola instead opts for making the opposing point, that photojournalists could be deterred from recording what they saw. Kurtz threatens

the photojournalist (as Conrad's Kurtz threatens the young Russian) *for tak-*
ing his picture—"If you take my picture again, I'm going to kill you"—suggesting that many U.S. atrocities committed in Vietnam and Cambodia went
unreported. But perhaps the most interesting and famous self-reflexive scene
in the film is Coppola's cameo appearance as a member of a television news
crew filming Colonel Kilgore's men after their mopping-up operation. "Don't
look at the camera," Coppola screams at Willard. "Just go past as if you were
fighting." The scene reminds us forcibly of how the presence of the camera
warped putatively documentary film and video footage in Vietnam, by inter-
polating self-consciousness into the pressure and opportunity to act the
scenes that were relayed to the home front. Coppola acknowledges in this
scene that *Apocalypse Now,* like photojournalism, is neither war nor simulation but a representation obliged to problematize itself. When the war in
Vietnam ended, not with apocalypse, as expected, but rather as T. S. Eliot
predicted in "The Hollow Men"—*"This is the way the world ends / This is the*
way the world ends / This is the way the world ends / Not with a bang but a
whimper" (59)—the photojournalists left, like the figure played by Dennis
Hopper in Coppola's film, "and with a whimper I'm fucking splitting, Jack."
But, in truth, photojournalism helped end the war, and Francis Ford Coppola, animated by the critical narrative of the invisible Joseph Conrad and
the poetry he inspired, obliged the United States to revisit this particular
heart of its darkness.

9

ONLY THE GUNS HAVE EYES

Military Censorship and the Body Count in the Persian Gulf War

War and Hyperreality

BY THE END OF THE TWENTIETH CENTURY, THE KNOWL-edge and representation of modern warfare had inevitably become inflected by dramatic changes in electronic communications technology and their effect on the perception of "reality" and the possibilities of truth. But if the Vietnam War of the 1960s and 1970s was a television war, its gritty images of close-up combat and injury brought into the American living room every night for more than a harrowing decade, the Persian Gulf War of the early 1990s was different: video within video, representations not of carnage but of technology, a media production of media that looked more like simulation than representation. As warfare, the brief, intense Persian Gulf War during six weeks of early 1991 superficially resembled the destructive strategic bombing attacks of World War II, with all the effects of Edith Wyschogrod's manmade mass death as maximum destruction delivered in the most compressed moment of time. But militarily, the production of this level of carnage as the opening maneuver of a conflict signaled a major policy shift whose frightening implications—"to grant permission for the large-scale *systematic* murder of a nation's populace"—Susan Jeffords describes as scientifically engineered and culturally sanctioned terror:

> What distinguishes the Persian Gulf War from earlier instances . . .
> is that the strategies of terror that are part of the death-world were
> used, not at the end of an already long and brutal war (as in the
> use of the atom bomb, the fire-bombing of Tokyo, the conflagra-
> tion of Dresden, the carpet-bombing of Hanoi, or the massacre at
> Wounded Knee), but as its initial strategy. In this way, the U.S. en-
> gagement in the Persian Gulf War moved warfare in the post–Cold
> War era into a distinctively different and more terrifying phase: the
> combination of the death-world and the technological world as a
> philosophy of war.

The Persian Gulf War reversed the narrative sense of the beginnings and
endings of war by making the depopulation that should mark the drama of
its end—the last resort and final outcome—its opening gambit.[1] But this
particular population cataclysm achieved its high popularity and approval
through a military censorship that made it, to the U.S. public, virtually
corpseless.[2] The synergistic relationship between military censorship and
media control produced a sensation of hyperreality that made the Persian
Gulf War strangely indeterminate with respect to "reality"—a problem that
became the flash point of bitter debate by contemporary critical theorists of
the postmodern condition. I intend in this chapter to use this debate to illuminate the human body's derealization by technological media under military control in warfare at the end of the twentieth century.

In a sense, the theoretical debates over postmodernism's enabling or
foreclosure of politically relevant criticism preceded the Persian Gulf War.
Christopher Norris, in *What's Wrong with Postmodernism?* urgently questioned the threat that skepticism about the adequacy of knowledge seems to
pose to the possibility of political praxis. He specifically deplored the cynicism toward political action produced by hypertextualist and hyperrealist
conceptions of culture that remove the ground of truth and reality from the
foundations of progressive action. Yet these debates on the enabling or dis-
abling of political activism by theory are most fruitfully conducted—as the
example of "nuclear criticism" has shown[3]—with reference to history. After
a number of pieces by Jean Baudrillard were printed on the Persian Gulf
War—one in the *Guardian* a few days before its outbreak, which predicted
that "this war would never happen, existing as it did only as a figment of
mass-media simulation, war games rhetoric or imaginary scenarios" (Norris,

11), and one published afterward in *Libération* called "The Gulf War Has Not Taken Place"—Christopher Norris was impelled to write a counterattack called *Uncritical Theory: Postmodernism, Intellectuals, and the Gulf War.* In the Postscript of this book, Norris excoriates the irresponsibility of Baudrillard's contention that "the true belligerents are those who thrive on the ideology of the truth of this war. . . . If we have no practical knowledge of this war—and such knowledge is out of the question—then let us at least have the skeptical intelligence to reject the probability of all information, of all images whatever their source" (193–94). I share Norris's dislike for reading a destructive historical event as a phenomenon of hyperreality, but at the same time I find Baudrillard's theory useful for explaining the Pentagon's new strategies for transforming war into a seemingly virtual event. I further wish to press beyond this point to analyze how the Persian Gulf War's hyper-realities were constructed out of a military press censorship whose agenda was to derealize casualties, to strip them of the impact of "reality" and thereby make Operation Desert Storm murderously destructive yet simultaneously corpseless.

The effect of this censorship on the transmission and perception of the war's "reality" raises questions about subtle possibilities of truth management beyond mere deception or disinformation. From the vantage of the public, did knowing that all the news was censored paradoxically serve to warrant a repressed truth and a hidden reality—say, the materiality of 100,000 dead Iraqi bodies? Did censorship thereby continually threaten to unmask the technological media extravaganza of Operation Desert Storm? From the Pentagon's vantage, was censorship used to create the illusion of reality, to make its layered series of simulacra appear real: the prepared maps, computer simulations, training rehearsals, televised briefings, and staged scenarios that gave the war all the trappings of a planned media happening? To ask the question more cynically, did censorship lend an aura of reality to a Pentagon public relations stunt designed to repair Vietnam's damage to the military image, in which the Iraqis were always already chiefly conscripted props or involuntary extras in an orchestrated Pentagon show? Has military censorship made it possible to replace the older, simpler forms of official lying known as "propaganda" with the state-of-the-art subtleties of image control that have taken the place of political debate in late twentieth-century presidential campaigns, as some critics charge? If censorship's purpose is lying and deceit, there remains hope of an unproblematic truth. But if its function is a performative aesthetics, a creative production of sentimental narratives ("support our troops") and sleek, monochromatic aesthetic effects (steel and "camies"), then the military has indeed textualized the war, staged the massive violence to produce a marketable scenario of "winning." In that case, both truth and reality are swallowed up in a play of scenes and signs whose *unreality* is all that can be disavowed. Was this censorship's job: to lend a patina of "real" war, of genuine superpower might, to a conflict that even *Newsweek*'s tame reportage characterized as colonial adventurism, likening it to "the use of air power by colonial forces in the 1930's: Italians beating up on defenseless Ethiopians"—"as if, one Marine put it, Rhode Island had taken on the United States" (Mar. 11, 1991, 42, 38)?[4] Richard Keeble expresses it even more dramatically: "There was no Gulf war of 1991. In the way in which the term is generally used and understood, what took place in the Persian Gulf in January–February 1991 was not a war at all. It was nothing less than a series of massacres" (5). If so, was the Pentagon's use of censorship wildly successful or not? In either case, academic criticism appeared required to intervene, intellectually, in an arena in which the press seemed constrained by its role as a principal in the war, and largely unwilling to demystify its own complicities while the conflict was in progress.[5] Stanley Cloud of *Time* wrote, "Throughout the long evolution of the Department of Defense pool, the press willingly, passively, and stupidly went along with it" (quoted in MacArthur, 35). And Richard Keeble said of the British press, "Many elite journalists were remarkably supportive of the government-censorship ground rules. Some were positively enthusiastic. An editorial in *The Economist* of 19 January 1991 commended opposition politicians for suspending 'the normal play of democratic argument'" (125).

The most remarkable feature of the new press censorship policy in effect during the Persian Gulf was its proleptic character, its emplacement in advance not only of the Iraq-Kuwait conflict but theoretically of all future wars. Malcolm W. Browne's account of the Sidle Commission traced the new system of press control to the news industry's protest of the total press exclusion in the Grenada "war" of 1983. "Their employers objected so strongly that the Pentagon convened a commission headed by Maj. Gen. Winant Sidle, retired chief of Army information, and made up mainly of military and Government public-affairs officials. It recommended that future wars be covered by pools of news representatives—selected, controlled and censored by the military" (29). The new censorship policy thereby functions as a programming of history, a maneuver that proleptically concedes the priority of history as text to history as experiential phenomenon. The conditions for the writing of history may always be suspected of being determinable and determined. But Pentagon press censorship renders this determination visible by giving historiography a different institutional mise-en-scène or staging: "In effect, each pool member is an unpaid employee of the Department of Defense, on whose behalf he or she prepares the news of war for the outer world" (Browne, 29). History may always be institutionally produced—by the academy, for instance. But its production before the facts, its writing in advance of its referent, is not considered traditional in a democracy.[6] Yet that is the effect of "pre-censorship," as Walter Cronkite called it in his testimony before the Senate Committee on Governmental Affairs: "I'd rather have post-censorship, where you could argue it out after you get your story" (Rosenstiel, "Senators Told"). Pre-censorship performs what Baudrillard calls "the precession of simulacra" that illustrates history's entry into the ontological space of the hyperreal: "It is the generation by models of a real without origin or reality: a hyperreal. The territory no longer precedes the map, nor survives it. Henceforth, it is the map that precedes the territory—*precession of simulacra*—it is the map that engenders the territory" (166). The new military censorship policy creates, in effect, the map that precedes the territory: the map of U.S. waged war as a technological miracle marked by the unlocatability of the dead. Military censorship produces the hyperreality of the most extreme maneuver of postmodern skepticism: the capture of death itself in the inescapable confines of rhetoric by denying it a material referent. When *Newsweek* writes the story of the Persian Gulf War under the headline "A Textbook Victory," the trope, marred only by its technological anachronism, functions as a tautology and a redundancy (Barry and Thomas, 38). Censorship makes all future U.S. wars potentially prewritten or scripted events by definition, since the unprogrammable experiential residue or excess—unpredictabilities, irregularities, mistakes, accidents, costs, atrocities, gratuitous destructions, uncontrollable consequences—can be pre-edited from the model text that writes its history in advance.

Military Censorship and the Press

Its new policy of proleptic censorship cost the Pentagon only the mark of its own self-reference: the price of concealment in the paradoxical visibility of the concealing gesture. In other words, in place of the censored foreign violence (the enemy body count, the witness of killing, the scenes of damage), a species of domestic violence was produced by censorship: a hobbled and gagged press complaining of its own constraint and abuse. But because the Sidle Commission policy allowed the military to introject and ingest the press ("Some reporters, hiding out in American Marine and Army field units, are meanwhile working in the guise of mascots, given G.I. uniforms and gear to look inconspicuous, enjoying the affection [and protection] of the units they're trying to cover" [Browne, 45]),[7] press stories about press censorship were treated as a kind of conscript complaint, a spoiled and insolent corps chafing and whining under newly imposed martial discipline. The Pentagon used its new powers to edit prose: "Even adjectives were edited: Frank Bruni of *The Detroit Free Press* wrote that pilots were 'giddy' on returning from early missions. Officers changed the word to 'proud'; they compromised on 'pumped up'" (Alter and Manegold, 61). The military delayed and rerouted copy ("Our stories have been sent instead to officials at the Tonopah Test Range in Nevada—the home base of the Stealth fighters" [Browne, 44]). And MPs disciplined fractious reporters ("I was spread-eagled across a Humvee [military vehicle] and searched and blindfolded" [Frantz, A15]). But reporters' complaints about their own treatment became the burlesque version ("I cannot tell you much about Army aviation at any price" [Balzar, "No War in Sight," A8]) of the off-stage tragedy of a country bombed back to the pre-industrial age—its people killed (100,000 dead, according to U.S. Defense Intelligence estimates) at the rate of about one per minute during a six-week period.

If military censorship allowed the Pentagon to script and stage the Persian Gulf War as a pre-edited performance, it simultaneously inscribed for the press a role not of adversarial resistance—not of aggressive investigative reporting to uncover the action behind the briefings and to fill in the gaps and silences—but of figures trapped in a *mise en abîme*. The press was left repetitively describing the bars of its cage and writing the story of its own failure: "Unfortunately, this is a story we cannot tell you much about " (Balzar, "No War in Sight," A8). In place of the story of the war ("Flying Blind to Tell the Story on Army Aviation"; "The Pentagon Strategy for the Press: Good News or No News"; "Just the Good News, Please") the press was obliged to present the public with a mirror of its own impotence. Indeed, journalism also scripted itself in advance as a proleptic burlesque—even in the academy. The *Columbia Journalism Review,* the profession's most respected academic organ, assigned its war correspondence to a writer who camouflaged himself in name and persona as the protagonist of Evelyn Waugh's satirical *Scoop:* "William Boot is the pen name of Christopher Hanson, the Washington correspondent for the *Seattle Post-Intelligencer.* He will be reporting on the gulf war from Saudi Arabia in the next issue" (Boot, 23). In place of a serious analysis of press options for eluding censorship to report, say, Iraqi casualty figures to the U.S. public, Boot gave the press mock-heroic advice drawn from the Hemingwayesque school of war correspondence: "They should get in their Land Rovers or onto their motorcycles and go where the action is. The public might hate them. The Pentagon might expel them. The Iraqis might even kill them. But at least they shall have acquitted themselves with honor" (24). Boot's metaphor ("Journalists accredited to the allied command in Saudi Arabia are, in effect, prisoners of war, trapped behind the barbed wire of reporting curbs" [24]) was eventually enacted by the CBS Middle East correspondent Bob Simon and his crew, who were captured by Iraqi patrols in an unauthorized zone near the border intersection of Iraq, Saudi Arabia, and Kuwait on January 21, 1991. The result of this maverick action was only self-reflexive news—the press reporting on itself: "Iraq Frees Captured CBS News Crew; Network Credits Soviet Intervention" (Fineman, A8). Military censorship traps the press in its own journalistic mirror.

When that mirror cracked only a little (and then after the fact), the truth it revealed—of what was censored and why—simultaneously revealed even more intractable blindness. The truth, of course, was no surprise: it was killing, and the image of the violently killed, that the Pentagon's elaborate press control mechanisms sought to keep out of sight. This was John Balzar's story of why his crew failed to get their story on Army aviation: "Maybe it was because of the stories two of us filed before the ground war began. The stories described vivid videotapes taken from Apache gun cameras during early patrols into Iraq. The video images were the first of the conflict to show, close up, the killing of individual soldiers" ("No War in Sight," A8). The Army is not ashamed of killing, but only of *being seen* killing.[8] But the gun camera video inscribes an even greater peril in the self-reference inherent in its optical "gaze." The viewer of the video assumes, literally, the gun's point of view of an actual killing—an experience that if it were made available to the public would force it to become the gun's "eye" and to assume the spatial position of the agency of killing, to stand in place as killer. In addition the viewing public would need to recognize or *see* itself as the ocularly instrumental agency of killing—the lethal eye of the U.S. gaze that kills. What is censored, then, is the extraordinary capability of video technology to re-introduce into modern mass warfare the ability to witness one's own act of killing, the self's lethality—for example, Paul Bäumer's stabbing of the Frenchman in *All Quiet on the Western Front*—which seemed to have been lost in the nuclear age. But by driving this peril of self-recognition under-ground (in a cultural sense), the Pentagon's press censorship transforms the restored significant moment of historical "witness" into the realm of an ob-scene textuality whose transgression resides in the fact that it has a "real" referent it is not supposed to have. In other words, military censorship has replaced open and public war correspondence with a species of secret snuff film. By extension, military censorship has shifted the witness of war from the realm of historiography to the realm of a classified, and therefore under-ground, pornography. When such footage does become available to the U.S. public—for example, in the images of charred bodies and killing obtained by Bill Moyers from *Newsday* and British television—truth remains under a mark of transgressive textuality and the viewer is placed in the position of a media voyeur.[9]

Counting the Dead

The crack in the mirror of censorship revealed only ghosts: John Balzar reporting stories he could not tell about scenes he did not see, whose residue is a rumored knowledge of classified Army footage of close-up killing that no one ever saw except the guns. But even the most aggressive investigative reporting to ferret out the censored enemy casualty figures seemed doomed to entrapment in the "precession of simulacra." In one of the most significant pieces of reporting on the Persian Gulf War, John H. Cushman Jr.'s story in the *New York Times* of February 3, 1991, explained the Pentagon policy that there would be no Iraqi casualty count during this war. Cushman delved into alternative possibilities for reconstructing enemy casualty information, but the suggestions he received and relayed relied on electronically inferred and produced data that owed their chief instruments, methods, and proce-dures to the very War College apparatus that produced the "textbook" in the first place. After speaking to Joshua Epstein, a military analyst at the Brook-ings Institution, Cushman reported:

> But other analysts noted that the Pentagon has a great deal of infor-mation, including photographs taken by satellites and aircraft, and

complete lists of targets hit and bombs dropped, that would allow it to make a reliable estimate, perhaps within a margin of error of several thousand. . . . A formula could be constructed based on a list of targets struck, estimated population densities at and near the targets, the lethal radius of the explosives dropped, and the accuracy of similar weapons in tests. (10)

As an aspect of BDAs (bomb damage assessments), the censored enemy dead return to their origin as ghosts in the electronic simulators that first engendered them theoretically at the War College in Leavenworth, Kansas. Duncan Moore describes this "graduate school for warriors":

Each of four battalion commanders sits at an oversized computer screen, giving directions to a keyboard operator who executes the order. The display shows a contour map of the battlefield. U.S. forces are blue markers; the enemy is red. The software replicates the soldier's weapons and its range. When a shot is fired, the computer gives a mathematical result based on the probability of hitting the target, and if hit, of killing it. (A1O).

War is literally preceded by simulacra, and the enemy dead are both before and after the fact figures of theory, hypothetical objects beforehand, and statistical folds or margins of error afterward. What they are *not* are figures of phenomenology, actual beings (subjective or objective) that are ontologically mortal, figures of empiricism, material objects of sufficient individuality to be either counted or represented. *Time* magazine reported on June 17, 1991, "The Defense Intelligence Agency last week released an internal estimate of 100,000 Iraqi soldiers killed, 300,000 wounded. But DIA said those figures had an 'error factor of 50% or higher'—to a statistician, a grotesque number. The Pentagon has little wish to refine its figures either" (26).[10] Which 50,000 Iraqis are the phantoms that live in the dimension of unknowability and unlocatability, and in the rhetorical carelessness of the "more or less" of a margin of error of 50 percent on a figure of 100,000 lives?

When censorship reduces the dead to phantoms of speculation, it shifts them from one language to another. Instead of objects of *destruction,* "evidence" (in empirical language) capable of serving as the locus of ethical address, the dead become objects of *deconstruction,* figures problematized in their unlocatability, and therefore unavailable to any intellectual scrutiny or discussion other than dispute of their existence. Censorship thereby plays a crucial role in the conscious philosophical shift in military theory that shaped Pentagon policy during the Persian Gulf War. Colonel Harry G. Summers Jr. (a retired military specialist who wrote theoretical military analysis for the *Los Angeles Times* during the war) traced the historical roots of the Pentagon's abandonment of the "body count" to a shift from one Napoleonic war strategist to another, from the empirical approach of Baron Antoine Henri Jomini, who urged understanding war in terms of mathematics, to the more psychological theories of Carl von Clausewitz, who emphasized the role of perception and morale in the achievement of victory. The Pentagon's own philosophical moves between the Vietnam War and the Persian Gulf War appear crudely to mirror the large shifts in academic social theory in the late twentieth century away from scientific positivism toward a more subtle Foucauldian grasp of the significance of institutional control over the production of knowledge. Censorship thus became the military's superweapon and metaweapon, its discursive "smart bomb," capable of guiding its technological fire power in the appropriate rhetorical and hermeneutical direction. Richard Keeble identifies *mediacentrism* as the locus of the shift from "militarism to new militarism": "Military strategy becomes essentially a media event: an entertainment, a spectacle. . . . Media manipulation becomes a central military strategy" (8).

Censorship, in fact, allows the Pentagon to deploy its control of knowledge selectively, in a way that invests its lethal activity with the intellectual legitimations of empiricism and the social authority of science while suppressing the representation of its effects. The mise-en-scène of the daily military briefing and press conference on C-SPAN during the Persian Gulf War became a theater of Enlightenment domination, a space where warrior scientists became pedagogues imparting to the public a knowledge "hard" and authorized because invested in the symbolic truth status of the empirical "facts" of quantifications and the occultations of a new technical language. This discourse was simultaneously supported by an apparatus of demonstration designed to confound representation and simulation in a performance of the indeterminate status of the "real." Thus the video clips of target hits were selected to replace the representational reference of the close-up killing in Balzar's snuff film with the simulatory figurations of electronic gaming, the miniaturized and abstracted dots and lines inside the cross-hairs that made General Norman Schwarzkopf's "luckiest man in Iraq," the tiny vehicle just safely crossing an exploding bridge, a Pac-man. Schwarzkopf's video of an actual bombing and an actual potential killing cannot be distinguished as a representation with a "real" or actual reference from a simulacrum or pure model of the same event. The Nintendo character of the Persian Gulf War merely signified the public's attempt to name its perception of the conflict's hyperreality. Indeed, the television graphics of the prize-nominated lead-in to CBS's *Showdown in the Gulf* was a highly sophisticated digitalized production, as described by its creator, a British graphics company called Quantel:

> To create the map and radar sweep, animator Steve Blakely sent a hi-con of the map and a moving line to 2-D. Then, Quantel Paintbox/Harry artist Don Butler painted the map to give it color and texture, and created a green trail of light to transform the moving line into a radar sweep. . . . At [Mitch] Friedman's request CBS news provided icons of war ships, jet fighters, and soldiers, which were manipulated in Paintbox and used in a variety of forms throughout this piece. (MacArthur, 83)

Censorship, then, has come to play a crucial role in the phenomenology of modern warfare by allowing the military to manipulate codes of the "real" for the purpose of controlling public perception and response. The operation of these "reality" manipulations have as their reference the figure of the killed or injured body for reasons that Elaine Scarry's explication of the metaphysics of martial killing makes very clear:

> That is, the outcome of war has its substantiation not in an absolute inability of the defeated to contest the outcome but in a process of perception that allows extreme attributes of the body to be translated into another language, to be broken away from the body and relocated elsewhere at the very moment that the body itself is disowned. . . . The force of the material world is separated from the fifty-seven thousand or fifty million hurt bodies and conferred not only on issues and ideologies that have as a result of the first function been designated the winner, but also on the idea of winning itself. (124)

Because of this power of the dead body's materiality to signify an excess of "reality" in its massed and accumulated effects, military discourse has historically developed conventions to simultaneously display and hide, acknowledge and disavow its presence. One of these strategies is a rhetorical convention that Scarry describes as the sublating of the body of the individual soldier into a collectivized metaphorical corpus that transforms the Army itself into an embodied colossus whose features lend anatomical personification to injury and disablement (the severed "arteries" of ruptured supply routes, "decapitation" by destruction of command headquarters, the maneuver of "outflanking" battalions by skirting their sides, etc.). Scarry adumbrates the ideological consequences of this "convention which assists the disappearance of the human body from accounts of the very event that is the most radically embodying event in which human beings ever collectively participate" (71). By replacing necrology with technology, contemporary censorship allowed the Pentagon to shift the embodied trope of the Army onto the cybernetic machine, transforming the enemy into a robotic body whose injury is best calculated by BDA's (bomb damage assessments) undistorted by body counts. "In military terms," John Cushman explains, "the number of dead is not considered as important as the number of hits against command centers, communication links, airfields, and major weapons"—targets whose translation reconstitutes them as the vital sites of a cybernetic robot: brain (command centers), speech (communication links), feet (airfields), and arms (major weapons). The logic of these translations was, in the Persian Gulf, to evoke precisely those popular cultural formations that are recognizable as simulacra (computer-generated "special effects" rather than representations) of futuristic warfare. Commentators called it "robowar" (Easterbrook) and invoked *Star Wars*: "Buck Rogers and Luke Skywalker would be at home in the Gulf War," Admiral Dunn reported.

Retroping the soldierly body as a collectivized robotic figure not only disembodies the killed human body twice over—materially and rhetorically—as Scarry suggests, but further transforms its ontological status according to the conventions of a postmodernistic logic. The dead enemy body becomes the product of chance and accident—as much a form of "collateral damage" as the civilian dead—and it thereby becomes noninstrumental, nonreferential, and formally irrelevant, its significance dispersed and unlocatable. The operation of censorship, which implements the dead enemy body's institutional irrelevance by denying the need to see it or know it or count it or commemorate it, colludes with its marginalization as a material excess or surplus, as bombing debris ("After bombing, they were moving this debris with shovels. . . . While [doing so], they see dead bodies—some legs, some heads. They remove these things" (Fineman), as technological garbage. This marginalization was confirmed in the aftermath of the conflict, when for a time the only attempts to produce or learn an official Iraqi body count were made by conservation agencies: Greenpeace had its director of military research produce an estimate, and the Natural Resource Defense Council used the Freedom of Information Act to compel an estimate from the Defense Intelligence Agency. Their efforts suggest, in addition to a humanitarian concern, the logic that the Iraqi dead ended up mattering chiefly as a potential pollutant and contaminant—the decay and degradation of 100,000 largely formally unburied corpses—of a fragile desert ecosystem. The minimal eyewitness journalism permitted after (but not during) the ground war on the highly localized highways inscribed in the timing of its utterance the effects of time and nature on the material degradation of the recently dead: "At one spot, snarling wild dogs have reduced two corpses to bare ribs," Bob Drogin wrote on March 10, more than a week after the fighting stopped. "Giant carrion birds claw and pick at another; only a boot-clad foot and eyeless skull are recognizable" ("On Forgotten Kuwait Road, A10).

These journalistic accounts of the carnage on the highway, the only graphic necrological accounts to come out of the Persian Gulf War, demonstrate how shrewdly the military controlled not only what it concealed but also what it permitted to have revealed. Virtually every report expended considerable prose on an inventory of looted consumer goods strewn about at the site, "new television sets and videocassette recorders; shirts in plastic wrappers; unopened bottles of Chanel perfume; children's bikes and baby strollers" (Drogin, "Images of War Carnage," A17) to tacitly suggest that the carnage signified the justice of a criminal execution meted out to looters guilty, presumably, of a capital offense.[11] The new style of war correspondence inaugurated by contemporary military censorship has created a *mise en abîme* of ideological consumption. The media's outrage over the Iraqi looters' violation of the consumer economy was buttressed by its own obedience to that same economy: a new compact between Pentagon and press that obliges journalism to package the news of war as other political news (campaigns, summit conferences, diplomatic travel, televised hearings) is packaged—for politically profitable purchase and consumption. "Convincing Americans to fight a war to liberate a tiny Arab sheikhdom ruled by a family oligarchy would require the demonization of Hussein in ways never contemplated by human rights groups. . . . The war had to be sold," John

246

MacArthur wrote. "Fortunately for the President, there was talented help at hand" (41). MacArthur went on to narrate how a Kuwaiti organization hired the American (British-owned) public relations firm of Hill and Knowlton at a cost of over $5 million to manufacture publicity items, including atrocity stories.[12]

Once Operation Desert Storm was under way, the daily Pentagon briefings took over the public relations project. Richard Keeble writes, "Schwarzkopf's performances were above all theatrical, straight out of the Hollywood tradition. . . . The 'Stormin' Norman Show' was perfectly suited to the largely male-dominated, chauvinist environment of the press conferences" (123). The easy selection of domesticated martial images in the war's aftermath— Norman Schwarzkopf in signature "camies" with stuffed bear at hand, tearful reunions of soldier families, yellow-ribboned parades—made the Persian Gulf War's assimilation to the genres of television entertainment smooth and seamless. Viewers soon saw Schwarzkopf's talk show interviews with Barbara Walters and David Frost, Jonathan Winters's parody of his briefing style for America West Airlines commercials, Schwarzkopf's entry into the Disneyland logo, the made-for-television movie (*Heroes of Desert Storm*), the *TV Times* discussions of Peter Arnett's celebrity. In a piece titled "Antihero" ("Danny Schechter Looks at an Unreported Casualty—The Death of a Free and Objective Television Press)" Schechter brutally indicted the television networks for the crass commercial exploitation of the war aftermath:

New[s] organizations ran promo after promo, pimping off the war's popularity. *Time* and *Newsweek* pumped out souvenir editions; the line between news, entertainment, and merchandising began to disappear. In New York City, a daily newspaper helped pay for the "victory parade." . . . ABC tried to cash in one last time with a prime-time movie of the week salute to "the heroes of Desert Storm," complete with President Bush as the MC. Footage of the real events and dramatized material were intermixed. In a sense this lack of distinction between fantasy and reality was consistent with the way network news treated the war. (54).

The curious effect of military censorship's transformation of the Persian Gulf War into a hyperreal event is that, while it spared the U.S. public the trauma of contending with a "real" war, it also failed to register as a significant and lasting political credit for the Bush administration. *Hyperreality* cuts both ways: if it removes historical information from the realm of refer-entiality into the realm of illusion that the electronic game machine industry has named "virtuality" (from "virtual reality" [Schwartz and Librach]), its derealization of the dead bodies and the suffering generated by the massive destruction simultaneously deprived the war of what Elaine Scarry calls the "anchor" for its issues (108). Precensorship's pre-editing of representation places not only the phenomenological events of the fighting but also the political and historical significance of the enterprise under erasure. The war passed through the public imagination and memory like a video phantom, unable—in the absence of any national pain or suffering—to imprint a last-ing inscription on either the national conscience or the national self-image. The result has been a political revisionism ("Did the fighting end too soon?" ["Day We Stopped the War"])that precisely misses the point. The argument that the war was unfinished because Saddam Hussein remained in power failed to grasp the metaphysics of military winning and losing. Wars are not won or lost because this or that political objective is realized; they are won or lost because the killing and destruction that are the military activities of war have lent those military objectives their own peculiar code of empirical reality. According to this logic, even a significant change in Iraqi leadership or political power—bought at the cost of, say, a doubling of Allied and Iraqi casualties—would not have made the outcome more "real" if press censor-ship and information control had continued to render it "virtual" (in the optical sense). Or *was* that precisely the hidden point of the revisionary criti-cism of the war's aborted aims? When the suppressed violence made visible by the ground war was retrieved and called carnage, slaughter, and massacre ("The way Colin presented it, to have pursued the campaign beyond where we did would have been just a massacre"[ibid.]), the "clean win" produced by censorship was made to seem less hyperreal. A year after the Persian Gulf War, critics of its premature end had to work hard to make it feel, retro-actively, more like a "real war."

The relationship between censorship and the burial of the enemy in un-marked graves is not merely one of analogy, a parallel production of a signi-fied made unknowable by the erasure of its signifier. In the case of the Persian Gulf War the relationship was causal, censorship in the service of permitting mass burial of the uncounted dead ("U.S. journalists have reported seeing American and British troops shovelling the dead into shallow graves without identification and registration" [Burkhalter]). Holly Burkhalter of Human

Rights Watch complained that while the United States long delayed normalizing relations with Vietnam until the remaining 2,300 soldiers missing in action were accounted for, the United States treated the Iraqi dead as worth neither counting nor burying. Furthermore, the United States' refusal to account for and properly bury the enemy dead violated the Geneva Convention. "Articles 15 and 16 of the 1949 Convention require belligerents to search for the dead and to record any information that might aid in their identification. Article 17 requires that bodies be buried individually in marked graves, and only after careful examination to establish identity and cause of death" (Burkhalter). But censorship made possible even more egregious violations, such as the burial of the living, as *Newsday* disclosed in September 1991: "Using plows mounted on tanks and combat earthmovers, the U.S. Army division that broke through Saddam Hussein's defensive front line buried thousands of Iraqi soldiers—some still alive and firing their weapons—in more than 70 miles of trenches, according to U.S. Army officials. . . . No Iraqi body count was possible after the assault" (Sloyan). Would this assault by the First Mechanized Infantry Division have been countenanced by the U.S. public had journalism reported it in narrative and pictorial form on the evening news? Until the leak through *Newsday,* censorship made it possible for the administration and the Pentagon to conceal the incident (which had no journalistic witness) from Congress ("Defense Secretary Dick Cheney made no mention of the 1st Division's tactics in a recent interim report to Congress on Operation Desert Storm. . . . The Pentagon has withheld details of the assault from both the House and Senate Armed Services committees, according to committee officials" [Sloyan]).

Military censorship could place the mark of skepsis on all news information and official announcements received by the public in time of war, and could thereby stimulate an intense interrogation of governmental and military policy. Instead, it seems to have translated history into hyperreality, with the effect of derealizing warfare to the point of blunting apprehension, conscience, and memory along with criticism. The uncomfortable confrontation of official and journalistic discourses that at the time of Vietnam provoked protest and debate could have done the same in the Persian Gulf War if censorship had not muzzled journalism. "Americans treat human life as our most precious value" ("Fitzwater's Remarks"), Marlin Fitzwater stated in the official White House response to the bombing of the Baghdad shelter on February 13, 1991. But the unedited CNN feeds shown in the United States could have been supplemented by the far more detailed and graphic footage of the bombing impact obtained by Jordan TV. According to Laurie Garrett, the medical reporter for *Newsday,* most of the world's public, including Jordanians, never saw this footage: "This reporter viewed the unedited Baghdad feeds the following day; they showed scenes of incredible carnage. . . . Among the corpses were those of at least six babies and ten children, most of them so severely burned that their gender could not be determined. Rescue workers collapsed in grief, dropping corpses; some rescuers vomited from the stench of the still-smoldering bodies." Garrett quotes Rabah Rousan, the anchor for the English-language broadcast on Jordan TV, remembering of the footage, "I saw a young child's body, completely charred, clothes and hair all burned off, and there was still smoke coming off him." Garrett and Rousan may appear to be using the highly charged image of the dead child to sensationalize their argument. Yet the fact remains that such explicit information and images of the Baghdad bombing could have provoked much sharper challenge to Fitzwater's pious cant about the sanctity of human life. Later admissions forced by disclosures from the *London Independent* confirmed that the Pentagon—aware that the Ameriyah facility had been used as a shelter during the Iran-Iraq War (Healy)—believed it was bombing the families of the Iraqi military elite (Nairn, 16).

The U.S. public apparently so strongly supported military censorship during the Persian Gulf War ("The survey found that a majority of nearly 2 to 1 felt that military censorship is more important than the media's ability to report important news" [Rosenstiel, "Americans Praise Media"]) that Bill Kovach of Harvard's Nieman Foundation has called the policy "a watershed that will change the flow of official information not only in the military, but throughout government, increasing officials' power to bend public opinion to their will" (DeParle, 388). In January 1991 a number of news organizations, including the *Nation,* the *Village Voice,* and *Harper's,* sued the Defense Department in U.S. District Court in New York for imposing unconstitutional restrictions during the Gulf conflict. But as Michael Massing points out, "In the current climate, the outcome of any contest between the *Nation* and the nation would seem foreordained." He was right: the press complaint was dismissed, even though the court conceded that the Pentagon could apply censorship and press restrictions in future wars ("DoD has admitted that the CENTCOM regulations have been 'lifted' but remain in place and may be reactivated. In fact, during the last three military efforts of the United States abroad, various types of pooling arrangements were utilized and the government concedes it is likely to follow this format in the future" [Sand, 409]). Future wars are likely to intensify the paradox that Elaine Scarry has identified as constitutive of the structure of war—that "while the central activity of war is injuring and the central goal of war is to out-injure the opponent, the fact of injuring tends to be absent from strategic and political descriptions of war" (12). Military press censorship will ensure that the fact of injuring and killing will also remain absent from news of war.

NOTES

1. Writing War in the Twentieth Century: An Introduction

1. Adorno's broader concern with the risks that artistic representation may demean victims through their stylization and inadvertently produce aesthetic pleasure when none is appropriate is thoughtfully contextualized in the larger discussion of Michael André Bernstein's chapter "Narrating the Shoah" in his *Foregone Conclusions,* 42–73.

2. See Christopher Norris's chapter "Baudrillard and the War That Never Happened" in his *Uncritical Theory,* 11–31.

3. Ian F. W. Beckett points out in "Total War" that these World War I casualty figures "usually exclude an estimated 1.5 million Armenians exterminated by the Turks in 1915" (9). I discuss the problem of categorizing genocidal victims among the war dead later in this chapter.

4. John W. Dower's *War without Mercy* is an exemplary study of the ideological manipulation of language and image in the discourses of war.

5. Michael André Bernstein elaborates this point when he writes, "Even the most scrupulous first-person 'factual' testimony does a certain injustice to the other victims, if only by making its narrator the primary observing consciousness of both the tale and the events, thereby slighting the anguish of everyone else to a certain degree" (46).

6. Ian Buruma, in his essay "The War over the Bomb," explores specifically how the predispositions of Nagasaki's Christian communities might have colluded with this neglect. In addition to a mood of religious resignation and acceptance, social factors might have prompted the city's survivors to keep their sufferings to themselves: "Like many Jewish survivors of the Holocaust who returned to their native countries in Europe, Nagasaki Christians did not wish to dwell on their suffering lest it expose them to the public gaze. They did not want to stand out in a society obsessed with bloodlines and social conformity. It was difficult enough finding marriage partners for your children; if you were a bomb survivor, being a Catholic could only make things worse. So there is something to the cliché that 'Hiroshima is angry, while Nagasaki prays'" (28).

7. Iris Chang writes in *The Rape of Nanking:* "The death of Nanking—one Chinese city alone—exceeds the number of civilian casualties of some European countries for the entire war. (Great Britain lost a total of 61,000 civilians, France lost 108,000, Belgium 101,000, and the Netherlands 242,000" (5).

8. See Derrida's essay "No Apocalypse, Not Now," in which he argues for the

humanities' rigorous interrogation of *competence* as the justification for its competence to engage in "nuclear criticism" (22).

9. Frances Ferguson's highly complex exploration of population discourses in the eighteenth and nineteenth centuries, and their poetic consequences, finds in the Enlightenment and post-Enlightenment age a shift: where the ancients saw in populousness a sign of civic success and national prosperity, the eighteenth century began to see large populations as a structural threat and psychological danger.

10. Matthew Arnold cites (without remarking whether they are playful or not) his father's sentiments toward irrationally roused populations in his *Culture and Anarchy:* "As for rioting, the old Roman way of dealing with *that* is always the right one; flog the rank and file, and fling the ring-leaders from the Tarpeian Rock" (203).

11. Perhaps one of the difficulties of empathizing with a dead enemy population results from the propagandistic equation of the enemy with death incarnate during the conflict. Sam Keen writes, in *Faces of the Enemy,* "Propaganda relegates the enemy to the role of agent of death. . . . His face is reduced to a skull, his body a dangling skeleton. We, the bearers of the 'indomitable spirit,' are the angels of life. . . . At its simplest, propaganda must switch the blame for the massive suffering and death from us to them. Although we also deal in death, we are not to blame because we are forced to defend ourselves against an enemy who is the incarnation of death" (64–65).

12. Owen's revisions of the poem "Strange Meeting"—which provided a text for Benjamin Britten's 1962 oratorio *War Requiem*—suggest that his expression was constrained by fear that empathy with the enemy dead could be construed as treasonous in the wartime context. In earlier versions of the poem, the famous line had been "I was a German conscript, and your friend" (*Penguin Book of First World War Poetry,* n.p. [197/198]).

13. The back cover of Christopher Norris's *Uncritical Theory* offers a succinct description of the Baudrillard position Norris felt compelled to attack: "Shortly after the cessation of hostilities, Jean Baudrillard published an article entitled 'The Gulf War Has Not Taken Place,' arguing that the conflict had been a 'hyperreal' event, a product of superinduced media illusion and saturation TV coverage. Moreover, there was something like a duty to abandon any belief in its real-world occurrence, since in Baudrillard's view 'the true belligerents are those who thrive on the ideology of the truth of this war.'"

14. Wyndham Lewis, in particular, made "The Crowd" one of his satirical objects, an aggregate of the victims of his aggression. Fredric Jameson describes the disturbing eventual backfiring of this satire:

> It is indeed as though Lewis were asking himself how it is possible for people who are not really alive—the mass-produced simulacra of modern civilization, the sham puppet-victims of his satire—to die. In what sense can death be real if life itself has been unreal? . . . To put it another way, if it can be shown that death itself is unreal, if it follows logically . . . that people who were never really alive in the first place cannot really die either, then the satirist is absolved of all his guilt for victims who have only undergone an appearance of death, and not its irrevocable reality. . . . Yet at this point something unaccountable begins to take place: as *The Human Age* progresses, it becomes only too clear that the resurrected dead of this afterlife can really die after all, and this time for good, in the horrors of Lewis's Auschwitz-Hell. (162)

15. Some historians dispute this perception of a generation destroyed by World War I. Ian Beckett concedes that "the idea of a 'lost generation' current in Britain in the

1920s and 1930s had some basis in fact" (10); but he nonetheless concludes that "the total war was not necessarily a cause of demographic loss overall" (9). Better wartime public health policies and new medical developments stimulated by the war may have offset reproductive losses in some countries, he argues.

16. I invoke "idealism" as a discourse of war and pair it with rationalism in a sense very different from that invoked by Jean Bethke Elshtain, when she poses "idealism" (e.g., pacifism or humanitarianism) as the alternative to "realism," which she calls "the discourse that had won the war":

> The alternative to this discourse of "realism," and its professionalization, was (what else?) "idealism," a potpourri of the writings of religious pacifists, of some if not all just-war thinkers (Augustine slipped into the realist camp on many readings), of liberals (Kant), of natural-law types (Grotius), and a smattering of world-federationalists, one-worlders, peace-through-understanding naifs, and contemporary behavior-modification enthusiasts out to deprogram the human race away from aggression—most well meaning, very few compelling, but all falling hopelessly wide of the mark where the matter of "why war?" is concerned. (87)

17. For the sake of a tight focus, my characterization of Clausewitz's rationalism is here as restricted as Barbara Ehrenreich's, when she writes, "The Napoleonic Wars, which bore along with them the rationalist spirit of the French Revolution, inspired the Prussian officer Carl von Clausewitz to propose that war itself is an entirely rational undertaking, unsullied by human emotion" (7). This view occludes one of Clausewitz's most important contributions to the theory of war: his stress on the psychological factor, the significance of morale, in military strategy.

18. I am particularly troubled by the romantic essentialism that colors John Keegan's theory of war and "warrior culture" when he writes, "Warfare is almost as old as man himself, and reaches into the most secret places of the human heart, places where self dissolves rational purpose, where pride reigns, where emotion is paramount, where instinct is king. . . . Man is a thinking animal in whom the intellect directs the urge to hunt and the ability to kill" (3).

19. In Allan Bloom's editorial preface to *Introduction to the Reading of Hegel* he reminds us that Kojève's book is the product of Raymond Queneau's collection of the 1933–39 lectures on Hegel that Kojève gave at the Ecole des Hautes Etudes. Bloom cites Aimé Patri's delineation of the clear lines of philosophical influence extending from Kojève's work: "This teaching [by Kojève] was prior to the philosophico-political speculations of J. P. Sartre and M. Merleau-Ponty, to the publication of *Les Temps modernes* and the new orientation of *Esprit,* reviews which were the most important vehicles for the dissemination of progressivist ideology in France after the liberation. From that time on we have breathed Kojève's teaching with the air of the times" (vii).

20. There is a large and important body of literature on war and gender in a diverse range of fields. I can point to only a few random examples here: such feminist studies as Cynthia Enloe's 1983 *Does Khaki Become You?;* Jean Bethke Elshtain's 1987 *Women and War;* Lynne Hanley's 1991 *Writing War;* Miriam Cooke and Angela Woollacott's 1993 collection *Gendering War Talk;* Margaret Randolph Higonnet's 1987 collection *Behind the Lines;* and Jean Gallagher's intriguing 1998 *The World Wars through the Female Gaze;* as well as books on masculinity and war by Klaus Theweleit (*Male Fantasies*) and Brian Easlea (*Fathering the Unthinkable*).

21. Atomic research, with its highly dangerous experiments, certainly entailed a risk to life, as did the flying of the bombing missions. But the source of the intrinsic risk to atomic scientists and technicians, comparable to the risks of all munitions makers, is so thoroughly displaced from the imagined combatant or opponent (who is reduced to a reified "target") that the gladiatorial model is nonetheless inoperative and irrelevant.

22. Elaine Scarry complicates this model even further when she argues that geno-cide should be perceived as "outside war and in the realm of atrocity"—a definition that would *include* the use of nuclear weapons against civilian populations: "So, too, the pos-sibility of genocide that arises with nuclear weapons has led humanity to the cry for their elimination. That is, so little is genocide (or the permanent elimination of the opponent's capacity to injure) a structural requirement of war that it in fact seems a deconstruction of war, a deconstruction of a deconstruction" (*Body in Pain,* 100).

23. "One city stood out above all others in light of the Committee's criteria," Martin Sherwin notes, "Kyoto, the ancient capital of Japan and the center of her civilization for more than a thousand years" (229). Furious at Stimson's refusal to approve the bombing of Kyoto, George Harrison, a special assistant to Leslie Groves, "wired Stimson at Potsdam that his military advisers wanted his 'pet city' reinstated as a target. But the old man stood firm. . . . Already planning to groom Japan as an outpost for American interests in the Far East, he feared that 'the bitterness which would be caused by such a wanton act might make it impossible during the long postwar period to reconcile the Japanese to us in that area rather than to the Russians'" (230–31).

24. In a later article ("Serbian Veterans") Paul Watson seems to elaborate this remark not only in the direction of the many "mistakes" of NATO bombings of civilians (cited in "Deadly Errors") but of the possibility of a far graver relationship between the bombings and killings on the ground: "As many as 11,000 ethnic Albanians died after the bombing began—more than five times the estimated 2,000 ethnic Albanians and Serbs who were killed in a single year of civil war that preceded NATO's airstrikes" (A20). The opening sentence of Tyler Marshall's "Anti-NATO Axis" suggests an even more ominous fallout from the bombing campaign: "U.S. foreign affairs specialists are monitoring the potential for increased cooperation between Russia, China, and India, amid a growing conviction in all three countries, especially after NATO's bombing campaign against Yugoslavia, that U.S. power must be checked."

25. Michael André Bernstein writes, "When an event is so destructive for a whole people, so hideous in its motivation, enactment, and consequences as was the Shoah, there is an almost irresistible pressure to interpret it as one would a tragedy, to regard it as the simultaneously inconceivable and yet foreordained culmination of the entire brutal his-tory of European anti-Semitism" (10).

26. Jean Gallagher, *The World Wars through the Female Gaze,* offers an illuminating analysis of the relationship between war and vision through the filter of gender.

27. The Russian novel, in particular, appears to Bernstein a powerful model with possibilities for ethical representation: "Nineteenth- and twentieth-century Russian litera-ture, to invoke a powerful supporting model, always kept alive a sense of the moral ac-countability of the act of writing, and in both prose and verse it managed to create a heritage of permanently renewed 'tales of the tribe' in which the trials and 'perplexity' of unmistakably individualized figures was immediately understood as emblematic of the nation as a whole" (123).

2. The Trace of the Trenches

1. Jean Baudrillard describes hyperreality as "the generation of models of a real without origin or reality: a hyperreal. The territory no longer precedes the map, nor survives it. Henceforth, it is the map that precedes the territory—*precession of simulacra*—it is the map that engenders the territory and if we were to revive the fable today, it would be the territory whose shreds are slowly rotting across the map" (166).

2. See Michael North's essay "Where Memory Faileth," on the problem of memory and forgetfulness in Pound's work.

3. Booth writes, "The extremely restricted space within which trench warfare was fought simultaneously ensured that Great War soldiers would live with the corpses of their friends and that British civilians would not see dead soldiers. . . . Soldiers inhabited a world of corpses; British civilians experienced the death of their soldiers as corpseless-ness" (21). What ensured that civilians did not see soldiers' corpses were governmental regulations that "soldiers would be buried where they died; families would not have the right to demand the return of combatants' bodies for burial" (24). Furthermore, no photographs or films of actual killings in combat or of corpses could be shown to the public (21).

4. Sebastian Knowles's project in *A Purgatorial Flame*—"to extend the compass of British modernism into World War II" (xv)—disputes this statement. Knowles argues that "the Second World War did not mark a hiatus in British literature; the progress of literary thought continued through into the forties. This study will center on the war work of seven British modernists: Woolf, MacNeice, Eliot, Tolkien, Lewis, Williams, and Waugh" (xiv). He goes on to note that "none of the seven is generally considered a war writer" and "only a handful of them are generally considered modernists" (xiv)—the received views he seeks to reverse in his study.

5. I use Jon Silkin's anthology of First World War poetry as a reference for many of the poems I discuss, both because this text is widely used as a teaching anthology and because I admire it for reasons I make clear later in the chapter.

6. The craft, care, and power of Owen's poetic practice come into clearer focus when we consider the wildly popular enlistment poems that were the explicit target of his resistance. Fred Crawford argues that Owen intended "Dulce et Decorum Est" to counter Jessie Pope's "The Call":

> Who'll earn the Empire's thanks—
> Will you, my laddie?
> Who'll swell the victor's ranks—
> Will you, my laddie?
> When that procession comes,
> Banners and rolling drums—
> Who'll stand and bite his thumbs—
> Will you, my laddie?
> (Crawford, 141)

Crawford also believes that "with the exception of Sir Henry Newbolt and W. B. Yeats, most readers responded favorably to Owen's work" (174), although he concedes that "critics addressing the war poets have varied greatly in their estimates of Owen" (173).

7. Samuel Hynes notes that "Rupert Brooke remained England's favourite war poet

after the war, as he had been through the fighting years. One might reasonably argue that in fact Brooke was not a war poet at all, in the sense that men like Owen and Rosenberg and Gurney were—he had never written from direct experience, and the five '1914' sonnets were the only poems he wrote that had anything at all to do with war. But it was those sonnets that sold his books; and they sold in very large numbers" (299–300).

8. The poem's utter domestication was marked by a cartoon sequence in Charles Schultz's *Peanuts* that appeared in syndication in the summer of 1998. "There are a lot of poppies growing here . . . I've been thinking of writing a poem about them," Spike tells Snoopy as they sit in a trench. "How does this sound? . . . 'In farmer's fields the poppies blow'?"

9. Although Jon Silkin does not impute the direct influence of Isaac Rosenberg on Pound's imagery of good and bad teeth in "Hugh Selwyn Mauberley," such an assumption would not be unreasonable, given Pound's familiarity with and promotion of Rosenberg's work (Silkin, 36–38). Silkin compares Pound's passage with these lines from Rosenberg's "August 1914":

> Iron are our lives
> Molten right through our youth.
> A burnt space through ripe fields
> A fair mouth's broken tooth.

See Silkin, 207–8, for the text of the entire poem.

10. Lewis, who noted in the editorial in the war issue of *Blast* that "Nietzsche has had an English sale such as he could hardly have anticipated in his most ecstatic and morose moments" (5), produced a series of texts dealing with the crowd and herd mentality. These include a 1915 Vorticist painting called *The Crowd;* "The Code of the Herdsman," published in *The Little Review* in 1917; and the 1926 book *The Art of Being Ruled,* with its explicit references to Arnold's *Culture and Anarchy.*

11. Citations to Eliot's *Waste Land* refer to the page number of the 1962 Harcourt Brace edition, followed by the line reference.

12. "Lines 8–16 were suggested by the Countess Marie Larisch's memoir, *My Past* (1913)," according to *The Norton Anthology of American Literature,* 2:1243.

13. Poems that Silkin includes less on poetic merit than because of their expression of the time's ethos he marks with an asterisk. There are five: Julian Grenfell's "Into Battle," John McCrae's "In Flanders Fields," Alan Seeger's "Rendezvous," Charles Hamilton Sorley's "All the hills and vales along," and—perhaps not surprisingly—Wilfred Owen's "Anthem for Doomed Youth" (76).

14. A remarkable characteristic of nearly all the poems in the Silkin anthology is the absence of animus toward the enemy. The enemy of most of this war poetry is war itself, not the warring opponent.

15. Stramm's extreme linguistic experiments also characterize his prewar and non-war poetry and dramas, and Patrick Bridgwater, in his essay "The Sources of Stramm's Originality," gives Stramm's poetic destructiveness a wide philosophical genealogy, including Nietzsche, Vaihinger, Mauthner, and Marinetti: "Now the poet who abandons 'logical' syntax does so because he has lost faith in conceptual thought or logic as such; if Stramm has followed Marinetti here, that is, if he agreed with the need to 'break apart the old shackles of logic,' he will have done so because Vaihinger and Nietzsche had already made logic suspect, while Mauthner . . . had shown 'syntax' to be an arbitrary affair" (Adler and White, 42).

3. The Novel as War

1. I am making here a more extreme and polemical statement of the disjunction between narrator and text that James Phelan calls *distance*—"the relation between Hemingway as author and Frederic as narrator; it is a function of the extent to which Hemingway endorses Frederic's understanding of and judgments about the events he reports" (54).

2. See the early reviews of the novel published in Robert Stephens's *Ernest Hemingway: The Critical Reception,* 69–104, which are, in general, marked by the tension of attempting to evaluate the crossing of the war story and the love story, and the strange disjunction of tone, sentiment, and philosophy this fusion or superimposition produces. My own response to this generic dilemma is to twist Robert Penn Warren's description of *A Farewell to Arms* as "the great romantic alibi for a generation" (36) by arguing that this operation of the romantic alibi, of translating one kind of story into another so that cruelties or moral bankruptcies can be disguised by romance and love, is immanent in the text and produced by its narrative and stylistic performance.

3. The stunning success of Erich Maria Remarque's graphically brutal *All Quiet on the Western Front,* published in the same year as *A Farewell to Arms,* proved wrong the assumption that a reading public would not listen to a grim war story. I will discuss this issue further in chapter 4.

4. Susan Beegel's extensive and useful treatment of the piece explores its critical neglect as a generic problem: "Yunck in particular dislikes this combination of genres, and objects to Hemingway's using a short story as a 'vehicle for miscellaneous criticism'" (32).

5. My reading of Hemingway's *Death in the Afternoon* makes a very different ethical judgment of his writing than the one I produce here. See chapter 9, "The Animal and Violence in Hemingway's *Death in the Afternoon*" (195–219), in my *Beasts of the Modern Imagination.*

6. In the short sketch "In Another Country," Hemingway imputes the same sort of candor to the young narrator: "I had been wounded, it was true; but we all knew that being wounded, after all, was really an accident. I was never ashamed of the ribbons, though, and sometimes, after the cocktail hour, I would imagine myself having done all the things they had done to get their medals" (369).

7. In chapter 4 I mention that Erich Maria Remarque may also have worn improper medals after his return from the war.

8. My argument adds textual incrimination to excellent readings of the problem of narrative unreliability, such as James Phelan's and Gerry Brenner's ("it is because he is preoccupied with his feelings and experience, rather than with our understanding, that Frederic is an inconsiderate, and ultimately an untrustworthy, narrator" [35]). My aim is to demonstrate that the text is contaminated by and replicates Frederic's narrative pliability as a character—his tendency to tell people what they want to hear—because the narrative issues of love and war exert tremendous ideological pressures both within and outside the text.

9. See, for example, Julian Smith, "Hemingway and the Thing Left Out," and Brenner, *Concealment in Hemingway's Works.*

10. Maud Ellmann's brilliant analysis of *The Waste Land* in *The Poetics of Impersonality* elaborates the implication of the war dead in the obsessional formal strategies ("The text's integrity dissolves under the invasion of its own disjecta" [98]) through which modernism sought to grapple with the abhorrence of filth, bodily effluvia, and verbal trash.

11. Although the only copy of *Wuthering Heights* Hemingway is known to have owned was the 1935 Cape edition (Brasch and Sigman, 49), published after the writing of *A Farewell to Arms,* this does not preclude his having read the book in high school (Oak Park High School owned ten copies of *Jane Eyre* [Reynolds, 42]) or borrowed it from Shakespeare and Company in the 1920s.

12. See "Military Law" in *The New Encyclopaedia Britannica,* 12:194–97. "In Great Britain, the United States, and other common-law countries, there is usually a right of appeal against summary punishment awarded through the military chain of command and extending to the highest authority. In other countries, the appeal will lie to a tribunal" (195).

13. If casual execution, like the sergeant's, is clearly incommensurate with a debatable desertion, still less can it be justified for looting. Hemingway, anticipating that the sergeant's looting would elicit a highly charged response ("Looting, Frederic knows, is a despicable act of greed" [Nolan, 271]), carefully writes in Bonello's counterlooting to test the ethics of adjudicating this issue. When Charles Nolan writes, "As a decent man and a man of honor, Frederic recognizes the inappropriateness of the sergeant's stealing and reprimands the engineer for it" (272), he fails to note that if he is indeed a decent man and a man of honor, Frederic nonetheless does not reprimand Bonello for looting the dead man's pockets. "Bonello, sitting behind the wheel, was looking through the pockets of the sergeant's coat. 'Better throw the coat away,' I said" (206). Frederic does not tell him to restore its contents first.

4. The Novel of Depopulation

1. Schwarz groups Oswald Spengler, Moeller van den Bruck, Carl Schmitt, Ernst von Salomon, Erich Edwin Dwinger, Ernst Niekisch, and Ernst Jünger among the militaristic writers, and Thomas Mann, Hermann Hesse, Ernst Wiechert, Carl von Ossietzky, Ernst Troeltsch, Arnold Zweig, René Schickele, Theodor Plievier, and Erich Maria Remarque among the pacifists (7–8).

2. Both Alfred Antkowiak (33) and Modris Eksteins (280) insist that in this review Remarque seemed indifferent to the considerable ideological and aesthetic differences among the writers he considered. Antkowiak points out that Remarque commented chiefly on the representations of the trench experience.

3. Owen gives the text of a rare interview in which Remarque discussed the genesis of the novel: "I suffered fairly [sic] of attacks of despair. At the attempt to overcome them, I sought out quite consciously and systematically the cause of my depressions. Through this deliberate analysis I hit upon my war experiences. . . . On the same day that I hit upon this thought, I began to write, without much premeditation. This went on for six weeks, every evening, when I came home from the office. And then the book was finished" (69). The interview was conducted by Axel Eggebrecht and "variously reprinted from *Die literarische Welt,* June 14, 1929" (Owen, 79).

4. Owen notes that "Remarque during his lifetime gave practically no information on or about his life, rarely expressed himself on private matters and his widow consistently refused to make access possible to Remarque's papers" (26).

5. This fact is remarkable as emerging from the Second World War—complicating the indisputable fact that modern wars have become increasingly more brutalized. "Marshall conducted both individual and mass interviews with over four hundred infantry

companies, both in Europe and in the Central Pacific, immediately after they had been in close combat with German or Japanese troops, and the results were the same each time. They were, moreover, as astonishing to the company officers and the troops themselves as they were to Marshall; each man who hadn't fired his rifle thought he had been alone in his defection from duty" (Dyer, 118). Marshall reasoned that men can refuse to fire only when they are unobserved, and that the combat conditions of World War II permitted greater opportunities for soldiers to isolate themselves from their comrades.

6. Theweleit discusses the role of the iron body in the work of Ernst Jünger: "The picture Jünger paints of the mechanized body is more evocative than descriptive; his more extreme depictions of the 'figure of steel' (*Stahlgestalt*) are never descriptions of actual soldiers. The steel figure is the soldier's utopia, a vision more general than Jünger's alone. It represents the man the soldier wished and was expected to be—though, in actuality, he barely approximated it" (206).

7. Remarque was trained as a teacher and received his teaching certificate. But his career in education took him to depressed rural villages as a substitute teacher, and ended after an unpleasant altercation with a village priest who interfered with Remarque's instruction and eventually brought him up on administrative charges (Owen, 29–32).

8. Owen cites an early 1929 review of Remarque's novel by Rudolf Binding, whom he describes as "a participant of the war and a man of letters." Binding's dismissive review particularly takes issue with the description of the screaming horses: "Dying horses do not scream as Remarque wants us to believe in his effect-seeking way. With almost closed mouth, barely audible, moaning lightly through the nose. . . . All of this unnecessary exaggeration makes so many parts of the book truly suspect" (123).

9. Remarque's novels *The Road Back* (1931) and *Three Comrades* (1938) treat the lives of veterans after the war, and are regarded by some as sequels (Schwarz, 30; Antkowiak, 51–72).

5. Unmaking and Remaking a World

1. *Thinking the Unthinkable*, edited by Roger S. Gottlieb, contains several discussions of the question of the uniqueness of the Holocaust and the issues of exceptionalism and universalism. See especially Gottlieb's introduction (1–21) and Joan Ringelheim's "Thoughts about Women and the Holocaust" (141–49).

2. See Jeff Sharlet's discussion of Peter Novick's 1999 *Holocaust in American Life* in the *Chronicle of Higher Education* of May 29, 1999: "The problem, as he sees it, is that by establishing the Holocaust as a moral standard, specific lessons, such as the need for worldwide response to genocide, can be nullified by the Holocaust's very extremity" (A16).

3. Dori Laub provides a penetrating discussion of the problem of discrepancies or inaccuracies in survivor accounts in *Testimony* (Felman and Laub, 59–63). Laub argues that the psychiatrist must contend with a different kind of historical "truth" in Holocaust testimony than the historian, and that subjective "truth" must be respected even if incomplete or objectively flawed. Historical errors or discrepancies in Holocaust testimony trouble historians, but Laub reports: "I had myself the opportunity of encountering—during the very process of the interviewing—questions similar in nature to these that the historians were now raising. And yet I had to deal with those objections and those questions in a different manner" (60).

4. Suppressions of the function of money and the body in stories of Holocaust survival would silence stories like Margot Schlesinger's: "Margot kept her valuables in a condom 'inside.' The only place that was safe was inside the body, but it was terrible. I had to sleep with it, eat with it. Even in Auschwitz, I had fifty dollars in a condom" (Brecher 131). When attention is drawn to the inside of the distressed and suffering body, it is drawn also to the feelings and sensations that attend it.

5. See Roger Gottlieb's excellent discussion of the complexities of resistance in "The Concept of Resistance: Jewish Resistance during the Holocaust" (Gottlieb 327–44).

6. In addition to Oskar Schindler, Keneally tells of the garment factory owner Julius Madritsch, and his manager, Raimund Titsch, who were honored as Righteous Gentiles by the State of Israel after the war; Sepp Aue, the *Treuhänder* for Itzhak Stern's original company (42); the Intelligence officer Eberhard Gebauer (66); the German Czech Cracow ghetto sentry, *Wachtmeister* Bosko, who eventually perished working for the Resistance (139); Herr Szepessi of the Cracow Labor Office, who died at Auschwitz (121); Erich Lange, the highly placed Armament Division official, who facilitated Oskar's move of his camp to Czechoslovakia (282); and many smaller players, like the chef and his girlfriend who smuggled little Olek Rosner out of the ghetto under a cloak before one of the police actions (117).

7. In *The Genocidal Mentality*, Robert Jay Lifton and Eric Markusen discuss the question of when Nazi policies became explicitly genocidal in the course of the war:

> For the Nazis, crossing the threshold was less a matter of a specific event taking place at a particular moment than of the point at which the momentum toward genocide became irreversible. . . . The immediate situation bearing on the crossing of the threshold was the Nazi quandary after the invasion of the Soviet Union: what to do with the increasingly large numbers of Jews under their control? In that sense, the Final Solution developed, as one German historian puts it, "not solely as a result of an ostensible will for extermination but also as a 'way out' of a blind alley into which the Nazis had maneuvered themselves." But, in maneuvering themselves into that "blind alley," the Nazis were indeed expressing something close to a "will to extermination." (170–71)

Raul Hilberg gives the more specific historical sequence behind the establishment of extermination camps in "Auschwitz and the Final Solution."

8. In the interest of tightening the script, Zaillian frequently compressed persons with similar functions into a single figure. Abraham Bankier and Itzhak Stern are compressed this way into the single figure of Stern in the film. Similarly, Schindler's two mistresses, the German Ingrid and the Polish Victoria Klonowska, are compressed into a single persona in the film.

9. The information in the chronology at the end of Stella Müller-Madej's memoir (275) suggests that 18,000 people lived in an area of less than half a square mile.

10. Keneally summarized the hardships of that first year and a half of occupation by using Juda Dresner as an example:

> The past year and a half had brought a bewildering succession of decrees, intrusions, and confiscations. He had lost his business to the Trust Agency, his car, his apartment. His bank account had been frozen. His children's schools had been closed. . . . He and his family were forbidden entry to the center of Cracow, denied any travel by train. . . . His wife and daughter and sons were subject to intermittent roundups for snow shoveling and compulsory labor. . . . Under this sort of regimen you felt that

life offered no footholds, and that you were slithering into a pit which had no bottom. (85)

Zaillian's footage of Mrs. Dresner's terrified efforts to keep her daughter Danka from seeing the murder of a man during one of the snow-shoveling details gives a painfully subjective dramatization to this account.

11. Keneally scrupulously concedes that he cannot substantiate the claim that Schindler compensated the evicted couple: "A number of Schindler's friends would later claim—though it is not possible to prove it—that Oskar had gone looking for the dispossessed Nussbaums at their lodgings in Podgórze and had given them a sum close to 50,000 złoty in compensation. With this sum, it is said, the Nussbaums bought themselves an escape to Yugoslavia" (51). Although Keneally cannot verify Schindler's having compensated the Nussbaums for the flat, the story seems not implausible given that it was Mr. Nussbaum who apparently suggested that Schindler contact Poldek Pfefferberg's mother for help with redecorating the apartment. "'You're Mrs. Pfefferberg?' the German asked. 'You were recommended to me by Herr Nussbaum. I have just taken over an apartment in Straszewskiego Street, and I would like to have it redecorated'" (53).

12. Zaillian tropes the fate of the cattle car deportees through their carefully and uselessly labeled luggage, which instead of going forward with them, as promised, goes backward into storage depots for chillingly methodical and professional plunder. The mound of teeth suddenly cast before one of the Jewish appraisers disrupts this narrative continuity, because it cannot belong to the deportees whose train has just pulled out and whose luggage is at that moment being despoiled. But the image reflects the actual experience of the jeweler Mordecai Wulcan, who—some six months after Bankier's near deportation—was made to grade gold and appraise valuables for the SS Economic and Administrative Main Office (Keneally, 151).

13. Perhaps because she was herself still nearly a child, Stella Müller-Madej was a particularly acute observer of children in the ghetto and the Płaszów camp. Since children had no place in the labor camps, parents smuggled them in backpacks and boxes and taught them to be silent, still, and inconspicuous, because their quasi-illicit status made them constantly vulnerable to deportation. Müller-Madej reports that this experience made some of the children pathologically quiet and rigid, like puppets, except when they scurried under beds and furniture to hide, on reflex, like mice (90).

14. Victor Lewis told Elinor Brecher a story that suggests that the hangings may have been the first in Płaszów, and may therefore have been an extraordinary shock to everyone: "Because there was a ghetto in progress, two girls went there and didn't come for the *Appell* [roll call] the next morning. Goeth saw that people were missing, so he called on Leopold Goldberg and Katz [Jewish policemen] and they gave a report. He told them to kneel down. First Katz was shot, [then] Goldberg was shot. They found those two girls, and they were hanged. This was the first hanging in Płaszów. We had all to watch it" (Brecher, 221).

15. Spielberg told *Newsweek's* David Ansen that working against his "command of the visual language" became one of his greatest challenges with *Schindler's List:* "I know how to put a Cecil B. DeMille image on the screen. I can do a Michael Curtiz. If my mojo's working I can put one tenth of a David Lean image on the screen. . . . And certainly not until 'Schindler' was I really able to not reference other filmmakers. I'm always referencing everybody. I didn't do any of that on this movie" (Ansen, 63).

16. See David Patterson's chapter "The Death of the Child," in his *Shriek of Silence,*

for a discussion of this difficult representational problem. "The Holocaust novel is as much a children's memorial as the Children's Memorial at Yad Vashem" (77).

17. More than one witness seems to have brought news of the crematoria at Belżec to the Jews outside. Raul Hilberg reports, "The next day, the thirteen year old son of one of the council functionaries (Wolsztayn) came back from the camp. The boy had seen naked people and had heard an SS man make a speech to them. Hiding, still clothed, in a ditch, the young Wolsztayn had crawled out under the barbed wire with the secret of Belżec" (3 : 493).

18. Franciszek Piper's "The System of Prisoner Exploitation" and Shmuel Krakowski's essay "The Satellite Camps," which describes industrial camps associated with Auschwitz, give an overview of the relationship between German industry and the concentration camps that makes it clear how exceptional the policies and practices of Schindler and Madritsch were.

19. During neither phase was it a designated extermination camp, even though the appendix to Stella Müller-Madej's memoir lists 8,000 people murdered at Płaszów during its relatively brief existence.

20. Helen Sternlicht Rosenzweig told the story to Elinor Brecher: "It was almost dawn and [Goeth] had company. One of the civilians—he was a frequent guest, a Gestapo who would bring out the orders—came out and said to Lisiek he needed transportation to go home. We knew him so well that Lisiek ran to the barn. A horse and carriage came. As soon as he left, Goeth [asked] Lisiek why he didn't check with him. He's the boss. He didn't give him a chance; he killed him instantly. It was in the yard, in back. I was standing there in the door to the kitchen, and I saw it all" (Brecher, 60). Witness accounts like Rosenzweig's and Müller-Madej's convey with greater immediacy the psychic trauma of seeing an actual killing than can Keneally's narrative. However, film—with its ability to show rather than tell—gives viewers vicarious access to the pain of witnessing. The murder of the architect Diana Reiter in the film produces such a traumatic moment of witnessing.

21. Although Keneally treats Chilowicz and his family chiefly as Göth tools and collaborators, Stella Müller-Madej describes how during one nerve-racking official inspection of Płaszów by German high officials, Chilowicz ran around like a man possessed trying to plan for the concealment of the children. He covered the windows of a barracks with paper and posted a sign, "Disinfection," in order to keep the inspectors out (Müller-Madej, 100). Roman Ferber claims his aunt, Cyla Wiener, confirmed that Chilowicz saved the children. Chaskel Schlesinger, however, said, "I was always afraid to look at this [Wilek] Chilowicz—he was also a monster" (Brecher, 132). Chilowicz may have played a dual role, making a brutal spectacle of himself in front of the Nazis but helping and meliorating behind the scenes.

22. According to Keneally, Schindler sent a list of the women detained at Auschwitz on their way to Brinnlitz to Erich Lange, to enlist his help in getting them out. This may account for a difference Elinor Brecher notes between the way men and women were organized on the list of April 18, 1945—"the women are listed alphabetically" (xxxi).

23. Several of the accounts in Brecher's book suggest that Emalia workers were deported in August 1944. Barry Tiger was one of those sent from Płaszów to Mauthausen (Brecher, 200). Sol Urbach, who actually remembers the "selection" of Emalia workers, describes being reprieved by Schindler, who recognized him (Brecher, 250). Although Keneally has Amon Göth describe the overheated Mauthausen transport as "partly

Płaszów people . . . and people from the work camp at Szebnie. And Poles and Jews from Montelupich" (265), Murray Pantirer remembers Emalia workers being in the transport: "The Germans had ordered Schindler to pare his workforce, and hundreds of Jews who'd worked at Emalia were sweltering and moaning inside locked cattle cars. 'Schindler came to see how his people were doing. . . . He got permission from Goeth, and he ordered some of us boys to stretch a hose to the cars and soak them with water. He himself was yelling, '*Mach schnell!*'" (Brecher, 180). If, as Pantirer suggests, the overcrowded boxcars were full of his own Emalia workers, Schindler's panic at seeing them blistering in the August heat becomes even more plausible.

24. Keneally's extensive research and interviewing suggested that there was definitely a reduction of the Emalia workforce that resulted in deportations, but not on the scale suggested by Elinor Brecher. Brecher makes the following strong assertion, but without providing documentation or identifying its precise source: "What's definite is that seven hundred Emalia workers were sent to death camps. Some survived; others didn't. There's no small amount of bitterness among the former and among the surviving relatives of the latter" (xxxv).

25. John Gross, however, reports that in a December 1993 interview in the *Daily Mail,* Emilie Schindler verified that the rescue of the women from Auschwitz "was accomplished by a friend of the family, a young woman who offered the functionaries her sexual favors" (Gross 15).

26. Keneally reports that Pfefferberg melted the doors with a welding torch, but Victor Lewis gives other details of the rescue of the "frozen transport": "We took straw and burned it underneath the cars. We tried to melt the ice [immobilizing the locks and latches]. Schindler said to take old mattresses—'tomorrow you get new.' Mrs. Schindler was there to help. When this melted and they opened the cars, people were lying on the floor, frozen" (Brecher, 224).

27. The *Schindlerjuden* interviewed by Brecher represent a wide range in their coping mechanisms and their postwar attitudes toward their experiences, toward Schindler, and toward their own visibility as *Schindlerjuden.* Leon Leyson surprised *People* magazine by refusing to participate in an article: "I told them I was not a *People* kind of person. I didn't care to be exhibited" (Brecher, 79). Helen Rosenzweig finds aspects of her celebrity extremely painful: "A ten-year-old once asked her if she ever thought about killing Amon Göth, and an eight-year-old wanted to know how badly she'd been beaten" (54). Henry Silver felt bitter enough about his whole trauma to refuse Paul (Pfefferberg) Page's request to help Keneally with Schindler's story: "A Nazi is a Nazi. Schindler did nothing wrong by me—he did good for me. But he was dead already by this time, and I thought, 'I've been through so much, to me the best German is a dead German'" (381). Celina Karp Biniaz and her family, on the other hand, spent two years in Mindelheim, Bavaria, after the war and felt "those two years among normal German families were my salvation. . . . I would have hated Germans for the rest of my life" (117). But the postfilm phenomenon was distressing to her "because of the memories" (122).

6. Dividing the Indivisible

1. Spencer Weart writes of nuclear physicists in *Scientists in Power:* "They meant to set in motion forces that would transform society for all time to come, and they did. They did not, in fact, keep control once they had set events in motion. Scientists like Halban

and Kowarski in Cambridge and Montreal, Szilard and his colleagues in Chicago, or Joliot and the Scientific Committee of the CEA in Paris, for all their efforts, personally controlled events only as long as matters moved in the direction desired by other, more powerful groups" (273).

2. One of Szilard's more misguided ideas was to approach, by way of an introduction from Einstein, the then very famous aviator Charles Lindbergh. Before this avenue was fully explored, Szilard sent Einstein a copy of a talk by Lindbergh (presumably urging U.S. neutrality in the war) accompanied by the rueful conclusion "I am afraid he is in fact not our man" (Szilard, 100).

3. The U.S. Strategic Bombing Survey, conducted after the end of the war, in the fall of 1945, essentially concurred. After "groups of engineers, doctors, architects, and other professionals probed the physical effects of atomic bombings, shot thousands of feet of motion-picture film, and studied the Japanese surrender," they made the following statement: "'The Hiroshima and Nagasaki bombs did not defeat Japan, nor by the testimony of the enemy leaders who ended the war did they persuade Japan to accept unconditional surrender.' The emperor and his top ministers 'had decided as early as May of 1945 that the war should be ended even if it meant acceptance of defeat on allied terms'" (Lifton and Mitchell, 82–83).

4. Lifton and Mitchell report a conversation between Groves and Oppenheimer (no source is cited) that suggests that the scientists were disappointed that the bomb was deployed in the early morning rather than at twilight or night, when the visual effect would have been even more dramatic:

Groves: Apparently it went with a tremendous bang.

Oppenheimer: When was this, was it after sundown?

Groves: No, unfortunately, it had to be in the daytime on account of security of the plane and that was left in the hands of the Commanding General over there. . . . (30)

5. The writer and atomic bomb survivor Yōko Ōta noted that "until dawn on August 6 Hiroshima had been left absolutely alone. No one understood why this was so. People sat around marveling at the fact. . . . The residents of the city also had pipe dreams that were even wilder. For example: Hiroshima was known as the city of water; it was a beautiful stretch of delta crossed by the seven rivers that flowed through the city. So the Americans would turn it into their residential sector" (166–67).

6. A notable exception was Joseph Rotblat, who, as early as December 1944, had "come to the conclusion that Hitler had made no progress towards the bomb, that Germany was due for defeat" (Reid, 181), and so returned to England. The only scientist to walk away from the Manhattan Project, he was barred from reentering the United States, and later played a leading role in the Nova Scotia Pugwash conferences promoting nuclear disarmament. In October 1995, Rotblat was awarded the Nobel Peace Prize for the work.

7. The concern, apparently, was not for the welfare of civilians but because "the specter of endless lawsuits haunted the military" (quoted in Lifton and Mitchell, 44). No news of fallout was ever officially reported to the U.S. public: "Even as the scientists celebrated their success at Alamogordo the first radioactive cloud was drifting eastward over America, depositing fallout along its path. When Americans found out about this, three months later, the word came not from the government but from the president of the Eastman Kodak Company in Rochester, New York, who wondered why some of his film was fogging and suspected radioactivity as the cause" (ibid.).

8. Laurence also betrayed that the power of the bomb gave him a virtually patho-

logical sense of megalomania. Speculating that Kokura would be destroyed, he wrote: "It was early morning; it was dark; and I was thinking of the town of Kokura being asleep and all the inhabitants having gone to bed, men, women, and children. . . . They were like a fatted calf, you know, saved for slaughter. . . . *And here I am. I am destiny. I know. They didn't know. But I know that this was their last night on earth.* . . . I was thinking: *there's a feeling of a human being, a mere mortal, a newspaper man by profession, suddenly has the knowledge which has been given to him, a sense—you might say—of divinity*" (quoted in Lifton and Mitchell, 17).

9. Lifton and Mitchell give a more sympathetic account of Oppenheimer and the Los Alamo contingent, reporting that the initial cheering and triumphant celebration over the technical success quickly turned into shock and depression as damage photos and information filtered back, and as Nagasaki was bombed. "A few days later Oppenheimer screened for Los Alamos scientists aerial footage of what was left of Hiroshima. No one spoke. Hans Bethe, the physicist, felt shock at the damage and pity for the victims" (31).

10. Lifton and Mitchell report that "Groves even wondered if there was 'any difference between Japanese blood and others'" (45; no citation given).

7. Writing the Apocalypse of Hiroshima

1. Robert Lifton reports a kinder interpretation of the incident: when the *Asahi Evening News* reported Lewis's words on August 19, 1959, many *hibakusha* were moved by what they took to be an expression of repentance (Lifton, 341).

2. Richard Minear says that Hersey's *Hiroshima* "was the first significant account in English of the devastation of Hiroshima; it remains an enormously influential book, the account that introduces Hiroshima to most Western readers" (7).

3. In treating only Hiroshima, and not Nagasaki, my own discussion exhibits some of the same truncation and incompleteness that afflict other writing about the atomic bomb experience. Many of the issues I discuss here—particularly the justification for the use of atomic weapons—take on a much sharper focus in relation to Nagasaki. For an excellent discussion of Nagasaki's neglect, see Ian Buruma's essay "The War over the Bomb."

4. Churchill rendered the argument in melodramatic and sentimental prose. The bomb ended the "nightmare picture" of a Japanese invasion, he wrote, and put in its place "the vision—fair and bright indeed it seemed—of the end of the whole war in one or two violent shocks. . . . To avert a vast, indefinite butchery, to bring the war to an end, to give peace to the world, to lay healing hands upon its tortured peoples by a manifestation of overwhelming power at the cost of a few explosions, seemed, after all our toils and perils, a miracle of deliverance" (quoted in Miles, 123).

5. The text of the canceled 1995 Smithsonian exhibit claims that at the meeting on June 18, 1945, Truman approved Operation DOWNFALL, which consisted of two parts: Operation OLYMPIC, the planned invasion of Kyushu, and Operation CORONET, the planned invasion of the Japanese main island, Honshu. However, the text concurs with Miles that the military "made no firm estimates for 'Coronet,'" and that the estimates discussed for Kyushu were "perhaps ten thousand American dead" (Nobile, 48–49).

6. Wyden also tells the story of a Japanese documentary filmmaker, Akira Iwasaki, who was filming a documentary on the bombed cities for the Japanese Ministry of Education when he was ordered to stop filming by U.S. Army officials. Since the U.S. Strategic

Bomb Survey team liked his footage, however, he was then ordered to continue. "When Iwasaki delivered a 15,000-foot film and 30,000 feet of negatives to the bomb survey officials, all of his work was confiscated, classified 'secret,' and shipped to Washington, where it disappeared from view for nearly twenty-five years" (327).

7. Robert Lifton, in his chapter "A-Bomb Literature" (398–450), discusses two novels by non-*hibakusha* writers that use the ABCC as their topos: Toshiyuki Kajiyama's *Experimental City* (415–16) and Hiroyuki Agawa's *Devil's Heritage* (424–32).

8. On September 8, 1945, Dr. Marcel Junod, chief representative of the International Red Cross, arrived in Hiroshima with 15 tons of medical supplies. The entrance to the Hiroshima Peace Park memorializes Junod's humanitarian response with a plaque.

9. A phenomenon analogous to the "expressionless face" occurred in the Nazi concentration camps in the form of a catatonia, whose victims were given the name *Musselmänner* (Muslims). The etiology of the Holocaust victims' condition is made different by the role that intense and sustained suffering rather than acute shock played in producing their "living dead" condition.

10. The realism of Ōta's accounts of survivors' response to radiation sickness has been occluded by a sentimental and inspirational counternarrative that has gained wide currency in the West. This is the story of twelve-year old Sadako Sasaki, who was exposed to radiation at the age of two, was diagnosed with leukemia in February 1955, and died in October at the Red Cross hospital. Sadako had faith that if she could fold a thousand paper cranes she would survive: "It's supposed to live for a thousand years. If a sick person folds one thousand paper cranes, the gods will grant her wish and make her healthy again" (Coerr, 18). According to Eleanor Coerr's children's book, Sadako folded 664 before her death, and her classmates folded the remaining 336 to bury with her. If my notes are accurate, however, the Hiroshima Peace Memorial Museum Exhibit claims that Sadako died even though she had folded 1,300 cranes.

11. Masuji Ibuse's *Black Rain* creates the most profoundly ironic representation of the terrible temporal torsion that continually forces *hibakusha* lives back to the moment of the blast as the determinant of their future. His character Shigematsu Shizuma writes a "Journal of the Bombing" in order to create a future for his ward, Yasuko—a memoir that will dispel the rumor of contamination and allow the young woman to marry into a future of normality and restored postwar life. Instead the writing proceeds apace with Yasuko's radiation sickness to assume the function of her requiem.

12. Nor, of course, did the effects of radiation cease with the first generation of *hibakusha*. Hersey, writing in 1945–46, lacked the foreknowledge of radiation's genetic effects when he wrote poetically but glibly, "And, as if nature were protecting man against his own ingenuity, the reproductive processes were affected for a time; men became sterile, women had miscarriages, menstruation stopped" (78). Betty Jean Lifton's 1985 photo essay, *A Place Called Hiroshima,* follows the sad legacy of the atomic bomb in the children of Hiroshima, the second generation of *hibakusha nisei,* and the third generation, the *hibakusha sansei.* She tells of the microcephalic children, exposed in utero and born with small heads and mental retardation, and of the Mushroom Club for forgotten *hibakusha* children who "are growing like mushrooms in the shade," afflicted with "eye problems, hip dislocation, epileptic fits, high blood pressure, kidney and liver disease" (80). She narrates fears of the second generation for the third: "Yukawa sees many of his *hibakusha nisei* friends having miscarriages and stillbirths, as well as retarded children like his own" (96).

13. The same trope fits Thomas Keneally's *Schindler's List,* of course, and underlies some of the criticism of his project. But the timing of Hersey's project in relation to history and Occupation politics gave it an urgency that perhaps made its ventriloquism more problematic.

14. "The critics have not been kind to Ōta Yōko," Richard Minear writes, and he calls the portrait Ōta's biographer, Akiko Esashi, creates of her "a nasty one." (Esashi stated flatly that "Yōko was not a talented writer" [Minear, 133]). Critics found Ōta's theme of atomic bomb damage insufficiently "literary," and Robert Lifton, whose portrait of her in *Death in Life* gave her wide exposure in the English-speaking world, represented her as an unattractive and maladaptive personality. John Whittier Treat concurs that Ōta's reputation has survived with difficulty the ravages inflicted by those who have written about her (223).

15. One might argue that surrealism invented the aesthetic ability to deconstruct form itself in a deferred response to the plasticity and mutability of form conceptualized by Darwinian biology. This ideological potential was explored in its artistic responses to world war, in poetry as well as art. (See Norris, *Beasts of the Modern Imagination.*) The problem with making surrealism—or the Gothic, for that matter—the expressive subjective mode of a phenomenon like Hiroshima is that its markers of unreality and fantasy compromise a simultaneous need to insist on the event's phenomenological reality, however labile its material referents have become.

8. Modernism and Vietnam

1. Although Coppola might be supposed to have understood the anthropology in Eliot's poetry, he apparently had to be reminded of the significance of the Fisher King by Dennis Jakob, his friend from film school. Michael Goodwin and Naomi Wise report that Coppola summoned Jakob when he had difficulty devising an ending: "Jakob was still a fanatic Nietzschean, who believed in the deep power of mythology, especially myths about supermen. He ordered Coppola to read the story in *The Golden Bough* about the corn king who must be sacrificed at the end of the year so that the crops will grow; whoever kills him becomes the new king" (229). The story foregrounds Coppola's interest in the mythological underpinnings of the quest motif.

2. According to Peter Cowie, John Milius in 1982 disclaimed the influence of *Heart of Darkness* on *Apocalypse Now.* But in 1986 Milius revised his story, casting his relationship to Conrad's text in tropes of combat and agon: "My writing teacher had told me that nobody could lick *Heart of Darkness.* Welles had tried it, and nobody could do it. So, as it was my favorite Conrad book, I was determined to lick it" (120).

3. As Seymour Hersh's account makes clear, one can only gloss rather than compare the momentary panic of the patrol boat's crew on the sampan, or even Willard's killing of the woman to prevent delay, and the deliberate, systematic, and gratuitous slaughter of about five hundred people, including mostly women, children, and old men, at My Lai.

4. Michael Herr writes in *Dispatches,* "Pacification, for example, was hardly anything more than a swollen, computerized tit being forced upon an already violated population, a costly, valueless program that worked only in press conferences" (230).

5. Michael Herr gives this line a literal meaning when he describes a "little boy of about ten" who "was laughing and moving his head side to side in a funny way. The fierceness in his eyes should have told everyone what it was, but it had never occurred to

most of the grunts that a Vietnamese child could be driven mad" (82). Coppola represents the murder of innocence by having his most benign figure, the surfer Lance Johnson, go mad after the massacre on the sampan. Lance is coded throughout the film as childlike— water-skiing, tanning, setting off flares, putting on face paint, breaking the little arrows that are aimed at the boat, and donning a broken one in a mock-piercing of his brain.

6. Jeffrey Chown's generally astute analysis of the film fails to extend to the film's gender politics when he produces a trivial and sexist reading of the USO show: "The sequence cogently underlines Willard's remarks about the absurdity of our involvement in the war: we tried to remain as comfortable as possible by not denying the soldiers the pleasures they were accustomed to having back home, which only made them more unhappy" (136).

7. Michael Herr says, "The Marines did not like the Cav, the 1st Cavalry Division (Airmobile) . . . and at the same time members of the Cav were beginning to feel as though their sole mission in Vietnam was to bail out Marines in trouble. They had come to help the Marines a dozen times in the past six months, and the last time, during the battle of Hue, they had taken almost as many casualties as the Marines had" (147).

8. Coppola apparently devalued use of the "Flight of the Valkyries" to invest the "psy-war" helicopters with primitive power to terrify. He was deeply disappointed when a screening questionnaire showed that people liked this scene—"which he considered merely an action scene, with no philosophical depth" (Goodman and Wise, 256)—best. Afterward Eleanor Coppola found a note in Francis's typewriter that read, "The movie is a mess. . . . Brando is a disappointment to the audiences—the film reaches its highest level during the fucking helicopter battle. . . . My heart is broken" (Coppola, 266). Intended or not, the Wagner interpolation perfectly advances the complex implications of "the mythical method" in the film. T. S. Eliot, too, incorporates Wagner into *The Waste Land*—although given his theme of impaired modern sexuality, he uses *Tristan and Isolde*. The *Ring*'s exaltation of Teutonic mythology and its historical and cultural role in promoting nationalistic fervor lends political relevance to Kilgore's use of the music in Coppola's film.

9. Michael Herr reports similar ironies: "Once or twice, when the men from Graves Registration took the personal effects from the packs and pockets of dead Marines, they found letters from home that had been delivered days before and were still unopened" (83).

10. I believe Renny Christopher, interesting though her book is, misreads the ironies of Coppola's film when she writes, "American films depict Vietnamese as other, but other in a specific way: as primitive in contrast to America's civilized technological, tall, clean-cut white boys. . . . These films simply cast Viet Nam as the heart of darkness, either self-consciously, as does *Apocalypse Now,* or unselfconsciously" (181).

11. Jeffrey Chown reports that in the original Milius script, "a Montagnard interpreter comes along on the voyage. He is portrayed as something of a mascot who does not help in any way and cowers in fear every time the boat is attacked. Nearing the Kurtz compound he inexplicably attempts to escape, and Willard orders Lance to machine-gun him. Because the Montagnard is the only Vietnamese character in the script, the interpretation comes across as racist" (131).

12. Lévi-Strauss opens the "Overture" to *The Raw and the Cooked* with the explanation, "The aim of this book is to show how empirical categories—such as the categories of the raw and the cooked, the fresh and the decayed, the moistened and the burned, etc., which can only be accurately defined by ethnographic observation and, in each instance,

by adopting the standpoint of a particular culture—can nonetheless be used as conceptual tools, with which to elaborate abstract ideas and combine them in the form of propositions" (1).

13. Although the murder of elephants is the violent link between Kurtz's colonialism and the musical culture of Europe implemented by the piano keys, Conrad's novella precedes modern moral judgments of colonialism's violence to African animal life and natural environment.

14. Jeffrey Chown writes: "The degree of personal risk Coppola took with this film cannot be minimized. In an attempt to retain control over the production, he mortgaged his house, his future earnings on the *Godfather* films, and he sold foreign distribution rights. His personal life and his problems with the film were placed in the public eye with the publication of his wife's book. . . . It is difficult to think of a successful director in the Hollywood context who has so risked that success as Coppola did with this film" (146). Peter Cowie concurs: "It was a profit achieved at great personal cost to Francis. The project sapped time, energy, and money on a prodigious scale. It almost wrecked the Coppola marriage. Production was so protracted that even close colleagues of Francis were doubtful it would ever be completed" (119). Coppola's biographers, Michael Goodwin and Naomi Wise, also cite friends and associates who believed *Apocalypse Now* ruined Coppola artistically: "In the jungle, Coppola decided he was a genius, and he never gave up this idea. It ruined him as an artist; it ruined his career" (272–73).

15. Joel Zuker's synopsis of the reviews of Coppola's *Apocalypse Now* throughout 1979 indicates far more disapproval than approval of the film's literary and poetic allusiveness. Vincent Canby's *New York Times* reviews are described as lauding the film but noting its imperfections: "Michael Herr's narration is appalling, Brando's performance a decided anti-climax, and Coppola's dependence on the Conrad novel and T. S. Eliot quotes a rip-off" (170). Richard Grenier's review in *Commentary* is said to conclude that Coppola was "too respectful" of his literary sources, "particularly of Conrad and Frazer, who have diverging viewpoints" (177). Stanley Kauffmann wrote in the *New Republic,* "Unlike Conrad, the experiences along the way do not knit toward a final episode of revelation, throwing retrospective light" (179). Rex Reed, in the *New York Daily News,* called the film "a mess," although he apparently liked the helicopter attack and the Playboy bunny sequence (187). Frank Rich, in *Time,* complained, Zuker reports, that "a major problem is the lack of depth in the characterizations and the use of Michael Herr's narration and Kurtz's quoting of Conrad and Eliot in an attempt to compensate for this" (187). Coppola's Kurtz, to be precise, does not, in fact, quote Conrad—a silence that I consider interesting and significant.

16. Goodwin and Wise are brutal in their dislike of Kurtz's reading of Eliot: "His dialogue is bombastically cultured; he reads aloud from T. S. Eliot's 'The Hollow Men,' a poem that draws its title from Conrad's description of Kurtz as a 'hollow man.' . . . As Brando intones his lines in a small treble voice, he sounds like a castrato who's been shooting Xylocaine" (269).

17. All references to Eliot's poetry in this chapter refer to *The Complete Poems and Plays, 1909–1950.*

18. Zuker notes that in his November 1, 1979, interview in *Rolling Stone,* Coppola discussed people's objections to giving Conrad a screen credit, which led to arbitration by the Writers' Guild and the decision to remove Conrad's credit from the film (183).

19. Jeffrey Chown quotes Sir James Frazer's reference to Cambodia as one of

the cultures in which mystic kings were ritually killed to permit the country's regeneration (144). The same reference was apparently cited earlier, in a piece in the *New York Times,* Oct. 21, 1979, by John Tessitore, "The Literary Roots of *Apocalypse Now*" (Zuker, 190).

20. Such snapshots and such albums may be the suppressed grisly residue of many wars. Haruko and Theodore Cook open their *Japan at War* with an anecdote about a Japanese keepsake photo album with shocking pictures of severed heads (5).

21. The point was repeated upon the reported capture of Pol Pot; Robert Scheer wrote in the *Los Angeles Times* of July 8, 1997, "The plight of the Cambodians is the direct consequence of three decades of U.S. policy. . . . In 1969, they [Kissinger and Nixon] unleashed the awesome might of B-52 carpet bombing against a people still tilling the soil with water buffalo. Fourteen months and 3,500 sorties later, 'Operation Breakfast,' the secret code name for the bombing, had totally destabilized Cambodia" (B7). The "killing fields" of Cambodia were not uncovered until after 1979—that is, after the making of *Apocalypse Now.* However, stories of Khmer Rouge murderousness were sufficiently rife for Coppola to make the allegorical point that secret U.S. military operations in the region contributed to the savagery that decimated the Cambodian population.

22. Hamlet pleads with Horatio: "I am dead, / Thou livest, report me and my cause aright. . . . O God, Horatio, what a wounded name, / Things standing thus unknown, shall live behind me. . . . And in this harsh world draw thy breath in pain, / To tell my story" (act 5, ll. 341–60).

9. Only the Guns Have Eyes

1. This strategy of treating conflicts with a rain of bombings and missile attacks has become conventional military practice, as evidenced in the bombing of Baghdad with Tomahawk missiles during the December 1998 retaliation by the United States for Iraq's obstruction of U.N. weapons inspections (Marshall, "U.S., British," A1).

2. Not only did the U.S. public see very few images of Iraqi dead and receive no count of Iraqi casualties, but by closing Dover Air Force Base to journalists, the Pentagon censored images of the coffins of dead U.S. soldiers. John MacArthur explains, "The Administration had banned journalists from Dover because in 1990 the networks had broadcast the embarrassing split-screen images of a Bush speech glorifying the Panama invasion alongside rows of coffins of soldiers killed in the fighting" (245).

3. See particularly J. Fisher Solomon's introduction to his *Discourse and Reference in the Nuclear Age* (5–17). Solomon discusses the connection of academic interests to matters of policy, and particularly military policy.

4. Lewis Lapham's essay "Trained Seals and Sitting Ducks" elaborates this argument in some detail. "The trick was to make the sitting duck look like a 6,000-pound gorilla," Lapham writes, as he describes Lt. Gen. Thomas Kelly conceding that "yes, sending B-52s to carpet bomb a single Iraqi Scud site was, come to think of it, 'a delightful way to kill a fly'" (261). In Lapham's assessment, "Had anybody been concerned with the accurate use of words, the destruction of Iraq and the slaughter of an unknown number of Iraqis— maybe 50,000, maybe 150,000—might have been more precisely described as a police raid, as the violent suppression of a mob, as an exemplary lesson in the uses of major-league terrorism" (257).

5. When, in January 1991, "a group of small, primarily left-wing weeklies and

monthlies . . . sued the Pentagon in New York federal court claiming that the Pentagon rules were unconstitutional . . . [the] big three television networks, as well as *The Washington Post, The New York Times,* and *Newsday,* all declined either to join the suit or to contribute friend-of-the-court briefs once the suit was filed," according to John MacArthur (34). Eventually a letter dated Apr. 29, 1991, addressed to the secretary of defense did denounce the press policies: "The Defense Department seems to think, as Pete Williams put it, that 'the press gave the American public the best war coverage they ever had.' We strongly disagree. Our sense is that virtually all major news organizations agree that the flow of information to the public was blocked, impeded, or diminished by the policies and practices of the Department of Defense. . . . The pool system was used in the Persian Gulf War not to facilitate news coverage but to control it" (Hedrick Smith, 378). Although the letter represented individuals and not their corporations, the signatories did belong to thirteen news outlets, including *Time* and *Newsweek,* the *Chicago Tribune.* the *Los Angeles Times,* the *New York Times,* the *Washington Post,* and the *Wall Street Journal,* as well as CBS, ABC, and NBC.

6. U.S. journalists appeared largely divided on the question of "press neutrality" after the CNN anchor Bernard Shaw refused to be debriefed by the U.S. military after returning from Baghdad ("Who does he think he is?" scoffed Charlton Heston. "Switzerland?" [Seelye and Polman, 371]). Stephen Aubin, for example, stated flatly, "This even-handed, 'neutral' approach was wrong then [during the Cold War], and it is wrong now. As for today's Gulf War, here's a news flash: there is virtually nothing in common between Iraq's practiced attempts to manipulate world opinion and the U.S. government's attempts to protect its operational security" (Aubin, 360). Ed Rabel complained sarcastically about Iraqi censorship of U.S. news stories: "After Najah's initial review, every story I transmit from Iraq is subject to censorship. Each word, each frame of videotape is monitored scrupulously by Dr. Saad Al-Hamadani, a high official of the Ministry of Information. The U.S.-educated Saad speaks flawless English and knows its American nuances. Nothing gets by Dr. Saad that he doesn't want to get by. In the grimy government TV transmission station, Saad's face is eerily lit by the glow from the monitor on which the night's images pass" (302).

7. Chris Hedges, a *New York Times* reporter, used the term "unilaterals" to designate reporters who managed to escape the pool system. "By this time I had my hair cut to military regulations, my jeep marked with an inverted 'V' that was on all military vehicles, and a large orange cloth tied to the roof," Hedges wrote in describing his camouflage before the ground war. With the ground war, however, unilaterals were outlawed. "No reporters were allowed to wear military dress, to use cellular phones to file stories, or to mark their vehicles" (29).

8. Jason DeParle adds further detail to Balzar's report: "The military also refused to make public vivid videotapes of Apache helicopter attacks on Iraqi positions, although when several reporters arrived at a forward unit without their escorts they got an unauthorized viewing from a commander proud of the machines' performance. John Balzar, of the *Los Angeles Times,* said the tape showed Iraqi soldiers 'as big as football players on the T.V. screen.' He added: 'A guy was hit and you could see him drop and he struggled up. They fired again and the body next to him exploded'" (387).

9. In an interview on *Special Report: After the War with Bill Moyers* on PBS, June 27, 1991, the Jordanian writer Fadia Faqir said of seeing the violence, "It was like watching pornography. You felt guilty watching it, but you can't help but watch it."

10. Richard Keeble gives a fairly comprehensive summary of various postwar casualty estimates:

A Saudi military source quoted on 1 March radio news bulletin a figure of 65,000 to 100,000 Iraqi casualties. Julie Flint, in the *Observer* of 3 March said 100,000 were killed and injured. By mid-March the figures were being revised upwards with the *Christian Science Monitor* reporting estimates of 100,000 to 200,000 while on March 20 the *Independent* reported that up to 190,000 Iraqi soldiers had not been accounted for. . . . Three months after the slaughter the US Defense Department estimated that 100,000 Iraqi troops had been killed. . . . Dr Sa'adoun Hammadi, deputy prime minister of Iraq, said that 22,000 civilians had been killed in air raids over Baghdad alone. . . . But the *Telegraph*'s defence editor and eminent military historian John Keegan . . . went so far as to say that there were no civilian casualties at all. (155)

11. Sgt. Mike Ange, whose National Guard unit followed the 24th Mechanized Infantry Division into Basra, reported in an interview on Bill Moyers's *Special Report* (see n. 9 above) that he examined some of the vehicles that had been "taken out" on the road, and found that they appeared to belong to fleeing refugees, loaded down with furniture, suitcases, and household goods. John MacArthur reports a further, highly ironic twist to the reporting of looting: "*Paris Match* published a photograph in its March 28, 1991, issue which was taken sometime during the Iraqi occupation of Kuwait and which appeared to show an Iraqi firing squad executing six blindfolded men in Kuwait City. In a caption above the picture, the *Paris Match* editors explained that the photo had first arrived at their office on November 30, 1990, and they had assumed that it depicted Iraqis shooting Kuwaiti resisters. The editors learned on December 1 that the firing squad was in fact executing disobedient Iraqi soldiers who had been caught looting Kuwait City" (75). *Paris Match* refused to run the picture at the time because it refused "to aid the image of Saddam Hussein" (76).

12. The most highly publicized of these tales was the notorious baby incubator story. According to MacArthur, "H[ill] & K[nowlton] sent a fifteen-year-old girl named 'Nayirah' [to the Human Rights Caucus of Congress], allegedly a Kuwaiti with firsthand knowledge of the situation inside her tortured land" (58). "Nayirah," who was later unmasked as the daughter of Kuwait's ambassador to the United States, told the Congress that "Iraqi soldiers came into the hospital with guns" and "took babies out of the incubators, and left the babies on the cold floor to die" (58). The story, repeatedly cited by George Bush as evidence of Hussein's Hitlerian nature, was repeated without substantiation by Amnesty International ("with tragic consequences for the organization's reputation for accuracy" [MacArthur, 59]). The civil rights organization Middle East Watch, however, refused to confirm it: "I have yet to come across the name of one family whose premature baby was allegedly thrown out of an incubator" (68).

BIBLIOGRAPHY

Adler, J. D., and J. J. White, eds. *August Stramm: Kritische Essays und unveröffentlichtes Quellenmaterial aus dem Nachlass des Dichters.* Berlin: Erich Schmidt, 1979.

Alter, Jonathan. "After the Survivors." *Newsweek,* Dec. 20, 1993. Reprinted in *Oskar Schindler and His List,* ed. Thomas Fensch, 196–201. Forest Dale, Vt.: Paul S. Eriksson, 1995.

Alter, Jonathan, and C. S. Manegold. "Showdown at 'Fact Gap.'" *Newsweek,* Feb. 4, 1991, 61–62.

Anderson, Benedict. *Imagined Communities: Reflections on the Origin and Spread of Nationalism.* London: Verso, 1991.

Ansen, David. "Spielberg's Obsession." *Newsweek,* Dec. 29, 1993. Reprinted in *Oskar Schindler and His List,* ed. Thomas Fensch, 56–64. Forest Dale, Vt.: Paul S. Eriksson, 1995.

Antkowiak, Alfred. *Erich Maria Remarque: Leben und Werk.* West Berlin: Verlag das Europäische Buch, 1983.

Apollonio, Umbro, ed. *Futurist Manifestos.* London: Thames & Hudson, 1973.

Arnold, Matthew. *Culture and Anarchy.* Ed. J. Dover Wilson. Cambridge: Cambridge University Press, 1971.

Aubin, Stephen. "Bashing the Media: Why the Public Outrage?" In *The Media and the Gulf War,* ed. Hedrick Smith, 358–61. Washington, D.C.: Seven Locks Press, 1992.

Balzar, John. "Daily Military Briefings: A Mixture of Substance and Smoke." *Los Angeles Times,* Feb. 12, 1991, A5.

———. "No War in Sight—Flying Blind to Report on Army Aviation." *Los Angeles Times,* Mar. 3, 1991, A8.

Barker, Christine R., and R. W. Last. *Erich Maria Remarque.* New York: Barnes & Noble, 1979.

Barker, Pat. *The Eye in the Door.* New York: Plume 1995.

———. *The Ghost Road.* New York, Plume 1996.

———. *Regeneration.* New York: Plume, 1993.

Barry, John, and Evan Thomas. "A Textbook Victory." *Newsweek,* Mar. 11, 1991, 38–42.

Baudrillard, Jean. *Selected Writings.* Ed. Mark Poster. Stanford: Stanford University Press, 1988.

Beach, Joseph Warren. "Style in *For Whom the Bell Tolls.*" In *Ernest Hemingway: Critiques of Four Major Novels,* ed. Carlos Baker. New York: Scribner's, 1962.

Beauvoir, Simone de. *The Second Sex*. Trans. H. M. Parshley. New York: Vintage Books, 1989.

Beckett, Ian F. W. "Total War." In *Warfare in the Twentieth Century,* ed. Colin McInnes and G. D. Sheffield. London: Unwin Hyman, 1988.

Beegel, Susan F. *Hemingway's Craft of Omission: Four Manuscript Examples*. Ann Arbor: UMI Research Press, 1988.

Bell, Millicent. "*A Farewell to Arms*: Pseudobiography and Personal Metaphor." In *Ernest Hemingway: The Writer in Context,* ed. James Nagel. Madison: University of Wisconsin Press, 1984.

Bernstein, Barton J. "The Struggle over History: Defining the Hiroshima Narrative." In *Judgment at the Smithsonian,* ed. Philip Nobile. New York: Marlowe, 1995.

———, ed. *The Atomic Bomb: The Critical Issues*. Boston: Little, Brown, 1976.

Bernstein, Michael André. *Foregone Conclusions: Against Apocalyptic History*. Berkeley: University of California Press, 1994.

Boot, William. "And the Press Stands Alone." *Columbia Journalism Review,* Mar./Apr. 1991, 23–24.

Booth, Allyson. *Postcards from the Trenches: Negotiating the Space between Modernism and the First World War*. New York: Oxford University Press, 1996.

Brasch, James D., and Joseph Sigman. *Hemingway's Library*. New York: Garland, 1981.

Brecher, Elinor J. *Schindler's Legacy: True Stories of the List Survivors*. New York: Dutton, 1994.

Brenner, Gerry. *Concealment in Hemingway's Works*. Columbus: Ohio State University Press, 1983.

Browne, Malcolm W. "The Military vs. the Press." *New York Times Magazine,* Mar. 3, 1991, 27–45.

Bundy, McGeorge. *Danger and Survival: Choices About the Bomb in the First Fifty Years*. New York: Random House, 1988.

Burkhalter, Holly. "Some Bodies Don't Count." *Los Angeles Times,* Mar. 12, 1991, B11.

Buruma, Ian. "The War over the Bomb." *New York Review of Books,* Sept. 21, 1995, 26–34.

Butz, Arthur R. *The Hoax of the Twentieth Century: The Case against the Presumed Extermination of European Jewry*. Torrance, Calif.: Institute for Historical Review, 1976.

Caruth, Cathy. *Unclaimed Experience: Trauma, Narrative, and History*. Baltimore: Johns Hopkins University Press, 1996.

Chace, William M. *The Political Identities of Ezra Pound and T. S. Eliot*. Stanford: Stanford University Press, 1973.

Chang, Iris. *The Rape of Nanking: The Forgotten Holocaust of World War II*. New York: Basic Books, 1997.

Chown, Jeffrey. *Hollywood Auteur: Francis Coppola*. New York: Praeger, 1988.

Christopher, Renny. *The Viet Nam War/The American War: Images and Representations in Euro-American and Vietnamese Exile Narratives*. Amherst: University of Massachusetts Press, 1995.

Cobley, Evelyn. *Representing War: Form and Ideology in First World War Narratives*. Toronto: University of Toronto Press, 1993.

Coerr, Eleanor. *Sadako and the Thousand Paper Cranes*. Ed. Hideko Midorikawa. Japan: Yamaguchi Shoten, 1977.

Compton, Arthur Holly. *Atomic Quest: A Personal Narrative*. New York: Oxford University Press, 1956.

Bibliography

Conrad, Joseph. *Heart of Darkness: A Case Study in Contemporary Criticism.* Ed. Ross C. Murfin. New York: St. Martin's Press, 1989.

Cook, Haruko Taya, and Theodore F. Cook, eds. *Japan at War: An Oral History.* New York: New Press, 1992.

Cooke, Miriam, and Angela Woollacott, eds. *Gendering War Talk.* Princeton: Princeton University Press, 1993.

Coppola, Eleanor. *Notes.* New York: Simon & Schuster, 1979.

Corliss, Richard. "Schindler Comes Home." *Time,* Mar. 14, 1994, 110.

Cowie, Peter. *Coppola.* New York: Scribner's, 1990.

Crawford, Fred D. *British Poets of the Great War.* London: Associated University Presses, 1988.

Cushman, John H., Jr. "Pentagon Seems Vague on the Iraqi's Death Toll." *New York Times,* Feb. 3, 1991, K10.

"The Day We Stopped the War." *Newsweek,* Jan. 20, 1992, 16–25.

"Deadly Errors." *Los Angeles Times,* May 31, 1999, A12R.

DeKoven, Marianne. "History as the Suppressed Referent in Modernist Fiction." *ELH* 58 (spring 1984): 137–52.

Deleuze, Gilles, and Félix Guattari. *A Thousand Plateaus: Capitalism and Schizophrenia.* Trans. Brian Massumi. London: Athlone, 1988.

DeParle, Jason. "Keeping the News in Step: Are Pentagon Rules Here to Stay?" In *The Media and the Gulf War,* ed. Hedrick Smith, 381–90. Washington, D.C.: Seven Locks Press, 1992.

Derrida, Jacques. *Cinders.* Trans. and ed. Ned Lukacher. Lincoln: University of Nebraska Press, 1991.

———. "No Apocalypse, Not Now (full speed ahead, seven missiles, seven missives)." *diacritics,* Summer 1984, 20–31.

Doctorow, E. L. "Mythologizing the Bomb." *The Nation,* Aug. 14/21, 1995, 149, 170–73.

Dower, John W. *War without Mercy: Race and Power in the Pacific War.* New York: Pantheon, 1986.

Drogin, Bob. "Images of War: Carnage, the Last Push, Nightmares." *Los Angeles Times,* Mar. 2, 1991, Al, A17.

———. "On Forgotten Kuwait Road. 60 Miles of Wounds of War." *Los Angeles Times,* Mar. 10, 1991, A1, A10.

Dunn, Vice Admiral R. F., USN (Ret.). "Early Gulf War Lessons." *Naval Institute Proceedings,* Mar. 1991, 25.

Dyer, Gwynne. *War.* New York: Crown, 1985.

Eagleton, Terry. *Criticism and Ideology: A Study in Marxist Literary Theory.* London: Verso, 1978.

Easlea, Brian. *Fathering the Unthinkable: Masculinity, Scientists and the Nuclear Arms Race.* London: Pluto, 1983.

Easterbrook, Gregg. "Robowar." *New Republic,* Feb. 11, 1991, 17–19.

Edvardson, Cordelia. "Der Film verletzt mich." Trans. Anna-Liese Kornitzky. *Publik-Forum* 11 (June 10, 1994). Originally published in *Svenska Dagbladet,* Mar. 13, 1994. Reprinted in *"Der gute Deutsche,"* ed. Christoph Weiss, 266–70. St. Ingbert: Werner J. Röhrig Universitätsverlag, 1995.

Ehrenreich, Barbara. *Blood Rites: Origins and History of the Passions of War.* New York: Henry Holt, 1997.

Eksteins, Modris. *Rites of Spring: The Great War and the Birth of the Modern Age.* New York: Doubleday, 1989.

Eliot, T. S. *The Complete Poems and Plays, 1909–1950.* New York: Harcourt Brace Jovanovich, 1967.

———. *Selected Prose of T. S. Eliot.* Ed. Frank Kermode. New York: Harcourt Brace Jovanovich, 1975.

———. *The Waste Land and Other Poems.* New York: Harcourt, Brace, 1962.

Ellmann, Maud. *The Poetics of Impersonality: T. S. Eliot and Ezra Pound.* Cambridge: Harvard University Press, 1987.

Elshtain, Jean Bethke. *Women and War.* New York: Basic Books, 1987.

Enloe, Cynthia. *Does Khaki Become You? The Militarization of Women's Lives.* London: South End Press, 1983.

Erbach, Karen. "*Schindler's List* Finds Heroism Amidst Holocaust." *American Cinematographer,* Jan. 1994. Reprinted in *Oskar Schindler and His List,* ed. Thomas Fensch, 99–109. Forest Dale, Vt.: Paul Eriksson, 1995.

Felman, Shoshana, and Dori Laub, M.D. *Testimony: Crises of Witnessing in Literature, Psychoanalysis, and History.* New York: Routledge, 1992.

Fensch, Thomas. "The Journalist Who Knew Oskar Schindler: An Interview with Herbert Steinhouse." In *Oskar Schindler and His List,* ed. Thomas Fensch, 3–19. Forest Dale, Vt.: Paul Eriksson, 1995.

———, ed. *Oskar Schindler and His List: The Man, the Book, the Film, the Holocaust, and Its Survivors.* Forest Dale, Vt.: Paul S. Eriksson, 1995.

Ferguson, Frances. "Malthus, Godwin, Wordsworth, and the Spirit of Solitude." In *Literature and the Body: Essays on Populations and Persons,* ed. Elaine Scarry. Baltimore: Johns Hopkins University Press, 1988.

Fiedler, Leslie A. *Love and Death in the American Novel.* New York: Stein & Day, 1966.

Fineman, Mark. "Iraq Frees Captured CBS News Crew; Network Credits Soviet Intervention." *Los Angeles Times,* Mar. 3, 1991, A8.

———. "Refugees from Iraq Describe Hellish Scenes." *Los Angeles Times,* Feb. 5, 1991, A10.

Fitzgerald, Frances. *Fire in the Lake: The Vietnamese and the Americans in Vietnam.* Boston: Little, Brown, 1972.

"Fitzwater's Remarks: 'Loss of Civilian Lives Is Truly Tragic.'" *Los Angeles Times,* Feb. 14, 1991, A6.

Frantz, Douglas. "Restrictions—and MPS—Have Journalists on Defensive." *Los Angeles Times,* Feb. 11, 1991, A15.

Frisch, Otto. *What Little I Remember.* Cambridge: Cambridge University Press, 1979.

Froula, Christine. *A Guide to Ezra Pound's "Selected Poems."* New York: New Directions, 1983.

Fussell, Paul. *The Great War and Modern Memory.* New York: Oxford University Press, 1975.

———, ed. *The Norton Book of Modern War.* New York: Norton, 1991.

Gallagher, Jean. *The World Wars through the Female Gaze.* Carbondale and Edwardsville: Southern Illinois University Press, 1998.

Garrett, Laurie. "The Dead." *Columbia Journalism Review,* May/June 1991, 32.

Gilbert, Martin. *The First World War: A Complete History.* New York: Henry Holt, 1994.

Bibliography

Goldhagen, Daniel Jonah. *Hitler's Willing Executioners: Ordinary Germans and the Holocaust*. New York: Vintage Books, 1997.

Goodwin, Michael, and Naomi Wise. *On the Edge: The Life and Times of Francis Coppola*. New York: Morrow, 1989.

Goralski, Robert. *World War II Almanac, 1931–1945: A Political and Military Record*. New York: Bonanza Books, 1984.

Gottlieb, Roger S., ed. *Thinking the Unthinkable: Meanings of the Holocaust*. New York: Paulist Press, 1990.

Gourevitch, Philip. "*Schindler's List*." *Commentary* 97:2 (Feb. 1994), 49–52.

Gross, John. "Hollywood and the Holocaust." *New York Review of Books*, Feb. 3, 1994, 14–16.

Groueff, Stephane. *Manhattan Project: The Untold Story of the Making of the Atomic Bomb*. Boston: Little, Brown, 1967.

Groves, Leslie R. *Now It Can Be Told: The Story of the Manhattan Project*. New York: Harper & Row, 1962.

Guthmann, Edward. "Spielberg's 'List.'" *San Francisco Chronicle*, Dec. 12, 1993. Reprinted in *Oskar Schindler and His List*, ed. Thomas Fensch, 50–55. Forest Dale, Vt.: Paul S. Eriksson, 1995.

Gutman, Yisrael, and Michael Berenbaum, eds. *The Anatomy of the Auschwitz Death Camp*. Bloomington: Indiana University Press, 1994.

Hachiya, Michihiko, M.D. *Hiroshima Diary: The Journal of a Japanese Physician, August 6–September 30, 1945*. Trans. and ed. Warner Wells, M.D. Chapel Hill: University of North Carolina Press, 1995.

Hanley, Lynne. *Writing War: Fiction, Gender, and Memory*. Amherst: University of Massachusetts Press, 1991.

Hara, Tamiki. *Summer Flowers*. In *Hiroshima: Three Witnesses*, ed. and trans. Richard H. Minear. Princeton: Princeton University Press, 1990.

Hartman, Geoffrey. "The Cinema Animal: On Spielberg's *Schindler's List*." *Salmagundi* 106–7 (spring–summer 1995), 127–46.

Healy, Melissa. "1000 Iraqi Civilians Died in Illegal Attacks, Rights Group Says." *Los Angeles Times*, Nov. 17, 1991, A4.

Hedges, Chris. "The Unilaterals." *Columbia Journalism Review*, May/June 1991, 27–29.

Heidegger, Martin. *Being and Time*. Trans. John Macquarrie and Edward Robinson. New York: Harper & Row, 1962.

Hemingway, Ernest. *Death in the Afternoon*. New York: Scribner's, 1960.

———. *A Farewell to Arms*. New York: Scribner's, 1957.

———. *Green Hills of Africa*. New York: Scribner's, 1963.

———. *Selected Letters, 1917–1961*. Ed. Carlos Baker. New York: Scribner's, 1981.

———. *The Short Stories of Ernest Hemingway*. New York: Modern Library, 1938.

Herr, Michael. *Dispatches*. New York: Avon, 1980.

Hersey, John. *Hiroshima*. New York: Vintage Books, 1989.

Hersh, Seymour M. *My Lai 4: A Report on the Massacre and Its Aftermath*. New York: Random House, 1970.

Hershberg, James G. *James B. Conant: Harvard to Hiroshima and the Making of the Nuclear Age*. New York: Knopf, 1993.

Hertz, Richard, and Norman M. Klein, eds. *Twentieth-Century Art Theory: Urbanism, Politics, and Mass Culture*. Englewood Cliffs, N.J.: Prentice Hall, 1990.

Hertzberg, Hendrik. "Theatre of War." *New Yorker,* July 27, 1998, 30–33.

Hewlett, Richard G., and Oscar E. Anderson Jr. *The New World, 1939/1946.* Vol. 1, *A History of the United States Atomic Energy Commission.* University Park: Pennsylvania State University Press, 1962.

Higonnet, Margaret Randolph, et al. *Behind the Lines: Gender and the Two World Wars.* New Haven: Yale University Press, 1987.

Hilberg, Raul. "Auschwitz and the Final Solution." In *The Anatomy of the Auschwitz Death Camp,* ed. Yisrael Gutman and Michael Berenbaum, chap. 5. Bloomington: Indiana University Press, 1994.

––––––. *The Destruction of the European Jews.* Rev. ed. 3 vols. New York: Holmes & Meier, 1985.

"How Many Iraqi Soldiers Died?" *Time,* June 17, 1991, 26.

Hynes, Samuel. *A War Imagined: The First World War and English Culture.* London: Bodley Head, 1990.

Ibuse, Masuji. *Black Rain.* Trans. John Bester. New York: Kodansha International, 1969.

In the Matter of J. Robert Oppenheimer: Transcript of Hearings Before Personnel Security Board. Washington, D.C.: U.S. Government Printing Office, 1954.

Jameson, Fredric. *Fables of Aggression: Wyndham Lewis, the Modernist as Fascist.* Berkeley: University of California Press, 1979.

Jeffords, Susan. "Rape and Resolution in Bosnia." Paper presented at "A Day of Peace," University of California, Irvine, May 15, 1993.

Kauffmann, Stanley. "Stanley Kauffmann on Films: A Predicament." *New Republic,* Dec. 11, 1995, 24–26.

Keeble, Richard. *Secret State, Silent Press: New Militarism, the Gulf and the Modern Image of Warfare.* Luton: University of Luton Press, 1997.

Keegan, John. *A History of Warfare.* New York: Knopf, 1993.

Keen, Sam. *Faces of the Enemy: Reflections of the Hostile Imagination.* San Francisco: Harper & Row, 1986.

Keller, Evelyn Fox. *Secrets of Life/Secrets of Death: Essays on Language, Gender, and Science.* New York: Routledge, 1992.

Keneally, Thomas. *Schindler's List.* New York: Penguin, 1983.

Klüger, Ruth. "'Wer ein Leben rettet, rettet die ganze Welt.'" *Deutsches Allgemeines Sonntagsblatt,* Feb. 13, 1994. Reprinted in *"Der gute Deutsche,"* ed. Christoph Weiss, 33–38. St. Ingbert: Werner J. Röhrig Universitätsverlag, 1995.

Knowles, Sebastian D. G. *A Purgatorial Flame: Seven British Writers in the Second World War.* Philadelphia: University of Pennsylvania Press, 1990.

Kojève, Alexandre. *Introduction to the Reading of Hegel.* Ed. Allan Bloom. Trans. James H. Nichols Jr. Ithaca: Cornell University Press, 1980.

Krakowski, Shmuel. "The Satellite Camps." In *The Anatomy of the Auschwitz Death Camp,* ed. Yisrael Gutman and Michael Berenbaum, 50–60. Bloomington: Indiana University Press, 1994.

Langer, Lawrence L. *The Holocaust and the Literary Imagination.* New Haven: Yale University Press, 1975.

Lanham, Fritz. "Keneally's Luck." *Houston Chronicle,* Apr. 24, 1994. Reprinted in *Oskar Schindler and His List,* ed. Thomas Fensch, 41–44. Forest Dale, Vt.: Paul S. Eriksson, 1995.

Bibliography

Lanzmann, Claude. "Ihr sollt nicht weinen." Trans. Grete Osterwald. *Frankfurter Allgemeine Zeitung,* Mar. 5, 1994. Originally published in *Le Monde,* Mar. 3, 1994. Reprinted in *"Der gute Deutsche,"* ed. Christoph Weiss, 173–78. St. Ingbert: Werner J. Röhrig Universitätsverlag, 1995.

Lapham, Lewis H. "Trained Seals and Sitting Ducks." In *The Media and the Gulf War,* ed. Hedrick Smith, 256–63. Washington, D.C.: Seven Locks Press, 1992.

Le Moyne, James. "Pentagon's Strategy for the Press: Good News or No News." *New York Times,* Feb. 17, 1991, E3.

Lévi-Strauss, Claude. *The Raw and the Cooked.* Trans. John and Doreen Weightman. New York: Harper & Row, 1969.

Lewis, Wyndham. *Blasting & Bombardiering.* London: Eyre & Spottiswoode, 1937.

———, ed. *Blast: Review of the Great English Vortex.* (1915.) Santa Barbara: Black Sparrow Press, 1981.

Liebow, Averill A. *Encounter with Disaster: A Medical Diary of Hiroshima, 1945.* New York: Norton, 1970.

Lifton, Robert Jay. *Death in Life: Survivors of Hiroshima.* New York: Random House, 1967.

Lifton, Robert Jay, and Eric Markusen. *The Genocidal Mentality: Nazi Holocaust and Nuclear Threat.* New York: Basic Books, 1990.

Lifton, Robert Jay, and Greg Mitchell. *Hiroshima in America: Fifty Years of Denial.* New York: Putnam, 1995.

Louvish, Simon. "Witness." *Sight and Sound,* Mar. 1994. Reprinted in *Oskar Schindler and His List,* ed. Thomas Fensch, 75–82. Forest Dale, Vt.: Paul S. Eriksson, 1995.

Lyotard, Jean-François. *The Differend: Phrases in Dispute.* Trans. Georges Van Den Abbeele. Minneapolis: University of Minnesota Press, 1988.

MacArthur, John R. *Second Front: Censorship and Propaganda in the Gulf War.* New York: Hill & Wang, 1992.

Macdonald, Dwight. "The Bomb: The Decline to Barbarism." In *The Atomic Bomb: The Critical Issues,* ed. Barton J. Bernstein, 142–50. Boston: Little, Brown, 1976.

Marshall, Tyler. "Anti-NATO Axis Could Pose Threat, Experts Say." *Los Angeles Times,* Sept. 27, 1999, A1, A14.

———. "U.S., British Pound Military Sites." *Los Angeles Times,* Dec. 18, 1998, A1, A17.

Massing, Michael. "Debriefings: Another Front." *Columbia Journalism Review,* May/ June 1991, 23.

McInnes, Colin, and G. D. Sheffield, eds. *Warfare in the Twentieth Century: Theory and Practice.* London: Unwin Hyman, 1988.

Menand, Louis. "Jerry Don't Surf." Review of *Saving Private Ryan. New York Review of Books,* Sept. 24, 1998, 7–8.

Meyers, Jeffrey. *The Enemy: A Biography of Wyndham Lewis.* London: Routledge & Kegan Paul, 1980.

Michaels, Walter Benn. "The Souls of White Folk." In *Literature and the Body: Essays on Populations and Persons,* ed. Elaine Scarry, 185–209. Baltimore: Johns Hopkins University Press, 1988.

Miles, Rufus E., Jr. "Hiroshima: The Strange Myth of Half a Million American Lives Saved." *International Security,* Fall 1985, 121–40.

Miller, J. Hillis. *The Ethics of Reading: Kant, de Man, Eliot, Trollope, James, and Benjamin.* New York: Columbia University Press, 1987.

Minear, Richard H., ed. *Hiroshima: Three Witnesses*. Princeton: Princeton University Press, 1990.

Mitchell, Greg. Review of *Hiroshima's Shadow*, ed. Kai Bird and Lawrence Lifschultz. *Los Angeles Times Book Review,* Aug. 9, 1998, 4.

Moore, J. Duncan, Jr. "A Graduate School for Warriors." *Los Angeles Times,* Feb. 21, 1991, A9–10.

Müller-Madej, Stella. *Das Mädchen von der Schindler-Liste*. Trans. (from Polish) Bettina Thorn. Augsburg: Ölbaum, 1994.

Nagel, James. "Hemingway and the Italian Legacy." In Agnes von Kurowsky, *Hemingway in Love and War: The Lost Diary of Agnes von Kurowsky, Her Letters, and Correspondence of Ernest Hemingway,* ed. Henry Serrano Villard and James Nagel, 197–269. Boston: Northeastern University Press, 1989.

Nairn, Allan. "When Casualties Don't Count." *The Progressive,* May 1991, 16–19.

Nathan, Debbie. "Just the Good News, Please." *The Progressive,* Feb. 1991, 25–27.

The New Encyclopaedia Britannica. 15th ed. Vol. 12. Chicago: Encyclopaedia Britannica, 1984.

Nichols, Maj. Gen. K. D., U.S.A. (Ret.). *The Road to Trinity*. New York: Morrow, 1987.

Nietzsche, Friedrich. *Ecce Homo*. Trans. R. J. Hollingdale. New York: Penguin, 1992.

Niven, William J. "The Reception of Steven Spielberg's *Schindler's List* in the German Media." *Journal of European Studies* 25:98 (June 1995), 165–89.

Nobile, Philip, ed. *Judgment at the Smithsonian*. New York: Marlowe, 1995.

Nolan, Charles J., Jr. "Shooting the Sergeant—Frederic Henry's Puzzling Action." *College Literature* 11:3 (Fall 1984), 269–75.

Norris, Christopher. *Uncritical Theory: Postmodernism, Intellectuals, and the Gulf War*. Amherst: University of Massachusetts Press, 1992.

———. *What's Wrong with Postmodernism: Critical Theory and the Ends of Philosophy*. Baltimore: Johns Hopkins University Press, 1990.

Norris, Margot. *Beasts of the Modern Imagination: Darwin, Kafka, Ernst, and Lawrence*. Baltimore: Johns Hopkins University Press, 1985.

———. "The (Lethal) Turn of the Twentieth Century: War and Population Control." In *Centuries' Ends, Narrative Means,* ed. Robert Newman, 151–59. Stanford: Stanford University Press, 1996.

North, Michael. "Where Memory Faileth: Forgetfulness and a Poem Including History." In *Ezra Pound: The Legacy of Kulchur,* ed. Marcel Smith and William A. Ulmer. Tuscaloosa: University of Alabama Press, 1988.

The Norton Anthology of American Literature. Ed. Ronald Gottesman, Laurence B. Holland, David Kalstone, Francis Murphy, Hershel Parker, and William H. Pritchard. 2 vols. New York: Norton, 1979.

Oppenheimer, J. Robert. *Robert Oppenheimer, Letters and Recollections*. Ed. Alice Kimball Smith and Charles Weiner. Cambridge: Harvard University Press, 1980.

Ōta, Yōko. *City of Corpses*. In *Hiroshima: Three Witnesses,* ed. and trans. Richard H. Minear. Princeton: Princeton University Press 1990.

Owen, C. R. *Erich Maria Remarque: A Critical Bio-Bibliography*. Amsterdam: Rodopi, 1984.

The Oxford Book of Modern Verse, 1892–1935. Chosen by W. B. Yeats. New York: Oxford University Press, 1937.

Ozick, Cynthia. "Who Owns Anne Frank?" *New Yorker,* Oct. 6, 1997, 76–87.

Bibliography

Paikert, G. C. *The German Exodus: A Selective Study on the Post–World War II Expulsion of German Populations and Its Effects.* The Hague: Martinus Nijhoff, 1962.

Patterson, David. *The Shriek of Silence: A Phenomenology of the Holocaust Novel.* Lexington: University Press of Kentucky, 1992.

Perloff, Marjorie. *The Futurist Moment: Avant-Garde, Avant Guerre, and the Language of Rupture.* Chicago: University of Chicago Press, 1986.

Phelan, James. "Distance, Voice, and Temporal Perspective in Frederic Henry's Narration: Successes, Problems, and Paradox." In *New Essays on "A Farewell to Arms,"* ed. Scott Donaldson. New York: Cambridge University Press. 1990.

Pimlott, John. "The Theory and Practice of Strategic Bombing." In *Warfare in the Twentieth Century: Theory and Practice,* ed. Colin McInnes and G. D. Sheffield, 113–39. London: Unwin Hyman, 1988.

Piper, Franciszek. "The System of Prisoner Exploitation." In *The Anatomy of the Auschwitz Death Camp,* ed. Yisrael Gutman and Michael Berenbaum, 34–49. Bloomington: Indiana University Press, 1994.

Ponce, Pedro E. "Making Novels of Life's Ethical Dilemmas." *Chronicle of Higher Education,* Feb. 2, 1994. Reprinted in *Oskar Schindler and His List,* ed. Thomas Fensch, 38–39. Forest Dale, Vt.: Paul S. Eriksson, 1995.

Pound, Ezra. *The Cantos of Ezra Pound.* New York: New Directions, 1970.

———. *Personae: The Collected Shorter Poems of Ezra Pound.* New York: New Directions, 1971.

———. *Selected Prose of Ezra Pound.* Ed. William Cookson. New York: New Directions, 1973.

Rabel, Ed. "Baghdad: The Ugly Dateline." In *The Media and the Gulf,* ed. Hedrick Smith, 300–307. Washington, D.C.: Seven Locks Press, 1992.

The Random House Dictionary of the English Language. New York: Random House, 1969.

Rassinier, Paul. *Debunking the Genocide Myth: A Study of the Nazi Concentration Camps and the Alleged Extermination of European Jewry.* Trans. Adam Robbins. Torrance, Calif.: Noontide Press, 1978.

Reid, R. W. *Tongues of Conscience: Weapons Research and the Scientists' Dilemma.* New York: Walker, 1969.

Remarque, Erich Maria. *All Quiet on the Western Front.* Trans. A. W. Wheen. New York: Fawcett Crest, 1991.

Reynolds, Michael. *The Young Hemingway.* New York: Basil Blackwell, 1986.

Rhodes, Richard. *The Making of the Atomic Bomb.* New York: Simon & Schuster, 1986.

Rieff, David. "What Went Wrong in Rwanda?" *Los Angeles Times Book Review,* Aug. 22, 1999, 6–8.

Rosenstiel, Thomas B. "Americans Praise Media but Still Back Censorship, Postwar Poll Says." *Los Angeles Times,* Mar. 25, 1991, A9.

———. "Senators Told of Press Curb Problems." *Los Angeles Times,* Feb. 21, 1991, A5.

Sand, Judge Leonard B. "Excerpts from the Court Opinion." In *The Media and the Gulf War,* ed. Hedrick Smith, 403–75. Washington, D.C.: Seven Locks Press, 1992.

Sanders, David. *John Hersey.* New York: Twayne, 1967.

———. *John Hersey Revisited.* Boston: Twayne, 1991.

Scarry, Elaine. *The Body in Pain: The Making and Unmaking of the World.* New York: Oxford University Press, 1985.

————, ed. *Literature and the Body: Essays on Populations and Persons.* Baltimore: Johns Hopkins University Press, 1988.

Schechter, Danny. "Antihero: On the Gulf War's First Anniversary." *SPIN* 7:11 (Jan. 1992), 54.

Scheer, Robert. "Cambodia's Anguish: Made in the U.S.A." *Los Angeles Times,* July 8, 1997, B8.

Schickel, Richard. "Heart of Darkness." *Time,* Dec. 13, 1993, 74–77.

Schiff, Stephen. "Seriously Spielberg." *New Yorker,* Mar. 21, 1994. Reprinted in *Oskar Schindler and His List,* ed. Thomas Fensch, 142–64. Forest Dale, Vt.: Paul S. Eriksson, 1995.

Schwartz, John, and Phyllis Brasch Librach. "Entering the Virtual Zone." *Newsweek,* Jan. 20, 1992, 45.

Schwarz, Wilhelm J. *War and the Mind of Germany.* Bern: Herbert Lang/Frankfurt am Main: Peter Lang, 1975.

Seaborg, Glenn T. *The Plutonium Story: The Journals of Professor Glenn T. Seaborg, 1939–1946.* Ed. Ronald L. Kathren, Jerry B. Gough, and Gary T. Benefiel. Columbus, Ohio: Battelle Press, 1994.

Seelye, Katharine, and Dick Polman. "Hindsight: Can the Press Be Free in Wartime?" In *The Media and the Gulf,* ed. Hedrick Smith, 371–75. Washington, D.C.: Seven Locks Press, 1992.

Serber, Robert. *The Los Alamos Primer: The First Lectures on How to Build an Atomic Bomb.* Ed. Richard Rhodes. Berkeley: University of California Press, 1992.

Sharlet, Jeff. "A Scholar Argues that Americans are Obsessed with the Holocaust." *Chronicle of Higher Education,* May 28, 1999, A15–16.

Sherwin, Martin J. *A World Destroyed: The Atomic Bomb and the Grand Alliance.* New York: Knopf, 1975.

Silkin, Jon, ed. *The Penguin Book of First World War Poetry.* 2nd ed. New York: Penguin, 1981.

Singer, Kurt, and Jane Sherrod. *Ernest Hemingway, Man of Courage: A Biographical Sketch of a Nobel Prize Winner in Literature.* Minneapolis: T. S. Denison, 1963.

Sloyan, Patrick J. "U.S. Tank-Plows Said to Bury Thousands of Iraqis." *Los Angeles Times,* Sept. 12, 1991, A1.

Smith, Hedrick, ed. *The Media and the Gulf War: The Press and Democracy in Wartime.* Washington, D.C.: Seven Locks Press, 1992.

Smith, Julian. "Hemingway and the Thing Left Out." In *Ernest Hemingway: Five Decades of Criticism,* ed. Linda Welshimer Wagner. East Lansing: Michigan State University Press, 1974.

Solomon, J. Fisher. *Discourse and Reference in the Nuclear Age.* Norman: University of Oklahoma Press, 1988.

Stein, Gertrude. *Picasso.* London: B. T. Batsford, 1946.

Stephen, Martin, ed. *Never Such Innocence: A New Anthology of Great War Verse.* London: Buchan & Enright, 1988.

Stephens, Robert O., ed. *Ernest Hemingway: The Critical Reception.* New York: Burt Franklin, 1977.

Stimson, Henry L. "The Decision to Use the Atomic Bomb." *Harper's* 194 (Feb. 1947), 97–107.

Bibliography

Stoff, Michael B., Jonathan F. Fanton, and R. Hal Williams, eds. *The Manhattan Project: A Documentary Introduction to the Atomic Age.* Philadelphia: Temple University Press, 1991.

Summers, Harry G., Jr. "Body Count Proved to Be a False Prophet." *Los Angeles Times,* Feb. 9, 1991, A5.

Szilard, Leo. *Leo Szilard, His Version of the Facts: Selected Recollections and Correspondence.* Ed. Spencer R.Weart and Gertrud Weiss Szilard. Cambridge: MIT Press, 1978.

Takahama, Valerie. "'Schindler's' Author Gives Film a Standing Ovation." *Orange County Register,* Jan. 2, 1994. Reprinted in *Oskar Schindler and His List,* ed. Thomas Fensch, 45–47. Forest Dale, Vt.: Paul S. Eriksson, 1995.

Theweleit, Klaus. *Male Fantasies.* Trans. Stephen Conway in collaboration with Erica Carter and Chris Turner. Vol. 2. Minneapolis: University of Minnesota Press, 1989.

Thompson, Anne. "How Steven Spielberg Brought 'Schindler's List' to Life." *Entertainment Weekly,* Jan. 21, 1994. Reprinted in *Oskar Schindler and His List,* ed. Thomas Fensch, 65–74. Forest Dale, Vt.: Paul S. Eriksson, 1995.

Tōge, Sankichi. *Poems of the Atomic Bomb.* In *Hiroshima: Three Witnesses,* ed. and trans. Richard H. Minear. Princeton: Princeton University Press, 1990.

Treat, John Whittier. *Writing Ground Zero: Japanese Literature and the Atomic Bomb.* Chicago: University of Chicago Press, 1995.

Tytell, John. *Ezra Pound: The Solitary Volcano.* New York: Anchor, 1987.

Van Pelt, Robert-Jan. "A Site in Search of a Mission." In *The Anatomy of the Auschwitz Death Camp,* ed. Yisrael Gutman and Michael Berenbaum, 93–156. Bloomington: Indiana University Press, 1994.

Virilio, Paul. *War and Cinema.* Trans. Patrick Camiller. London: Verso, 1989.

von Kurowsky, Agnes. *Hemingway in Love and War: The Lost Diary of Agnes von Kurowsky, Her Letters, and Correspondence of Ernest Hemingway.* Ed. Henry Serrano Villard and James Nagel. Boston: Northeastern University Press, 1989.

Warren, Robert Penn. "Ernest Hemingway." In *Five Decades of Criticism,* ed. Linda Welshimer Wagner. East Lansing: Michigan State University Press, 1974.

Watson, Paul. "Serbian Veterans Recount Their Side of Kosovo War." *Los Angeles Times,* Aug. 14, 1999, A1, A 20, A21R.

———. "A Witness to War." *Los Angeles Times,* June 20, 1999, A1, A32–34.

Weart, Spencer R. *Scientists in Power.* Cambridge: Harvard University Press, 1979.

Weiss, Christoph, ed. *"Der gute Deutsche": Dokumente zur Diskussion um Steven Spielbergs "Schindlers Liste" in Deutschland.* St. Ingbert: Werner J. Röhrig Universitätsverlag, 1995.

White, Armond. "Toward a Theory of Spielberg History." *Film Comment,* Mar.–Apr. 1994, 51–56.

Wloszczyna, Susan. "Spielberg Strikes a Blow for Black-and-White Films." Gannett News Service. *Houston Post,* Jan. 30, 1994. Reprinted in *Oskar Schindler and His List,* ed. Thomas Fensch, 110–11. Forest Dale, Vt.: Paul S. Eriksson, 1995.

Woolf, Virginia. *Mrs. Dalloway.* New York: Harcourt Brace, 1990.

———. *To the Lighthouse.* New York: Harcourt Brace, 1989.

Wyden, Peter. *Day One: Before Hiroshima and After.* New York: Simon & Schuster, 1984.

Wyschogrod, Edith. *Spirit in Ashes: Hegel, Heidegger, and Man-Made Mass Death.* New Haven: Yale University Press, 1985.

Yeats, William Butler. *The Letters of W. B. Yeats*. Ed. Allan Wade. New York: Macmillan, 1955.

———. *Selected Poems and Three Plays of William Butler Yeats*. Ed. M. L. Rosenthal. 3rd ed. New York: Collier, 1986.

Zuker, Joel. *Francis Ford Coppola: A Guide to References and Resources*. Boston: G. K. Hall, 1984.

INDEX

Index

Ibuse, Masuji, 268 n. 11
idealism, 14, 16, 20, 255 n. 16
ideology, military, 87
Ifugao, 221
Iliad, 24, 37
imaginable community, 86
"In Another Country" (Hemingway), 72, 259 n. 6
incommensurability of art to modern warfare, 1
Independent (London), 250
India, 212
"In Flanders Fields" (McCrae), 41, 258 n. 8
I-novel, 191
interchangeability of figures, 27–28
Interim Committee, 157, 158–62, 166, 168
international relations (IR), 14–15
Iraq, 272 n. 1
"Irish Airman Forsees His Death, An" (Yeats), 39–41
irony, 80
irrationalism, 15
ivory, 221, 271 n. 13
Iwasaki, Akira, 267 n. 6

Jakob, Dennis, 269 n. 1
Jameson, Fredric, 43, 254 n. 14
Japan: bombing of, 159–60, 167; defeat of, 163, 167, 177, 266 n. 3; planned invasion of, 176, 267 n. 5; victims of, 150, 272 n. 20
Japan at War (ed. Cook), 272 n. 20
Japanese people, 13, 27; blood, 181, 267 n. 10; doctors, 169; medical treatment, 185; military leadership, 161; postwar recovery, 175; press, 178, 181; testimonies, 191
Jeffords, Susan, 3, 234–35
Jena, Battle of, 16
Jesuit Report to the Holy See (Siemes), 186
Jesuits, 186, 190; mission in Tokyo, 27, 186–87, 190
Jews, genocide of. *See* Holocaust
Jews, and identity in *Schindler's List,* 109
Joliot-Curie, Frédéric, 149
Jomini, Antoine Henri, 243
journalism, 21–22, 190–91, 193, 207, 208, 240, 246, 273 n. 6
Judenrat, 120, 123
judgment, 229–30
Jünger, Ernst, 81, 84, 93, 260 n. 1, 261 n. 6
Junod, Marcel, 268 n. 8

justification for use of atomic weapons, 163, 175–78, 267 n. 3
just war, 28

Kael, Pauline, 103
Kaiser-Wilhelm-Institut, Berlin, 149–50
Kajiyama, Toshiyuki, 268 n. 7
Kaminski, Janusz, 104
Karp, Phyllis, 123
Kauffmann, Stanley, 103, 217 n. 15
Keeble, Richard, 237, 243, 247, 274 n. 10
Keegan, John, 255 n.18, 274 n. 10
Keen, Sam, 254 n. 11
Keller, Evelyn Fox, 4, 168
Kelly, Thomas, 272
"Keloid Girls," 173, 195, 202–3
Keneally, Thomas, 13, 23, 99–142, 264 nn. 22, 23, 265 nn. 24, 26, 269 n. 13
Khmer Rouge, 228, 272 n. 21
killing: of the Frenchman in *All Quiet on the Western Front,* 97, 241; of the sergeant in *A Farewell to Arms,* 72–76; soldiers refusing, 84; of the water buffalo in *Heart of Darkness,* 221; witnessed, 241
Killing Fields, The (film), 228
Kimura, Yasuko, 199
Kleinsorge, Father Wilhelm, 188, 190, 192, 201
Klemm, Wilhelm, 55–56
Klüger, Ruth, 100, 138
Knowles, Sebastian, 257 n. 4
Kojève, Alexandre, 16–17, 255 n. 19
Kokura, 266 n. 8; Arsenal, 157
Koreans, in Hiroshima, 191
Korean War, 7, 170, 207
Körte, Peter, 134
Kovach, Bill, 250
Kuwait, 247, 274 nn. 11, 12
Kyoto, 19, 157, 159, 166, 256 n. 23
Kyushu, 176, 267 n. 5

Ladenburg, Rudolf, 155
Lange, Erich, 133, 264 n. 22
Langer, Lawrence, 102–3
Lanzmann, Claude, 2, 7, 100, 102–3, 108, 111, 115, 118, 128
Lapham, Lewis, 272 n. 4
Larisch, Countess Marie, 50–51, 258 n. 12
Laub, Dori, 15, 30–31, 141, 261 n. 3
Laurence, William, 165–66, 168, 266 n. 8
law, military, 74, 260 n. 12

293

Index

CULTURAL FRAMES, FRAMING CULTURE

Books in this series examine both the way our culture frames our narratives and the way our narratives produce the culture that frames them. Attempting to bridge the gap between previously disparate disciplines, and combining theoretical issues with practical applications, this series invites a broad audience to read contemporary culture in a fresh and provocative way.